D1295582

artibus et historiae

an art anthology

IRSA

nr 16 (VIII)
firenze—wien
1987

EDITORIAL BOARD:
A-1030 WIEN, KRUMMGASSE 3/18, AUSTRIA. Tel. 0043/ 222/ 827197

PUBLISHER:

IRSA VERLAG GMBH
A-1130 WIEN, AUHOFSTR. 112/5, AUSTRIA

PRINTER:

ABC TIPOGRAFIA Snc., 50019 SESTO FIORENTINO (FIRENZE)

LAYOUT:

MARIA BOGNA GRABSKA

DISTRIBUTION AND SUBSCRIPTIONS:

IRSA VERLAG GMBH
A-1130 WIEN, AUHOFSTR. 112/5, AUSTRIA

DISTRIBUTOR FOR ITALY:

LIBRERIA COMMISSIONARIA SANSONI (LICOSA), S.p.A.
50121 FIRENZE, VIA LAMARMORA, 45

ISBN 3-900731-05-5

4

5

artibus et historiae nr 16, 1987

Contents:

JÓZEF GRABSKI

The Corsini *Flagellation* Group by Alessandro Algardi

The Corsini *Flagellation* group [Fig. 1], until now known to scholars only from occasional references,[1] seems to offer new chances of solving some of the questions related to this three-figure composition, which gained a popularity unmatched in the post-Renaissance, not only during the 17th, but throughout the entire 18th century as well - with echoes of it even in the 19th century.

The gilded-bronze Corsini group[2] is on a pear-wood base, painted black and waxed, making it look like ebony, and rests on four small, gilded-bronze spheres, one located on each of the four corners of the base. The three-part composition of the sculptures is echoed in the three architecturally structured projections of the base, one under each of the three figures. The focus on the figure of Christ is strengthened by the Corinthian column He is tied to, which is inlaid with brownish marble between bronze flutings; the base and capital of the column are also gilded-bronze. The Christ figure is situated on a platform and is slightly taller than the two flagellators on either side of Him.

From direct examination of the three figures one can observe that they are all of the same type of cast, with the surfaces showing that they have been worked on with the same tools, i.e., with at least three different types of chisels and a fine file. The techniques of execution are quite similar to those employed in the Cambridge example (Fitzwilliams Museum).[3] All three figures show traces of similar corrosion in basically the same places, for instance, at the upper edge of the loin-cloth. But most important, the modelling of the torso, the muscles of the arms and legs, the veins on the feet and arms, as well as the form of the fingers are alike, and the rendering of the hair is similar as well. But not only was the initial modelling and the final

casting of all three figures definitely the same, even the finishing and gilding is identical. The minute details like the fingernails and toenails, the navels, or the busy elaboration of the beards, moustaches, sideburns, as well as the underarm hair of the flagellator on the right [Figs. 2, 3] surpass in quality the group in the Kunsthistorisches Museum in Vienna,[4] until now considered the best example. There are, though, also some slight differences in the elaboration of certain details in each figure. For example, the loincloth pattern is different: 1) Christ's consists of small, lightly struck hammer blows, 2) the the flagellator's on the right shows irregular points roughly made with the point of a chisel, and, finally, 3) the flagellator's on the left exhibits small regular circles. The difference in effect produced by these patterns lends variety to an essentially unified scheme. The execution reveals the work of an experienced, highly trained craftsman.

In order to find some solution to the complex problems connected with the *Flagellation*, one needs to examine it within the general context of the art scene in Rome of the 1630s, a time in which Bernini was unquestionably the foremost sculptor, but also the dominant figure in the area of sculptural commissions. In fact, certain questions can be answered by comparing the Corsini composition with some of Bernini's works of the early 1620s. An analysis of the Corsini group in this context may also aid in resolving the controversy concerning the identity of the artist in the various versions of this composition, disputed as being either by F. du Quesnoy or by A. Algardi.

Differences in opinion go as far back as Bellori,[5] continue on through 18th-century inventories, to Planiscig and Schlosser, and right up to modern-day scholars like Nava Cellini, Eglinski, Montagu, and Heimbürger Ravalli.[6]

It is Jennifer Montagu, however, who has devoted the closest attention to this problem in her two studies relating to the topic. In her first article, published in 1967, on two versions of the *Flagellation* group, she agreed with Bellori, who spoke of du Quesnoy as the inventor of the composition, and she attributed the figure of Christ in both versions to du Quesnoy. She reached her conclusion mainly by comparing it with the figure of Christ in *Christ at the Column* which du Quesnoy did for Hesselin,[7] a work unfortunately now lost, and some reflection of which she felt might be found in the terracotta Christ formerly in the Girardon collection (also now lost but known from an engraving by Nicholas Chevallier[8]), and with the bronze figure of Christ in the Metropolitan Museum in New York.[9] In the same study she proposed to distinguish two versions which she called type "A" and type "B", with the Christ figures remaining the same in both cases, but distinguishable by the pairs of flagellators being distinctly different, and which she said were "two quite distinct interpretations of the theme"[10]:

1) of type "A" are the examples in which she felt all three figures were modelled by du Quesnoy. The sculpture of highest quality here would be the one in the Musées Royaux d'Art et d'Histoire in Brussels [Fig. 4];
2) of type "B" are the cases in which she saw the figure of Christ as du Quesnoy's work, but the figures of the two flagellators as Algardi's. She thought the best piece here was in the Kunsthistorisches Museum in Vienna [Fig. 5].

The comparison of these versions led her to the conclusion that: "these two pairs of *flagellators* could not have been conceived by the same mind, nor could the original models have come from the same hands".[11]

Later, in her excellent 1985 monograph on Algardi, Montagu slightly revised her conclusions of 1967. She still maintained that there were two artists at work, du Quesnoy and Algardi, but, on second thought, after comparing the torso of Christ with the ones in Algardi's *Pietà* reliefs,[12] she changed her mind and said the figure of Christ had also been modelled by Algardi. Thus in her revised opinion of 1985:

1) in type "A", the figure of Christ is by Algardi, but the two flagellators are by du Quesnoy, and,
2) in type "B", all three figures are Algardi's;

this was a change from her opinion of 1967; she now no longer agreed with Bellori and attributed the whole group "B" to Alessandro Algardi.[13]

What led Montagu to conclude that there were two different artists involved were the basic differences between the two versions regarding their overall conception:

1) in type "A", there is a graceful balance of movement, with the content of the scene subordinated to the studied beauty of form (qualities she considered typical of du Quesnoy), and;
2) in type "B", the figures are more dynamic, and the more dramatic movement stresses the violence of the scene (qualities she considered typical of Algardi).

Thus, according to Montagu, the Corsini *Flagellation* is a group halfway between types "A" and "B", and, in fact, in her 1985 monograph she mentions it in the catalogue as *Christ, and a Flagellator, in a Flagellation Group*, and attributes only Christ and flagellator on the left to Agardi, but supposes du Quesnoy modelled the flagellator on the right.[14] She herself, however, stresses that she was not able to examine the group directly, so her conclusions are only hypothetical.

Since the Corsini *Flagellation* group has recently come to light and can be examined, it may now be possible to reconsider Jennifer Montagu's hypothesis.[15]

Montagu's work has been the basis for the present study, but after examining the Corsini group in its overall context, I, unlike her, propose to attribute both versions to Algardi. In my opinion, there is the same basic conception underlying both examples, and they are the work of, and seem to reflect inner struggles in the creative process of the same artist who attempts different approaches to the theme, in search of the best possible solution. The artist proposes different versions, perhaps slightly distant in time, and lets the viewer choose which he prefers, according to his taste. And, no less important for the artist at the time, he shows potential patrons, or collectors, his professional skill, and flexibility in being able to treat a commissioned theme according to varying requirements. He also offers a possible choice of castings to goldsmiths, silversmiths, and bronze-founders to fit the varying demands of the art market.

The Corsini group is a new configuration, combining the two types, and the question arises as to Algardi's motivation in offering all these different variations of the same composition. We can follow the artist's creative process by examining the way he modified the different versions of the subject. The thinking behind this artistic method, however, must be considered in light of his feeling of rivalry towards Gianlorenzo Bernini.

When Alessandro Algardi arrived in Rome in 1625, Maffeo Barberini had already been reigning in the Vatican for two years as Pope Urban VIII, and his *protégé* Bernini had begun to dominate the artistic life of the City. In particular in 1629, when after Maderno's death Bernini became the architect of St. Peter's, practically all major commissions in sculpture and architecture went to Bernini, or passed through his hands on to others. His recommendations were taken into serious consideration, and almost no one could be appointed to any

1) A. Algardi, The Corsini «Flagellation», New York, private collection.

2) A. Algardi, «The Flagellation» (detail: a flagellator at the left), Vienna, Kunsthistorisches Museum.

3) A. Algardi, The Corsini «Flagellation» (detail: a flagellator at the left), New York, private collection.

4) A. Algardi, «The Flagellation», Brussels, Musée Royaux d'Art et d'Histoire.

5) A. Algardi, «The Flagellation», Vienna, Kunsthistorisches Museum.

major sculptural project in Rome without his approval. In such a closed society a foreign artist had little chance to receive a major commission. But there were still two opportunities open to young, capable sculptors: the restoration of ancient works, which even Bernini did as a young man, and the creation of small but original sculptures, either religious ones for private devotion, or secular ones for decoration or as gifts. Small models of this kind were supplied to bronze-founders and silversmiths, and casts of them were sold anonymously. Even though Algardi had come to Rome with a letter of introduction to Cardinal Ludovisi, of the prominent Bolognese family, such assistance was only of use at the beginning to give him a hand in starting off on his new artistic activity, but was hardly sufficient to place him in a position to compete with Bernini and thus receive any of the more challenging commissions. As a sample of his work he carved two ivory Crucifixes for Cardinal Ludovisi in 1625, and two years after that a *putto*, which the Cardinal ordered to complement another one already in his collection which Bernini had done for him earlier. This first confrontation of his work with Bernini's seems not to have turned out especially to Algardi's

advantage, since after this *putto* Ludovisi commissioned him to do no other works. We may most likely suppose, therefore, that at the beginning of his stay in Rome he did some small models for castings, which he had already had considerable practice in doing previously during his stay at the Gonzaga court in Mantua, for example, as Bellori tells us. This would have given him a chance to earn some money, but more important to show what he could do as an artist and to exhibit that he had talents deserving of major commissions, perhaps more convincingly than the now lost Ludovisi putto did, which even Bellori could not manage to praise. Whether he wanted to or not, Algardi must have felt such a presentation of himself in his early works as a kind of challenge to Bernini, and since Algardi was excluded from more substantial opportunities at the time, the *Flagellation* may be considered his own modest response to Bernini's earlier works for Cardinal Scipione Borghese. Bernini had created these stylistically and thematically homogeneous sculptures, e.g., the *Rape of Proserpina* (1621-1622), *David* (1623)[Fig. 6], and *Apollo and Daphne* (1622-1625), a few years before Algardi came to Rome, and they had brought

6) G. L. Bernini, «David», Rome, Galleria Borghese.

7) A. Algardi, The Corsini «Flagellation» (detail: a flagellator at the left), New York, private collection.

8) A. Algardi, «Triumph» (detail), drawing, Copenhagen, Statens Museum for Kunst.

9) A. Algardi, «Hercules Shooting the Stymphalian Birds» (detail), stucco relief, Rome, Villa Doria Pamphilij.

Bernini an unequaled but well-deserved reputation, opening all doors to him. His revolutionary works had become required study for other artists as an example to follow for quality in sculpture. It was not easy to start a career in the shadow of such a personality, and it must have been difficult for Algardi, since as a matter of fact he was unable to realize any ideas of the same quality. From the very beginning of his stay in Rome, Algardi was confronted with Bernini's works. In fact, Bernini's *Rape of Proserpina*, with its dramatic study of dynamic figures, belonged to Algardi's powerful protector, Cardinal Ludovico Ludovisi, to whom Cardinal Scipione Borghese had passed it on in 1622.[16] As is well documented, *Apollo and Daphne* was greatly admired for its balanced, graceful movement.[17] The figure of Apollo was a model for many sculptors, and its influence can be seen in Algardi's more graceful "A" version of the Flagellation. But the strongest influence came from Bernini's

David, in which, as Wittkower noted, the "figure striding through space almost menacingly engages the observer".[18] Algardi's two different solutions of the flagellators obviously can be felt as a challenge to the prevailing influence of Bernini's *David*, with all its expressive force. And Algardi's response is of quite good quality.

Even if he did not possess an imagination as forceful and creative as Bernini's, there is all the same in Algardi's works a good sense of composition, movement, and space that was to set an example for generations of artists to come. A study of movement like that which we see in the *Flagellation* group can be found in works throughout Algardi's career, and this is an additional argument in support of his authorship of both versions. Comparing even the few samples of his other works I have chosen [Figs. 7 - 15] makes clear his constant search for varying solutions to a single artistic problem, as in the multiple

15

10) A. Algardi, «Bust of Urbano Mellini» (detail), marble, Rome, Santa Maria del Popolo.

11) A. Algardi, «Beheading of St. Paul» (detail), gilded bronze, Bologna, San Paolo Maggiore.

12) A. Algardi, «Beheading of St. Paul» (detail), marble, Bologna, San Paolo Maggiore.

13) A. Algardi, «Executioner», terracotta, Leningrad, The Hermitage.

17

14) A. Algardi, «Venus and Amor at the Forge of Vulcan» (detail), Darmstadt, Hessisches Landesmuseum.

15) After Algardi, «Venus and Amor at the Forge of Vulcan» (detail), Barlaston, Wedgwood Museum.

versions of the *Flagellation*. And much later too, in the mid 1640s, Algardi's stucco reliefs on the vault of the Villa Doria Pamphilj in Rome appear almost to be a pattern-book,[19] a recapitulation of his previous experience in studying bodies in movement, and to reflect to his familiarity with ancient art.

In spite of Algardi's attempts to prove himself as an artist in his own right, Cardinal Ludovico Ludovisi, his first patron, chiefly had him restore works in his important collection of ancient sculptures. We should not underestimate, though, the experience Algardi received in his restoration work for the Cardinal. Just a glance at some of the works he restored proves how useful this experience was for his own works, the

Flagellation included. Even as early as 1626, in his first job for Cardinal Ludovisi, the restoration of the *Torchbearer* (coll. Ludovisi, Museo Nazionale d'Arte Antica, Rome),[20] provides us with useful material for comparison. Algardi's flame-like shaping of the hair is very similar to the curled hair of the Corsini flagellators [Fig. 16], as well as the way he himself a little later sculpted the hair on the stucco head of *St. John the Evangelist*, located in the church of S. Silvestro al Quirinale, Rome, or that of *San Concordio*, one of the *Three Martyr Saints*, situated in the church of SS. Luca e Martina, Rome, or that of the ephebes [Fig. 17, 18] gracefully supporting the *Borghese Table* found in a private collection, Rome. Note how the studied grace of these

16) A. Algardi, The Corsini «Flagellation» (detail: a head of the flagellator), New York, private collection.

17) A. Algardi, «Borghese Table» (detail), private collection.

18) A. Algardi, «Borghese Table» (detail), private collection.

19

19) A. Algardi, «Christ Liberating Soul from Limbo» (detail), terracotta, London, Victoria and Albert Museum.

20) A. Algardi, The Corsini «Flagellation» (detail: a flagellator at the right), New York, private collection.

Algardi figures corresponds to the graceful movement of the right flagellator in the Corsini group. This same graceful movement, which led J. Montagu to conclude that du Quesnoy was the author of what she called the works of type "A", is to be found in many other of Algardi's figures too, both in his drawings as well as in the sculptures he actually completed as, for example, the figure of Christ in his *Christ Liberating Souls from Limbo* [Fig. 19], in the Victoria and Albert Museum, London, which could almost be a complement to the Corsini flagellator on the right [Fig. 20].[21]

In addition to this restoration work for Ludovisi, Algardi was also offered other chances to show what he could accomplish. In 1628 he restored the *Four Seasons Sarcophagus* (Palazzo dei Conservatori, Roma). At first glance there appears to be no direct relationship between this architecturally structured sarcophagus [Fig. 22] and the *Flagellation* group. Upon closer analysis, however, the symmetrical, three-part composition of the sarcophagus, with the young, nude ephebes standing in contraposto between the columns on either side of the door and looking toward the door in the middle, suggests there is, after all, some connection. The slightly opened door is located in the middle of the front of the sarcophagus and is iconographically the most important part, symbolizing the crossing over from this world to the hereafter, and opens almost invitingly to the small figure of the deceased, for whom the cosmic cycle of the changing seasons has already come to an end.[22] It is not altogether impossible that this ancient sarcophagus was also present in the artist's mind as he worked on the *Flagellation*. The symmetrical, three-part composition, the movement of the side figures toward the center, as well as the main iconographical focus on the middle with Christ tied to the column symbolizing Fortitude, are all obviously not just coincidental analogies of conception. Even the black, ebony-like base of the Corsini group has a three-part division like the sarcophagus Algardi restored.

A similar three-part architectural base with a Corinthian column as the axis of symmetry (for the figures) can also to be observed in a *Flagellation* in Brussels, another in the Schatzkammer, Vienna, and yet another in the church of Notre-Dame-des-Doms in Avignon. It is no accident that all these groups with similar bases belong to type ''A'', though, of course, there may also be additional examples of this type, in which the original base has been lost and the group has been arranged in a different way. On the other hand, the works of type ''B'' have very different bases, with respect to material (marble, wood, bronze, semiprecious stones), form (on a plain, moulded, or non-architectural pediment, like for example the one in the Fitzwilliam Museum, Cambridge, and color (green, white, blue, brown, gold). Unlike type ''A'' which has a tall classical column, type ''B'' has a small, non-classical one, sometimes carved out of semiprecious stones like agate. All these differences between the various versions lead me to suppose that Algardi created them at different, though not necessarily distant periods of time.

Type ''A'', with its stiller, more static, and well-balanced composition, and the classical column as the axis of the harmonious symmetry for the whole group, is more traditional in its expression. The iconography of this type is also more literary and classical, with a centripetal movement toward the

21) A. Algardi, The Corsini «Flagellation», New York, private collection.

22) «Four Seasons Sarcophagus», restored by A. Algardi, Rome, Palazzo dei Conservatori.

In type "B" there is more dynamic movement, less narrative, and it is more intrinsically aesthetic. The smaller size or even elimination of the column and the symbolism connected with it place more emphasis on dramatic expression and sheer movement. Stylistically this "B" version is later, more "Baroque"; its composition is less tranquil, but more open (in Wölfflin's sense of the word). The omission of the symbol of Fortitude is surely not accidental, but indicative of a different underlying concept.

It appears we can safely venture the hypothesis that what Montagu called the "A" was the earlier version, completed ca. 1628-1630.[23] In the second version, Algardi left the figure of Christ unchanged but felt the need to give more expression to His tormentors, to lend them more dramatic movement. Only he himself would have dared to modify his already respected work. One can hardly imagine some other sculptor taking Algardi's Christ, leaving it untouched, and changing not the substance of the other figures, but instead simply giving them more move-ment and more expression. Another artist would most certainly have changed more, including the Christ figure. It seems much more plausible in this case that Algardi is challenging himself to give further proof of his artistic skill by continuing and elabora-ting on his previous works.

The second version should be dated ca. 1632-1635, before the *Beheading of St. Paul* for the church of S. Paolo Maggiore in Bologna [Fig. 12], in which the figure of the executioner reflects the experience acquired by representing movement in these *Flagellation* figures. This second version is close in time and can be stylistically compared to the *Tomb of Pope Leo XI*, in St. Peter's, especially to the allegorical figure of Liberality, as well as to the *Scenes of Cardinal de' Medici's Legation to France.*

Before being commissioned to design and carry out these more important works, Algardi had to demonstrate professional skill and sufficient preparation. I assume that apart from his restorations of ancient sculptures like the *Torchbearer* and the *Four Seasons Sarcophagus*, it was precisely these small works, that Algardi executed on his own, which brought him to public notice. The *Flagellation* group was one of these successful demonstrations of his *maestria* and inventiveness. Its relatively small size and shape made it especially suited to family devotion on the small altar of a private chapel. Owing to its devotional expressiveness as well as its mobility, it was an ideal gift for both the clergy and laymen, as attested by inventories, letters, and other sources of the time.[24] Widespread appreciation of his talents brought him considerable renown as early as the 1630s, and enabled him to gradually disrupt the practice of exclusively commissioning Bernini, who was already overloaded with work. But ultimately it was the small *Flagellation* group, one of his chief artistic achievements, which guaranteed Algardi some important commissions.

23) A. Algardi, The Corsini «Flagellation», Cambridge, (detail: Christ at the Column), New York, private collection.

figure of Christ. The tall column focuses attention on His central role, symbolizes the Christian virtue of Fortitude, and functions mainly as a support, not only literally, but also symbolically. The tortures Christ is subjected to are not only shown artistically, but as part of a symbolic, theological narrative.

[1] L. Planiscig, *Die Bronzeplastiken: Statuetten, Reliefs, Geräte und Plaketten*, (Kunsthistorisches Museum Wien, Publikationen aus den Sammlungen für Plastik und Kunstgewerbe, Vol. IV), Vienna, 1924, p. 182; J. Montagu, "A Flagellation Group: Algardi or du Quesnoy?", *Bulletin des Musées Royaux d'Art et d'Histoire*, 4e série, XXXVIII-XXXIX, 1966-1967, p. 166.

[2] The figure of Christ is 22.1 cm. high, the flagellator on the left, 23.2 cm., the one on the right, 22.1 cm., the column 25.8 cm, and wooden base including the ball supports, 21.5 cm. high. The letters P and C carved on the calves of each figure indicate the Corsini provenance of this group. At this point we should recall the notation in the 1713 inventory of Prince Ferdinando de' Medici in the Archivio di Stato di Firenze, Guardaroba 1222, found by Montagu, *op. cit.*, Vol. II, p. 321, 9.L.C., no. 9: "Tre figurette di bronzo dorato, uno che rappresenta nostro Sig.re Giesù Christo nudo legato alla colonna in mezzo à due manigoldi nudi in atto di flagellarlo [...] posano sopra una base di pero tinto di nero".

[3] I would like to thank Michael Jaffé for his cordiality and helpfulness during my visit to the Fitzwilliams Museum.

[4] I am grateful to the sculptures curator of the Kunsthistorisches Museum in Vienna, Dr. Manfred Leithe-Jasper, for all his professional help and many fruitful observations.

[5] G. P. Bellori, *Le vite de' pittori, scultori e architetti moderni*, ed. E. Borea, Turin, 1976, pp. 301-302.

[6] H. Zimerman, "Inventare, Acten und Regester aus der Schatzkammer des Allerhöchsten Kaiserhauses, etc.", II. Theil", *Jahrbuch der Kunsthistorischen Sammlungen des Allerhöchsten Kaiserhauses*, XVI, 1895, pp. i-lix; J. von Schlosser, *Werke der Kleinplastik in der Skulpturensammlung des A. H. Kaiserhauses*, I, Vienna, 1910, pl. XLIII; A. Weixlgärtner, *Führer durch die geistliche Schatzkammer*, Vienna, 1929, p. 60, no. 183, p. 70, no. 221; E. Eglinski, "A Flagellation Group by Algardi", *Register of the Museum of Art*, The University of Kansas City, III, Dec. 1963, pp. 18-23; H. Fillitz, *Kunsthistorisches Museum: Schatzkammer*, Vienna, 1963, p. 58, no. 107; *idem, Kunsthistorisches Museum: Katalog der weltlichen und der geistlichen Schatzkammer*, Vienna, 1971, p. 78, no. 107; A. Nava Cellini, "Duquesnoy e Poussin: nuovi contributi", *Paragone*, 195, 1966, pp. 30-59, esp. p. 55; Montagu, *op. cit.*; H. R. Weihrauch, *Europäische Bronzestatuetten 15.-18. Jahrhundert*, Braunschweig, 1967, pp. 243-244; M. Heimbürger Ravalli, *Alessandro Algardi scultore*, Rome, 1973, pp. 181-182.

[7] G. P. Bellori, *Vite dei pittori, scultori, etc.*, Pisa, 1821, Vol. II, p. 16: "Circa la medesima grandezza di tre palmi, è la statua di Cristo ignudo di marmo con le mani avanti legate alla colonna, fatto per il Signore Esselin, che era Gran Maestro dell'Erario della Camera del Re Cristianissimo".

[8] Some bronze casts based on this figure are still extant: cf. Montagu, *op. cit.*, p. 158, note 20.

[9] J. G. Phillips, "Note: Two Statuettes by Duquesnoy", *Bulletin of the Metropolitan Museum of Art*, XXXV, 1940, pp. 126-129.

[10] Montagu, *op. cit.*, 1967, p. 153.

[11] *Ibidem*, pp. 154-155.

[12] E. g., the *Pietà* in the Victor Spark Collection, New York, or the one in the Carlo Bertelli Collection, Milan.

[13] Montagu, *op. cit.*, 1985, p. 316.

[14] Montagu, *op. cit.*, 1985, Vol. I, p. 292: "Corsini Collection (formerly): *Christ and a Flagellator* by Algardi"; *idem*, Vol. II, pp. 319-320, no. 9. C. 23.

[15] Montagu, *op. cit.*, pp. 153-193, *idem, Alessandro Algardi*, New Haven-London, 1985, Vol. II, pp. 315-321.

[16] I. Faldi, "Note sulle sculture borghesiane del Bernini", *Bollettino d'Arte*, XXXVIII, 1953, pp. 140-146; J. Pope-Hennessy, *La scultura italiana. Il Cinquecento e il Barocco*, Vol. II, Milano, 1966, p.438.

[17] F. Baldinucci, *Vita del Cavaliere Gio. Lorenzo Bernino, etc*, Florenze, 1682, p. 9: "Il volere io qui descrivere le maraviglie, che in ogni sua parte scuopre agli occhi d'ognuno questa grande opera, sarebbe un faticare assai per poi nulla concludere; perché l'occhio ne può formar concetto bastante. Conciossiacosaché e per il disegno e per la proporzione e per l'arie delle teste e squisitezza d'ogni parte e per la finezza del lavoro, elle è tale che supera ogni immaginazione e sempre sarà agli occhi de'periti e degl'indotti nell'arte un miracolo dell'arte: tanto ch'ella dicesi per eccellenza la Dafne del Bernino senz'altro piú: e bastimi solamente il dire, che non solo subito ch'ella fu fatta veder finita, se ne sparse un tal grido che tutta Roma concorse a vederla per un miracolo, ecc".

[18] R. Wittkower, *Art and Architecture in Italy, 1600-1750*, Harmondsworth, 3rd ed. 1973, p. 98.

[19] O. Raggio, "Alessandro Algardi e gli stucchi di Villa Pamphili", *Paragone*, 251, 1971, pp. 3-38; Montagu, *op. cit.*, 1985, Vol. I, pp. 94-110, and Vol. II, pp. 454-456.

[20] I. Faldi, "Il mito della classicità e il restauro delle sculture antiche nel XVII secolo a Roma", *Atti del IV convegno di studi promosso ed organizzato dal Comitato degli Studi sull'Arte dell'Accademia Polacca delle Scienze e della Fondazione Giorgio Cini di Venezia*, Warsaw, 1974, pp. 57-69; B. Palma, *Museo Nazionale Romano, le sculture, I, 4. I marmi Ludovisi, storia della collezione*, Rome, 1983, pp. 25, 72, 86, 95, 124, 139, 177; Montagu, *op. cit.*, 1985, Vol. II, p. 401-402.

[21] The *St. Proculus*, Oratory of Sta. Maria della Vita, Bologna; the already mentioned *St. John the Evangelist*, S. Silvestro al Quirinale, Rome; the already mentioned *St. Concordio* in SS. Luca e Martina, Rome; *The Baptism of Christ*, of which one is in the Vatican and another in the Cleveland Museum of Art; the numerous stucco figures in the reliefs in the Villa Doria Pamphilj, Rome; the drawing with an *Allegory* in The Art Institute of Chicago; the angels in the drawing for a *Float* (Christ Church, Oxford); and several others.

[22] See J. Białostocki, "The Door of Death. Survival of a Classical Motif in Sepulchral Art", *Jahrbuch der Hamburger Kunstsammlungen*, XVIII, 1973, pp. 7-32, esp. pp. 12-13.

[23] I would not exclude that the two generic remarks in the 1629 inventories, one for Cardinal G. G. Mellini, and the other for Cardinal Ottavio Bandini, and quoted by Montagu, *op. cit.*, 1985, p. 321, refer to Algardi's "invenzione". The more precise description of 1632 leaves no doubt that at this time the group was already highly appreciated by more sophisticated art collectors, like Bernini's patron Cardinal Scipione Borghese, who in that same year probably acquired the type "A" version: "Sene compro un Cristo con due farisei che lo Battono il tutto dargento con una Colonna d'Ebano profilato dargento con suo piedestallo d'ebano" (*loc. cit.*, 9. L. C., no. 3).

[24] As we know from the inventories of Cardinal Scipione Borghese, Cardinal Francesco Barberini, Prince Ferdinando de' Medici, and others, and quoted by Montagu, *op. cit.*, 1985, Vol. II, p. 321.

LEO STEINBERG

"How Shall This Be?"
Reflections on Filippo Lippi's *Annunciation* in London
, Part I

When Mary responded to the archangel's message, saying, "How shall this be, since I know not a man?" – was she asking, incredulously, how this were possible, that is to say, how, in the absence of its necessary cause, this consequence could arise? Was she protesting that she had vowed perpetual virginity? Or did she offer instant faith and compliance so that only curiosity remained to be satisfied: "Quomodo," she asks in the Vulgate; in the Douay translation, "How shall this be done" – in other words, by what means?[1]

It was evidently in this operational sense that the angel construed Mary's query for, as the Fathers and Doctors would point out again and again, the question Gabriel answered was not *whether* it would be done, but *in what manner*. To describe what God was about to do, Gabriel summoned two active verbs. The impregnation, he explained, would be accomplished by the Holy Ghost "coming upon" her, and by the power of the Highest "overshadowing" her.

We read that the answer satisfied Mary; but Christian imagination was not appeased. Of the two metaphors adduced by the angel, the first, the *superveniet in te*, was too vague to silence a well-meant "how"; and the *odumbrabit tibi* resists visualization: no Christian artist would see the event as casting Mary in shadow. Both terms beg the question in that they keep aloof from the virginal body, the site of the miracle. For to "come upon" is not to inhabit; to "overshadow" is not to enter. About the quomodo, the means that effected the Incarnation, the translation from pole to pole, godhead to maiden womb, nothing at all has been said.

To amend Gabriel's dodge, Western Christianity has resort-ed to natural similes of contact and penetration, analogical figures among which three are preeminent. God's working on Mary's womb was likened to an infusion of breath, to sound entering by the ear, and to the vivifying action of dew. In the words of St. Bernard: "Was it not into her womb that the fullness of Divinity descended, even as the heavens let fall their dew?"[2]

The metaphor of the dew appealed chiefly to poets; pictorial practice hardly responded to it. More pervasively influential was the idea of fertilization by divine breath, an early legacy from universal mythology. Even Celsus, the pagan skeptic whom Origen in the 3rd century refuted at famous length, took it for granted that this is how Christians imagined the miraculous impregnation: "If he [God] did wish to send down a spirit from himself, why did he have to breathe it into the womb of a woman?"[3] Some eight centuries later, when the *spiritus sanctus* in the form of a dove had become a regular visitant in depicted Annunciation scenes, the notion of divine exhalation was conveyed, as it were, by etymology, that is, by the literal meaning of *spiritus* – breath of air. And if this intimation did not suffice, then the begetful ray on which the Dove glides toward Mary could be shown issuing from God's mouth [Figs. 1, 2]. In naive or staunchly literal representations, God could appear aloft, blowing down through a tube [Fig. 3]; or exhaling the Dove itself.[4] Sometimes, in mid-Quattrocento painting, the Dove's beak expels its own rays.[5] In the imagery of Filippo Lippi, these rays may relay or double the jet discharged by the Father, as if to diagram the event as the cooperant work of the Trinity [Figs. 4, 5].

Question: what form should this inspiriting radiance take? For

1) Jacopo Torriti,«Annunciation», 1295, Rome, Sta. Maria Maggiore.

centuries past it had proceeded toward the Madonna in fine rods of metallic gold, or single file, like coherent radiation with a point focus. But the Madonna, from halo down, was a large target, and their pictures are evidence that some Renaissance painters wanted a narrower mark. Accustomed by perspective practice to tracing directional lines that converged with precision, they began answering curious questions. For instance: should those heaven-sent streamers be allowed to diffuse and shed about Mary's head, or should they collect in a single beam? And this more delicate question, hardly thought of by painters until well into the Quattrocento: should a narrowly focused light bypass the Virgin's head and aim at her bosom, or should it target her womb – as indeed it does in a Gentile da Fabriano panel [Fig. 6][6], in Piero's *Annunciation* (Arezzo), and again in Lippi's Doria panel [Fig. 4]? And if the Dove, or its breath, was the procreant agent, how close should it come? Would the avian sign of the Holy Ghost forfeit its ethereality if it came nearly touching, like a tame bird? Of all Christian mysteries none demanded more tact in the telling, for surely the very purpose of ascribing the wonder of Mary's pregnancy to the breath of God was to shield an unsearchable secret from too diligent investigation.[7] Accordingly, in traditional exegesis, inquisitiveness was deflected, and the sensuous imagination was disoriented, by citing successively the types of the Virgin's conception prefigured in the Old Testament: her womb, it was

said, was bedewed like Gideon's fleece; enkindled like the burning bush seen by Moses; budded without cultivation like Aaron's rod, and so forth.

But painters must make decisions which more modest Christians are spared; and it is remarkable to see Fra Filippo Lippi – the sweet purveyor of Victorian bondieuserie – emerge as the keenest in seeking to visualize what previously had been veiled and misted in figures of speech.

The celestial rays which in thousands of conventional Annunciation scenes from the 11th century onward dart toward Mary may be qualified in several ways, most obviously as divine light. In a few instances, where the rays start from God's hands, they denote divine operation, or more abstractly, directional vectors.[8] Only when they leave the mouth of the Father or the bill of the Dove are the rays interpretable as afflatus, and even then they allow yet another meaning. They may signify the Word of his mouth, the Word tilting wombward to perform the Creator's greatest deed, his descent into his creature's condition, entering a sealed virgin womb.

But by what route? To answer the question without scanting the supernatural character of the event, the Latin Church Fathers evolved their acoustical metaphor. They taught that the Virgin conceived through the ear, the right ear. And this fantasy - - *Gaude Virgo, mater Christi, quae per aurem concepisti*[9] – was to haunt the popular and poetic imagination of Western Catholicism down to W. B. Yeats. His poem "The Mother of God" (1931) gives voice to Mary's subjective experience:

The threefold terror of love; a fallen flare
Through the hollow of an ear....[10]

The genesis of this fantasy is surprisingly bookish – it does not lie in remote myths of miraculous impregnation.[11] The Mariological doctrine of the *conceptio per aurem* was forged by theologians bent over Scripture and resolved to match the Old Testament to the New. In their anxiety to present the Christian salvation as the fulfillment of what had long been prefigured, the earliest Christian Apologists searched the two Testaments for hidden typological parallels. Thus Justin Martyr (mid-2nd century), recalling St. Paul's apposition of Christ to Adam, propounded a comparable polarity of Mary and Eve by contrasting the Annunciation with the Temptation. For just as the virginal Eve had conceived the word of the serpent, thereby engendering disobedience and death, so Mary, a virgin again, conceived faith and joy when the angel brought the glad tidings.[12]

In St. Irenaeus (Bishop of Lyons, d. c. 200), the typology of the two virgins is further elaborated. As summarized by von Campenhausen: "Just as the one brought on death for herself and the whole human race, so the other became the cause of salvation for herself and all humankind. Eve was averted from God by an (evil) 'angel'; Mary listened to the joyful angelic message and received God himself. Everywhere, therefore, there is the most exact correspondence as if reflected in a mirror. The disobedience of the one virgin was to be set right by the obedience of the other; for the knot that held our fetters had to be loosened again in the way in which it was tied."[13] Note that in Irenaeus' text – "Mary listened [...] *and* received God himself" – the ear's hearing and the womb's act of conceiving are successive moments that have not yet coalesced. Mary's listening still conforms to the ear's natural function.

Similarly, Tertullian (d. 220):

Eve was yet virgin when the death-bearing word stole into her; therefore in like manner the life-bringing word of God had to enter into a virgin, so that what had been led to perdition through the female sex might, through the same sex, be led to salvation. Eve believed the serpent, Mary believed Gabriel. What the one had credulously committed, this other, in faith, redressed.[14]

So far, the typological antithesis of Eve and Mary offers this constant: both lent their ear to persuasion – the one in credulity to the fiend, the other to the angel of God.[15] As yet, none of these early Apologists has Mary's ear serve as the actual conduit of fecundation. It is only in the formulations of the latter 4th century that the act of listening is itself mystified and the auricular conception becomes explicit. Disengaged from its typological motivation, the *conceptio per aurem* now assumes a life of its own and, with it, the semblance of an authentic myth, comparable to, yet (in the displacement of the receptive organ) surpassing, earlier wonderful impregnations by, say, the North Wind or by showers of gold.[16] But the impulse was dialectic, not mythopoeic. If the ear was invoked as the proper inlet for the entering Word, the *topos* was purely verbal, a homiletic device – no visualization intended. And yet, as the *conceptio per aurem* metaphor underwent repetition, the wording became increasingly carnal.

St. Zeno, Bishop of Verona (d. 372), has Christ himself, not merely the angel's message, "entering by the ear." Similarly, St. Ephraem Syrus (d. c. 373):

In the beginning the serpent, getting possession of the ears of Eve, thence spread his poison throughout her whole body; today Mary through her ears received the champion of everlasting bliss.[17]

2) Melchior Broederlam, «Annunciation», 1392-99, Dijon, Musée des Beaux-Arts.

From Augustine onward, the "myth" of aural impregnation appears detached from its typological origin: "Deus per angelum loquebatur et Virgo per aurem impregnebatur."[18] There can be no doubt that Augustine intended the formula in a spiritual sense. His phrase "God spoke through the angel" was to be causally understood; it meant that the very words heard by Mary were the seeding by which she conceived. But other exegetes, evading the Augustinian equation, preferred to separate Gabriel's speech from the entering godhead. For St. Gaudentius (Bishop of Brescia, c. 400, and friend of St. Ambrose), the trope has become wholly physical:

None other was born of Mary than He who glides in through the motherly ear to fill the Virgin's womb.

3) Würzburg Cathedral tympanum, «Annunciation», stone, 1430-40.

A century later, in the words of St. Eleutherius (bishop-martyr of Tournai, c. 500), even the Augustinian formula is eroticized:

> O blessed Virgin [...] made mother without cooperation of man. For here the ear was the wife, and the angelic word the husband.

And by Carolingian times, the locus of Christ's point of entry could be specified by a saintly bishop (St. Agobard of Lyons, d. 816) as if it were part of the Creed:

> He, light and God of the created universe, descends from heaven, sent forth from the breast of the Father [*missus ab arce patris*]; having put on the purple stole, he enters our region through the ear of the Virgin, and exits through the golden gate.[19]

In the Eastern Church, the *conceptio per aurem* fantasy never flourished; perhaps because the Greek term for the godhead that took flesh from the Virgin was *Logos*. Given the vast connotations of *Logos* in Greek philosophy – as reason and inward thought, creative principle and indwelling rationality of the cosmos – the term may have seemed too abstract to assort with an auditory event; to a speaker of Greek, the *Logos* was not to be scooped by an ear.

But Latin, in "the poverty of its language" (Quintilian), lacked the abstracting powers of Greek.[20] Thus in the Vulgate, *Logos* translates into *Verbum*, and *Verbum*, to users of Latin, suggests more readily than the Greek *Logos* that which is merely audible. The consequent slippage from *Logos* to vocal speech was, as it were, preconditioned by the respective languages used. Accordingly, it seemed fitting to Latin Christians preaching the mysterium of the Incarnation that the *Verbum*, the Word, should be conceived as sound penetrating through the receptive organ of hearing. In this confounding of the wordless Word with audible speech, no matter how spiritually intended, the Latins – as the Greeks would have judged them – claimed to know more about the mysterious quomodo of the Incarnation than was divulged in the mute scriptural term "overshadow."

Whatever the reason, the Latin *conceptio per aurem* proved unacceptable to Greek Orthodox Christendom. The caution against seeking such topical knowledge as the doctrine pretended is sounded by St. John Chrysostomos, who would have the faithful content with received Scripture, without embarrassing the Evangelist and troubling him with unopportune questions.

> Proceed no further, neither require any thing more than what hath been said; neither say thou, "But how was it that the Spirit wrought this of a Virgin?" For if, when nature is at work, it is impossible to explain the manner of the formation; how, when the Spirit is working miracles, shall we be able to express these? And lest thou shouldest weary the Evangelist, or disturb him by continually asking these things, he hath said Who it was that wrought the miracle, and so withdrawn himself. "For I know," saith he, "nothing more...." Shame on them who busy themselves touching the Generation on high.[21]

In a sermon of St. Hesychius (d. after. 451), the check to excessive curiosity is administered by the angel himself. Rather than answer the Virgin's plea for enlightenment, Gabriel urges her to join him in contented unknowing: "More," he confides, "I am unable to announce. For I have no mandate to say the manner how, O Virgin [...]. Be in amazement therefore with me at the mystery, and receive the good tidings without doubting."[22]

4) Filippo Lippi, «Annunciation», c. 1445-50, Rome, Galleria Doria.

Finally, Photius, Patriarch of Constantinople, incorporates implicit criticism of the Western tradition in a homily on the Annunciation preached in 862.[23] He scorns the *per aurem* fiction and reverts to the original Eve-Mary typology formulated by the Apologists and sustained by early Greek Fathers – formulations that respect the ear's natural function.

Do they say in the West that Christ entered Mary's body by way of the ear? Photius objects and leaves ears to their task of hearing. What the Virgin received through the ear was not the Christ, but the announcement of Christ's conception. And where the ear of Eve had absorbed the serpent's poison of disobedience, we, by the office of Mary, ''are enabled to submit and hearken only to the commands of our Creator'' (Homily VII). But by what route Christ came to inhabit the Virgin's womb we neither know nor aspire to know.

A passage in the fifth homily expands the Gospel's dialogue between Mary and Gabriel to include an almost forthright rebuke. Photius' angel has closed his initial address to the Virgin as follows: ''Whom the heavenly vault could not contain [...] Him thou shalt conceive in thy womb.'' The homilist then proceeds:

But what did the most-holy Virgin reply to this? Was she immediately softened by these words, and having opened her ears wide with pleasure, did she allow her thoughts to give assent without scrutiny? Not at all. But what says she? ''Now I know clearly that thou describest to me conception, pregnancy and the birth of a son, but thou hast increased my

5) Pesellino (formerly ascribed to Lippi), «Annunciation», London, Courtauld Institute Galleries.

perplexity all the more. For how shall this be to me, seeing I know not a man? For every birth comes from intercourse with a man, while abstention from relations with a man does not so much as permit one even to hear of conception. How then shall I have offspring, whose begetter is unknown? How shall this be?''

The reply which Photius puts in the angel's mouth is extraordinary; Gabriel seems almost to chide the Virgin's inquisitiveness, avowing that even he does not know and would not dare ask.

Who is able to relate the manner of the strange birth? Who has the strength to scrutinize an inscrutable mystery? How

shall this be? One thing I know, one thing I have been taught, one thing I have been sent to tell […]. The Holy Ghost shall come upon thee, and the power of the Highest shall overshadow thee. It is that which shall teach thee how thou shalt be pregnant. It shall interpret how thou shalt conceive. […] I praise the miracle in song, and worship the birth, but I am at a loss to tell the manner of the conception.

Is Photius' archangel here refusing to tread where the Western Fathers with their *conceptio per aurem* had already trespassed? He instructs Mary to rest content with the predictive signs supplied by the Old Testament – the miracles of Aaron's rod, of the burning bush, and Gideon's fleece – ''these things which prefigured thy conception,'' and which represent her pregnancy

6) Gentile da Fabriano, «Annunciation», c. 1421-25, London, Thos. Agnew & Sons Ltd.

''from afar.'' All further questioning is dispraised as idle curiosity. May one suspect that the great Byzantine patriarch who, five years after preaching this homily, excommunicated the pope and first opened the East-West Schism, was delegating the angel of the Annunciation to accuse the West of a heterodox innovation?

The Latin West continued to cherish its auricular myth. We hear it restated in the 12th century by St. Bernard, then by Walter von der Vogelweide (c. 1200), then in a dozen known 13th- and 14th-century hymns and songs.[24] A 14th-century German scourging song asserts clearly enough that Mary's ear received more than the angel's tidings: ''The message entered through her ear, and the Holy Ghost flew in with it, and so worked in her body that Christ became God and man.''[25] Down

7) **Benedetto Bonfigli, «Annunciation», Perugia, Galleria Nazionale dell'Umbria.**

to the 17th century the *topos* recurs in sermons and devotional poetry. A French 17th-century version of the *Gaude Virgo* apostrophe reads:

> Rejouyssez-vous, Vièrge, et Mère bienheureuse,
> Qui dans vos chastes flancs conçeutes par l'ouyr,
> L'Esprit-Sainct opérant d'un très-ardent désir,
> Est l'Ange l'annonçant d'une voix amoureuse. [26]

On the other hand, the attitude of artists seems to have been somewhat guarded. Annunciation scenes in which conception through the ear is indicated without equivocation are surprisingly rare. [27] Simone Martini's picture in the Uffizi may be alluding to it: here the angelic salutation, spelled out in lettered sequence, travels from Gabriel's mouth to the Madonna's right ear. But whether we are thereby shown what Mary was hearing

or Gabriel's speech as the actual agent of impregnation is left undecided. Fifteenth-century painters sometimes beam the divine ray to the auricle, yet invariably they keep it respectfully distant; contact is hinted at, never consummated. [28] Never once is the ray allowed to touch or to enter the ear (as rays from Christ's stigmata may be shown transfixing the sites of St. Francis' wounds; or as the Trinity's darts impale St. Augustine's breast in Lippi's predella panel of the saint in his study). Even Lippi's small *Annunciation* panel of c. 1440 in the Frick Collection, New York [Fig. 11], escapes the indiscretion of actual penetration, though few 15th-century renderings of the subject come so close to suggesting a Holy Ghost near enough to whisper Christ into the Virgin: even here, the Dove's golden jet steers clear of its mark. And though Lippi returns to the subject again and again, testing the expressibility of its mystery, he does not revert to the *per aurem* fiction. It is as though the doctrine were acknowledged only to be played down. By and large, artists shunned the motif long before Rabelais burlesqued it in the birth of Gargantua from the left ear of his dam. [29]

We can only speculate on the reasons for this resistance.

Did artists wisely recognize the purely verbal, i. e., the aniconic, non-visual character of the metaphor – best left unrealized? Did they shrink from the indelicacy of depicting the impregnation of a young woman, no matter whither the receptive organ had been displaced? Did they think the *per aurem* motif ineffectual, because the device of the Dove at the ear was a commonplace, after all, in images of Old Testament Prophets, or of Pope Gregory, serving there as a token of mere inspiration in composing a text? Did Renaissance artists, in the manner of Photius, resist the motif as a vain novelty and gross superstition? Was it offensive to their growing respect for human anatomy? Or was it rejected on theological grounds?

The case for a theological qualm could be argued somewhat as follows. The anatomic miracle in the dogma of the Incarnation is God's personal inhabitation of a sealed chamber; and that is wonder enough. [30] Mary's body itself must not be marvelous, since its office was precisely to lend God her common humanity. Why then miraculize her internal anatomy by positing an unnatural passage from ear to womb? Is it because the Logos-Verbum-Word had been punningly linked to audition and thus engaged to the ear – piling paronomasia upon parthenogenesis? Granted that God can work miracles, but since God's purpose in the Incarnation was to submit to the laws of nature and to a womb's natural mothering, what cause is served by fantasizing an eccentric detour? Why not allow the divine influence direct access?

We assume reasoning of this sort to find the probable motivation behind three remarkable images created in Florence between c. 1421 and the 1450s: the first by Gentile da

8) Francesco di Gentile, «Annunciation», c. 1460-80, Florence, Villa I Tatti.

9) Mantuan tapestry, «Annunciation», 1506-19, The Art Institute of Chicago; Bequest of Mr. and Mrs. Martin A. Ryerson.

Fabriano, the two latter by Fra Filippo Lippi. Gentile's *Annunciation* panel [Fig. 6] begins upper left with God the Father attended by seraphim [Fig. 12] – a broad beam of golden light issuing from his breast (*ab arce patris*). Through a sixfoil tracery window, the beam pours into the Virgin's chamber, carries the Dove along, and comes to rest under her heart, settling there in the cusped shape of the oculus through which it had passed, with the Dove's wingspread shadow at center impressed on the Virgin's womb like a photogram, a foreshadow of the Advent. It could be Gentile's way of honoring, for the first time, Gabriel's word ''overshadow.'' And it prepares the ground for the leaps to be taken by Filippo Lippi.

During his thirty-odd productive years, Lippi turned at least ten times to the subject of the Annunciation, searching the mystery and proposing original symbols. He appears as a radical innovator in a long-neglected predella panel at the Metropolitan Museum of Art, an image wherein Gentile's projected imminence becomes boldly actual [Fig. 13].[31] The work is in lamentable condition, its paint surface badly rubbed, and its status as an autograph Lippi unsettled. But one of the picture's outstanding features – its central symbol, the unheard-of intimacy of the bird – has not been considered in the debate over its authenticity. Yet it deserves to be noticed. The hands of the kneeling Mary, folded in prayer, canopy the arrived Holy Ghost who, heaven-sent and spread-eagled, presses breast and wings to her womb. What is the artist trying to tell us? That the Virgin conceived, not by the Spirit's breath, whisper, or shadow, but by imparted warmth? Surely no Christian painting, before or since, dared close the distance between the begetful spirit and its destination.[32]

The Metropolitan Museum predella of the mid-1440s is not Lippi's last word on the subject. It was followed more than a decade later by the large *Annunciation* lunette in London, a work whose central metaphor mysteriously reconciles worshipful distance with penetration [Fig. 15]. This is the picture which first directed our interest to the quomodo question as a problem for Renaissance art.

One tends not to see it at once: but looking fixedly at the London *Annunciation*, one observes sooner or later that the Dove of the Paraclete – discharged from the hand of God at top center – has relinquished its normal high-flying station [Fig. 16]. Instead of looming aloft, or descending to hover in the vicinity of an ear, it comes vailed in profound condescension, leveled with Mary's womb, and not twelve inches away. Look closer, and you discern a spray of rare golden motes – an emanation of particles from the Dove's mouth – aimed at the Virgin's belly; then notice that the Virgin's dress parts over the abdomen, opening in a tiny slit to release a burst of similar gold-dotted rays [Fig. 17]. What is it we are seeing? A discreet tryst of photons in the stretch between bird and womb?

That the artist, a Carmelite friar committed to public orthodoxy, was rethinking the familiar event with astonishing independence of mind is apparent from his disregard of the scriptural text – the one certainty to hold on to. The Holy Ghost, the angel told Mary, would "overshadow" her, would literally "come upon" her; and the prefix in the term *supervenio* is not to be thought away. Accordingly, every earlier image of the Annunciation had pitched the Spirit in superior position. Lippi alone brings it down to earth and profiles the Dove in the nether zone reserved for the flooring.[33] Moreover, he ousts rival metaphors of fecundation, so that the operant Logos is made to work solely by silent light. We may or may not want to read these decisions polemically; but interpret we must. And we are faced with three choices, the first pair offered by well-meaning *advocati diaboli*.

First: May the light from the Virgin's womb betray the divine presence within? In this interpretation, the rays from the Dove would be assigned to convention, while attention is focused on the gleam issuing from the Madonna – the sign of the Word's brightness shining in darkness. "Mary, though pregnant, joyed with healthful lightness," wrote St. Fulgentius (468-533), "for the Light she bore within could have no weight. She became the window of heaven [...]."[34] Visual parallels for such symbolism exist, but they are rare and somewhat unorthodox. For we read in the Fathers that the enwombed Christ, whether thought of as Light or Word, was effectively hidden from sight ("He hides himself, about to become man," wrote St. Zeno;[35] and Milton's Samson assures us that "inward light, alas, puts forth no visual

10) Jacob Matham after Giuseppe Valeriano, «Annunciation», engraving, Hollstein 30.

beam.") Nevertheless, it is thinkable that a painter would choose radiant light to suggest that the godhead, newly incarnate, shines forth from its tabernacle. Could this suffice to explain what Lippi intended?

I think not, because such partial reading dismembers the given encounter. The plummeting of the Dove, though unprecedented, is not taken into account; nor the fact that the respective effulgences from Dove and womb are consubstantial, reciprocal, and about to commingle.

Second alternative: If we are seeing one compound event, may we interpret the action as a collapsed temporal sequence? The angel has spoken; he has won Mary's consent; now spends the Spirit and sets the womb aglow with the Word's presence.

11) Filippo Lippi, «Annunciation», c. 1440, New York, The Frick Collection (copyright).

12) Gentile Shop, «Annunciation», c. 1421-25,
Rome, Pinacoteca Vaticana (detail).

13) Filippo Lippi, «Annunciation», c. 1445,
New York, The Metropolitan Museum of Art;
Bequest of Maitland Fuller Griggs.

14) Virgin of the Annunciation, stone, c. 1360, from the Nuremberg Frauenkirche, Nuremberg, Germanisches Nationalmuseum.

Perhaps. But note that the sequence breaks; the crucial link in the causal chain is passed over. We see radiation from the Dove bound for the womb, and see the cloistered godhead allegedly sparkling back from within through a slit in the Virgin's dress. But how the radiant Word entered remains undeclared. Nor is it clear why the Second and Third Persons of the Trinity should, at this denouement, persist in flashing light signals at one another. Yet this improbability is what the proposed alternative would have us see.

Our preferred reading repletes the omission in the foregoing. The picture appears to us to be rendering the "How" of Mary's virginal impregnation in symbolic analogy with the process of vision – that is to say, in analogy with the optical apperception of light as understood in 15th-century Florence: visual rays exiting from the eye mingle with oncoming rays to constitute sight. This lucid simile is so apt that one marvels to be seeing it here in what is probably a unique instance. But then Lippi is merely clarifying — or thinking through to a necessary conclusion — a proble long dormant in Annunciation imagery: the problem of naming the matter, the quiddity of the procreative energy represented. For the golden beams that speed toward Mary in thousands of earlier *Annunciations* symbolize divine light, and this light should be all-sufficient; therefore, strictly speaking, these beams should deter all alternative metaphors, such as quickening moisture, leaping flame, voiced utterance, or a breeze from God's mouth. In paintings of the Annunciation, the ethereal stream falling from heaven is rendered as an emission of luminous energy, even when aimed at the ear.

Yet the sense of hearing is not responsive to brightness; light in the ear is not potent. Were those golden tracers, then, drawn in synaesthetic confusion, in a *dérèglement de tous les sens*, somewhat as in poor Bottom's post-somnial rave in *A Midsummer Night's Dream* (IV, 1, 211) – "The eye of man hath not heard, the ear of man hath not seen; man's hand is not able to taste [...]," and so on? Or was the bond passing from God to Mary designed to neutralize sense by confounding our specialized sensory apparatus? When the expounders of biblical verses say that God speaks or blows, illumines or fructifies, they do not imagine the divine operation strained through sensory channels, but employ bodyless figures of speech. And so the seeming anomaly of a darting ray for the inspiriting breath of God coming upon the Virgin "as dew in April," or "like a divine fire" (St. Bonaventure), or as a voice, or again as "a fallen flare through the hollow of an ear" is not anomalous after all, poetically speaking.

But the Renaissance master painter, committed to the priority of his art, thinks otherwise. It is as if Lippi protested: why risk synaesthesia at all? Do they take sight itself, sight unassisted, to be somehow deficient? Is the visual spectacle

15) Filippo Lippi, «Annunciation», c. 1449-60, London, National Gallery.

spread before our eyes spread too thin? And are pictures inadequate unless eked out with a borrowed metaphoricity? What need is there to think Christ enfleshed by way of breath or acoustics? Suppose the sole and sufficient symbol of fecundation were light. Is it not purest light that materializes in scores of pious pictures of the Annunciation, where the divine effluence assumes the similitude of ethereal gold? Is not this what Gentile da Fabriano conveys in his little *Annunciation* panel – a broad, unswerving sunbeam settling on Mary's womb [Fig. 6]? And is not light of all substances the most spirit-like and God's most sensible attribute? Because light is empowered to pass without violation through glass and crystal, it is the preeminent figure of Mary's virginal impregnation. Therefore, says the painter, we who are called to envision the Incarnational moment prefer the visible propagation of light to all verbal fancies of fertile utterance or fecund breath. Then let the painter depict God's imminent humanation as a radiance from the Holy Ghost finding the Virgin's womb. And what follows? How is that emanation received? Why, in responsiveness, even as the eye receives light – by reciprocation.

In the London *Annunciation*, Mary's womb is impregnated by light as the eye is by sights received. Lippi's symbol of a uterine radiance drawn forth by approaching light represents a precisely visualized mechanism: it reflects a theory, widely held in

medieval and Renaissance speculation, concerning the nature of visual perception.

From the time of the Ancients, learned men – pagan, Christian, and Arab – had debated whether seeing occurs by Intromission or Extramission. In the former view, advanced by Aristotle and the great Arab philosophers Avicenna, Alhazen, and Averroes, the act of seeing occurred as an impression made *on* the eye as it passively receives the ''species'' – that is, the image, or visible aspect – of an illumined body. The alternative doctrine – propounded by Galen, by the Stoics and Neo-Platonists, and by men of influence from St. Augustine to Milton – explained the act of vision as a radiant emission issuing from the eye. There seemed to be evidence for both views.[36]

In the 13th century, Roger Bacon had proposed a compromise, a synthesis of visual reception and ocular radiation. He speculated that, when the eye beholds, a power issuing from it ''alters and ennobles the medium and renders it commensurate with sight, and thus it prepares for the approach of the species of the visible object.''[37]

Bacon's synthetic theory was variously restated in the two following centuries and gained wide acceptance. As Samuel Edgerton's part of the present essay will demonstrate, the theory appealed especially to mid-15th-century theologians. We believe that this contemporary understanding of light and

16) Detail of Fig. 15.

perception gave Lippi his operational metaphor for the phenomenon of the Incarnation. Edgerton shows that the Dove's
loss of altitude – unknown elsewhere in Christian art – is
dictated by Bacon's geometric optics, and that even the plotted
course of the Dove's earthward journey follows the notion of
"the approach of the species." The theory allowed Lippi to gaze
upon – in Milton's phrase, to "express unblamed" – the
actuality of the miraculous impregnation; making it happen as
vision occurs, not passively, but in consequence of an interaction. The Virgin's responding womb, like the eye when it hails
the light, "alters and ennobles the medium" through which the
quickening ray is brought home.

It would not be the last time that a painter resorted to science
for its metaphoricity. But it was the last time that the mystery of
the virgin conception engaged this precise symbol. Perhaps
Lippi's discreet example went by unnoticed. Perhaps it was
scientifically superseded. Lippi's recourse to a mixed diagram-
matic mode may have seemed recondite, unacceptable. And
the image may have raised theological scruples, since Mary's
womb must be only receptive, not reaching out. To which last
objection, however, Lippi might have replied that Mary's active
consent to the angel's proposal was prerequisite to God's
scheme of salvation. Her willing faith – which would make her
co-redemptrix with Christ – elicited the Incarnation, much as the
shining eye invites kindred light.

Lippi's metaphor is marvelously consistent. As the eye is
unhurt by the piercing ray, so the numinous light left Mary *virgo
intacta*. As the eye conceives unsubstantial species by vision,
so her virgin womb conceived soul, not semen. As light is the
world's noblest substance and its cognate, vision, the noblest
sense, so their mutual coupling is fittest to serve as a symbol of
sacred union. And as the eye is the proper portal of love, so the
mating of sight with light is the appropriate figure for the
exemplary love act – God's espousal of human nature.

Finally, Lippi, like Leone Battista Alberti, would have held
to the view that the manifestations of light, and they alone,
define the painter's true province. Drawing on the boundless
sufficiency of the visible, says the painter, we affirm and flesh
out the truths of the faith far beyond the flimsy constructs of
poets. For as the eye outranks the ear, so does the painted
image surpass poetic diction: a claim for the supremacy of the
painter's art in which Lippi anticipates a younger Florentine –
Leonardo da Vinci.

In Robert Browning's splendid dramatic monologue "Fra Lippo
Lippi" (1855), the painter is cast as a natural genius, rash,
garrulous, lovable, not above whoring, and impatient of learning. Browning has him say:

Such a to-do! they tried me with their books.
Lord, they'd have taught me Latin in pure waste!

How likely is it that this genial monk would have delved into
exotica such as the Baconian theory of perception? With this
rhetorical question, I yield the floor confidently to my partner.

40

17) Detail of Fig. 15.

ACKNOWLEDGMENTS

The writing of this article was pleasantly eased by the counsel of cherished friends: Lillian Feder, Distinguished Professor, Queens College and Graduate Center, City University of New York; Susan Koslow, Brooklyn College, CUNY; Wayne Dynes, Hunter College, CUNY; Andrea Kirsh, Curator at the Lowe Art Museum, University of Miami; and, not least, my co-pilot, Sam Edgerton. And I acknowledge with gratitude the courtesies of Mr. Mario Modestini, and of Dr. Keith Christiansen and Dr. Charles Little, both of the Metropolitan Museum of Art.

[1] The first alternative, which imputes incredulity to Mary, is not part of acceptable Christian tradition. It is suggested in the two accounts of the Annunciation which appear in the Koran, 3: 41, 19: 20. In the latter passage, the spirit of God, who "took for her the semblance of a well-made man," declares: "I am the messenger of your God to give you a pure son." To whom Mary: "How can I have a son when no man has touched me, and when I am no harlot?"

For St. Augustine, and explicitly for St. Bernard, Mary's response to the angel expresses concern over her vow of virginity. Bernard has her say: "If it behooves me to break my vow in order to bear such a son, I both rejoice in the son and grieve at the disposition. His will be done. But if I may conceive virginally and virginally give birth, which, if it please Him shall not be impossible, then shall I know that He has truly regarded the low estate of His handmaid" (*Super missus est*, hom. IV, 3, *Pat. lat.* 183, col. 80).

The third alternative is the canonic. Thus St. Ambrose: "She doubted not of the effect, but only inquired as to the mode of that effect" (*De spirito sancto*, III, 11; trans. Thomas Livius, *The Blessed Virgin in the Fathers of the First Six Centuries*, London, 1893, p. 131). As summarized by Yrjö Hirn, *The Sacred Shrine: A Study of the Poetry and Art of the Catholic Church* (1909), Boston, 1957, p. 287: Mary's question "gave rise to long and ingenious explanations," none of which "imagined that Mary faithlessly doubted [...]."

[2] *Super missus est*, hom. II, 7, *Pat. lat.* 183, col. 64; trans. Samuel J. Eales, *Life and Works of St. Bernard*, London, 1896, III, p. 303.

[3] Origen, *Contra Celsum*, VI, 73; trans. Henry Chadwick, rev. ed., Cambridge, England, 1965, p. 386.

[4] In addition to Figs. 1 and 2, the following are outstanding examples of Annunciation scenes with rays issuing from God's mouth: Bernardo Daddi's panel in the Louvre; the Parement Master, Très Belles Heures de Notre-Dame, Paris, Bibliothèque Nationale, nouv. acq. lat. 3093, fol. 2; a popular Swabian woodcut of c. 1450, Schreiber 27a; Gerolamo di Giovanni (act. 1449-73), Camerino, Pinacoteca Civica; and the late 15th-century panel by Benedetto Bonfigli [Fig. 8].

The motif of the Dove proceeding as though by exhalation from the mouth of God occurs in Lorenzo Veneziano's *Annunciation* of 1357 at the Venice Accademia; and in the *Virgin and Child* fresco fragment by Domenico Veneziano, London, National Gallery. Remarkable instances of the Dove proceeding, by exhalation, both from the Father and from the Son (*filioque*) are the Avignon School *Retable de Bourbon* in the Louvre, and, probably, the *Coronation* by Enguerrand Quarton, Villeneuve-les-Avignon.

[5] Rays issuing from the mouth of the Dove occur in the *Annunciations* by the Master of the Barberini Panels and by Filippo Lippi (both in the National Gallery of Art, Washington, D.C.); by Ghirlandaio, San Gimignano; and in Filippino Lippi's St. Thomas Aquinas Altar, Rome, Sta. Maria sopra Minerva.

[6] The picture reproduced in Fig. 6, presently in the possession of Thos. Agnew & Sons, Ltd., is a recently discovered version of a composition long known from an inferior copy in the Vatican Pinacoteca. The Agnew panel has suffered some losses in the upper left corner, rendering the figure of God the Father unrecognizable. In the Vatican version, Fig. 12, this detail is clear.

[7] Cautions against misdirected curiosity and "imprudent investigations" resound throughout the Christian tradition. A serious recent contribution to the subject is Carlo Ginzburg, "High and Low: The Theme of Forbidden Knowledge in the Sixteenth and Seventeenth Centuries," *Past & Present*, no. 73 (November 1976), pp. 28-41.

[8] Two fine examples of rays starting from the hands of God are the Aix *Annunciation* and Piero della Francesca's *Annunciation* at Arezzo.

[9] For the *Gaude Virgo* hymn and its popularity, see Hirn, *op. cit.*, p. 297.

[10] The early reception of the Yeats poem betrays the collective amnesia which had overtaken the aural myth and Yeats' own gloss indicates unawareness of its ample sources, and some confusion. He commented in 1932: "In 'The Mother of God' the words 'A fallen flare through the hollow of an ear' are, I am told, obscure. I had in my memory Byzantine mosaic pictures of the *Annunciation*, which show a line drawn from a star to the ear of the Virgin. She received the word [*sic*] through the ear, a star fell, and a star was born"; quoted in A. Norman Jeffares, *A Commentary on the Collected Poems of W. B. Yeats*, Stanford, 1968, p. 359. I have been unable to find Byzantine mosaic *Annunciations* of the type Yeats thought he remembered. Standard Byzantine Annunciation iconography shows not a star but the hand of God emerging from a token heaven. The poet may have conflated this imagery with the Byzantine type of *Nativities* (e. g., the mosaic at the Martorana, Palermo), where a ray falls from a star upon the newborn Christ Child.

[11] A direct derivation of the *per aurem* theme from ancient pre-Christian myths is wrongly assumed in Ernest Jones, "The Madonna's Conception Through the Ear: A Contribution to the Relation between Aesthetics and Religion" (1914), reprinted in Jones, *Essays in Applied Psychoanalysis*, London, 1951, II, p. 269.

[12] Justin Martyr, *Dialogus cum Tryphone Judaeo*, 100, *Pat. gr.* 6, cols. 709-12. The Eve-Mary antithesis in the context of the Annunciation is discussed -- without special attention to the *per aurem* motif -- in Ernst Guldan, *Eva und Maria: Eine Antithesis als Bildmotiv*, Graz-Cologne, 1966, pp. 26-29; and in Hans von Campenhausen, *The Virgin Birth in the Theology of the Early Church*, London, 1964, pp. 38-41.

[13] Irenaeus, *Adversus omnes haereses*, 5, 19, 1, *Pat. gr.* 7, col. 1175. For the relevant text *in extenso*, see von Campenhausen, *op. cit.*, p. 38 n. 1.

[14] Tertullian, *De carne Christi*, 17, CSEL 70, pp. 232-33.

[15] The correspondences between Eve and Mary were imaginative Patristic inventions. That both were virgins was wishful thinking: nothing in Scripture asserts that Adam and Eve abstained from fulfilling God's first commandment before the serpent's advent. (In *The City of God*, XIV, 26, St. Augustine argued that Edenic intercourse must have been non-violent and without injury to the hymen.) The remaining antitheses of disobedience/obedience, gullibility/faith, perdition/salvation were entirely abstract -- except insofar as both virgins listened. Hence the importance of their respective ears to the working of the typology.

[16] For a select list of unnatural pregnancies, see chapter 14 of Joyce's *Ulysses* (lines 242-247), where Stephen Dedalus, in a drunken display of exorbitant erudition, speaks of "bigness wrought by wind of seeds of brightness or by potency of vampires mouth to mouth or, as Virgilius saith, by the influence of the occident or by the reek of moonflower or an she lie with a woman which her man has but lain with, *effectu secuto*, or peradventure in her bath according to the opinions of Averroes and Moses Maimonides."

[17] Zeno of Verona, *Tractatus*, XIII, 10, *Pat. lat.* 11, col. 352: "And because the devil, creeping in through the ear by temptation, had wounded and given death to Eve, Christ, entering by the ear to Mary, dried up all the vices of the heart, and cured the woman's wound by being born of the Virgin" (trans. Jones, *op. cit.*). Ephraem Syrus, *De divers. serm. I, Opp. Syr.*, p. 607; trans. Jones, *op. cit.*, p. 292.

[18] Quoted in Hirn, *op. cit.*, p. 296.

[19] *Ibid.*, for the passage from St. Gaudentius. St. Eleutherius, *Serm. in Annunt. Fest.*, LXV, quoted in Livius, *op. cit.*, p. 140. The Latin text of the quotation from St. Agobard, from *De correctione antiphonarii*, 8, appears in Jones, *op. cit.*, p. 269: "Descendit de coelis missus ab arce patris, introivit per aurem Virginis in regionem nostram indutus stola purpurea et exivit per auream portam lux et Deus universae fabricae mundi." Lost in translation is the punning assonance between *aurem* and *auream*, ear and gold.

For the translation of *ab arce patris* as "from the breast,"see C. Du Cange, *Glossarium mediae et infimae latinitatis*, Paris, 1840, I, p. 363, def. 7 – a medieval usage reflected in several iconographies, as when in Adorations of the Child the divine rays descend upon the Infant from the breast of the Father; see, for example, the Cologne School panel of c. 1415-20, reprod. in *Vor Stefan Lochner: Die Kölner Maler von 1300 bis 1430*, exh. cat., Cologne, Wallraf-Richartz-Museum, 1974, no. 28 and p. 168. For the *ab arce patris* motif in Annunciation scenes, see Fig. 12.

[20] Quintilian, *Institutio oratoria*, VIII, 3, 33, trans. H. E. Butler, Cambridge, Massachusetts, 1920; see also II, 14, 1-4. The Greek Bible writes *logos* at the opening of St. John's Gospel. But in Luke's wording of Mary's submission (1:38) – "be it done according to thy word" - "word" is rendered as *rhema*, i. e., that which is spoken. In the Vulgate, where *verbum* is used in both places, the distinction between *logos* and *rhema* is canceled. The same impoverishment occurs in the Latin translation of a passage in St. John Chrysostomos, referring to the Eve-Mary typology: "Eve, having been deceived, brought forth the word [*rhema*] which brought us death; Mary, receiving the happy tidings, bore the Word [*logos*] in the flesh" (*In salvatoris nostri Jesu Christi nativitatem oratorio, Pat. gr.*, 56, col. 392). The Latin translation in Migne employs *verbum* in both instances.

For a naively literal representation of *verbum* in medieval imagery, see the 13th-century stone sculpture at Bamberg Cathedral, where the beak of the descending Dove clamps down on one end of Gabriel's *Spruchband* or banderole, bearer of words; reprod. in Gertrud Schiller, *Iconography of Christian Art*, I, Greenwich, Connecticut, 1971, fig. 89.

[21] John Chrysostomos, *In Matt.*, hom. IV, 5-6, trans. *The Homilies of S. John Chrysostom [...] on Matthew*, Oxford, 1843, p. 48. Cf. the Dordrecht Confession, 1632, of the Anabaptists: "But how, or in what manner, this worthy body was prepared, or how the Word became flesh, and He Himself man, we content ourselves with the declaration which the worthy evangelists have given and left in their description thereof"; trans. B. A. Gerrish, ed., *The Faith of Christendom*, Cleveland, 1963, p. 221.

[22] Hesychius, *De sanct. Maria deip.*, IV, *Pat. gr.* 93, col. 1453; trans. Livius, *op. cit.*, p. 141.

[23] Cyril Mango, trans., *The Homilies of Photius, Patriarch of Constantinople*, Cambridge, Massachusetts, 1958, Homily V, pp. 118-20.

[24] St. Bernard, *Sermo II in festo Pentecostes, Pat. lat.* 183, col. 327: "missus est interim Gabriel angelus a Deo, ut verbum patris per aurem virginis in ventrem et mentem ipsius eructaret, ut eadem via intraret antidotum, qua venenum intraverat" – i. e., the antidote to Eve's temptation enters by the same port as had the poison; in this respect, Bernard recalls St. Zeno's commentary, quoted above, n. 17. For these connections, see Hirn, *op. cit.*, p. 298.

The lines from Walter von der Vogelweide read: "Dur ir ôre empfinc si den vil süezen" ("through her ear she conceived the most sweet"); quoted in Karl Künstle, *Ikonographie der christlichen Kunst*, I, Freiburg i. Br., 1928, p. 339.

For the *Gaude Virgo* hymn, see above, n. 9.

[25] "Diu botschaft gie zeîr oran in der hailig gaist flos damit in der worht in ir libe daz das cristus got und mensche waz"; quoted in Hirn, *op. cit.*, p. 298.

[26] Quoted in Jones, *op. cit.*, p. 269. In a sermon preached on March 13, 1661, Bossuet spoke of "her who first conceived the Son of God through the ear"; see Lucien Febvre, *The Problem of Unbelief in the Sixteenth Century: The Religion of Rabelais* (1942), trans. Beatrice Gottlieb, Cambridge, Massachusetts, 1982, p. 162 n. 20.

[27] Schiller's *Iconography of Christian Art, op. cit.*, reproduces a selection of medieval examples that show more or less direct approaches to the ear; see especially her figs. 85 (from the Klosterneuburg Altar) and 105 [our Fig. 3], the absurdly telephonic Würzburg Cathedral tympanum, where God blows down through a tube that presumably attaches to Mary's right ear.

[28] Quattrocento *Annunciations*, displaying as usual the Madonna's left side, sometimes direct the divine ray to the presumed location of the unseen right ear; for especially graphic examples, see Francesco di Gentile's panel at the Villa I Tatti, Florence [Fig. 7], and Gerolamo di Giovanni's panel in Camerino, Pinacoteca Civica. See also the *Annunciations* by Crivelli (London), Benedetto Bonfigli [Fig. 8], and the early 16th-century Mantuan tapestry, made for Francesco Gonzaga, now in The Art Institute of Chicago [Fig. 9]. A striking late 16th-century instance (to which Mr. Robert Dance kindly drew my attention) is Jacob Matham's engraved *Annunciation* [Fig. 10] after Giuseppe Valeriano's altarpiece in the Gesù, Rome.

[29] Rabelais, I, 6: "[...] the cotyledons of the matrix were loosened at the top, and the child leapt up through them to enter the hollow vein. Then, climbing through the diaphragm to a point above the shoulders where this vein divides in two, he took the left fork and came out by the left ear" (trans. J. M. Cohen, Harmondsworth, 1955, p. 52). Lucien Febvre, *op. cit.*, p. 162, argues somewhat too strenuously that this Rabelaisian spoof can have no bearing on the Marian myth under discussion, because Rabelais is not describing a conception but a miraculous birthing, whereas the course of Mary's confinement was normal. It seems to us that in this rare instance the great savant, bent upon proving that Rabelais was not anti-Christian (agreed), misdirected his zeal. The Gargantuan satire was aimed at a vulgar superstition, not at an article of Christian faith. It claims that if a womb's impregnation had once been effected by way of the ear, then Gargantua could avail himself of the same route in reverse.

[30] A further miracle involving the generation of Christ was produced by a Scholastic syllogism. Its major premise: souls are infused into the fetus only when the body is fully formed. Minor premise: it was Christ's soul that entered the Virgin's womb at the moment of his conception.

Conclusion: Christ did not pass through the normal stages of embryonic development, but was a perfect body joined to its soul and complete in all the parts of a man from the instant of his conception. However, this reasoning does not alter the physiology of the Virgin, which submitted to the single sufficient miracle of the unbroken hymen.

[31] The Metropolitan Museum panel entered the museum collection in 1943 with an attribution to the workshop of Fra Filippo Lippi, an earlier ascription to Pesellino being generally discarded. In 1963 and again in 1971, Federico Zeri upgraded the attribution, calling the panel "typical of Fra Filippo Lippi's work in the middle of the 1440s"; F. R. Shapely concurred; see Zeri, *Italian Paintings [...] The Metropolitan Museum of Art, Florentine School*, New, York, 1971, p. 63, with full bibliography. Nevertheless, the panel was consigned to storage. In Jeffrey Ruda's forthcoming Lippi monograph, it is described as dependent on Lippi in composition, but not by the master's hand.

Summer 1986, the panel emerged from its long years of occultation to be hung in the museum's "Study Collection." The accompanying label tentatively disattributes it, describing its composition as "weak and ill-conceived." Yet I find it nobly conceived – firm and subtle. Contrary to what has been written, the design is not simply "symmetrical"; it counterpoints bilateral symmetry with a strong rightward drift. (Ruda rightly observes that Lippi's compositions "are more asymmetrical than most by his contemporaries.") The effect – as in Lippi's *Madonna Enthroned* (Metropolitan Museum), in the *Barbadori Altarpiece* (1437, Louvre), and in the San Lorenzo *Annunciation* – is to combine apparent stability with felt movement (an effect loosely sought also by Domenico Veneziano, e. g., in the *Annunciation* predella at the Fitzwilliam Museum, Cambridge, and magnificently achieved both in Leonardo's *Last Supper* and Michelangelo's *Last Judgment*.) In this respect alone, and for all its apparent modesty, Lippi's Metropolitan panel reveals bold pictorial thinking. It is equally inventive and subtle in harmonizing perspectival illusionism with surface shape (the placing of Gabriel's wings is as enchanting as the step-up flow of the Madonna's robe). And it is boldest in its unique symbolism touching the Incarnation. The unprecedented motif of the Dove pressed against Mary's womb is a thought characteristic of Lippi's yearning to see. It is less likely to come from an anonymous hand in his workshop, from Pesellino, or from "an artist between Fra Filippo Lippi and Pesellino" (Berenson).

[32] One earlier image may be relevant here. Nuremberg's Germanisches Nationalmuseum preserves a life-size stone-carved *Annunciation* group of c. 1360, acquired in 1927 from the Nuremberg Frauenkirche [Fig. 14]; see The Metropolitan Museum of Art, *Gothic and Renaissance Art in Nuremberg 1300-1550*, exh. cat., New York, 1986, no. 5, with bibliography, to which should be added Gregor Martin Lechner, *Maria Gravida: Zu Schwangerschaftsmotiv der bildenden Kust*, Zürich, 1981, p. 17 and no. 10. The statue of the Annunciate shows her, proleptically, in advanced pregnancy – the type of the *Madonna gravida*. In its present, reworked condition, the Virgin's belly supports her left hand. But the hand is modern. According to Kurt Martin (*Die Nürnberger Steinplastik im XIV. Jahrhundert*, Berlin, 1927, no. 55), it is the result of an alteration ordered by the local clergy in 1879-80. In the original state, it was the Dove of the Holy Ghost that perched on the belly. Unfortunately, this crucial feature is not well attested. Martin's information was received orally from one Baumeister Göschel, recounting a recollection then nearly half a century old. How reliable was Göschel's recall? We know of no other *Annunciation* wherein the Dove of the Holy Ghost is visualized as a brooding bird, fecundating by intimate contact. One thinks, anachronistically, of Milton's address to the Holy Ghost (*Paradise Lost*, I, 18-21):

[...] thou from the first
Wast present, and with mighty wings outspread,
Dove-like sat'st brooding on the vast Abyss,
And mad'st it pregnant [...]

Or of the closing words of Gerard Manley Hopkins' "God's Grandeur":

The Holy Ghost over the bent
World broods with warm breast and with ah! bright wings.

My phrase "imparted warmth" as a euphemism for fecundation is adapted from Dryden's "Absalom and Architophel," line 8.

[33] The Dove's radical self-abasement is projected with keen pictorial intelligence. The third person of the triune godhead appears incongruously trapped between verticals, pressed down under multiple horizontals beneath an upright wall panel: a normally free-coasting bird narrowly quartered.

[34] St. Fulgentius, Sermon 36, *De laudibus Mariae ex partu Salvatoris*; trans. Livius, *op. cit.*, p. 138.

[35] St. Zeno, *Tractatus*, II, 8, 9, *Pat. lat.* 11, cols. 413-17; trans. Livius, *op. cit.*, p. 126.

[36] See David C. Lindberg, *Theories of Vision from Al-Kindi to Kepler*, Chicago, 1976, *passim*.

The Extramission theory may once have relied on naive observations – e. g., that the eyes of cats shine in the dark. More important for its tenacious hold down to the 17th century is our subjective conviction that visual attention, the act of focusing or fixating, is an outgoing energy. As Donne's ecstatic lovers gaze upon one another "our eye-beams twisted, and did thred / our eyes, upon one double string [...]." Blind Milton loses the power of sight when his "light is spent." A glance that "sweeps" sky or horizon goes forth like a searchlight. A look may be caressing or piercing; either way, it is felt to impinge, to weigh on its object. Even the photographic camera is said to "shoot." It is in fact difficult to avoid feeling that one's focused look is active out there, like one's grasp, one's raised voice, or blown breath.

[37] Lindberg, *op. cit.*, p. 115.

44

SAMUEL Y. EDGERTON, JR.

"How Shall This Be?"
Part II

The Virgin Mary's innocent question, "how shall this be, seeing I know not a man (*quomodo fiet istud quoniam virum non cognosco*)?," was surely one of the most tantalizing in theological history. The archangel's evasive response, as Steinberg has just shown, thereafter engendered all manner of curious exegeses on her miraculous fecundation. Not only did theologians attempt to satisfy inquisitive ears with circumspect verbal explanations, but medieval artists took the further liberty of inventing pictorial metaphors to image this most sensitive of all Christian mysteries before profane eyes. Renaissance artists then added a new dimension – the third – which unexpectedly changed the heretofore discreet rules for envisioning her intimate story. In the hands of Quattrocento and Cinquecento painters, skilled in the art-science of *prospettiva*, pictures of the Annunciation began to look so "real" that viewers might believe they were actually seeing the substance that passed between God and Mary at the moment of Jesus's miraculous conception.

I should like to argue, as my contribution to our joint examination of Fra Filippo Lippi's extraordinary painting of the subject [Fig. 15], that this versatile Florentine painter not only applied all the tricks of by-now *de rigueur* linear perspective in his usual original way, but went further, adapting to his art yet another, even more complex aspect of medieval optical geometry. I intend to compare certain pictorial details of Lippi's London Annunciation with some written documents concerning the science of optics available in Florence during Lippi's lifetime. Moreover, these same documents were read and glossed for publication by a contemporary colleague, Lorenzo Ghiberti (1378-1455), a man in position to exert considerable influence on Lippi. I repeat below the particular images in the picture that attract our attention. Unfortunately, they are difficult to discern, not only in our accompanying photographs but in the actual painting itself. Much of Lippi's original oil gilding, at one time brightly conspicuous has flaked off. What remains is difficult to discern especially in photographic reproduction. However, close examination, especially with a magnifying glass, clearly reveals:

1) an array of overlapping gilded rings marking the Holy Spirit's descent from God's hand at the top of the picture to where it appears as a dove in the center just opposite the Virgin's womb,

2) dual sprays of golden dots that fan out reciprocally from the head of the dove and Mary's womb,

3) a deliberately painted opening in the Virgin's garment at the place where the gilded dots make contact with her body.

What do these strange details mean? Steinberg is the first modern historian to have noticed them. They have never been remarked upon in print before. They are unique as far as we can tell in the entire history of *Annunciation* painting.[1] To begin my part of our joint analysis then, I beg the reader accept the conventional art historical wisdom that Lippi painted his London *Annunciation* for the Medici family sometime between 1449 and 1460.[2] A precise date within this spread is not important to our arguments since the relevant scientific ideas about to be compared with the picture were prevalent in Florence during all those years. It is important, however, that the Medici were the patrons. They would most logically have provided Lippi with the material in the manuscript sources, and access to a prestigious personality who may also have stimulated the artist to this unusual solution.

This person was Antonino Pierozzi, Dominican priest and

Prior of the Convent of San Marco from 1439 until 1444 during its Medici sponsorship. In 1446, he was appointed Archbishop of Florence, a post which he held with distinction until his death in 1459. So esteemed was he that the Church rewarded him with sainthood in 1523. In his lifetime, Archbishop Antonino was also regarded as a powerful and prolific preacher. From his pulpit in the Duomo, he delivered sermon after sermon to the Florentine faithful on every imaginable subject from female dress habits to capitalist economics. His words, neatly blending Christian piety with Florentine civic pride, were perfectly in tune with the politics of Cosimo de'Medici, and he soon became a close family advisor, especially to Lucrezia Tornabuoni, wife of Cosimo's son Piero (and mother of Lorenzo and Giuliano).[3] She commissioned at least two paintings from Fra Filippo Lippi in the late 1450's, both entitled *Madonna Adoring the Christ Child* (one now in the Dahlem Museum, Berlin, and the other in the Uffizi, Florence[4]) and both bearing resemblance to the London *Annunciation*.

Towards the end of his Life, Antonino collected his sermons into a huge tome he called the *Summa theologica*, a Thomistic conceit, since the Archbishop intended to formulate a set of moral guidelines that would transform his beloved Florence into a true New Jerusalem, heaven on earth *in figuram*.[5] While the subjects covered in his opus are diverse and legion, two threads relevant to our arguments run throughout. The Archbishop was fascinated with the metaphor of light as metaphysical vehicle, and also with every aspect of the life of the Virgin Mary. Regarding light, Antonino took pleasure in the fact that he knew the current scientific literature of the subject. He wrote a sermon "On the Twelve Properties of Divine Grace and their Similarity to Material Light" (*De duodecim proprietatibus divinae gratiae ad similitudinem lucis materialis*). Concerning the eleventh "property," he observed how God's grace is like a ray of sunlight at high noon that *magis directe reverberat terram*, "strikes the earth at right angles," thus releasing its greatest intensity according to the principles of geometric optics.[6]

Antonino was captivated by the story of the Virgin Mary. Fully an eighth part of his *Summa* is devoted to her, including of course a long disquisition on the Annunciation.[7] He discussed the Virgin's appearance, the color of her hair and skin according to current Galenic humoral theory, and also at what age she would be physiologically most fecund. He argued further about the date of the Annunciation, March 25, and whether this was also the same day as Jesus's Passion. Did both events occur at noon, he asked, again making analogy to laws of geometric optics. At that time the sun "produces the most heat on the earth" (*maximum calorem generat super terram*). *Calor*, he averred in this context, symbolized *caritas*, Jesus's supreme

charity to mankind when he sacrificed himself on the cross.[8]

Frequently, Antonine employed the prepositional phrase *in figuram*, "into a figure," by which he meant that his listeners should convert his words in their own mind's eye and imagine just what the Annunciation scene must have looked like –but not in terms of contemporary painting. The Archbishop's imagination remained ever abstractly Augustinian rather that pictorially Albertian; for example, he described the *species* of the announcing angel who, though appearing in human form, nonetheless was able to pass through the closed door of the Virgin's chamber. Since he was composed of divine and not earthly material, Gabriel had no need of either teeth or palate. Thus he spoke not from his mouth but transcommunicated the "voice from heaven [...] in the air" (*vox de caelo [...] in aere*) by means of an *illuminatione invisibili* so that the Virgin's mind was "illuminated and inflamed by God" (*illustrabatur et inflammabatur a Deo*[9]).

Concerning the *modus* of her impregnation, when the Holy Spirit *supervenit in Mariam*, Antonine was just as circumspect as all previous church fathers. He offered a particularly Dominican analysis, part of his special emphasis on the revival of writings by Aquinas and Albertus Magnus. Following these fathers, Antonine wished to make it explicitly clear that the divine begetting took place *in utero* not *in uterum*, the ablative case underscoring Mary's virginity both before and after her pregnancy. Antonine wondered further as to whether this divine union occurred *secundum naturam* as with normal wives, or *supra naturam*. Certainly not the former, he concluded. When the Holy Spirit came upon her, Mary did not feel "the heat of sexual desire" (*calorem concupiscentiae*), but rather "coolness" (*refrigerium*) from the "overshadowing," as Gabriel said, of the "power of the highest." Antonino explained that shadow results from a body in light, and in such manner the "body of humanity raised up in her the incorporeal light of God."[10] In ordinary wives, moreover, impure blood "descends into the place of begetting with a certain kind of sexual desire" (*descendit in locum generationis cum quadam concupiscentia*), whereas Jesus was formed in *utero virginis* from only the "most pure and chaste blood."[11] Finally, after having denied the Virgin's fecundation *secundum naturam*, Antonino abstracts from Gabriel's term "overshadow" the very root of the word, dwelling on its correlation with *light*, thereby implying that the Holy Spirit came upon her in some way analogous. At that point, Antonino tactfully dropped the matter altogether, nor did he ever mention the ear, leaving the artisan-minded in his audience still pondering his light analogy *in figuram*.

We may assume that Fra Filippo Lippi often listened to sermons like these. The charismatic Archbishop's Sunday preachings were certainly discussed and argued in the streets for days afterward. One might also presume the artist's frequent patrons, the Medici, urged him to pay attention. If venal ''Brother Lippo'' (*qua* Browning's Victorian portrait) did grow bored with painting ''saints and saints and saints again,'' he managed nonetheless to limn every one of his dozen known *Annunciations* with striking variety, especially the mechanics of God manifesting the Holy Spirit to Mary. This was clearly one of his most saleable subjects. Would he not have had special reason to hear about it from the most admired theological expert in all of Florence?

Nevertheless, Antonino's verbal descriptions, while picturesque, were not easily picturable. How would an ingenious artist like Fra Filippo Lippi, if he were inspired by such eidetic words, have then translated them into pictorial *invenzioni*? Steinberg and I believe that some time in the late 1450's, the artist, ever looking for a more convincing way to depict the Virgin's sacred fecundation, decided to try something unexampled in the history of both art and science. Whether motivated by Antonino or not, Lippi surely did investigate further Antonino's own analogue, the science of optics (called *perspectiva* in medieval Latin), in order to adapt more of its concepts to this commission. Especially interesting to him was that part of the discipline which attempted to explain how visual images pass through the air into the human eye. This, as Steinberg has already pointed out, would have offered the painter an ideal model for demonstrating explicity yet without breach of decorum how the Holy Spirit ''came upon'' Mary.

Representative manuscripts of all the medieval optical classics were unquestionably in wide circulation in mid-Quattrocento Florence. We know this because the sculptor Lorenzo Ghiberti translated many excerpts, or copied them from someone else's Italian translation into Book III of his *Commentarii*, written in the early 1450's.[12] We have no idea what Ghiberti intended to do with this material, or whether he shared it with fellow artists. For reasons about to be discussed he was particularly interested in the writings of the English Franciscan Roger Bacon (ca. 1220-ca. 1292), though he never referred to Bacon by name, only by the anonymous title *auctore della prospettiva*.

The latter, about 1267, had written a lengthy compendium covering a variety of subjects called *Opus majus* which he sent to Viterbo in an effort to help Pope Clement IV organize a new crusade. Bacon believed that all prior crusades had failed because Christians lacked sufficient scientific learning, especially of geometry and optics. This science he found interesting because, among other things, it could teach Christians how to build giant burning glasses for destroying Moorish ships. He developed these ideas in several tracts relating to optics, the most important being *De multiplicatione specierum*, ''On the Multiplication of Species,'' and *Perspectiva* (actually Part V of his *Opus majus*).[13] No one knows what Pope Clement made of Bacon's work (he died in 1268 shortly after assuming office), but eventually manuscript copies showed up in libraries all over Europe. Bacon's optics not only amalgamated the classical, Arab, and medieval Christian traditions, but newly expanded the concept of radiating light to more universal application.

Bacon began by appropriating an idea earlier proposed by Robert Grosseteste (ca. 1168-1253) that light, created by God on the first day of Genesis, was the essential medium through which every forceful action everywhere in heaven and on earth takes place, including the spreading of God's divine grace to mankind.[14] Since luminous bodies like the sun propagate light in rectilinear rays in all directions without loss of substance, Bacon concluded that every physical and spiritual object in the world also gives forth from itself similarly a uniform but invisible force. He termed it in Latin *species*, that is, ''likeness'' or, as he refined the meaning, ''visual ray.'' *Species* then ''multiply'' throughout the medium, interacting with one another, the stronger *agens* forcing a qualitative change in the weaker *patiens*, as fire consumes wood for example.

Bacon's ''multiplication of *species*'' was clearly dependent on the geometrical theorems of Euclid and Ptolemy which had already explained how visual rays both enter and leave the eye collectively in the form of a cone. In classical optics it was believed that only the ray which passes directly from the center of the object seen to the sensitive center of the eye, making perpendicular contact with both surfaces, could ''certify'' the image clearly. All other oblique rays in the visual cone must either transmit weaker visual details or become reflected away or refracted.[15] Ever since the ancients discovered that light falling at right angles upon a transparent surface passes through unrefracted, or, if the surface is opaque and inflammable, causes burning, Western philosophers equated this process with divine and moral power. Indeed, as the German mystic Meister Eckhart (1260?-1328?) wrote, the soul ''sees'' God just as the eye receives direct light.[16]

Bacon never explained exactly the corporeal nature of *species*, other than claiming it had *longitudinem latitudinem et profundum*. However, he carefully avoided likening it to physical atoms such as the Stoics had argued were the essence of light. His theory, as David Lindberg has shown, was basically Aristotelian and anti-Platonic (or better anti-Plotinus) insofar as it postulated that light must have a material medium through which to pass, and that the *species* are corporeal entities actualized from the substance of that medium.[17] Bacon was therefore concerned with how *species* moves through the medium, whether the medium be uniform such as air, or changing as between the spiritual realm to the mundane world.

Here is what he says:

"But a species is not a body, nor is it moved as a whole from one place to another; but that which is produced [by the *agens*] in the first part of the air [or other medium] is not separated from the part, since form cannot be separated from the matter in which it is unless it should be mind; rather, it produces a likeness to itself in the second part of the air, and so on. Therefore, there is no change of place, but a generation multiplied through the different parts of the medium; nor is it body which is generated there, but a corporeal form that does not have dimension of itself but is produced according to the air; and it is not produced by a flow from the luminous body, but by a drawing forth out of the potentiality of the matter of the air."[18]

Bacon's *species* theory was extraordinarily compelling to thinkers in the late Middle Ages, since it so clearly postulated the physics of vision as microcosm of God's own creative process. A copy of *De Multiplicatione specierum* was purchased for the San Marco Library, either by Cosimo de'Medici or Antonino himself when he was Prior of the convent.[19] The Medici Laurentian Library still possesses three Baconian manuscripts, two of the *Perspectiva* and another of the *De multiplicatione specierum* that were probably in Florence during the fifteenth century. The Biblioteca Riccardiana owns two more fourteenth-century editions of the *Perspectiva*.[20] No Florentine, however, left more documentation of this Baconian interest than Lorenzo Ghiberti. His third *Commentario* is filled with relevant quotations, sometimes garbled, sometimes translated *verbatim* from Bacon or Bacon's chief followers, Witelo (d. after 1281) and John Pecham (ca. 1235-1292)[21] These excerpts have to do with the nature and material of *species* (or *spetie* in Italian), how it carries images through the air to the eye, and what happens within the eye itself. Ghiberti also cited many passages from Bacon and other opticians concerning the necessity for visual rays to be *perpendiculari* in order to produce clear vision. "If one wishes to certify the forms of things seen," he quoted from the Arab Alhazen, "one moves [the eye] so that the center of it is opposite each part of the thing seen [...]."[22] And again from Bacon:

"And because this line [visual ray] is perpendicular and direct and very strong, as we have said above in the things about multiplication of *species*, and this is necessary to vision in order that it comprehend very certainly [...] what it is [that is seen]."[23]

During Ghiberti's busiest years in Florence from 1425 to 1452 when he was designing and casting the ten valves for his

18) A printed diagram (from Witelo, *Opticae libri decem*, F. Risner, ed., Basel, 1572, Book III, p. 87) illustrating the anatomy of the eye as understood by Ghiberti and Fra Lippo Lippi in the fifteenth century. Perpendicular light rays enter the eye through the *foramen* (marked "f" in the diagram) in the *tunica uvea*, and through the *humor aqueus*. They next fall upon the *humor crystallinus*, which we now know to be the focussing lens but then understood as the most sensitive part of the eye, receiving and displaying in miniature the incoming image. The denser *vitreus humor* behind was supposed to refract the visual rays and keep the image from inverting as happens in a regular *camera obscura*. The image would then be transmitted upright through the hollow *nervus opticus* to the brain for final cognition.

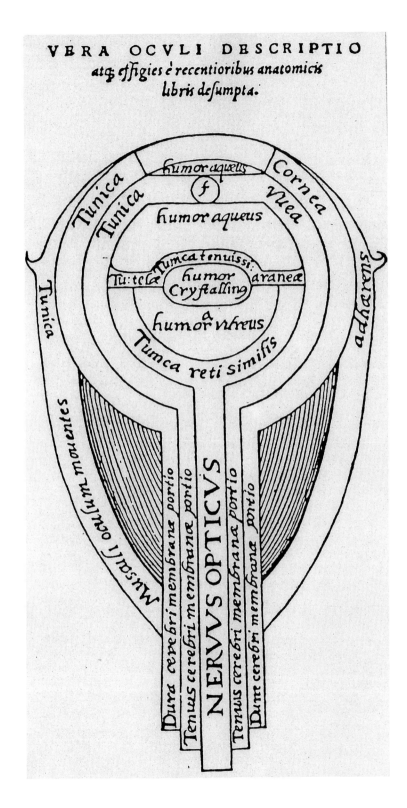

"Gates of Paradise," his large and open *bottega* opposite the Hospital of Santa Maria Nuova served as a kind of meeting place for painters and sculptors to gossip and talk shop. We can be sure that the amiable Brother Lippo was a frequenter, and that he was present when other optical experts like Leon Battista Alberti also stopped by. Is it not possible that Fra Filippo Lippi, once stimulated by an exciting sermon on the Annunciation by Archbishop Antonino, also listened carefully to Ghiberti's own disquisitions on the science of optics?

It is time now to look at Lippi's painting. We notice at the very top of the picture that the artist has shown the hand of God emerging from a bit of cloud surrounded by a halo-like ellipse rimmed by tiny gilded dots. Below this, as if generated by God's haloed hand, are a series of descending circles likewise rimmed in golden dots. They seem to overlap one another, exuding thinner streams of gilding from their upper edges as they gravitate to where the dove is centered just opposite the Virgin Mary [Fig. 15, p.; 16, p.; 17, p.]. How should this strange dispersion of geometrical figures be interpreted? Why would Lippi want to show the dove in this lower position, since the common convention, often employed by Lippi himself, was to have it elevated and emitting rays diagonally toward the Virgin?

We are convinced that Lippi thought out this pictorial solution within the classical and medieval framework of Bacon's "multiplication of *species*" theory. Surely, when the artist painted his dove facing Mary's womb, he was thinking, just as Ghiberti's glosses stressed, about what the medieval opticians called "certification"; that is, how distinct vision occurs only when, as Bacon stated, the visual object "confronts" the eye (*quod est oppositio visibilis respectu visus*), and the visual rays are allowed to enter at right angles to the sensitive *glacialis*, or *humor crystallinus*, what we understand today as the focussing lens which at that time was thought to be in the center rather than in the forepart of the eyeball [Fig. 18].[24] Not only did Bacon believe this certifying power to be basic to vision, but he wished to amplify the concept, applying it as a law of nature, just as Archbishop Antonino adapted the metaphor of the perpendicular ray to argue how Christ crucified gave his charity to mankind at high noon. Notwithstanding, Fra Filippo Lippi emerges as the most versatile thinker of all upon this arcane subject. He attempted, as no one else before him had ever done, to relate this same principle of perpendicularity to Mary's miraculous fecundation.

Having decided this, Lippi had the problem within the same optical context of showing the *species* of the Holy Ghost moving from ethereal through terrestrial atmosphere. His pictorial response, as we see, follows closely the verbal logic of Bacon's just-quoted explanation from his *Perspectiva*. The artist did not show the Holy Spirit departing from God's offering hand in the earthly form of a dove, but rather as an ethereal halo that

49

appears to "produce a likeness of itself in the second part of the air [...] a generation multiplied through the different parts of the medium." Moreover, the gilded motes composing these descending haloes could be described as an artistic representation of *species* having, as Bacon stated above, "no dimensions of itself but produced according to the air [...] by a drawing forth out of the potentiality of the matter of air."[25] In the lowest of these "multiplying" haloes, just before the Virgin's womb, Lippi indicated that the Holy Spirit had at last materialized as the familiar dove.

We look more closely at Lippi's image of the dove *cum* Holy Spirit (see detail, Fig. 16). From its head there seems to radiate another array of gilded dots. There is of course nothing unusual about this. Painted *Annunciations* commonly show such clusters of golden rays fanning out from the symbolic dove, a conventional pictorial metaphor of celestial communication. What is unusual, as Steinberg has observed, is that from the Virgin's abdomen, just opposite the dove, flows an even more sharply formed *reciprocating* pyramid of clustered rays. Moreover, it emerges from a short vertical opening deliberately painted in the Virgin's garment.

While the rays from the dove are depicted in long wavy lines of gilded dots, those coming from the Virgin are shorter and somewhat straighter. None from either side are indicated as making contact with each other – save one issuing from the center of the cluster around the dove's mouth and reaching toward another from the center of the cluster at the parting of Mary's dress. Here we have two more remarkable clues that the artist was following Bacon's optical model.

In both his *De multiplicatione specierum* and *Perspectiva*, Bacon theorized that *species* do not act upon the eye in only one direction. Since the eye is such a special organ it must exert some kind of counter-force upon the incoming *species* of things seen. I repeat below the passage from Bacon's *Perspectiva* already noted by Steinberg:

> "Therefore vision must perform the act of seeing by its own force. But the act of seeing is the perception of a visible object at a distance, and therefore vision perceives what is visible by its own force multiplied to the object. Moreover, the species of the things of the world are not fitted by nature to effect the complete act of vision at once because of its nobleness. Hence these must be aided and excited by the species of the eye, which travels in the locality of the visual pyramid, and changes the medium and ennobles it [...] and so prepares the passage of the species itself of the visible object, and, moreover, ennobles it, so that it is quite similar and analogous to the nobility of the animate body which is the eye."[26]

The second hint of Lippi's debt to Bacon's optics is the way he represented the *species* coursing from the dove to the Virgin. Only one ray issuing from the dove's mouth connects with the center of the pyramid at Mary's womb. It is also the most nearly "perpendicular." Bacon explained that *species* even of this all-important certifying ray might be bent while progressing from a rare to dense medium, "as is the case in descending from the sky to [...] lower objects." When passing into the eye itself, *species* must follow a "twisting path (*linea tortuosa*) [...] as the actions of an animated being require."[27] Oblique rays, just as we see here in the dove's pyramid, are too sharply refracted by the change of medium and lose their power. Ghiberti noted further that non-perpendicular *species* falling on the eye "are broken up [...] and don't appear manifest to the eye" (*romperannosi [...][et] non appariscono manifeste all'occhio*).[28] Again, as we observe in Lippi's painting, the twisted, oblique rays coming from the dove fall short and do not penetrate to the Virgin's womb.

Finally, we consider the little cut Lippi depicted in Mary's garment. Why did the artist paint this? Certainly his patrons would never have permitted such a provocative detail if anything other than a *nihil obstat* meaning were intended. Once more, however, we find plausible explanations in the then-current, acceptable science of optics. Let us first suppose that the artist, having already equated Mary's impregnation with visual rays entering the eye, intended this opening represented in the Virgin's dress simply to remind his viewers of the pupil, or, as Ghiberti called it, *il foro*, "the opening" in the forepart of the *uvea*, the second of the three membranous "tunics" medieval opticians believed covered the eye. We note that in Lippi's time, the Latin and Italian word *tunica* had two well-understood meanings. It was the common term for a long dress belted below the bosom just as the Virgin wears in our London painting, and it was also the scientific expression for each of the layered integuments protecting the eye. Lorenzo Ghiberti frequently used the word in its latter sense, as he recited below Bacon's description of the *foro dell'uvea*:

> "[...] this [...] tunic [...] is called the *uvea* because it is similar to a grape [*uva*] since it has an opening in its anterior part like that left in a grape when the stem is removed [...]. [The] pyramid [...] perpendicular to the eye [...] falls into the opening of the *uvea* and is placed directly opposite the opening; that is, the center of the eye, and thus makes vision and the act of seeing good and principal."[29]

Nonetheless, even if Lippi did intend such a comparison between the *uvea* tunic of the eye and Mary's dress, why did he not paint the "pupil" in its usual circular form? Why did he shape it somewhat like an almond, or, more precisely, like a short, vertical vent in a piece of cloth? I can only surmise that Brother Lippo would have thought it distasteful if not brazenly suggestive to represent a sharply rounded hole in the Virgin's tunic.

Perhaps he was moved by yet another *figura*. Just as the pupillary opening in the *uvea* tunic of the eye reminded medieval opticians of the hole in the end of a plucked grape, so it also reminded medieval preachers of Jesus's wound, the similarly shaped gash in his right side. As the thirteenth-century Franciscan Peter of Limoges wrote in his *De oculo morali* ("On the Moral Eye"), an extraordinarily popular source-book for optical metaphors in sermons:

"The *foramen* [as in the eye] that we ought to gaze upon most frequently is the wound of Christ who was pierced on the cross [...]. Anyone can [...] mediate in his mind's eye on Christ' wound so that he conforms to Christ's sufferings through his model."[30]

Still, Lippi in his particularized image of this optical metaphor was reminded of how such a tear in a garment also follows the grain of the cloth. By disguising his detail in this way, it would look less conspicuous, indeed so much so that it has escaped notice ever since. In fact, do we not have here a Florentine case of multi-layered typology, "reality and symbol," just as in contemporary, fifteenth-century Northern art? As Erwin Panofsky revealed in his famous study of early Netherlandish painting, artists like Jan van Eyck frequently painted highly realistic physical details in their pictures in order to camouflage abstract religious ideas. Panofsky, quoting Thomas Aquinas, subtitled his appropriate chapter: *Spiritualia sub metaphoris corporalium*, "Corporeal Metaphors of Thing Spiritual," but he could just as easily have cited St. Antonine, who expressed the same thought in Quattrocento Florence: *Mensurare temporalia facit geometria spiritualis*, "Spiritual geometry works to measure temporal things."[31]

In sum, what we contemplate in Fra Filippo Lippi's London *Annunciation* is an elegant analogy relating Jesus's miraculous *in utero* conception, as described theologically by Archbishop Antonino, to the optical reception of images in the eye following the scientific explanations of Roger Bacon. According to Bacon and as interpreted by Ghiberti, the process of seeing begins with an object before the eyes emitting *species* from every point on its surface. This *species* immediately becomes invisible and dissolves in the intervening medium, continuing to regenerate or "multiply" itself according to the inherent "potentiality" of that medium. When arriving at the surface of the eye, and permitted to penetrate the *uvea* by the eye's "ennobling" power, the incoming *species* encounters the denser humoral medium of the inner eye which has its own potentiality. Upon the anterior surface of the sensitive *crystallinus*, the *species* actualizes as the original likeness, or rather as separate likenesses in the *crystallinus* of each eye which then pass through the individual optic nerves to the *nervus communis*, the

joined "common nerve" in the brain. There - *in nervo* in Bacon's Latin ablative – occurs final cognition.[32]

This same mechanistic rationale had also, about 1425, inspired Filippo Brunelleschi (1377-1446) to work out the rules for linear perspective in art, which he applied to his small, now-lost picture of the Florentine Baptistery.[33] Especially interesting to Brunelleschi was the optical explanation of how the *species* of a large object can produce a small image, still in scale and tiny enough to enter the pupil. He then adapted the Euclidean principle accounting for this to the similar problem in painting in order to depict a realistic likeness upon a smaller picture surface. Brunelleschi cut a little hole in the back of his first perspective painting. He wanted to convince his viewers, as they looked through the hole in order to see a mirror reflection of the picture in front, that the manner in which they were seeing the picture was just the same as if they were looking through the pupil in the *uvea* and beholding what the inner eye displays upon the surface of the glacial membrane.

Dare we assume that Fra Filippo Lippi, thinking about Brunelleschi and his application of the rules of optical science to painting, postulated a wonderful and completely original connection between Jesus's miraculous conception *in utero* and the Baconian mechanistic theory of visual conception *in nervo*, indeed, even likening the optic nerve in the eye to the umbilical cord from the Virgin's navel to her womb? Could it be that Lippi, theorizing how God sent forth His own *species* to Mary, ingeniously imagined that the Father then seeded His likeness in the sacrosanct womb of Mary, just as nature reproduces its likeness in the marvelous recesses of the human eye? And just as a Renaissance painter creates by applying perspective principles in a picture?

Unfortunately, as far as we know, Fra Filippo Lippi's ingenious imagery in the London *Annunciation* was never repeated. Was it too scientific, too arcane for ordinary understanding? Or was it because Bacon's writings were under suspicion by his own Franciscan Order? Perhaps such explicit application of his theories to so delicate a subject was deemed indiscreet by the local authorities.[34] After all, neither Antonino not Ghiberti ever mentioned Bacon by name.[35] It is also possible that the blatant Aristotelianism inherent in Bacon's theories, and by extension in Lippi's London *Annunciation*, became unfashionable in Medici circles after 1460, when Marsilio Ficino began to turn his patrons' attention to Plato. By the end of the Quattrocento in Florence, a more subjective, philosophic style in tune with Renaissance Platonism (as in Botticelli) had replaced the mechanistic, Aristotelian approach of artists during the first half-century. In any case, for the next five hundred years, Lippi's remarkable imagery was destined to remain not only unique but unobserved.[36]

[1] My sincere thanks to Dr. Ashok Roy, Head of the Scientific Department, National Gallery of Art, for permitting this examination of Lippi's *Annunciation* and discussing with me the artist's painting methods, and also to Ms Elspeth Hector, Head Librarian, for making available the Conservation Department reports and other relevant files concerning the picture. Regarding oil-gilding as applied here by Lippi, see J. Plesters and A. Roy, "The Materials and Techniques: Cennino Cennini's Treatise Illustrated," *National Gallery Technical Bulletin*, 9, 1985, pp. 26-35.

[2] The painting, 666 in the London National Gallery, is of identical size (68.5 by 152 cms.) and lunette-shape as another in the same museum entitled *Seven Enthroned Saints*. Both apparently were commissioned by Cosimo de'Medici as part of his furnishings for the new Palazzo Medici on the Via Larga (now Cavour). In our *Annunciation* a diamond ring with three feathers, an *impresa* often associated with his grandson Lorenzo, is clearly depicted as an illusionistic carving on the balustrade separating Gabriel from Mary. Martin Davies, in his *National Gallery Catalogue: The Earlier Italian Schools*, London, 1961, pp. 293-296, argues that the painting therefore should be dated no earlier than 1449, the year of Lorenzo's birth. However, he also avers not so reasonably that the picture was commissioned for that very occasion. In my opinion, the painting represents Lippi's style of the late 1450's, being similar to his Berlin *Madonna Adoring the Christ Child*, also painted for the Medici Palace. For further arguments concerning the dating, see G. Pudelko, "Per la datazione delle opere di fra Filippo Lippi", *Rivista d'Arte*, 18, 1936, pp. 47-56; R. Oertel, *Fra Filippo Lippi*, Vienna (Anton Schroll), 1942, p. 41; and M. Pittaluga, *Filippo Lippi*, Florence (Del Turco), 1949, pp. 202-203. For a brief summation, see G. Marchini, *Filippo Lippi*, Milan (Electa Editrice), 1975, pp. 206-207.

[3] On Antonino's relationship to the Medici and concerning his influence on Florentine art and culture in general, see F. Hartt, *History of Italian Renaissance Art*, Englewood Cliffs, N. J. (Prentice-Hall/Abrams), 1979, second edition, pp. 229-230 and *passim*. Professor Hartt is currently preparing an entire book on St. Antonino in this respect. See also C. Gilbert, " The Archbishop and the Painters of Florence, 145," *The Art Bulletin*, 41, 1959, pp. 75-87.

[4] See also M. A. Lavin, "Giovannino Battista: A Study in Renaissance Religious Symbolism," *The Art Bulletin*, 37, 1955, pp. 85-101.

[5] Originally transcribed in the 1450's, Antonino's *Summa* was finally published in the eighteenth century and recently reissued as *Sancti Antonini Summa Theologica*, Verona, 1740, fascimile edition, Graz, 1959, 4 vols.

[6] *Ibidem*, Vol. tit. 8, cap. 1, cols. 461-468.

[7] I have already analyzed Antonino's Annunciation remarks (*Summa, op. cit.*, Vol. IV, tit. 15, cap. 8, col. 957-985) elsewhere; see S. Edgerton, "'Mensurare temporalia facit geometria spiritualis': Some Fifteenth-Century Italian Notions about When and Where the Annunciation Happened," in I. Lavin and J. Plummer, eds., *Studies in Medieval and Renaissance Painting in Honor of Millard Meiss*, New York (New York University Press), 1978, Vol. I, pp. 115-130.

[8] *Summa, op. cit.*, Vol. IV, tit. 25, cap. 9, col. 970.

[9] *Ibidem*, Vol. IV, tit. 15, cap. 9, col. 973.

[10] *Ibidem*, Vol. IV, tit. 15, cap. 10, col. 981: *[...] corpus humanitatis in [Mariam] suscipiet incorporem lumen deitatis. Umbra enim a lumine formatur et corpore [...]*.

[11] *Ibidem*, Vol. IV, tit. 15, cap, 10, col. 980. Concerning the relationship of medieval moral codes generally to women's *menses*, see Ch. T. Wood, "The Doctors' Dilemma: Sin, Salvation, and the Menstrual Cycle in Medieval Thought," *Speculum*, 56.4, 1981, pp. 710-727.

[12] See J. von Schlosser, ed., *Lorenzo Ghibertis Denkwürdigkeiten*, Berlin, 1912, Vol. 1, pp. 55f.; for a concordance of Ghiberti's sources, see G. Ten Doesschate, *De derde commentaar van Lorenzo Ghiberti in verband met de mildeleeuwsche optiek*, Utrecht, 1940. My sincere thanks to Mr. Scott Opler, candidate for the Master's Degree in Art History at Williams College, for his considerable help in tracking down relevant references in the writings of Ghiberti and Antonino.

[13] For modern editions and translations of these writings, see J. H. Bridges, ed., *The Opus Majus of Roger Bacon*, Oxford, Eng. (Clarendon Press), 1897, 2 vols.; R. Belle Burke, *The Opus Majus of Roger Bacon*, Philadelphia (University of Pennsylvania Press), 1928, 2 vols.; and D. C. Lindberg, *Robert Bacon's Philosophy of Nature; A Critical Edition, With English Translation, Introduction and Notes, of "De multiplicatione specierum [...]"*, Oxford, Eng. (Clarendon Press), 1983.

[14] See A. C. Crombie, *Robert Grosseteste and the Origins of Experimental Science*, 1100-1700, Oxford, Eng. (Clarendon Press), 1961, pp. 99-104.

[15] Concerning classical, Arab, and medieval optical theory in general, see D. C. Lindberg, *Theories of Vision from Al-Kindi to Kepler*, Chicago (University of Chicago Press), 1976.

[16] F. Pfeiffer, ed., *Meister Eckhart*, Leipzig, 1857, sermon XLI. Dante the poet, was also intrigued, writing in his *Il convivio* that the same power explains why "looking someone straight in the eye" is virtuous (E. Moore and P. Toynbee, eds., *Le opere di Dante Alighieri*, Oxford, 1924, pp. 261-262). Perhaps the most popular and widely disseminated of all such applications of optical science to moral philosophy during the Middle Ages was the tract *De oculo morali*, written in the late thirteenth century by another Franciscan monk named Pierre Lacepierre de Limognes. Over a hundred manuscript copies still survive, and after first printing in Augsburg, 1495, three more editions were published including one in Italian (see D. L. Clark, "Optics for Preachers: The *De oculo morali* by Peter of Limognes," *Michigan Academician*, 9.3, 1977, pp. 329-343).

[17] D. C. Lindberg, "The Genesis of Kepler's Theory of Light: Light Metaphysics from Plotinus to Kepler," *Osiris*, 2, 2nd Series, 1986, pp. 5-42.

[18] *Perspectiva* (*Opus majus*), Part V, Distinction 8, Chap. 4. This translation is quoted in Lindberg, *op. cit.*, 1983, p. lxiii. A slightly different version is offered by Burke, *op. cit.*, Vol. II, pp. 489-490.

[19] The manuscript has been dated about 1450 (see D. C. Lindberg, *op. cit.*, 1983, p. lxxvi), and is catalogued as MS Conv. soppr. J.IV.29 in the Biblioteca Nazionale, Florence. A good example of Baconian influence on Antonino himself is seen in the following passage from his *Summa, op. cit.*, Vol. I, tit. 2, cap. 6, cols. 88-93, from a sermon entitled *De Phantasie, seu imaginativa*:

Sicut enim res sensibilis, quum videtur, multiplicat speciem suam, idest similitudinem usque ad potentiam visivam, mediante qua similitudine oculos videt; [...] sic ipsa potentia phantastica repraesentat tales similitudines, quae dicuntur phantasmata seu imaginationes intellectui, et in illis intelligit.

[20] D. C. Lindberg, *A Catalogue of Medieval and Renaissance Optical Manuscripts*, Toronto, 1975, p. 40. Both the Laurentian copies of Bacon's *Perspectiva* are catalogued under the same rubric: MS Plut. 29. Also in the Laurenziana is MS Ashburnham 957, a copy of *De multiplicatione specierum*. The Riccardiana copies of the *Perspectiva* are MS 885 and MS 1223 (II).

[21] Bacon's ideas in fact received their widest proliferation through the contemporary writings of fellow English Franciscan John Pecham,

Archbishop of Canterbury and author of *Perspectiva communis*, undoubtedly the most popular treatise on the subject during the late Middle Ages and Renaissance everywhere in Western Europe (see D. C. Lindberg, *John Pecham and the Science of Optics: "Perspectiva communis"*, Madison, Wis. (University of Wisconsin Press), 1970).

[22] Schlosser, *op. cit.*, p. 86:

"Et quando arà uoluto certificare la forma della cosa uisa, si mouerà sicchè il mezo sia opposita a ciascheduna parte della cosa uisa [...]."

[23] *Ibidem*, p. 78:

"Et perchè questa linea è perpendiculare et diritto et fortissimo, come se auuto nelle cose abbiamo dette di sopra della multiplicatione delle spetie, et questo è necessario al uedere acciochè egli comprenda certissimamente et fortissimamente quello è."

Ghiberti's statement, inscribed in Florence at about the same time that Lippi was painting his London *Annunciation*, ought to offer as solid textual evidence as any historian could hope for to explain why the artist placed the dove in such an unusual position before the Virgin's womb (see *infra*).

[24] Burke, *op. cit.*, p. 475; Bridges, *op. cit.*, Vol. 2, p. 56.

[25] D. C. Lindberg, in his "Genesis of Kepler's Theory," *op. cit.*, p. 15, quotes below from J. McEvoy, *The Philosophy of Robert Grosseteste*, Oxford, Eng., 1982, pp. 65-67, 136. While the passage refers to the specific theories of Grosseteste, it is also relevant not only to Bacon but to Lippi's image in the London *Annunciation*:

"Light streaming from a source tends to form a hierarchy of diminishing power, and the created lights in their varying degrees of participation imitate the nature of the source of light, each shining or reflecting upon the next light which it has itself received from above [...]. The generation and extension of light downwards from this spiritual sun leaves it in itself unchanged, undivided, and still transcendent to the hierarchy formed by its effusion [...]. Since all light comes from [...] the Father of Lights, the work of the assimilation and transmission of light within the grades of the hierarchy, down even to the lowest, is as much the activity of the *lux suprema* as of the lowest beings themselves."

[26] Burke, *op. cit.*, Vol. II, p. 471.

[27] D. C. Lindberg, *op. cit.*, 1983, pp. lxiv-lxv; Burke, *op. cit.*, Vol. I, p. 131-136.

[28] Schlosser, *op. cit.*, pp. 94-95.

[29] Schlosser, *op. cit.*, pp. 70-71, 94:

"[...] questa [...] tunica si chiama uuea però che'lla è simile alla uua, Però che'lla lascia nella sua parte dinanci el foro si come si lascia nella uua, quando si leua del ramo d'apiccarla [...]. [La] piramide [...] perpendiculare sopra all'occhio [...] cade nel foro dell'uuea et è dirittamente contraposto al foro cioè el centro dell'occhio et però fa la cisione et l'atto dello vedere buono et principale [...]."

[30] As quoted in D. Clark, *op. cit.*, p. 338 (see note 16 *supra*).

[31] *Summa, op. cit.*, Vol IV, tit. 16, cap. 1, col. 1265. Aquinas's Latin quotation is part of the title of Chapter V of Panofsky's *Early Netherlandish Painting*, Cambridge, Mass. (Harvard University Press), 1958, Vol. I, pp. 131-148. Lippi's debt to Netherlandish painting has frequently been noted. In his earlier, ca. 1440, *Annunciation* painted for the Medicean Church of San Lorenzo in Florence, he depicted a crystal flask filled with water in the foreground, very much in the manner of Jan van Eyck and with obvious optical iconographic significance as a symbol of the Virgin birth. See F. Hartt, *op. cit.*, p. 226.

[32] J. H. Bridges, *op. cit.*, Vol. II, pp. 32-33.

[33] See S. Y. Edgerton, Jr., *The Renaissance Rediscovery of Linear Perspective*, New York, 1976.

[34] D. C. Lindberg, *op. cit.*, 1983, pp. xxv-xxvi. My special thanks to Professor Lindberg for reading an early draft of this paper and offering excellent ideas and well-taken comments.

[35] Powerful clerics in fifteenth-century Florence often lashed out against inappropriate or potentially heretical artistic representations of religious subject matter. Archbishop Antonino offered a sermon on the problem; see Creighton Gilbert's interesting analysis of it in his article, "The Archbishop and the Painters of Florence," *loc. cit.*

[36] This paper has also profited from helpful comments made when delivered as a public lecture on three different occasions in 1986-87: during a *convegno* entitled "L'Annunciazione in Toscana nel rinascimento," held at the Villa I Tatti (The Harvard University Center for Italian Renaissance Studies) and the Istituto Francese di Firenze on October 29-31, 1986; and again at the American Academy in Rome on November 24, 1986; and with Leo Steinberg at the University of Pennsylvania, Philadelphia, on March 17, 1987. I am also indebted to Dorothy D. Edgerton and Karen Kowitz for their excellent editorial criticisms.

WALTER CAHN

Moses ben Abraham's *Chroniques de la Bible*

For Rachel Wischnitzer

In the Royal Library at The Hague, there is a little-known manuscript with illustrations of the prophecies of Daniel, a singular work probably executed in northeastern France or Flanders around the year 1300.[1] As will be seen below, it has some interest, albeit tangential, for the study of Jewish art, to which Rachel Wischnitzer has made both pioneering and fundamental contributions. The text of the Hague manuscript is a French paraphrase of the Bible, with special emphasis on the Books of Daniel and Maccabees. The translator and compiler identifies himself and his patron in the prefatory opening passage, which may be translated as follows: "My Lord, Count William of Auvergne, who wanted to have for himself and to know the beginning and the unfolding of the lineages since the creation of the world, as well as the battles which were fought in ancient times, had this book written. And I, Moses, the son of Abraham, the redhead and Jew, applied himself to put this matter into plain French."[2] The work comes to an end with the subscription "Explicit la bible en franchois" written in the hand of the original scribe, followed by the words in a *batarde* script of the fifteenth century: "selon la descricion veritable de Josephus par forme de chroniques en ce compris lexposition des visions de Daniel le prophete hystoriees destranges figures." The manuscript was formerly in the collection (Ms. 175) of the *landsadvocat* Jacob Visser, who died in 1804, and was acquired five years later by the Royal Library. Nothing is known of its earlier history.

As we learn from Moses ben Abraham himself, the sources of his chronicle were the Bible, Josephus – whose writings are referred to in the opening statement and elsewhere in the text as "la verite de Josephe" – and the Alexander legend.

The author's avowed aim to trace the lineages of noble clans and peoples back to their Biblical origins, to recount the struggles of ancient empires and speculate on marvels still to come governs the selection of his material.[3] There is no reference to the Creation of the World, and the opening prologue leads without a break of any kind to an enumeration of the descendance of Adam through Noah and his three sons, Shem, Ham and Iaphet, the traditional progenitors of peoples in the Medieval tripartite division of mankind. In this interpretation, the peoples of Europe are held to be descendants of Iaphet, and those of Gaul in particular, of the first of Iaphet's seven sons, Gomer.[4] Our chronicler, however, says nothing of the *Galli,* and instead rather boldly makes of Gomer the parent of Francus or Francio, the legendary founder of the Franks: "le premier fils de Iaphet, Gomer, engendra 1 fils qui ot a nom Francion. Et cil vint en la terre de France. Et par son nom fu apeles France. Et ler terre siet sur le fleuve de Seine."[5] It is worth noting that this view of Frankish origins is at variance with the much bruited account of the Trojan legend, enshrined in the *Grandes Chroniques de France,* which claims that Francio was a son of Hector, who fled westward with his followers after the fall of Troy.[6] But the author on the whole stays fairly close to the Biblical narrative, and I have not found anything else in the text that might be said to promote dynastic claims or the special interests of the Count of Auvergne, his putative patron.

The writer's further account of Iaphet's progeny and that of his two brothers in the different parts of the inhabited world touches on the history of the Babylonian and Persian empires as it is reflected in the Scripture, notably in the Books of Daniel and Esther. What follows (fols. 18-24) is a brief summary of the contents of each of the books of the Old Testament, and after this, two short sections on Christians and Muslims (24v). These passages differ markedly from one another in substance and tone. That which is devoted to the Christian side is not much more than a recital of the books of the New Testament, their authors and the intended beneficiaries of their exhortations. The writer also explains that the preaching of the Apostles had the effect of eradicating the idolatrous worship of the ancient gods and of substituting Christian festivals for them, but a certain distance, or even a touch of irony, may be detected in his declared intention "to deal only briefly with the Evangelists' assertion that they had heard and even seen the deeds and sayings of Jesus Christ and of others they had heard from the Apostles [...]."[7] By contrast, the section devoted to the Muslims deals concretely with their beliefs. Muslims, the writer states, adhere to the law of Moses. Muhammad commanded them not to eat ritually impure meat and prohibited the cult of stars to which they were accustomed to offer fasts and sacrifices. But Muhammad himself, who was learned in astronomy, the natural sciences and the magical arts, did not scruple to put these skills to use in order to make prognostications or to determine the appropriate time to wage a successful war against one's enemies.[8]

Without much of a transition, the chronicle once more takes up Daniel, who, according to the writer, "had foreseen with greater clarity than the other prophets the coming judgment of peoples, the salvation of the just and the destruction of the wicked." First (fols. 25-25v), Nabuchadnezzar's dream of the composite colossus with feet of clay and its destruction are recounted, followed by Daniel's interpretation (2:1-49). The writer then relates the Prophet's vision of the four beasts (7:1-28), which is explained to him by an angel (fols. 25v-28). This explanation corresponds to the exegesis of the vision diffused in the Medieval West chiefly through the agency of Jerome's *Commentary on Daniel,* where it is held that the beasts stand for the four ancient empires which succeeded one another, Babylon, Persia, Greece and Rome.[9] We then (fols. 28-30v) hear of Daniel's vision of the combat between a ram and a one-horned he-goat, and the former's defeat by the latter (8:1-27), symbolizing the struggle between the Persians and the Greeks and the victory of Alexander over Darius. Moses ben Abraham's explanation of this prophecy is drawn out at great length, since it includes the traditional speculation on the meaning of the Seventy Weeks (9:24) and the two thousand and three hundred days (8:14) for the reckoning of the duration of time that must elapse before the restoration of the Temple in Jerusalem and the onset of the Messianic age.[10] The author's calculations lead him to conclude

that the critical event will take place in the year 1290, and the new age be definitively ushered in forty-five years later, in 1335.[11]

Alexander's conquest of Persia having been adumbrated, the text takes up the career of the Macedonian (fols. 39v-50), of whom the author furnishes an engagingly fantastic portrait: "He was very wise and strong and brave (*preus*) in everything that he undertook... He did not resemble father or his mother, but rather had the appearance of a lion. His eyes shone. The right one was black and looked to the fore, while the left one was yellow, like the eye of a cat, and looked back. His teeth were sharp like the teeth of a dog, and he was brave and just like a lion already in young age."[12] The text follows Josephus (*Ant. Iud.* XI, 8) in the relation of the hero's march on Jerusalem and his respectful attitude toward the God of Israel and the priests of the Temple.[13] The Alexander romance supplied the information for the extraordinary adventures of the Greek campaign in the East.[14] The division of Alexander's empire among four successor kings provides the author with another opportunity to document for the reader the progressive unfolding of history according to Daniel's prophecy. The text now chronicles the agitated history of the Hellenistic rulers in the Holy Land, based on the two Books of Maccabees and the parallel narratives found in Josephus' *Jewish Antiquities* and the opening chapters of the *Jewish Wars.*[15] This section of the work, nearly two thirds of its entire length, comes to an end somewhat abruptly with the story of the struggle between Herod and his sons, and the king of Cappadocia Archelaus' guileful deflection of Herod's anger against his son Alexander (*Bellum Iud.* I, 508).

The manuscript is written in a not very regular Gothic *littera textualis,* with much abbreviation. The text is introduced by a historiated initial, eleven lines high, with a portrait of the author seated at a pulpit, and depicted in the act of writing, in the manner of a learned man or philosopher (Fig. 1). The figure, whose face and hands are unfortunately lost through accidental or deliberate abrasion, wears a mauve-colored mantle draped over a red robe, and a pink bonnet.[16] On the upper right arm, there is a circular, white-rimmed badge, the *rouelle,* which identifies him as a Jew. The Third Lateran Council (1215) had decreed that Jews should be required to wear distinctive garb. According to U. Robert, the use of the wheel (*rota, rotella*) as an identifying sign for Jews seems to be of French origin.[17] The synodal statutes of the bishop of Paris Eudes of Sully (d. 1208) stipulate the wearing by Jews of a *rota,* usually made of cloth or parchment and fastened on the outer garment, and this prescription was repeated by later church assemblies. The rule was given official sanction for the entire kingdom through a decree of Louis IX, issued in 1269, and later confirmed by Philip the Fair.

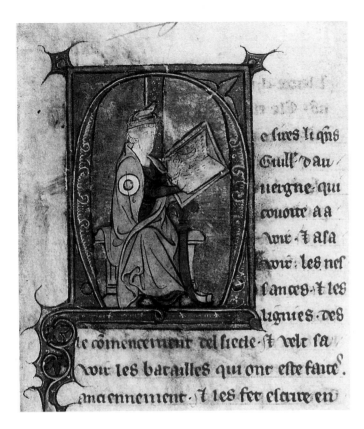

1) Moses ben Abraham, *Chroniques de la Bible*, «Author Portrait», The Hague, Royal Library, Ms. 131 A 3, fol. 1, (Photo: Koninklijke Bibliotheek).

While the opening initial of the manuscript is a fully painted design, making use of body color, the other illustrations in the work, though in my judgment executed in a comparable style and perhaps by the same painter, are carried out in a freer, almost wash-like technique, handled with impressive brio. These *etranges figures,* as they are called in the fifteenth-century addition to the original subscription, all concern Daniel's prophecies. They are placed in specially tailored spaces within the text or in the margins, and stand in isolation on the parchment, without a frame or an indication of the setting. Some of the images are accompanied by explanatory inscriptions, some formulated in French, others in Latin.

The first of these illustrations (Fig. 2), also damaged by rubbing, concerns the great statue of Nabuchadnezzar's dream, reduced to dust and carried away by the wind (2:3 1ff). The head of fine gold is envisioned by the artist as having been crowned. The arms are of silver, as indicated in the Biblical text, and the belly and thighs of brass are rendered in red.

2) Moses ben Abraham, *Chroniques de la Bible*, «Nabuchadnezzar's Statue», The Hague, Royal Library, Ms. 131 A 3, fol. 25, (Photo: Koninklijke Bibliotheek).

The iron legs are shown in blue, with red dots on the blue ground to show the mixture of iron and clay in the feet. While the text of the Latin Vulgate speaks of the destruction of the statue by a stone which struck its weakest part, the feet ("et percussit statuam in pedibus eius"), this verse does not occur in Moses ben Abraham's French version. The omission probably explains the fact that in the picture, the stone strikes the head or neck of the image, and suggests that the artist relied for guidance on the translation and not on the more authoritative scriptural source. The interpretation of the wind ("un tourbillons de vent" in the translation) in the margin below and on another page of the manuscript (fol. 26. Fig. 3) also deserves to be noted. It departs from the ancient and medieval habit of personifying winds in the guise of bearded and horn-blowing divinities,[18] and substitutes for this anthropomorphic convention a more "literal", graphically mimetic ideogram, a large, drop-like form shaded with wavy lines and tones that are meant to evoke the movement of air.

A second set of illustrations (Fig. 3) is devoted to Daniel's vision of the four beasts, surrounded on the page by the four winds which announced the appearance of these fantastic creatures of the sea. The first beast is described in the Latin Vulgate as being "like a lioness" ("quasi leaena"), with the wings of an eagle: "I beheld till her wings were plucked off, and she was lifted from the earth, and stood upon her feet as a man, and the heart of a man was given to her" (7:4). The French text, here at odds with Jerome as well as later interpreters, but significantly faithful to the meaning of the Hebrew 'aryeh, calls the animal a lion ("un lyon").[19] The painter (Fig. 3, left) once again followed the vernacular translation on this point, with which the rubric leo, visible just above the wings of the animal, agrees. His lion has a golden head with a crown, and a grey body. The man's heart on its breast oddly bears the features of a youthful face.[20] The beast is also equipped with human hands and feet, and so it would seem, human rather than leonine pudenda. I have no really satisfactory explanation for this puzzling aspect of the image. It may well be, however, that the mixture of human and animal features in the characterization of the beast was encouraged by an ambiguity in the translator's rendering of the Biblical "et cor eius datum est ei" as "et avait cors de homme", since the word cors can be read in the vernacular as either heart (coeur) or body (corps).

The second creature (bottom, center), described as resembling a bear (7:5), is silver-colored. In the place of three rows of teeth mentioned in the Vulgate ("et tres ordines erant in ore eius et in dentibus eius"), three horn-like protrusions depart from the snout, inspired once more by the French version of the same passage, which reads "et avait III. grans cornes en la bouche". Behind the animal, the curious and fiercely dramatic head of a man in profile seen in the act of speaking or shouting, stands for the mysterious voice with proclaims "Arise, devour much flesh." The third beast (right), a leopard-like animal with four heads and four bird's wings (7:6), is red and sports golden crowns, the latter perhaps meant to express the power given it, which extended, as the text states "dusques aux quatres angles de la terre". The fourth creature, called Bestia decem cornuum and the most ferocious of all (7:7-8) has a dark grey body with a barbed reddish spine (right, bottom). Three of its horns have been severed, and in the midst of the remaining seven, there is a human head, which stands for the little horn that sprang up between them, "with eyes like the eyes of a man... and a mouth speaking great things."

The third group of illustrations refers to the Prophet's vision of the struggle of the ram and the he-goat (8:3ff). In the first pair of miniatures (Fig. 4), we see the one-horned goat as it makes its charge against the ram, descending upon it from above in a diving thrust, for "un de ses pies ne touchait terre". On the opposite page (Fig. 5), the animals are depicted again, the more placid, prancing ram at the top and the goat breaking the horns of its defeated opponent below. The sequence continues on the verso of the same sheet (Fig. 6), where in the first episode, the ram's horn is now broken. The reader is told that he may see its fall to the ground in the picture.[21] In the second stage, the horn has been replaced by four new ones (8:8), and in the third, the little horn which came forth in their midst (8:9) has sprouted between them, animated, like the fourth beast of the earlier version, by human features. Throughout the entire sequence, the goat is red in color and has a blue horn, while the ram is blue and has golden horns. Setting aside the color the portrayal of these familiar animals, lively and relaxed, makes a more naturalistic impression than the fantastic creatures depicted on the previous page of the manuscript, of necessity remote from experience.

The last two illustrations of the chronicle only repeat some of the images which have already been described. This occurs in connection with the writer's desire to draw out or to underscore the meaning of the prophecy, showing it to have been truly fulfilled or soon about to be. The ten-horned beast from the vision regarding the succession of the world empires (7:7) and the goat with four horns from the subsequent prophecy (8:8) thus appear together in the context of the author's prognostications concerning the coming end of time, "le temps des temps et le dernier des temps" (fol. 34). His purpose is here to demonstrate that although the visionary creatures may be different, they signify the same thing, pointing both to Rome's assumption of world power in the reign of Titus as the fourth and final regnum. The picture of the ram's defeat by the he-goat is repeated at a point in the course of the life of Alexander (fol. 39), when the priests of the Temple

3) Moses ben Abraham, *Chroniques de la Bible,* «Vision of the Four Beasts», The Hague, Royal Library, Ms. 131 A 3, fol. 26, (Photo: Koninklijke Bibliotheek).

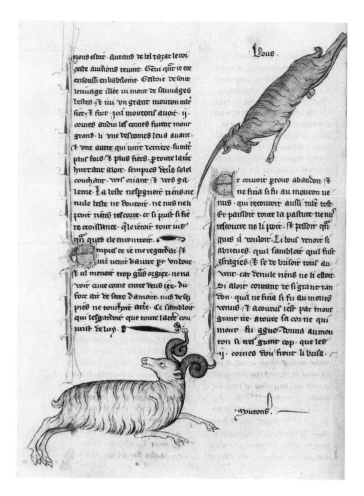

4) Moses ben Abraham, *Chroniques de la Bible*, «Combat Between Ram and Goat», The Hague, Royal Library, Ms. 131 A 3, fol. 28v, (Photo: Koninklijke Bibliotheek).

5) Moses ben Abraham, *Chroniques de la Bible*, «Defeat of the Ram by the Goat», The Hague, Royal Library, Ms. 131 A 3, fol. 29, (Photo: Koninklijke Bibliotheek).

in Jerusalem, questioned by the ruler, assure him on the basis of Daniel's prophecy that he will indeed prevail over Darius.

These illustrations have some antecedents, chiefly in the art of the earlier Middle Ages. Daniel's vision of the four beasts and the combat of ram and he-goat are depicted in the Roda Bible (Fig. 7), a manuscript from Catalonia thought to have been executed in the first half of the eleventh century, presumably on the basis of an older archetype.[22] The dream of Nabuchadnezzar's statue and the visions of the four beasts and ram-goat combat are found among the illustrations of Jerome's Commentary on Daniel inserted in the group of manuscripts, designated as Branch II, of the Commentary of Beatus on the Apocalypse (Figs. 8 and 9).[23] There is a separate tradition for the depiction of the vision of the four beasts in

Byzantine art, exemplified among the illustrations of Cosmas Indicopleustes' *Christian Topography*, and codified in the Mt. Athos *Painter's Manual*.[24] In the Spanish miniatures, the beasts alone are depicted. In the Byzantine iconography, on the other hand, each animal has its rider, the ruler who incarnates one of the four world empires of the prophecy: Nabuchadnezzar (Babylon), Darius (Persia), Alexander (Greece), and Augustus (Rome). This Byzantine tradition appears to stand behind the several representations of the theme on a monumental scale that are documented in the territories of the German Empire during the twelfth and thirteenth centuries: the lost ceiling paintings in the choir of the church of St. Emmeram at Regensburg,[25] the frescoes of the lower church at Schwarzrheindorf near Bonn, the wall paintings in the Charnel House

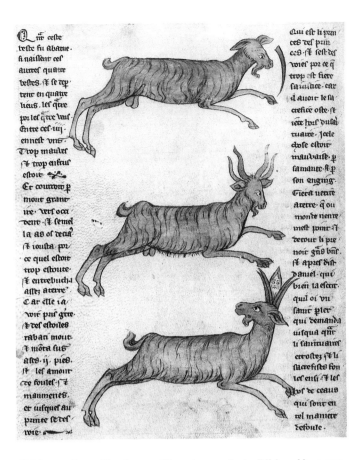

6) Moses ben Abraham, *Chroniques de la Bible*, «He-goat with Four New Horns», The Hague, Royal Library, Ms. 131 A 3, fol. 29v, (Photo: Koninklijke Bibliotheek).

"leap" over time and space in the copying of the manuscript could not be regarded as altogether out of the question.[27] If, ultimately, the issue of the painter's source or sources must remain unresolved, we have noted that in a number of details, he was guided by the phraseology of the translation, and therefore not slavishly dependent on an older model that would of necessity have been prepared in association with the Latin Vulgate text.

What can be said of the date of the manuscript and the place where it was written remains equally conjectural. I can think of no comparable gallery of animal pictures in book illumination of the thirteenth and fourteenth centuries. However, there are some indications, in the finely delineated head which functions as the lion's heart, for example (Fig. 3, left), that the illuminator was distantly touched by the innovations in Parisian painting around the year 1300 that are associated with the activity of Master Honoré.[28] Both the nature of the work and some aspects of its style are also apt to call to mind the series of illustrated Apocalypses made in England during the second half of the thirteenth century, or their Continental offshoots, though it would be more accurate to speak here of a parallel development than of direct connections.[29] The style of the painted and minor calligraphic initials, or of an incidental feature of the decoration like the ornamental border composed of short flourished pen strokes in alternating colors aligned vertically along the left side of the text column (Figs. 2, 4) make it very likely that the manuscript originated within the same rough chronological and geographical coordinates.[30]

Who was Moses ben Abraham, and who was the man for whom he claims to have prepared his work? Several authors so named are recorded, but all, with one exception, lived well after our manuscript was made. The exception is Moses ben Abraham of Pontoise, who flourished in the twelfth century. A pupil of Jacob Tam (c. 1100-1170), he is remembered chiefly as a Tosafist, or commentator of the Talmud (or of the interpretation of the Talmud by earlier commentators). He also wrote a number of liturgical poems, and he is believed to be the author of a commentary on the Pentateuch, now apparently lost.[31] It is not known if he ever wrote in any language beside Hebrew. This point set aside, what the compiler of our chronicle himself says or implies speaks against the idea that he and his namesake might be one and the same man. In the context of his calculations regarding the impending onset of the last days, he seems to indicate that he was writing in the year 1244, or possibly 1246, which would have been well after the Pontoise Tosafist's career had likely come to an end.[32]

In our eyes, he is bound to look like a peculiar kind of Jew, though he might well have been a less exceptional figure in his than in our time. He knew Latin and sometimes quotes it

adjacent to the church of Hartberg (Styria) and the sculpture of the facade of Regensburg Cathedral.[26]

It seems clear that the rider-less miniatures of Moses ben Abraham's chronicle adhere to the western rather than the Byzantine formula. Yet it has to be admitted that our evidence is too sparse to permit the assumption that the Book of Daniel was illustrated in a stable and sustained way during the Middle Ages. The sequence of Beatus manuscripts in which the comparable illustrations of Daniel's visions are found does not extend beyond the end of the twelfth century, and it is difficult to make the leap from this almost exclusively Hispanic enterprise to the very different northeastern French milieu in which the Hague codex was produced. There is, it is true, the interesting case of a Pamplona Bible, copied in northeastern France for a prince of Champagne at the beginning of the fourteenth century, which indicates that such an improbable

7) *Roda Bible,* «Daniel Scenes, Vision of the Four Beasts» (third tier), Paris, Bibl. Nat. lat. 6 (3), fol. 66, (Photo: Bibliothèque Nationale).

8) *Beatus of Saint-Sever*, «Vision of the Ancient of Days and the Four Beasts», Paris, Bibl. Nat. lat. 8878, fol. 235, (Photo: Bibliothèque Nationale).

9) *Beatus of Saint-Sever*, «Combat Between Ram and Goat», Paris, Bibl. Nat. lat. 8878, fol. 239, (Photo: Bibliothèque Nationale).

for its more authoritative effect, but makes no overt reference to the *Hebraica veritas*. Although not overly partisan or polemical in spirit, he gives what is basically a Christian reading of Hebrew prophecy, anticipating, for example, the coming of Antichrist.[33] Yet there is no indication whatever that he might have been a convert.[34] Even the precise nature of the work that he performed is by no means wholly clear. In his own words, he "arranged to put into plain French" (lai tretie a metre en plain francois") a book written at the behest of his patron, the Count of Auvergne. His activity might thus best be described as that of a translator or general editor, though it would seem reasonable to suppose that the qualifications which particularly recommended him for this task were not so much those of a stylist than of a man who, as a Jew, could lay special claim

to familiarity with the language and background of the Biblical text.[35]

The county of Auvergne was established as a separate entity following the dislocation of the duchy of Aquitaine during the later years of the tenth century. It never achieved in the course of its existence the importance of other feudal principalities like the duchies of Berry, Burgundy or Champagne, and its history, taken as a whole, is not very well documented. The account of the fortunes of the princely house written by the famous jurist and historian Etienne Baluze and published in 1708 remains to this day the most detailed treatment of the subject.[36] It is known that around 1155, following a quarrel between two members of the reigning house who both bore the name William, the county was divided. The older claimant

(Guillaume le Vieux) perpetuated the name of the dynasty and as William VIII, established himself at Clermont-Ferrand, while his younger rival settled in neighboring Montferrand and founded a new line known as the Dauphins d'Auvergne.[37] A new quarrel between one of William's grandsons Count Guy II and his brother Robert, the bishop of Clermont, led to the intervention of Philip Augustus and the conquest of the county on Philip's behalf by the lord of Bourbonnais, Guy de Dampierre (1212). After peace was finally made in 1230, the larger part of Auvergne was absorbed into the royal domain, while Count William was able to retain for his clan only the smaller parcel of land remaining around the county stronghold of Vic-le-Comte. But William was able to improve his situation through an advantageous marital alliance with the heiress of the county of Boulogne, Alix of Brabant, whose lands were united after her death (1260) with the Auvergnat domain.[38]

After William's death in 1247, there were only two counts of that name that need be mentioned, William XI, who seems to have held the title for less than a year (1277), and William XII, whose late dates, from 1326 to 1332, probably disqualify him from any connection with the making of the manuscript.

It should be noted, too, that after 1260, the incumbents styled themselves Counts of Auvergne and of Boulogne, while the opening address of our chronicle makes reference only to the first-named territory. It must therefore be concluded that the work could only have been composed for one of three men, William VIII, who is last heard of in 1182, his son William IX (d. before 1195) or William X, his grandson (1229-47). But since, following his own testimony, the author was involved in the composition of his chronicle in the year 1244, William X must be our man.

An important corollary to emerge from these deductions is that the Hague manuscript cannot be the original draft of the work or a contemporaneous reflection thereof, but must represent a later copy, perhaps made for one of the descendants of Moses' patron or a member of the same princely house. The fact that the chronicle puts the beginning of the forty-five year period before the final reckoning in 1290 would have made the work acutely topical at this time, and when, moreover, the impact of Joachim de Fiore's prophecies had procured for eschatological speculation a devoted audience.[39]

[1] The Hague, Royal Library, Ms. 131 A 3 (124 fols., 230 x 151 mm). *Catalogus codicum manuscriptorum Bibliothecae Regiae,* I, The Hague, 1922, p. 245, No. 696. The manuscript is cited by A. Jubinal, *Lettres à M. le Comte de Salvandy sur quelques-uns des manuscrits de la Bibliothèque Royale de La Haye,* Paris, 1846, pp. 18-19, and E. Brayer, "Jubinal et les manuscrits de la Bibliothèque Royale de la Haye," *Bulletin d'information de l'Institut de recherches et d'histoire des textes,* 3, 1954, p. 79. It is described in the exhibition catalogue *Schatten van de Koninklijke Bibliotheek,* The Hague, 1980, pp. 66-67, No. 26.

[2] "Mesires li quens Guillaume dauvergne qui convoite a avoir et a savoir les nessances et les lignies des du commencement del siecle et velt savoir les batailles qui ont este faites anciennement et les fet escrire en cest livre. Et ie moyses fils abraham, le rous le yuif lai tretie a metre en plain francois selonc les estoires de la bible." In this and other citations from the manuscript, I have respected the orthography of the scribe, but expanded the abbreviations. On the medieval association of red hair with Jews, see the study of R. Mellinkoff, "Judas's Red Hair and the Jews," *Journal of Jewish Art,* IX, 1982, pp. 31-46.

[3] The development and significance of family history (*histoire lignagère*) in the High Middle Ages are the subject of studies by G. Duby, "Remarques sur la littérature généalogique en France aux XIe et XIIe siècles," *Hommes et structures du moyen âge,* Paris-The Hague, 1973, pp. 287-98, and "Structures de parenté et noblesse dans la France du Nord aux XIe et XIIe siècles," *Idem,* pp. 267-85.

[4] D. Hay, *Europe: the Emergence of an Idea,* Edinburgh, 1957, pp. 37ff.

[5] Fol. 1v.

[6] See on this topic the studies of M. Klippel, *Die Darstellung der antikischen trojaner Sage in Geschichtschreibung und Dichtung vom Mittelalter bis zur Renaissance in Frankreich,* Marburg, 1936; A. Bossuat, "Les origines troyennes: leur role dans la littérature historique du XVe siècle," *Annales de Normandie,* VIII, 1958, pp. 187-97; J. P. Bodmer, "Die französische Historiographie des Mittelalters und die Franken," *Archiv für Kulturgeschichte,* XLV, 1963, pp. 91-119; C. Beaune, "L'utilisation politique du mythe des origines troyennes en France à la fin du moyen âge," *Lectures médiévales de Virgile* (Collection de l'Ecole française de Rome, 80), Rome 1985, pp. 331-55.

[7] "Nos le traitons cortement quant li evangeliste distrent quils avoient oi et veu des faits et des dits de iesus christ et des autres quil avoient quoneu des apotres..." (fol. 24v).

[8] For these and other ideas concerning Islam that were current in the Latin West, see R. W. Southern, *Western Views of Islam in the Middle Ages,* Cambridge, 1962, and N. Daniel, *The Arabs and Medieval Europe,* New York, 1979.

[9] Jerome, *Commentaria in Danielem, Pat. lat.* XXV, pp. 528-29; C. Trieber "Die Idee der vier Weltreiche," *Hermes,* XXVII, 1892, pp. 321-44; H. H. Rowley, *Darius the Mede and the Four World Empires in the Book of Daniel: A Historical Study of Contemporary Theories,* Cardiff, 1935; C. Gellinek, "Daniel's Vision of the Four Beasts in

Twelfth-Century German Literature," *Germanic Review*, 41-42, 1966/67, pp. 5-26, reprinted in the author's *Essays zur Literaturkritik des europäischen Mittelalters*, Poznań, 1980, pp. 67-88.

[10] On speculation concerning this prophecy, see L. Bigot's article "Les soixante-dix semaines du prophète," *Dictionnaire de théologie catholique*, IV, Paris, 1939, pp. 75-103. R. Lerner, "Refreshment of the Saints: the Time after Antichrist as a Station for Earthly Progress in Medieval Thought," *Traditio*, XXXII, 1976, pp. 97-144, and B. McGinn, *Visions of the End. Apocalyptic Traditions in the Middle Ages*, New York, 1979, p. 26.

[11] On the Jewish side, the author's prediction has a parallel in the opinion of Abraham ben Samuel Abulafia (1240-after 1291), who also announced the coming of the Messianic age in the year 1290 (5050 in the Hebrew calendar). There is no indication, however, that Moses ben Abraham knew of Abulafia's doctrine. (On this figure, see the articles of H. H. Ben Sasson, "Messianic Movements," *Encyclopedia Judaica*, XI, 1971, 1424, and G. Scholem, "Abulafia, Abraham ben Samuel," *Encyclopedia Judaica*, II, 185-86. In Christian eschatological speculation, the end of the thirteenth century was associated with the hopes for the coming of an Angelic Pope, centering on the figure of Celestine V (1294).

[12] Fol. 40: "Il estoit sages et fors et preus et vaillans en tout quil que il faisoit et son maistre avoit non aristotes et il ete sages outre mesure ne Alexandre ne resembloit de chiere na son pere na sa mere. Car sa chiere resembloit chiere de lyon et li oeuil li luisoient son oel destre estoit noirs et regardoit contre val et son oeuil senestre fu gausne et sembloit oeuil de chat et regardoit contre mont et ses dents erent agues comme dens de chiens et il estoit preus et justes comme un lyons des que il fu petis."

[13] G. Cary, "Alexander the Great in Medieval Theology," *Journal of the Warburg Institute*, XVII, 1954, pp. 98-114, and *Idem, The Medieval Alexander*, Cambridge, 1956, pp. 118-30.

[14] On the Alexander legend, see Cary's book cited in the preceding note and the numerous studies of D. J. A. Ross, of which there is a list in P. Noble, L. Polak and C. Isoz, eds., *The Medieval Alexander Legend and Romance Epic: Essays in Honour of David J. Ross*, Millwood, N. Y., and London, 1982, xi-xviii.

[15] The interest in Josephus and the translation of his works during the Middle Ages has not yet been dealt with in a comprehensive manner, though the rather superficial works of H. Schreckenberg, *Die Flavius-Josephus Tradition in Antike und Mittelalter*, Leiden, 1972, and *Rezeptionsgeschichte und Textkritische Untersuchungen zu Flavius Josephus*, Leiden, 1977, (esp. pp. 43 ff.), bearing on this subject should be mentioned. For the interest in the Maccabees, see J. Dunbabin, "The Maccabees as Exemplars in the Tenth and Eleventh Centuries," *The Bible in the Medieval World. Essays in Memory of Beryl Smalley*, ed. K. Walsh and D. Wood, Oxford, 1985, pp. 31-41.

[16] Ruth Mellinkoff assures me that this cap designates the figure as a Jew. See her valuable article on this subject "The Round, Cap-Shaped Hats Depicted on Jews in BM Cotton Claudius B.iv," *Anglo-Saxon England*, II, 1973, pp. 155-65.

[17] U. Robert, "Etude historique et archéologique sur la roue des juifs depuis le XIIIe siècle," *Revue des études juives*, VI, 1882-3, pp. 81-95, and VII, 1883, pp. 94-102. See also on this topic the study of G. Kisch, "The Yellow Badge in History," *Historia Judaica*, IV, 1942, pp. 95-144 (repr. in *Historia Judaica*, XIX, 1957, pp. 89-146).

[18] Th. Raff, "Die Ikonographie der mittelalterlichen Windpersonifikationen," *Aachener Kunstblätter*, XIX, 1957, pp. 89-146, and for Daniel, pp. 102-4.

[19] In making the beast a lioness, Jerome follows the Septuaginta, which is at variance with the Hebrew text on this point. In his commentary on Daniel (*Pat. lat.* XXV, 628), he makes much of the female sex of the creature in order to characterize Babylon's special wickedness: "Regnum Babylonium propter saevitiam, et luxuriam, sive propter crudelitatem, et vitam libidini servientem, non leo, sed leaena appelatur." In Comestor's *Historia Scholastica (Pat. lat.* CXCVIII, 1453), the beast is also called a lioness, and so it is also in Guyart des Moulins' French translation of this work. For advice on this matter, I am indebted to my colleague Steven D. Fraade of the Department of Religious Studies, Yale University.

[20] A somewhat similar device, though in another context, is found among the illustrations of the thirteenth-century North Italian Chansonnier in the Pierpont Morgan Library, Ms. 819, fol. 16. A. Rieger, "'Ins e. 1 cor port, dona, vostra faisso'. Image et imaginaire de la femme à travers l'enluminure dans les chansonniers des troubadours," *Cahiers de civilisation médiévale*, XXVIII, 1985, pp. 385-515.

[21] Fol. 29: "... li froissa corne... ensi comme vous le poes par de la veoir comme ell lui chiest de la teste a la terre."

[22] Paris, Bib. Nat. lat. 6; W. Neuss, *Die katalanische Bibelillustration um die Wende des ersten Jahrtausends und die altspanische Buchmalerei*, Bonn-Leipzig, 1922, and P. Klein, "Date et scriptorium de la Bible de Roda: état de recherches," *Cahiers de Saint-Michel de Cuxa*, No. 3, June 1972, pp. 91-102.

[23] On the Daniel illustrations of the Beatus manuscripts, see J. Williams, "The Beatus Commentaries and Spanish Bible Illustration," *Actas del Simposio para el Estudio de los Codices del'Comentario al Apocalypsis de Beato de Liebana*, Madrid, 1980, pp. 211 ff., and Y. Zaluska, "L'image de Babylone et le cycle de Daniel," *El 'Beato' de Saint-Sever, Ms. lat. 8878 de la Bibliothèque Nationale de Paris*, Madrid, 1984, II, pp. 315-24.

[24] For Cosmas, see W. Wolska, *La topographie chrétienne de Cosmas Indicopleustès*, Paris, 1962, pp. 14, 90; for the Mt. Athos handbook, P. Hetherington, ed., *The 'Painter's Manual' of Dionysius of Fourna*, London, 1974, p. 25, No. 70.

[25] J. Endres, "Die Reiterfiguren der Regensburger Domfacade im Lichte mittelalterlicher Kirchenpolitik," *Zeitschrift für christliche Kunst*, XII, 1900, pp. 363-76, and E. Marsch, *Biblische Prophetie und chronographische Dichtung* (Philologische Studien und Quellen, Heft 65), Berlin, 1972, pp. 74-86.

[26] Marsch, *op. cit.*, pp. 86-103. According to R. Will, the theme may also have been depicted in wall paintings of the choir of the church of Marmoutier in Alsace ("Une oeuvre d'art romane disparue: les peintures murales de l'ancien choeur de l'abbatiale de Marmoutier," *Archives de l'église d'Alsace*, XXII, 1975, pp. 15-33.

[27] On this manuscript in the collection of the New York Public Library (Spencer Ms. 22), see F. Bucher, *The Pamplona Bibles*, New York, 1970, pp. 61 ff. Prof. Peter Klein, in an as yet unpublished paper which he kindly permitted me to read, argues that a copy of the Beatus commentary reached England in the thirteenth century and affected the illustration of some English Apocalypse manuscripts.

[28] E. G. Millar, *The Parisian Miniaturist Honoré*, London, 1959. A monograph on this artist by Ellen V. Kosmer is awaited.

[29] P. Klein, *Endzeiterwartung und Ritterideologie. Die englischen Bilderapokalypsen der Frühgotik und Ms. Douce 180*, Graz, 1983, offers the most recent ovierview of this series of manuscripts. For a Continental offshoot, see A. H. Bober, "The Apocalypse Manuscript of the Bibliothèque Royale de Belgique," *Revue belge d'archéologie et d'histoire de l'art*, X, 1940, pp. 11-26.

[30] This type of calligraphic ornament is found, for example, in a *Legenda sanctorum* from France dated 1312 in the British Library, Add. 11.882 (S. H. Thompson, *Latin Bookhands of the Later Middle Ages*, 1100-1500, Cambridge, 1969, No. 15); in a copy of works of

Boethius and Macrobius dated 1298 in the Bibliothèque Nationale, lat. 16.678 (Thompson, *op. cit.,* No. 14); in an English *Flores historiarum* dated 1293-1307 (Private Collection, on deposit at the Getty Museum, Malibu, No. 84 MP. 111); and in the *De natura avium* and other works of Hugh of Fouilloy, attributable to northeastern France and dated 1270, in the Getty Museum, Ms. Ludwig XV, 3 (A. von Euw and J. Plotzek, *Die Handschriften der Sammlung Ludwig,* IV, Cologne, 1985, pp. 172 ff.).

[31] On this figure, see the entries in the *Jewish Encyclopedia,* New York and London, 1905, IX, p. 62, and the *Encyclopedia Judaica,* XII, 1971, p. 416, where further bibliography is given.

[32] Fol. 34v: "Or vous dirons combien il a passe de cete destruction de tytus (of Jerusalem) et combien il ia a venir des que iesu christ nasqui conte lan M. CC. XLIIII." Further on in the same passage, the writer says that "selon le conte des ebrieux il a des que tytus destruit Jerusalem M C et LXXVI, and since this destruction took place in the year 70 C.E., this would imply that the author was writing in 1246.

[33] Fol. 32v: "Car a cest derrenier terme sont toutes ces choses passees et de helyas le prophete et de antechrist..." Another formulation of the writer (fol. 31) "... que la sainte loy est escrite par la bouche au saint esperit..." has an equally Christian ring.

[34] I must acknowledge the very helpful advice of Prof. Michael A. Signer of Hebrew Union College, Los Angeles, on this question, and on the state of scholarship regarding the knowledge of Latin by Jews in the Middle Ages.

[35] For a somewhat similar case, see C.-O. Nordström, *The Duke of Alba's Castilian Bible (Figura. Uppsala Studies in the History of Art, N.S. 5),* Uppsala, 1967.

[36] E. Baluze, *Histoire généalogique de la maison d'Auvergne,* Paris, 1708. More recent studies are H. F. Rivière, *Histoire des institutions de l'Auvergne,* Paris, 1874; P.-F. Fournier, "La conquête de l'Auvergne pour Philippe-Auguste, 1211-1212. Récit de Guillaume le Breton," *L'Auvergne littéraire, artistique et historique,* XIV, 1937, No. 3, pp. 79-87; E. Jarry, *Provinces et Pays de France,* Paris, 1943, II, pp. 283-330; B. de Fournoux, "Le comté d'Auvergne de 1213 a 1437," *Positions de thèses... de l'Ecole des Chartes,* 1946, pp. 63-71; R. Sève, "La seigneurie épiscopale de Clermont des origines à 1357," *Revue d'Auvergne,* XCIV, No. 1, 1980, pp. 85-268.

[37] P. F. Fournier, "Le nom du troubadour Dauphins d'Auvergne et l'évolution du mot 'Dauphin' en Auvergne au Moyen Age," *Bibliothèque de l'Ecole des Chartes,* XCI, 1930, pp. 66-99.

[38] P. Heliot, *Histoire de Boulogne et du Boulonnais...,* Lille, 1937, pp. 82.

[39] On Joachim and his influence, see M. Bloomfield, "Joachim de Flora: a Critical Survey of his Canon, Teachings, Sources and Influence," *Traditio,* XIII, 1957, pp. 249-311, and M. Reeves, *The Influence of Prophecy in the Later Middle Ages. A Study of Joachimism,* Oxford, 1969.

JOSEPH GUTMANN

The Sacrifice of Isaac in Medieval Jewish Art*

The Jewish pietist, Eleazar ben Judah ben Kalonymus, who lived in the 12th-13th-century Rhineland, advised his followers to emulate Abraham at the Sacrifice of Isaac (*Akedat Yitzhak* = Binding of Isaac): "The root of [proper] fear [means] that it is difficult for [the Pietist] to perform [a virtuous act] and yet he still resists [the lures of] his passion and evil impulses because of fear of [God's] Name. His only fear is that he might not be [as] perfect [in his devotion] to the Lord as was Abraham [when Abraham did not hesitate to obey the Lord even by sacrificing his beloved son Isaac, and God said to him:] 'For you are one who fears the Lord' [*Genesis* 22:12]. This was the most demanding of Abraham's trials [and by proving equal to it, Abraham, manifested his fear of God.]"[1]

On the second day of the New Year holiday (*Rosh Hashanah*), during the morning worship service, pious Jews recite: "May God account to His people the sacrifice (literally, binding) of Isaac according to Your oath, and reverse Your decree from stern judgment to mercy."

And the modern Israeli poet Shin Shalom, in his poems entitled "The Songs of the Akedah," recreates the episode: "From the time / my eye was opened / as witness, / from the time / the body stood on his feet – / I lead / day by day to the sacrifice / my body / and soul in this world. / Alone, straight ahead, / asking nothing, / I carry the fire / and tie the rope. / Wherever my foot treads / is Mount Moriah, / everywhere is arranged for me / the altar of pain."[2]

Without question the dramatic narrative of *Genesis* 22 is one of the most important themes in Judaism. In each age, whether it was a medieval German Jewish Pietist seeking a model to inspire faith, a traditional Jew fervently praying for forgiveness of his sins on *Rosh Hashanah*, or a sensitive contemporary Israeli poet reflecting on his destiny, all have seen their lives refracted in the ancient biblical story of the Binding of Isaac. Many *piyyutim* (liturgical poems), commentaries, books and articles have been devoted to the subject, but relatively little has been written on how the Sacrifice of Isaac is treated in ancient and medieval Jewish art. Of the two depictions found in early Jewish art, one is a painting at the Dura-Europos synagogue of 244/45 – the earliest dated figuration in art. It reveals Isaac lying atop the faggots on an altar. Abraham, knife poised, is facing him; a ram is standing next to a tree, while the hand of God (symbolic of the *bat-kol* = voice from heaven) is emerging from the sky to interrupt the intended slaughter. Both the *bat-kol* (the hand) and the ram standing next to a tree are rabbinic interpolations into the biblical story. Direct intervention by the Deity has been substituted for the angel, and the ram, instead of being represented as caught by chance in the thicket, has become a ram patiently standing alongside a tree. This ram, especially prepared by God at twilight on the first Sabbath Eve, was grazing in paradise awaiting its future destiny. Early Western Christian, Byzantine and Jewish depictions of the Sacrifice of Isaac do not follow the artistic format of the Dura-Europos synagogue,[3] but some Eastern Christian works of art from fifth-century Sasania reveal close analogies.[4]

The second Jewish example from antiquity, a synagogue mosaic from the Beth-Alpha synagogue in ancient Palestine, dating from the second half of the sixth century, continues both the hand of God (the *bat-kol*) and the ram, this time actually tethered to a tree, but the fire on the altar and Abraham with aureole, grasping the ends of a blindfold by which he holds Isaac suspended in mid-air, follow a well-established

2) Bible, Würzburg area, 1236/38, Milan, Biblioteca Ambrosiana, Ms. B. 30 Inf., fol. 102r (Appendix I, No. 2).

1) Commentary to Bible, Würzburg area, 1232/33, Munich, Bayrische Staatsbibliotek, Cod. Hebr. 5/I, fol. 18v (Appendix I, No. 1).

3) Mahzor, Southern Germany, early 14th century, Oxford, Bodleian Library, MS Laud. Or. 321, fol. 184r (Appendix I, No. 3).

Christian iconographic type of Sacrifice, found especially in North African models dating from the second half of the sixth century.[5]

No other Jewish representations of the Sacrifice appear to have survived in Jewish art until we come to thirteenth-century

Germany. Of some twenty-seven illustrations extant from the thirteenth to the fifteenth century, most stem from the Franco-German region known in medieval Hebrew sources as *Ashkenaz*. One miniature is probably from Naples and three are from Spain (known as *Sepharad*). (All numbers in parenthesis used here

4) Pentateuch, etc., Southern Germany, ca. 1300, Jerusalem, Israel Museum, MS 180/52, fol. 18v (Appendix I, No. 4).

5) Collection of liturgical text, Southern Germany, late 13th century, New York, Library of the Jewish Theological Seminary of America, MS 8972, fol. 121r (Appendix I, No. 5).

refer to Appendix I). They reveal so many variations in detail that it is impossible to posit one source for all of them (cf. Appendix II). Though, in many cases, inspired by contemporary Christian examples of this theme, they do display unique Jewish iconographic details in several instances. No artistic relationship can be established between the two early Jewish depictions and the medieval Jewish illustrations. Indeed, seldom in medieval specimens is the ram shown standing next to or tethered to a tree, while it is not the hand of God (the *bat-kol*), but an angel or angelic wings which we generally find illustrated.[6] The early portrayals of the Sacrifice of Isaac appear on the walls or mosaic floors of synagogues, but all the medieval Jewish Sacrifice of Isaac illustrations are found in Hebrew manuscripts: Bibles, *Mahzorim* (festival prayer books) and *Haggadot* [private liturgical books used during the *Seder* (the Jewish Passover Eve home celebration)]. Several of the miniatures appearing in Bible manuscripts accompany the text of *Genesis* 22 (cf. Appendix I, Nos. 1, 4, 7, 8, 12, 25, 26). In one miniature (No. 12), which has the intercalated *Targum Onkelos* (the Aramaic paraphrase of the Hebrew Bible) and the commentary of Rashi (an eleventh-century Franco-German Hebrew Bible commentator) in the margin of the manuscript, the fact that a tree (*'ilan*) is

6) Birds' Head Haggadah, Rhineland, early 14th century, Jerusalem, Israel Museum, MS 180/57, fol. 15v (Appendix I, No. 6).

7) Mahzor, Southern Germany, first quarter of 14th century, Leipzig, Universitätsbibliotek, MS V. 1102/II, fol. 66r (Appendix I, No. 8).

8) Mahzor, Southern Germany, first half of 14th century, Oxford, Bodleian Library, MS Reggio 1, fol. 159v (Appendix I, No. 11).

shown, rather than the biblical thicket, clearly reflects the *Targum* and the Rashi Commentary. That Isaac's "hands and feet [are bound] behind him" (in the same No. 12) may also be due to the accompanying Rashi Commentary on *Genesis* 22:9. Whether Rashi's Commentary on *Genesis* 22:14: "The Lord [on account of the Binding of Isaac] will forgive Israel every year and rescue them from trouble," is implied in No. 12 and other such Hebrew Bible manuscripts with Rashi's Commentary (Nos. 1, 26) is difficult to determine.

9) Mahzor, Southern Germany, first half of 14th century, Wrocław, University Library, MS Or. I/1, fol. 46v (Appendix I, No. 9).

10) Pentateuch, etc., Germany, March 3, 1340, Oxford, Bodleian Library, MS Opp. 14, fol. 120r (Appendix I, No. 13).

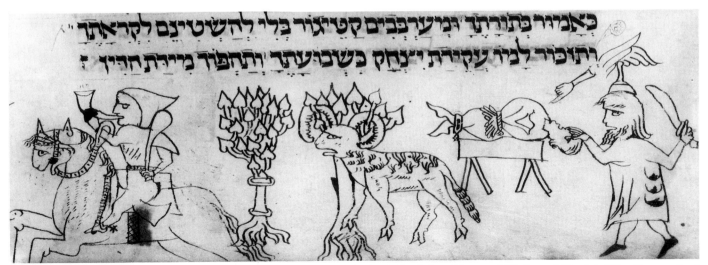

11) Mahzor, Southern Germany, first half of 14th century, Oxford, Bodleian Library, MS Can. 140 fol. 35v (Appendix I, No. 10).

13) Mahzor, Hammelburg, Germany, 1347/48, Darmstadt, Hessische Landes- und Hochschulbibliotek, MS Or. 13, fol.202v (Appendix I, No. 14).

12) Pentateuch, etc., Germany, March 3, 1340, Oxford, Bodleian Library, MS Opp. 14, fol. 22v (Appendix I, No. 12).

Two miniatures render the Sacrifice of Isaac at the opening of the *Book of Leviticus* (Nos. 2, 13), since chapter one of *Leviticus* deals with the proper way to sacrifice burnt offerings (*'olot*), and Isaac was to have been the perfect *'olah* (Genesis 22:2, 6, 7, 13). *Leviticus* was also the first book of the Pentateuch Jewish children learned in schools "because children are pure and the sacrifices are pure, let the pure ones come and occupy themselves with the pure ones."[7] It may have served to remind the children of the patriarch Isaac. As he was a willing and pure offering (*'olah*), so should the children be by emulating his noble example.

Most of the Sacrifice of Isaac miniatures are found in Franco-German (*Ashkenazic*) prayerbooks, especially *Mahzorim* (Nos. 3, 8, 9, 10, 11, 14, 15, 16, 27). According to rabbinic tradition, the Sacrifice took place at the New Year (*Rosh Hashanah*) and served as an eternal instrument of vicarious

14) Miscellany, Middle Rhine region, second quarter of 15th century, Hamburg, Staats- und Universitätsbibliotek, Cod. Hebr. 37, fol. 1r (Appendix I, No. 15).

16) Second Nuremberg Haggadah, Southern Germany, second half of 15th century, Jerusalem, Schocken Institute for Jewish Studies of the Jewish Theological Seminary of America. MS 24087, fol. 31r (Appendix I, No. 17).

15) Mahzor, Germany, first half of 15th century, Budapest, Library of the Hungarian Academy of Sciences, MS A 387, fol.403v (Appendix I, No. 16).

17) Haggadah, Sephardic rite, Castile (?), first quarter of 14th century, London, British Library, MS Or. 2737, fol. 93v (Appendix I, No. 20).

18) Sarajevo Haggadah, Catalonia, third quarter of 14th century, Sarajevo, Yugoslavia, National Museum, fol. 8r (Appendix I, No. 22).

atonement for the sins of the children of Israel. Some of the texts surrounding the *Mahzor* miniatures (Nos. 9, 10) specifically refer to the Sacrifice of Isaac – for example, the concluding prayer (*silluk*) from the morning service of the second day of *Rosh Hashanah,* when Jewish worshippers appeal to God "to account to His people the Sacrifice of Isaac according to Your oath, and reverse [Your decree] from stern judgment to mercy." There are also miniatures in which the Sacrifice of Isaac is implied (Nos. 15, 27), in keeping with the circumstance that the second benediction in the *Amidah* prayer for *Rosh Hashanah* became linked with Isaac's resurrection after the *Akedah.*[8] Furthermore, the connection of the Sacrifice with the blowing

of the *shofar* (ram's horn, Nos. 10, 11, 15) illustrates the firm belief that the *Akedah* not only occurred on *Rosh Hashanah* but serves as a reminder that the ram was sacrificed in place of Isaac.[9] On the second day of *Rosh Hashanah,* in the liturgical poem (*yotzer*) of the morning service, we read: "The season is come to sound the ram's horn, and thus recall for His tried ones [Abraham's offering of] the ram caught by its horns in the thicket." This ram, created according to rabbinic lore on the first Sabbath Eve at twilight – i.e., on the sixth day of creation – is quietly standing by, awaiting its divinely ordained destiny (Nos. 11, 15, 17).[10] The ram also calls up in the pious viewer's mind the tradition that its large right horn (called

74

19) Haggadah, Sephardic rite, Catalonia, ca. 1320/30, London, British Library, MS Add. 27210, fol. 4v (Appendix I, No. 21).

20) Miscellany, Northern France, late 13th century, London, British Library, MS Add. 11639, fol. 521v (Appendix I, No. 23).

shofar) will ultimately be sounded to signal the ingathering of the exiles and to usher in the advent of the Messiah. Rabbinic fancy has it that the smaller, left horn of the ram was sounded during the theophany at Sinai.[11]

The scales, whereon the individual's merits, or good deeds, and demerits, or evil deeds, are weighed, play an important role on *Rosh Hashanah*. In one manuscript (No. 15) which has an *Akedah* illustration, we see the scales held by an angel – while a black, hairy devil is desperately trying to pull down the left-hand pan of the scales, the pan of demerits. As the zodiacal sign for the Hebrew month of *Tishri* (*Rosh Hashanah* falls on the first of *Tishri*) is the scales (*moznayim*), the image expresses an essential rabbinic idea, that human deeds are weighed on the scales of judgment. The additional, or *Musaf*, service of the first day of *Rosh Hashanah* clearly underscores this idea: "This day has been ordained of old as a day of reckoning, when the deeds of man are weighed and judged."[12] Rabbinic sources explain that "expiation will be won for you 'in the Balance,' that is, in the month whose zodiacal symbol is the Balance. What month is that? *Tishri.*"[13]

Not all rabbinic commentators associate the *Akedah* with *Rosh Hashanah*. Some have taught that the Sacrifice took place on the afternoon of *Yom Kippur* (the Day of Atonement). Hence, we find one depiction of the Binding of Isaac inserted into the *Amidah* prayer of the afternoon (*Minhah*) service of *Yom Kippur* (No. 16). According to the accompanying text, Jews pray: "Remember unto us the Binding of the only one and forgive us all of our sins because of the righteousness of a perfect man."[14]

The *Akedah* is also linked with the late spring *Shavuot* (Pentecost) holiday and is illustrated in one manuscript (No. 5) next to an Aramaic liturgical poem on the *Akedah* theme. The poem follows the recitation of the Fifth Commandment "Honor your father and mother" – as *Shavuot*, in rabbinic tradition, commemorates the revelation of the Ten Commandments at Mount Sinai – and serves as an exemplar of filial piety.[15]

Although the *Akedah* was originally linked with the Hebrew month of *Nisan*, the month in which Passover falls, the *Haggadah* (the liturgical book used for the ritual meal which welcomes the holiday) differs from the *Mahzor* in that the *Haggadah* makes no direct reference to the Sacrifice of Isaac,

21) Maimonides, Mishneh Torah, Book X, Lorraine region, early 14th century, Budapest, Library of the Hungarian Academy of Sciences, MS A 77/III, fol. 81r (Appendix I, No. 24).

though the headgear is also employed on occasion for New Testament personages like Saint Joseph, Pontius Pilate and even Jesus.[17]

Unique to Hebrew manuscripts is the representation of the angel as a bearded male (Nos. 12, 13) – an image already prefigured in the third-century Dura-Europos synagogue, where angels are depicted as non-winged males.[18]

Most unusual in medieval Hebrew manuscripts are several miniatures of the Sacrifice of Isaac which endow either all of the participants with animal faces (No. 3) or bird heads (No. 6), or the angel alone with an eagle head (Nos. 5, 6). Appearing primarily in Southern German Hebrew manuscripts from about the thirteenth to the mid-fourteenth century, these zoocephalic figures have yet to be satisfactorily explained. Animal-headed figures are, of course, apparent in Christian manuscripts in connection with the four evangelists, often shown with human bodies surmounted by the head of their respective symbolic animals, while Saint Christopher is sometimes shown dog-headed, but their meaning in Hebrew miniatures is not clear and the theories offered to date are not convincing. In two manuscripts, for instance, only the faces of the angels – heavenly beings – are avoided, while in another Hebrew manuscript (No. 6) the angel is the only figure with a human head – all the others are bird-headed. Whether legal proscription or fear of the image is involved, or whether it is rooted in mystical Judeo-German pietism or both is worthy of detailed investigation.[19] No doubt the elimination of the facial features of human beings (Nos. 1, 2, 9) may express iconophobia, as the depiction of the *parzuf adam* (the features on the face of a human being) is forbidden by some contemporary Franco-German rabbinic authorities.[20] In medieval Christian manuscripts, such figures as the whore of Babylon, the devil and Judas are sometimes found defaced or mutilated.[21] In the latter case, however, hatred of evil figures and not iconophobia is the determinant reason.

Although Jewish sources and medieval Hebrew miniatures prefer the knife [*ma'akhelet,* which the medieval Jewish commentator Rashi explains as denoting a knife (*sakin*), Commentary to *Genesis* 22:6], usually held in Abraham's right hand,[22] we also find the sword (*herev;* Nos. 6, 7, 8, 9, 24, 26) used in Hebrew sources and medieval artistic renderings.[23]

Highly symbolic is the prayer shawl (*tallit*) that Abraham wears in the Sacrifice of Isaac (No. 26). This may suggest that Abraham's role in the scene is akin to that of the high priest (*kohen gadol*). In fact, several Hebrew sources allude to Abraham having worn a *tallit* at the Sacrifice.[24] It is undoubtedly related to contemporary Jewish history, as *kiddush ha-shem,* sanctification of God's Name through martyrdom, was an important belief in medieval Franco-German (*Ashkenazic*) Jewish communities. Many Jews, by imitating and recalling

though illustrations of the *Akedah* appear in it before the text itself or in the margins (Nos. 6, 17, 18, 20, 21, 22). The depiction of the Binding of Isaac is at times more closely related to contemporary Christian Psalter and Bible miniatures than to the Hebrew text, since Christian works, Psalters, for instance, were sometimes embellished with the Sacrifice of Isaac in the margins or in front of the text proper.[16]

More or less distinctively Jewish features which appear in medieval illustrations of the *Akedah* include Abraham depicted as wearing the funnel-shaped Jew's hat, the medieval *cornutum pileum* (Nos. 4, 5, 6, 10, 14), which *Ashkenazic* Jews were forced to wear following the 1215 decree of the Fourth Lateran Council. Sometimes, to be sure, in medieval Christian art, too, Abraham wears the Jew's hat, probably for polemical purposes and to denote Jews as sinners, villains and heretics,

22) Pentateuch, etc., Eastern France, around 1300, Paris, Bibliothèque Nationale, MS hebr. 36, fol. 283v (Appendix I, No. 25).

23) Pentateuch, etc., Brussels, 1309, Hamburg, Staats- und Universitätsbibliotek, Cod. Levy 19, fol. 34v (Appendix I, No. 26).

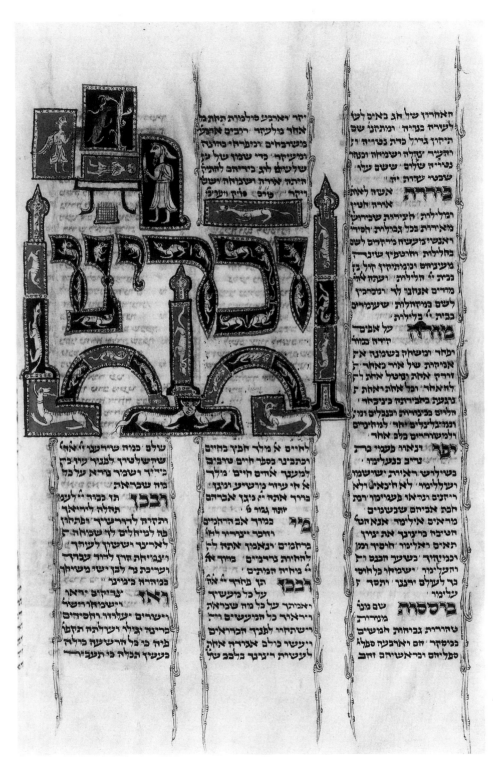

24) Siddur, Franco-Germany (?), early 14th century, Parma, Biblioteca Palatina, MS Parm. 3518, fol. 25v (Appendix I, No. 27).

Abraham's sublime example, willingly took their own lives and the lives of their families rather than submit to the conversion forced upon them by Christian mobs during the brutal massacres of the Crusades. Thus we read: "When were there ever a thousand and a hundred sacrifices in one day, each and every one of them like the *Akedah* of Isaac, son of Abraham?"[25] Or the story of Meshullam bar Isaac of Worms (in 1096) who "bound his son Isaac, and picked up the knife to slay his son, and recited the blessing appropriate for the slaughter [of cattle and fowl]. And the lad replied 'Amen.' And the father [perhaps wearing the *tallit*] slew the lad."[26]

These sacrificial victims, ritual sacrifices as they saw themselves, stretched forth their necks to have their throats cut, as is evident in some medieval *Ashkenazic* miniatures (Nos. 12-13): "for the sanctification of Him who Alone lives Eternally."[27] In keeping with a source like the medieval commentary of Rashi to *Genesis* 22:9, we note (Nos. 12, 17) that Abraham "bound [Isaac's] hands and feet behind him, his hands and feet together – this is *Akedah*."[28] That the left hand and foot tied together (No. 23, cf. No. 17) allude to the ritual prescription of "*akud*... tying hand and foot together", the "fore and hind leg [of the lamb] tied together like the Binding of Isaac," or, as Rabbi Ephraim of Bonn envisages it in his twelfth-century poem, that Abraham "bound him hand and foot like the perpetual offering [the *tamid*]"[29] is a distinct possibility. Many of the medieval Jewish depictions show either both hands and feet tied or hands alone tied – in keeping with Jewish sources (cf. Appendix II). Christian miniatures and literary sources, it should be noted, also show both hands and feet tied or simply the hands.[30]

Frequently, medieval Jewish illustrations reveal Isaac as a young boy, although No. 22 represents him as a babe. This ambivalence is reflected in Jewish sources where the age of Isaac varies from that of an infant to a child of 5, to young and aging men of 13, 23, 25, 26, 37 and 40. The same ambivalence to age also occurs in Christian art and literature, where it is claimed that Isaac was an infant, or that he was 8, 13, 15, 16, 17, 30, 32 or 35 years of age.[31] Most of the medieval Jewish depictions have the ram caught in the branches of a tree, although the thicket also appears (Cf. Appendix II). Both the tree and the thicket appear in Christian art.[32] In only a few miniatures (Nos. 5?, 12, 13, 20), in keeping with Jewish sources, is Isaac lying on top of an altar built of stones.[33]

Some unusual scenes appear in connection with the Sacrifice of Isaac. In one medieval Jewish depiction of the Sacrifice (No. 4), we note to the right of the Sacrifice a devilish-looking figure lifting high a woman with outstretched arms. In an apparently unpublished legend recorded in the second column of a manuscript (Munich, Bayrische Staats-bibliothek, Cod. Hebr. 5/I, fol. 18v), the following comment on Genesis (it may be by Joseph Kara and comes after Rashi's Commentary to Genesis 23:1-4) is recorded: Satan came to Sarah to inquire if she knew the real reason for Abraham's mission, then told her that "they went to slaughter him [Isaac], to kill him, to offer him as a burnt offering. Immediately, she trembled greatly. Satan seized her and lifted her upwards [as in our miniature] until she saw him being slaughtered. Immediately, her soul fled and she died."[34]

Another manuscript (No. 15) shows us a haloed angel guiding Isaac out of what appears to be a dark cavern, a scene which may allude to Isaac's return to earth from paradise (*Gan Eden*),where angels had carried him and where he had sojourned for several years recuperating from the wound inflicted by Abraham before the angel stopped him. According to medieval rabbis, Isaac had died and was resurrected.[35] It may also appear here because the Second Benediction of the prayer called *Shemoneh Esreh* (18 Benedictions) became associated with Isaac (Nos. 15, 27) and thus has an illustration of the Sacrifice of Isaac. According to legend, "Rabbi Judah said: when the blade (i.e., the sword) touched Isaac's throat his soul fled and departed, but when He let His voice be heard between the Cherubim, 'Do not raise your hand against the boy' his soul returned to his body. Then Abraham unbound him and Isaac rose, knowing that in this way the dead would come back to life in the future; whereupon he began to recite: 'Blessed are You, O Lord, who revivest the dead!' "[36]

Many of the miniatures were probably made by Christian artists or by Jews copying medieval Christian models. This is evident, for example, in (No. 1)[37], (No. 19)[38] and (No. 24).[39] It is also not surprising, therefore, that Christian elements and symbols are discernible in our miniatures. That is surely why the faggots appear arranged in the form of a cross (No. 1), or an angel's hand is depicted bestowing the Christian blessing (No. 25), or Isaac is seen folding his hands in the Christian gesture of prayer (Nos. 8, 19, 24), and angels are represented as wearing an aureole (Nos. 15, 24, 25, 26)[40] – all common practices encountered in medieval Christian art of the Sacrifice.

Some medieval Jewish manuscripts even show Isaac on a Christian altar covered with a white altar cloth (Nos. 3, 7, 11, 25). As the Sacrifice of Isaac has eucharistic implications and is recited at the Church altar in the *supra quae* prayer of the Roman Canon of the Mass (*supra quae propitio* –"Be pleased to look upon these offerings with a gracious and favorable countenance, accept them even as You were pleased to accept... the sacrifice of our patriarch Abraham..."), the draped altar refers, of course, to the new Isaac, the son of God. The Sacrifice is thus for medieval Christians merely a prefiguration, a foreshadowing of the one perfect sacrifice, Christ, whose death brought healing and redemption to the world.

Similarly, the ram suspended vertically from a tree or thicket in Hebrew miniatures may have been modelled on an allusion to Christ crucified (Nos. 8, 12, 13, 14, 21, 27) – "a sign that the lamb of God (= Christ) would also be hung from the cross." This lamb would make atonement for universal sins.[41]

Christ is also called the Paschal Lamb, as the Sacrifice of Isaac is linked with Passover in Christianity – the time when Christ was crucified.[42] *Genesis 22*, the story of the Sacrifice of Isaac, was read during the Easter Vigil service and a Paschal candle was lit. Hence, the large candle near the altar in a Hebrew manuscript (No. 9) is the Paschal candle, lit at the beginning of the Easter Vigil or Holy Saturday. It stands frequently in a special candlestick at the gospel-side of the altar, as in our miniature, and symbolizes Christ as the light of the world.[43]

The 27 extant Sacrifice of Isaac renderings in medieval Hebrew manuscripts thus form a unique chapter in the fascinating and complex history that the Sacrifice of Isaac played not only in Jewish but in Christian and Muslim art as well.[44] It is not astonishing to discover the involvement of the Jewish minority in medieval Christian civilization reflected in the adaptation of Christian models. What is novel are the many distinct Jewish iconographic features introduced to make the theme of the Sacrifice of Isaac (*Akedat Yitzhak*) relevant to and expressive of the unique Jewish experience in medieval Christian Europe.

APPENDIX I
Sacrifice of Isaac Depictions in Hebrew Manuscripts.

GERMANY

1. Munich, Bayrische Staatsbibliothek, Cod. Hebr. 5/I, fol 18v. Commentary to Bible, *hayyei Sarah* (*Genesis* 23), Würzburg area, 1232/33. The framed panel carries the opening Hebrew word *wayyihyu*, *"And* the life of Sarah *was."* (*Genesis* 23:1) [The depiction should illustrate *Genesis* 22]. A winged angel arrests the right hand of Abraham, which holds the sacrificial knife; the left hand unveils an empty scroll. Abraham looks towards the ram caught in what appears to be a tree, on the left, and places his left hand on Isaac's head. Isaac sits semi-nude on top of the faggots on the altar. His hands appear to be tied in front

and his feet are crossed. The faces are without features.
T. Metzger, "Le manuscrit enluminé Cod. Hebr. 5 de la Bibliothèque Nationale d'Etat à Munich, " *Etudes de civilisation médiévale (IXe-XIIe siècles). Mélanges offerts a Edmond-René Labande* (Poitiers, 1974), p. 543.

2. Milan, Biblioteca Ambrosiana, MS. B. 30 Inf., fol. 102. Bible, *Leviticus*, Würzburg area, 1236-1238.
The framed panel carries the initial Hebrew word, *wayikra* ("The Lord *called..."*), the opening word of the *Book of Leviticus* [the Hebrew letter *alef,* at the end of the word *wayikra,* is traditionally written in smaller script]. Above *wayikra* we see, on the right, Isaac crouching on an altar. Before the altar the faggots are ablaze. Abraham, in the center, wearing a tunic belted at the waist, a surcoat and skull cap with piping, looks toward the winged angel emerging from the clouds, who arrests Abraham's uplifted hand holding the knife with his right hand and points to the ram standing upright in the tree. Abraham appears to be holding down Isaac's head with his left hand. The faces are often blank or covered.
A. Luzzatto and L. Mortara Ottolenghi, *Hebraica Ambrosiana* (Milan, 1972), p. 120; B. Narkiss, "The Iconography of the Illustrations," in M. Spitzer, ed., *The Birds' Head Haggada* (Jerusalem, 1967), I, p. 96 [hereafter *Bird*]; K. Schubert, ed., *Judentum im Mittelalter.* Catalog of exhibition held in Schloss Halbturn (Burgenland, 1978), pp. 212-13 [hereafter *JM*]; J. Gutmann, "Joseph ben Kalonymus: The Enigma of a Thirteenth-Century Hebrew Scribe," *Festschrift für Stephen Kayser* (in press).

3. Oxford, Bodleian Library, MS Laud Or. 321, fol. 184. *Mahzor,* Southern Germany, early 14th century. The framed central panel has the opening word *melekh* of the *piyyut* beginning with *"O King,* Your word stands steadfast from of yore," recited during the morning service of the second day of *Rosh Hashanah.* Outside the panel, we see on the left the ram standing upright in vine branches with grape clusters. On the right, a nude Isaac is insecurely squatting on a draped altar. Abraham grasps Isaac's hair with his left hand. In his right hand is the uplifted knife. From a cloud, a winged angel emerges who points with his right toward the ram. All figures have animal faces.
B. Narkiss, *Hebrew Illuminated Manuscripts* (New York, 1969), p. 94 [hereafter *HIM*]; T. and M. Metzger, *Jewish Life in the Middle Ages* (New York, 1982), p. 306, No. 159 [hereafter *JL*]; G. Sed-Rajna, *Le mahzor enluminé* (Leiden, 1983), plate XXII, fig. 44 and pp. 64ff. [hereafter *Me*].

4. Jerusalem, Israel Museum, MS 180/52, fol. 18v. Pentateuch, etc., Southern Germany, ca. 1300. The text below the framed picture is *Genesis* 22:1-5. Isaac is crouching on the altar. Abraham is wearing a Jew's hat and looks toward the winged eagle-headed angel who grasps the tip of Abraham's knife (?) with his right hand. Abraham places his left hand on Isaac's head. The ram, on the right, is standing between the branches of a tree (?). To the right is a small panel which depicts a large devilish-looking figure holding aloft a woman, whose hands are spread in surprise. This is a legendary elaboration of the devil lifting up Sarah to witness the Sacrifice.
Narkiss, *HIM,* p. 98; Schubert, *JM,* p. 215; Metzger, *JL,* p. 302, No. 58.

5. New York, Library of the Jewish Theological Seminary of America, MS 8972 (Acc. No. 0017), fol. 121. Collection of *piyyutim* and other liturgical texts for the special Sabbaths and holidays, Southern Germany, late 13th century. The framed miniature is above the Aramaic *piyyut* to the morning service of *Shavuot.* It follows the recitation of the Fifth Commandment: "Honor your father and mother (*Exodus* 20:12 and *Deuteronomy* 5:16)," and begins with: "Isaac said to Abraham, his father: 'What a lovely altar you built for me father...'"
The miniature itself is surrounded with verses taken from *Genesis* 22:12-13, and the last sentence of the liturgical poem reads: "The Almighty said to him (to Abraham), Don't harm the child, for I'm His redeemer and I shall redeem you." The ram on the right is caught in a tree (?) by its horns. Abraham, wearing a medieval Jew's hat, has a large knife poised in his right hand, while his left hand is placed on the head of Isaac. Isaac is reclining on the stone altar, his hands tied. A crowned, eagle-faced angel points with his right hand towards the ram and is about to grasp Abraham's knife.
J. Bloch, *The People and the Book* (New York, 1954), pp. 56-58; Metzger, *JL,* p. 305, No. 138; I. Davidson, *Thesaurus of Medieval Hebrew Poetry* (New York, 1924), I, 5812; *Mahzor Vitry,* p. 341; B. Narkiss, "Illustrations of the Ten Commandments in a Tiny Mahzor of the Thirteenth Century," in B.-Z. Segal, ed., *The Ten Commandments as Reflected in Tradition and Literature of the Middle Ages* (Jerusalem, 1985), pp. 401f. (in Hebrew).

6. Jerusalem, Israel Museum, MS 180/57, fol. 15v.
"Birds' Head Haggadah," Germany, Rhineland, early 14th century. The picture is inserted in the Haggadah text, which reads: "God heard our voice as we read: 'When God heard their groaning He remembered His covenant with Abraham [Isaac and Jacob].'" Cf. *Exodus* 2:24. On the left we see a ram standing between the branches of a tree (?). Abraham with Jew's hat raises a sword with his right hand and grasps Isaac by the hair with his left hand. Isaac appears to have his hands and feet tied and is crouching on an altar. A winged angel appears on the right, grasps Abraham's sword and points to the ram with his left hand. All figures have bird heads with the exception of the angel.
Narkiss, *HIM,* p. 96; Narkiss, *Bird,* p. 35 and pp. 94 ff.; Metzger, *JL,* p. 302, No. 61.

7. Jerusalem, Schocken Institute for Jewish Studies of the Jewish Theological Seminary of America, MS 14840, fol. 1v. Bible, Southern Germany, early 14th century.
Bereshit, "When God *began,"* the opening word of the book of *Genesis* is in the central panel. Roundel 8, read from right to left, has the Sacrifice of Isaac. Isaac is crouching on a draped altar. Abraham has a sword in his right hand and his left appears to be grasping Isaac's hair. The winged angel arrests the sword and points to the ram suspended by its horns from a bush (?).
Narkiss, *HIM,* p. 102; J. Gutmann, *Hebrew Manuscript Painting* (New York, 1978), pp. 74-75.

8. Leipzig, Universitätsbibliothek, MS V. 1102/II, fol. 66. *Mahzor,* Southern Germany, first quarter of 14th century. Next to the text for the *Musaf* service of the second day of *Rosh Hashanah,* "I will praise my God, and sing of His might, I will tell of His glory", is the Sacrifice of Isaac. From the clouds emerge two hands of an angel (?). The right hand seizes the sword of Abraham, who looks upwards, and the left points to a ram suspended from a branch of a tree. Isaac is kneeling on an altar, his hands folded in a gesture of prayer. Abraham is placing his left hand on the head of Isaac. All faces have animal features.
B. Narkiss in *Machsor Lipsiae,* ed. E. Katz (Leipzig, 1964), pp. 97-98; Metzger, *JL,* p. 303, No. 87; E. Roth, "Rosch Haschana im Machsor Lipsiae," *Israelitisches Wochenblatt für die Schweiz* (24 September 1965), pp. 51ff.
[Cf. also fol. 26v of the same manuscript. In a frame is the word *melekh,* the opening word of the *piyyut* recited during the morning service of the first day of *Rosh Hashanah,* beginning with "O King, girt with power, Your name is great in strength; Yours is the arm of triumph." To the left is a Jew wearing a Jew's hat and blowing a shofar. To the right, outside the frame, is a blue ram standing against a tree, whose roots are visible. Cf. also Oxford, Bodleian Library MS Mich. 619, fol. 5v, *Mahzor,* Southern Germany, second quarter of 14th century. A

blue ram is standing with its horns in a leafy branch of a small tree. The illustration accompanies the same text as Leipzig, MS V. 1102/II, 26v.

Narkiss, *HIM,* p. 104; Sed-Rajna, *Me,* plate XXII, fig. 42; Metzger, *JL,* p. 306, No. 164.

London, British Library, MS Add. 15282, fol. 28, Pentateuch, etc., Southern Germany, first quarter of 14th Germany, reveals again a ram, drawn in masoretic micrography, which is entangled by its horns in the branches of a tree. The marginal illustration accompanies the text of *Genesis* 22. Metzger, *JL,* p. 303, No. 95].

9. Wrocław, University Library, MS Or. I/1, fol. 46v. *Mahzor,* Southern Germany, first half of 14th century. The text is from the morning service of the second day of *Rosh Hashanah,* when the Jew appeals to God to "account to His people the Sacrifice of Isaac according to Your oath, and reverse [Your decree] from stern judgment to mercy." A bearded Abraham on the left takes Isaac's left arm with his right hand and lovingly guides his son to the scene of the Sacrifice atop Mount Moriah. Isaac is lying on the altar, hands and feet (?) tied, eyes shielded from the sight of the sword by Abraham's left hand. In his right hand Abraham holds the sword which is intercepted by the right hand of a winged angel. With his left hand the angel points to a blue ram standing upright in a bush (?). Next to the altar is a large candle. Below are the two servants – one with a stick and two red barrels strapped over his shoulder; the other servant prods the donkey with a stick. The donkey carries the container with faggots on his back. The facial features appear to have been effaced. M. Plessner, "Eine illustrierte deutsche Machsor Handschrift in Breslau," *Menorah,* 5 (1927), pp. 88-89; Metzger, *JL,* p. 310, no. 258; J. Gutmann, "Rosh Hashanah in Art," in *Rosh Hashanah Anthology,* ed. P. Goodman (Philadelphia, 1970), pp. 167-68 [hereafter *RH*]; Sed-Rajna, *Me,* plate XXIII, fig. 45, pp. 67ff.

10. Oxford, Bodleian Library, MS Or. 140, fol. 35v. *Mahzor,* Germany, first half of 14th century. The crude sketch accompanies the same text as No. 8 (the Leipzig *Mahzor*). Isaac, hands and feet bound, lies on a trestle. A bearded Abraham, wearing a Jew's hat, shield's Isaac's eyes with his left hand. In his right he holds a knife. An arm with wings (probably of the angel) points to a large ram caught by its horns in the branches of a tree (?). To the left is a hunter galloping away on horseback, while blowing a horn (*shofar?*).

Metzger, *JL,* p. 306, No. 156.

11. Oxford, Bodleian Library, MS Reggio 1, fol. 159v. *Mahzor,* Germany, first half of the 14th century. The red and black sepia–ink illustration has the word *melekh* in the center. This is the opening word of the *piyyut* recited on the first day of the morning service of *Rosh Hashanah:* "O King, girt with power, Your name is great in strength; Yours is the arm of triumph (stressing sovereignty of God over men and nature)." Isaac is crouched on an altar draped with a cloth. A bearded Abraham holds a knife in his right hand and points to Isaac with his left. He looks upward toward a winged angel emerging from a cloud. With his left hand the angel points to the ram standing in the center. On the right a man is blowing a shofar. Gutmann, *RH,* p. 167; Metzger, *JL,* p. 307, No. 173.

12. Oxford, Bodleian Library, MS Opp. 14, folios 22v. Pentateuch with *Targum* and Rashi, etc., Germany, March 3, 1340. Isaac is lying on a stone altar, his hands and feet tied together from behind (cf. Commentary of Rashi to *Genesis* 22:9). Isaac's neck is stretched out ready to receive the cut (*shehitah*) from Abraham's knife, held in his right hand. A bearded angel towers above pointing to the ram suspended by its horns from one of the branches of a tree.

13. Oxford, Bodleian Library, MS Opp. 14, fol. 120. Pentateuch with *Targum* and Rashi, etc., Germany, March 3, 1340. A similar scene to the one described above is used to introduce the book of *Leviticus.* The major difference is that Isaac's hands and feet are tied separately from the front. Cf. also Milan, No. 2.

Metzger, *JL,* p. 306, No. 166.

14. Darmstadt, Hessische Landes- und Hochschulbibliothek, MS Or. 13, fol. 202v. *Mahzor,* Hammelburg, Germany, 1347/48, *Rosh Hashanah,* second day, *Musaf* service. The "Sacrifice of Isaac" is on top of a mountain. A bearded Abraham is on the left wearing a Jew's hat. He lifts his right hand bearing the knife and with his left attempts to shield Isaac's eyes. Isaac lies on top of a huge bundle of faggots, his hands and feet tied. A winged angel swoops down from above and grasps Abraham's knife while pointing to the ram suspended by its horns from the branches of a tree (?). One servant with a hatchet is about to chop down a small tree and a donkey with faggots strapped to his side is seen below.

Metzger, *JL,* p. 301, No. 40; Sed-Rajna, *Me,* pp.75-76.

15. Hamburg, Staats-und Universitätsbibliothek, Cod. Hebr. 37,

fol. 1. Miscellany, Middle Rhine region, second quarter of 15th century.

The miniature accompanies the text of the *Amidah* recited on *Rosh Hashanah*: "Blessed are You, O Lord our God, and God of our fathers, Abraham, Isaac and Jacob.... Remember us unto life, O King, who delights in life and inscribe us in the Book of Life.... You are mighty forever.... Blessed are You, O Lord, who revives the dead." The scene is to be read in a circular fashion beginning on the left margin with Sarah bidding her son Isaac goodbye (?) (badly effaced). The two servants are seen with the donkey; one servant carries an axe. In the center is Isaac, hands and feet bound, lying on top of the faggots of an altar. A bearded Abraham with a large knife in his right hand touches Isaac's head with his left hand. To the right is a young man with a lance (perhaps one of the servants?). Three winged angels with aureoles are seen, two are in the starry sky above. The angel on the right blows the *shofar* and holds the scales of judgment with his left hand, as the *Rosh Hashanah* liturgy reads: "This day has been ordained of old as a day of reckoning, when the deeds of man are weighed and judged." We see a hairy, black devil trying to pull down the left pan of the scales, as it bears the evil deeds of man. [In a *Mahzor* (Vienna, Österreichische Nationalbibliothek, Cod. Hebr. 174, fol. 1v), dated first half of 14th century, Germany, the left pan of the scales is labelled *hovot* (guilts). Cf. also the devil pulling down the left pan of the scales (Oxford Bodleian Library, MS Reggio 1, fol. 207v), in a *Mahzor* from Germany, 14th century. Metzger, *JL*, p. 247, fig. 363. The illustration accompanies the *piyyut* recited on the second day of the *Rosh Hashanah* holiday: "O King, Your word stands steadfast..." The zodiacal sign of the month of *Tishri (Rosh Hashanah* falls on the first of *Tishri)* is the scales. Thus we note in a *Mahzor* (Dresden, Sächsische Landesbibliotek, MS A46a, fol. 133v) from the second quarter of 14th-century Germany that the scales reveal a winged angel standing on the right pan, while a devil is trying to pull down the left pan.] The central angel hovering over the Sacrifice points to the ram standing on the mountain and another angel returns Isaac from paradise, where according to tradition his soul fled after the Sacrifice. At the bottom of the folio are the two servants with the donkey. Narkiss, *HIM*, p. 118; Gutmann, *RH,* p. 165; Schubert, *JM,* pp. 236-237; Metzger, *JL*, p. 301, No. 49.

16. Budapest, Library of the Hungarian Academy of Sciences, MS A 387, fol. 403v. *Mahzor*, Germany, first half of 15th century. The text of the unfinished sketch in the margin is from the *Amidah, Yom Kippur minhah* service: "Remember unto us the Binding of the only one and forgive us all of our sins because of the righteousness of a perfect man." Above the word *Akedat* (Binding), Isaac appears to be lying half nude on top of a bundle of faggots on the altar. A bearded Abraham places his right hand on the head of Isaac and raises his left hand, bearing the knife (?). Metzger, *JL*, p. 300, No. 23.

17. Jerusalem, Schocken Institute for Jewish Studies of the Jewish Theological Seminary of America, MS 24087, fol. 31; "Second Nuremberg Haggadah", Southern Germany, second half of 15th century. Isaac is lying bound on a trestle, one hand and one foot tied together. Abraham is placing his left hand on his head and raises the knife (?) with his right. The knife (?) is arrested by the right hand of a winged angel descending from the clouds. With his left hand he points to the donkey below. Above is a ram caught in a thicket.

The rhymed inscription next to the ram reads:
"A ram by his horns in the thicket was caught,
God from his habitation had the ram brought,
Created by God on Sabbath's twilight,
He among ten things was a delight."
Next to the angel is the inscription:
"As the ruler of the world divined
That father and son were of one mind,
His angel He sent the knife to restrain
That Isaac's skin should unharmed remain."
The rhyme near Abraham reads:
"Abraham his pain from his son well hid,
He listened to his Maker's bid.
The knife he took in hand quickly
His darling son to slaughter fitly."
Below Isaac the inscription records:
"As a burnt offering Isaac was bound
God's command appeared very sound."
The inscription near the donkey reads:
"God, Abraham tried,
Your son, he asked, your pride,
Take him, without deceit
To Mount Moriah, My seat."

18. Jerusalem, Israel Museum, MS 180/50, fol. 30. "Yahuda Haggadah", Southern Germany, second half of the 15th century. The text is the *Hallel* of the Passover Haggadah in both manuscripts. The depiction is similar to No. 17, except that the winged angel points to the ram. Isaac appears to be lying on a table. It is difficult to tell if he is bound, as the illustration is badly effaced. The rhymed

inscriptions are almost identical to No. 17. Narkiss, *HIM*, pp. 120-122; Metzger, *JL*, p. 302, No. 56 and p. 303, No. 84. B. Narkiss and G. Sed-Rajna, eds., *Iconographical Index of Hebrew Illuminated Manuscripts* (Munich, 1981), II. 2, Card Numbers 131-32 and II. 3, Card Numbers 134-35.

ITALY

19. Jerusalem, Library of the Schocken Institute for Jewish Research of the Jewish Theological Seminary of America, MS 24085, fol. 31. Haggadah, Ashkenazic rite, Naples (?), second half of 14th century.
The text above the miniature comes from the Grace after the meal: "Our God and God of our fathers...." Isaac is standing on a hillock with trees, his hands folded in an attitude of prayer. A bearded Abraham places his left hand on the head of Isaac and with his right is about to kill Isaac with a knife (?). A winged angel is behind Abraham and appears to be bringing the ram.
B. Narkiss, *Illuminated Manuscripts from Jerusalem Collections.* Catalog of exhibition at Israel Museum, No. 40 (October-November, 1970), No. 14. Metzger, *JL*, p. 303, No. 82; J. Gutmann, "The Sacrifice of Isaac: Variations on a Theme in Early Jewish and Christian Art," *Thiasos ton Mouson: Studien zu Antike und Christentum. Festschrift für Josef Fink zum 70. Geburtstag,* ed. D. Ahrens (Cologne, 1984), p. 118, n. 8.

SPAIN

20. London, British Library, MS Or. 2737, fols. 92-93v. Haggadah, Sephardic rite, Castile (?), first quarter of 14th century.
Folio 92 shows Abraham and Isaac riding on the donkey; on the left the two servants follow them. The text inscribed above the miniature is from *Genesis* 22:3. Folio 92v reveals a donkey feeding from a feed bag; two servants are behind the donkey. The text is from *Genesis* 22:5. Fol. 93 has Abraham taking Isaac by the hand; Isaac carries the faggots on his shoulder. The text above the miniature is from *Genesis* 22:4. Fol. 93v has a bearded Abraham with a knife in his right hand. Isaac is lying on top of a stone altar, his hands bound. Abraham pushes Isaac's face down with his left hand to bare the neck for the ritual cut (*shehitah*). A winged hand (of an angel?) emerges from the clouds and points to the ram caught in the thicket behind Abraham. The inscription is from *Genesis* 22:9 "And Abraham built an altar there; he laid out the wood, and he bound his son Isaac."
M. Metzger, *La Haggada enluminée* (Leiden, 1973), p. 413; Metzger, *JL*, p. 304, No. 115; B. Narkiss, *Hebrew*

Illuminated Manuscripts in the British Isles. A Catalogue Raisonné (Volume I, The Spanish and Portuguese Manuscripts) (Jerusalem and London, 1982), I, p. 50.

21. London, British Library, MS Add. 27210, fol. 4v. Haggadah, Sephardic rite, Catalonia, ca. 1320-1330. The inscription above the miniature reads: "You stay here with the ass" (*Genesis* 22:5); "behold, a ram" (*Genesis* 22:13); "he bound his son Isaac" (*Genesis* 22:9).
Isaac, his hands appear to be bound (?) in front, reclines on a rocky landscape. A bearded Abraham, wearing an apron, kneels beside him. His knife is in his right hand. He looks toward the winged angel appearing in the clouds who points to the ram suspended vertically from the branches of a small tree. Two servants with the ass are on the right.
B. Narkiss, *The Golden Haggadah* (London, 1970), p. 25; Gutmann, *HMP*, pp. 61-62; Narkiss, *Catalogue Raisonné*, p. 60.

22. Sarajevo, Yugoslavia, National Museum. "Sarajevo Haggadah", fols. 7-8. Catalonia, third quarter of 14th century. Fol. 7 has Abraham's servants with the ass, on the left. Abraham holds the sacrificial knife and a fire bowl (*Genesis* 22:6). He is preceded by Isaac who bears the fire wood. Fol. 8 has the following text above the miniature: "Behold, a ram caught in the thicket by its horns" (*Genesis* 22:13) and "Binding of Isaac". There are two mountain tops. On the left mountain top is Isaac as a young nude child lying on top of the faggots of the altar. His hands may be tied (?). Both Isaac and Abraham look toward the pointing hand (of the angel?) emerging from the cloud. Abraham places his right hand on the head of Isaac as he prepares to cut his throat with the knife held in his left hand.
Narkiss, *HIM*, p. 60; Metzger, *JL*, p. 309, No. 236; Gutmann, *HMP*, pp. 68-72; C. Roth, *The Sarajevo Haggadah* (New York, 1963), pp. 18-19; E. Werber, *The Sarajevo Haggadah* (Beograd, 1985), p. 27.
Cambridge University Library, MS Add. 652, fol. 13v, a Pentateuch with Hagiographa, Castile (?), early 14th century, reveals in the right-hand margin, a ram caught by its horns in a tree. Both the tree and the ram are drawn in masoretic micrography. The text of the page begins with *Genesis* 22:7ff. Narkiss, *Catalogue Raisonné,* I, pp. 35ff; II, fig. 53.

FRANCO-FLEMISH

23. London, British Library, MS Add. 11639, fol. 521v. Miscellany, Northern France, late 13th century.
Abraham raises his knife with the right hand and places

his left hand on the head of Isaac. Isaac sits on the high altar, his left foot bound to his left hand. A bundle of faggots and the fire are to the left of the altar. A winged angel appears from the clouds to arrest Abraham's knife and to point to the ram caught in the thicket. The inscription reads: "This is the Binding of Isaac on the altar and the ram caught by its horns." (*Genesis* 22:13). Z. Ameisenowa, "Die hebräische Sammelhandschrift Add. 11639 des British Museum," *Wiener Jahrbuch für Kunstgeschichte*, 24 (1971), pp. 30-31; M. Metzger, "Les illustrations bibliques d'un manuscrit hébreu du Nord de la France," *Mélanges offerts à René Crozet* (Poitiers, 1966), pp. 1239ff.; G. Sed-Rajna, "The Paintings of the London Miscellany, British Library Add. MS 11639," *Journal of Jewish Art*, 9 (1982), pp. 24ff.; T. and M. Metzger, "Les enluminures du Ms. Add. 11639 de la British Library, un manuscrit hébreu du nord de la France (fin du XIIIe siècle – premier quart du XIVe siècle," *Wiener Jahrbuch für Kunstgeschichte*, 38 (1985), pp. 89f.

24. Budapest, Library of the Hungarian Academy of Sciences, MS A 77/III, fol. 81. Maimonides, *Mishneh Torah*, Book X (*Taharah* = Purification), Lorraine region, Northeast France, early 14th century.
   Abraham has a sword in his left hand and has his right hand on the head of Isaac. Isaac sits on the altar, his hands folded in prayer. A nimbed angel arrests Abraham's sword and points to the ram caught in a bush next to the altar. The bundle of faggots is visible to the left of the altar. It has been suggested that the end of the ninth book deals with substituted sacrifices; the artist may have introduced the "Sacrifice of Isaac" at the beginning of the tenth book.
   G. Sed-Rajna, "The Illustrations to the Kaufmann Mishneh Torah," *Journal of Jewish Art*, 6 (1979), p. 76.

25. Paris, Bibliothèque Nationale, MS hébr. 36, fol. 283v. Pentateuch with *Targum*, etc., Eastern France, Poligny or Foulenay, around 1300. The text was completed on Thursday, June 30, 1300 = 12 *Tammuz* 5060.
   Abraham places his right hand on the draped altar and has the knife in his left hand. Behind him are the two servants with the ass (?). Isaac lies partly nude upon the altar, his hands and feet appear to be tied. He looks up to the nimbed, spread-winged angel who points to Abraham with his left hand and gives the Christian benediction to the ram which appears to be still running as it is being entangled in the bush by its horns. Narkiss, *HIM*, p. 88; Metzger, *JL*, p. 307, No. 187.

26. Hamburg, Staats-und Universitätsbibliothek, Cod. Levy 19, fol. 34v. Pentateuch with *Targum*, Rashi Commentary, etc., Brussels (Brabant), 1309. The text is *Genesis* 22 with Rashi Commentary. A bearded Abraham, wearing a short hood, its liripipe falling freely in the back, is enveloped by a *tallit* (prayer shawl).
   He has a sword in his right hand and grasps Isaac's hair with his left hand. Isaac is lying nude on the faggots of the altar, his hands and feet tied together. A nimbed, winged angel seizes Abraham's sword and points to the ram, whose horns are caught in a bush. Metzger, *JL*, p. 301, No. 51.

27. Parma, Biblioteca Palatina, MS Parm. 3518, fol. 25v. *Siddur*, Franco-Germany (?), early 14th century.
   The text surrounding the miniature is from the *Rosh Hashanah* liturgy: "Remember us unto life, O King, who delightest in life and inscribe us in the Book of Life." Above the Hebrew word *zahrenu* (remember us), the four chief characters of the Sacrifice are placed in four separate panels. To the right is Abraham holding the knife in his right hand. To the left stands a winged angel. On top of a table lies Isaac, whose hands may be tied or in a gesture of prayer. The fire is underneath the table (=altar). The panel above Isaac shows the ram suspended upright from the branches of a tree. (Cf. British Library, MS Add. 18424, a *halakhic* work done around 1307 by the same artist). Gutmann, *RH*, p. 167; Metzger, *JL*, p. 309, No. 228; G. Margoliouth, *Catalogue of the Hebrew and Samaritan Manuscripts in the British Museum* (London, 1905), II, pp. 143 ff., No. 538.

APPENDIX II

ABRAHAM

1 Abraham touches head of Isaac 1, 2, 4, 5, 7, 8, 12, 15, 16, 17, 19, 22, 23, 24.
2 Abraham pulls hair of Isaac 3, 6, 26.
3 Abraham shields eyes of Isaac 9, 10, 14.
4 Abraham looks tward angel 2, 4, 5, 6, 7, 8, 9, 11, 21, 22, 23, 25, 26.
5 Abraham looks toward ram 1, 3, 10, 25.
6 Abraham holds weapon in his left hand 16, 22, 24, 25.
7 Abraham about to cut neck of Isaac 12, 13, 20.
8 Abraham uses sword 6, 7, 8, 9, 24, 26.
9 Abraham kneels 21.

10 Abraham not bearded 2, 3, 5, 17, 18.
11 Abraham wears apron 21.
12 Abraham wears Jew's hat 4, 5, 6, 10, 14.
13 Abraham wears *tallit* 26.
14 Abraham points to Isaac 11.

ISAAC

1 Isaac crouches on altar 2, 4, 6, 11.
2 Isaac kneels on altar 3(?), 8.
3 Isaac lies on altar 5, 9, 10, 17, 18, 25.
4 Isaac on top of faggots 1, 14, 15, 16, 22, 27.
5 Isaac sitting on altar 1, 23, 24.
6 Isaac nude 1, 3, 22, 25, 27.
7 Isaac lying on ground 21.
8 Isaac standing 19.
9 Isaac, hands and feet tied 6, 9, 10, 12, 13, 14, 25, 26.
10 Isaac hands tied 1 (?), 5, 16, 20, 21(?), 22 (?), 27 (?).
11 Isaac, one foot and hand tied together 12, 17, 23.
12 Isaac praying 8, 19, 24.

ANGEL

1 Winged angel pointing to ram 2, 3, 5, 6, 7, 8, 9, 11, 12, 13, 14, 15, 18, 20, 21, 23, 24, 25, 26.
2 Hand of winged angel arresting Abraham's weapon 1, 2, 4, 5, 6, 7, 8, 9, 14, 17, 18, 23, 24, 26.
3 Winged hand of angel pointing 10, 20.

4 Hand of angel pointing 8, 22.
5 Winged angel with eaglehead 4, 5.
6 Winged standing angel 27.
7 Winged angel brings ram 19.
8 Male winged angel with beard 12, 13.
9 Angel with scroll 1.
10 Angel with aureole 15, 24, 25, 26.
11 Angel holding scale 15.

RAM.

1 Standing with hind legs on ground, front legs raised in tree 2, 3, 4, 5, 6, 7, 9.
2 Ram suspended vertically from tree 8, 12, 13, 14, 21, 27.
3 Ram entangled in tree or thicket 1, 10, 17, 18, 20, 22, 23, 24, 26.
4 Ram running toward bush 25.
5 Ram standing by 11, 15, 17.

ALTAR

1 Faggots on altar 1, 14, 15, 22, 26.
2 Faggots next to altar 23, 24.
3 Altar draped with cloth 3, 7, 11, 25.
4 No altar 19, 21.
5 Altar of stones 5 (?), 12, 13, 20.
6 Fire under altar 2, 15, 27.
7 Candle near altar 9.

*I am greatly indebted to my good friend, Prof. Stanley F. Chyet, for reading this paper and for making many suggestions for its improvement.

[1] I. G. Marcus, *Piety and Society* (Leiden, 1981), p. 35.

[2] N. M. Waldman, "The Akedah in Modern Midrash," *The Reconstructionist,* 44 (1978), p. 15. Cf. also M. Brown, "Biblical Myth and Contemporary Experience. The Akedah in Modern Jewish Literature," *Judaism,* 31 (1982), pp. 99-111; E. A. Coffin, "The Binding of Isaac in Modern Israeli Literature," *Michigan Quarterly Review,* 22 (1983), pp. 429-45.

[3] Cf. J. Gutmann, "The Sacrifice of Isaac: Variations on a Theme in Early Jewish and Christian Art," *Thiasos ton Mouson: Studien zu Antike und Christentum. Festschrift für Josef Fink zum 70. Geburtstag,* ed. by D. Ahrens (Cologne, 1984), pp. 115 ff.; L. H. Feldman, "Josephus' Version of the Binding of Isaac," *Society of Biblical Literature 1982 Seminar Papers,* 21 (1982), p. 126, and *idem,* "Josephus as Biblical Interpreter: The *'Aqedah',*" *The Jewish Quarterly Review,* 75 (1985), p. 247.

[4] J. A. Lerner, "Christian Seals of the Sasanian Period," *Nederlands Historisch-Archaeologisch Instituut te Istanbul,* 41 (1977), pp. 18-22 and J. Gutmann, "The Dura-Europos Synagogue Paintings: The State of Research," in *The Synagogue in Late Antiquity,* ed. L. I. Levine (Philadelphia, 1987), p. 69, n. 1.

[5] Gutmann, "Sacrifice of Isaac," *op. cit.,* pp. 120ff.

[6] A hand is shown pointing a finger in the Sarajevo Haggadah, folio 8v (No. 22). It is difficult to tell if the hand represents God or an angel. In other depictions of the Sarajevo Haggadah, God is usually represented by a series of emanating rays (fols. 2, 3, 21, 30); angels are shown faceless, but winged (fols. 10, 30). In two manuscripts (Nos. 10, 20) we see an arm with wings – its hand with pointing finger – emerging from the clouds. The angel intervening is often identified in Jewish and Christian texts as Michael [*Pesikta Rabbati, Piska* 40:6]. Cf. N. Cohen, "Heeding the Angel's Cry: A Modern Midrashic Reading of Abraham's Life," *Journal of Reform Judaism,* 30 (1983), p. 14, n. 38; U. Schwab, "Zum Verständnis des Isaak-Opfers in literarischer und bildlicher Darstellung des Mittelalters," *Frühmittelalterliche Studien,* 15 (1981), p. 456. Some sources claim that it was

the angel Raphael, cf. P. Matenko and S. Sloan, eds., *Two Studies in Yiddish Culture: 1. The Aqedath Jishaq* (Leiden, 1968), p. 62; R. Stichel, "Zur Ikonographie der Opferung Isaaks in der romanischen Kunst Spaniens und in der byzantinischen Welt," in *Actas del XXIII congreso internacional de Historia del Arte* I (Granada, 1973), p. 529. Still other sources state that it was the angel Gabriel, cf. *Neweh Shalom*, 51; J. R. Elliot, Jr. "The Sacrifice as Comedy and Tragedy," *North Carolina University – Studies in Philology,* 66 (1969), p. 40 and M. Grünbaum, *Neue Beiträge zur semitischen Sagenkunde* (Leiden, 1893), pp. 112 ff., for Islamic sources.

[7] *Leviticus Rabbah* 7:3 and H. Schauss, *The Lifetime of a Jew* (Cincinnati, 1950), pp. 312-13. Cf. also the parallel between *Leviticus* 1:7 and *Genesis* 22:10 that the sons of Aaron shall "lay out wood upon the fire." It is noteworthy that the priests shall "offer the blood [of the *olah*], dashing the blood against all sides of the altar" (*Leviticus* 1:5). Like priests of old, rabbis during the Christian massacres of the Middle Ages would sometimes sprinkle the blood of the human offerings (the new *Akedot* made to prevent apostasy or forced conversions at the hands of Christians) on the pillars of the Torah ark of synagogues. Cf. S. Bernfeld, *Sefer Hadma'ot,* I (Berlin, 1923), p. 173 and M. Habermann, *Sefer Gezerot Ashkenaz we-Tzarefat* (Jerusalem, 1945), p. 37.

Cf. F. Garnier, *Le langage de l'image au moyen âge* (Paris, 1982), fig. 89 for the Sacrifice of Isaac depiction in the initial letter of *Leviticus* in a 13th-century Christian Bible.

[8] S. Spiegel, "A Fragment from the Legends of the Akedah," *The Abraham Weiss Jubilee Volume* (New York, 1964), pp. 553 ff. (in Hebrew).

[9] Cf. J. Gutmann, "Rosh Hashanah in Art," in *The Rosh Hashanah Anthology,* ed. by P. Goodman (Philadelphia, 1970), pp. 165-68; G. Vermes, *Scripture and Tradition in Judaism* (London, 1961), pp. 195, 207, 211, 213; S. Spiegel, *The Last Trial* (Philadelphia, 1967), p. 55 n. 14; G. Stemberger, "Die Patriarchenbilder der Katakombe in der Via Latina," *Kairos,* 16 (1974), p. 70; L. Ginzberg, *The Legends of the Jews* (Philadelphia, 1947), I, p. 285 and V, pp. 252-53, n. 248. Some Church Fathers – Peter Comestor, for one (*Historia scholastica, P. L.* 198, cols. 1105C-D) – were also aware that for Jews "the sound of the ram's horn is in memory of the ram on [*Rosh Hashanah.*]" ("Diem autem liberationis Isaac dicunt Hebraei primam diem Septembris. Unde in eo solemnizant, et clangunt cornibus pecorinis in memoriam arietis"). Cf. also U. Schwab, "Zum Verständnis des Isaak-Opfers in literarischer und bildlicher Darstellung des Mittelalters," *Frühmittelalterliche Studien,* 15 (1981), p. 477. Jewish biblical commentators generally avoided explaining why both the words *seh* (sheep) and *ayil* (ram) are employed in the *Genesis* 22 chapter [R.-P. Schmitz, *Agedat Jishaq. Die mittelalterliche jüdische Auslegung von Genesis 22 in ihren Hauptlinien* (Hildesheim, 1979), p. 163]. The reason for the rabbinic silence may have been that Jesus was equated with the lamb-ram. Melito of Sardis in the second century already explained: "For as a ram he (Jesus) was bound... and as a lamb he was shorn and as a sheep he was led to the slaughter and as a lamb he was crucified," cf. S. G. Hall, ed., *Melito of Sardis on Pascha and Fragments* (Oxford, 1979), pp. 74-75; D. Berger, *The Jewish-Christian Debate in the High Middle Ages* (Philadelphia, 1979), pp. 243-44.

[10] Rashi's Commentary to *Genesis* 22:13 and Gutmann "Sacrifice of Isaac," *op. cit.,* p. 118, n. 8.

[11] Spiegel, *Last Trial, op. cit.,* p. 39.

[12] The left pan of the scales is actually labelled *hovot* (demerits) in a *Mahzor* from the first half of the 14th century (Vienna, Österreichische Nationalbibliothek, Cod. Hebr. 174, fol. 1v). The illustration appears next to the word *melekh,* the opening word of

the *piyyut*: "O King, girt with power," recited during the morning service of the first day of *Rosh Hashanah.* Cf. also the devil pulling down the left pan of the scales in another 14th-century *Mahzor* (Oxford, Bodleian Library, MS Reggio 1, fol. 207v). The illustration (cf. Gutmann, "Rosh Hashanah," *op. cit.,* p. 33) accompanies the text for the morning service of the second day of *Rosh Hashanah,* a *piyyut* beginning with "O King, your word stands steadfast..." As the zodiacal sign for *Tishri* is the scales (and *Rosh Hashanah* falls on the first of *Tishri*), we find a devil trying to weigh down the left pan of the scales within the zodiacal sign of the month *Tishri.* Cf. the *Mahzor,* second quarter of the 14th century, Dresden, Sächsische Landesbibliothek, MS 46a, fol. 133v, in G. Sed-Rajna, *Le mahzor enluminée* (Leiden, 1983), plate XXXVII. The scales, usually held by the archangel Michael, are also depicted in medieval Christian art. In Romanesque and Gothic tympana, we often see a devil pulling down the left pan of the scales which holds the *peccata* (sins); the right pan of the scales contains the *virtutes* (virtues), which an angel, at times, tries to support. Cf. L. Kretzenbacher, *Die Seelenwaage* (Klagenfurt, 1958), pp. 95 ff.; "Michael, Erzengel," in *Lexikon der christlichen Ikonographie* (Freiburg, 1971), III, pp. 255 ff; J. B. Russell, *Lucifer, The Devil in the Middle Ages* (Ithaca, 1984), pp. 129 ff.

[13] *Pesikta de Rab Kahana,* Piska 23:8; *Leviticus Rabbah* 29:8. Cf. also the blindfolded figure, *Justitia,* holding the scales in a Christian depiction of the Sacrifice of Isaac, from the 12th-century Mosan area, in J. Squilbeck, "Le sacrifice d'Abraham dans l'art mosan," *Bulletin des musées royaux d'art et histoire,* 37 (1965), p. 91, fig. 8.

[14] Cf. Spiegel, *Last Trial, op. cit.,* p. 55, n. 14.

[15] Cf. Appendix I, No. 5.

[16] B. Narkiss, *The Golden Haggadah* (London, 1970), pp. 65 ff.

[17] Cf. B. Blumenkranz, *Le juif médiéval au miroir de l'art chrétien* (Paris, 1966), pp. 41ff., 79 ff.

[18] The angel, called *malakh,* in the Hebrew Bible is a man. Cf. F. Landsberger, "The Origin of the Winged Angel in Jewish Art," *Hebrew Union College Annual,* 20 (1947), pp. 230 ff. On the bearded non-winged male angel in early Christian art, cf. L. Kötzsche-Breitenbruch, *Die neue Katakombe an der Via Latina in Rom* (Münster, 1976), pp. 97 ff.

[19] Cf. J. Gutmann, *Hebrew Manuscript Painting* (New York, 1978), pp. 25-26; B. Narkiss, "On the Zoocephalic Phenomenon in Medieval Ashkenazi Manuscripts," in *Norms and Variations in Art. Essays in Honor of Moshe Barasch* (Jerusalem, 1983), pp. 49-62.

[20] I. Z. Kahana, "Synagogue Art in Halakhic Literature," in *Bet ha-Keneset,* ed. M. Hakohen (Jerusalem, 1955), pp. 257 ff. (in Hebrew).

[21] H. Epstein, "Meyer Schapiro: 'A Passion to Know and Make Known,'" *Art News* (May, 1983), pp. 61-62.

[22] In Nos. 16, 22, 24, 25 the weapon is held in the left hand.

[23] Gutmann, "Sacrifice of Isaac," p. 116, n. 4. Although the Vulgate translates *ma'akhelet* as *gladius* (sword), and the sword is preferred in medieval Christian depictions, we also find the knife (*coulter*) used. Cf. the literary sources in H. J. Geischer, "Heidnische Parallelen zum frühchristlichen Bild des Isaak-Opfers," *Jahrbuch für Antike und Christentum,* 10 (1967), p. 134, n. 48.

[24] *Pirkei de Rabbi Eliezer,* 31; *Yalkut Shimoni, Wa-Yera* # 101; *Midrash Bereshit Rabbati,* 91. Cf. Spiegel, *Last Trial, op. cit.,* pp. 69, 143; Ginzberg, *Legends,* I, p. 274 and V, p. 249, n. 231. Abraham, the priest, is cited in such sources as *Yalkut Shimoni, Wa-Yera* # 96; *Pirkei de Rabbi Eliezer* 31; *Leviticus Rabbah* 25:6; Babylonian Talmud, *Nedarim* 32b; *Pesikta Rabbati,* Piska 40:6.

[25] Spiegel, *Last Trial, op. cit.,* p. 20.

[26] *Ibid.,* p. 24.

[27] *Ibid.,* pp. 19 and 17ff. Cf. *Yashar, Wa-Yera* 46a, *Pesikta Rabbati*

40:6; Schmitz, *Aqedat Jishaq*, pp. 141, 137.

28 It should be noted that hand and foot are also tied together from behind in the 12th-century Klosterneuburg altar panel of the Sacrifice of Isaac, cf. Squilbeck, "Sacrifice d'Abraham," *op. cit.*, p. 88, fig. 6.

29 Babylonian Talmud, *Shabbat* 54a; Babylonian Talmud, *Tamid* 31b; Spiegel, *Last Trial, op. cit.*, p. 147.

30 *Pirkei de Rabbi Eliezer*, 31; *Tanhuma, Wa-Yera* 46; *Pesikta Rabbati*, Piska 40:6; *Midrash Haggadol*, 354; *Yalkut Shimoni, Wa-Yera* # 101 speak of binding hands and feet. Some of the *Targumim* to *Genesis* 22:10 have "bind my hands." I am indebted to Michael Klein for this information. Cf. Stemberger, "Patriarchenbilder," pp. 62f.; Spiegel, *Last Trial, op. cit.*, pp. 147 f.; Ginzberg, *Legends, op. cit.*, I, p. 280 and V, p. 251, n. 242. For Christian sources, cf. Schwab, "Verständnis," *op. cit.*, p. 450; M. E. Wells, "The Age of Isaac at the Time of the Sacrifice," *Modern Language Notes*, 54 (1939), p. 580; Geischer, "Heidnische," *op. cit.*, p. 135, n. 50.

31 Ibn Ezra, Commentary to *Genesis* 22:4, reports that most rabbis claim Isaac was 37. [Since Sarah was 90 (*Genesis* 17:17) when Isaac was born and she died at age 127 (*Genesis* 23:1), which according to the *midrash* resulted from her hearing of Isaac's impending death, Isaac was 37 years old (127–90=37)]. Others claim that Isaac was 5, and Ibn Ezra believes he was 13. Cf. also Babylonian Talmud, *Sanhedrin* 89b, which states that Isaac was a child, and *Genesis Rabbah* 56:8 gives his age as 26. Josephus, *Antiquities* I.XIII.2 (=I.227) has 25. Cf. also Stemberger, "Patriarchenbilder," pp. 55-56; Spiegel, *Last Trial, op. cit.*, pp. 49, 103; Feldman, "Josephus", *op. cit.*, pp. 121-22; Schmitz, *Aqedat*, p. 138. S. Brock, "Genesis 22 in Syriac Tradition," *Mélanges Dominique Barthélemy* (Göttingen, 1981), pp. 6-7; Wells, "Age," *op. cit.*, pp. 580-81. Cf. also R. Woolf, "The Effect of Typology on the English Mediaeval Plays of Abraham," *Speculum*, 32 (1957), p. 817.

32 Rashi, Commentary to *Genesis* 22:13; *Targum*, Pseudo-Jonathan, *Genesis* 22:13; *Yalkut Shimoni, Wa-Yera* # 101. The tree is also found in Christian art and literature, Gutmann, "Sacrifice," *op. cit.*, p. 116, n. 3.

33 *Genesis Rabbah* 56:5; *Yalkut Shimoni, Wa-Yera* # 101; *Tanhuma, Wa-Yera* 23. Cf. Stemberger, "Patriarchenbilder," *op. cit.*, p. 62; Spiegel, *Last Trial, op. cit.*, p. 36. Only Nos. 5 (?), 12, 13, 20 show the altar built of stones, as Jewish legends would have it. Cf. Ginzberg, *Legends, op. cit.*, p. 280 and V, p. 250, n. 241.

34 *Targum* Pseudo-Jonathan, *Genesis* 22:20; *Yalkut Shimoni, Wa-Yera* # 98; *Pirkei de Rabbi Eliezer* 32; *Midrash Haggadol* 360 for other stories of Sarah and the devil (Satan). Cf. also Ginzberg, *Legends, op. cit.*, I, p. 278 and V, pp. 249-50, n. 235, 256, n. 259.

35 Cf. *Midrash Haggadol* 360; *Yalkut Shimoni, Hayyei Sarah* # 109; Ginzberg, *Legends, op. cit.*, I, p. 282 and V, p. 252, n. 243; Spiegel, *Last Trial, op. cit.*, pp. 5-7; Schmitz, *Aqedat*, p. 59.

36 *Pirkei de Rabbi Eliezer*, 31; *Yalkut Shimoni, Wa-Yera* # 101; *Midrash Haggadol*, 355; *Midrash Wa-Yosha* (A. Jellinek, *Bet ha-Midrash* I, 38); Spiegel, *Last Trial, op. cit.*, pp. 29 ff.; Ginzberg, *Legends, op. cit.*, I, p. 285 and V, pp. 254 f., n. 255.

37 Cf. the contemporary depiction of the Sacrifice of Isaac in the Wechselburg Schlosskirche, fig. 12, in J. Gutmann "Medieval Jewish Image: Controversies, Contributions, Conceptions," *Aspects of Jewish Culture in the Middle Ages*, ed. P. E. Szarmach (Albany, 1979), p. 144.

38 Cf. the contemporary depictions from 14th-century Naples in Gutmann, "Sacrifice," *op. cit.*, p. 118, n. 8.

39 Cf. the Christian miniature in a 13th-century Moralized Bible (Oxford, Bodleian Library, Ms. 270b, fol. 16) in M. Schapiro, *Words and Pictures* (The Hague, 1973), p. 66. Cf. also the adaptation of Christian models (in Nos. 4, 6, 7), such as the Sacrifice of Isaac in the Psalter of St. Louis of ca. 1260 (Paris: Bibliothèque Nationale, Ms. lat 10525, fol. 10), in M. Thomas, *Der Psalter des Ludwig des Heiligen* (Graz, 1985), plate 10.

40 In medieval Christian manuscripts, Abraham usually has an aureole. In Jewish art, Abraham has an aureole only in the 6th-century Beth-Alpha synagogue mosaic, cf. Gutmann, "Sacrifice," *op. cit.*, plate 7.

41 Brock, "Genesis," pp. 16 ff.; F. Nikolasch, "Zur Ikonographie des Widders von Genesis 22," *Vigiliae Christianae*, 23 (1969), pp. 212 ff.; Hall, *Melito, op. cit.*, pp. 76-77; Vermes, *Scripture, op.cit.*, pp. 216, 225 ff. Spiegel, *Last Trial, op. cit.*, pp. 84 ff.

42 Originally Passover was associated with the *Akedah* in Jewish sources, but this association was probably suspended and suppressed by the rabbis when Christianity linked the Sacrifice of Isaac with Christianity at Easter time. Cf. Vermes, *Scripture, op. cit.*, pp. 215 f.; Spiegel, *Last Trial, op. cit.*, p. 56; Stemberger, "Patriarchenbilder," *op. cit.*, p. 70; Feldman, "Josephus," *op. cit.*, p. 119; J. Danielou, *The Bible and the Liturgy* (Notre Dame, 1956), pp. 162 ff.

43 H. Thurston, "Paschal Candle," *The Catholic Encyclopedia*, XI (New York, 1913), pp. 515-16; D. Atwater, "Paschal candle," *A Catholic Dictionary* (New York, 1961), p. 369. Cf. W. Neumüller, *Speculum Humanae Salvationis* (Graz, 1972), II, p. 31, fol. 27v for a Sacrifice of Isaac. It has the draped altar, a ram suspended from a bush and the paschal candle.

44 Gutmann, "Sacrifice," *op. cit.*, for an extensive bibliography on the Sacrifice of Isaac in Jewish, Christian and Islamic art.

CHRISTIANE L. JOOST-GAUGIER

Lorenzo the Magnificent and the Giraffe as a Symbol of Power

When Giorgio Vasari painted the portrait of Lorenzo di Piero de' Medici [Fig. 1] for the apartments of Duke Cosimo I in the Palazzo Vecchio in Florence he was working from an old image of Lorenzo "il Magnifico", by that time dead about sixty-four years.[1] Though according to his own statement his visual source was a portrait executed by Sandro Botticelli, the rugged features of Lorenzo's head suggest that Vasari may as well have taken into account portraits by contemporary sculptors, such as Andrea del Verrocchio who, despite his treatment by this family, was also one of the favorites of Lorenzo.[2] In portraying Lorenzo in the act of receiving gifts from his ambassadors,[3] Vasari was also suggesting in accessible visual terms that the rule of this collateral kinsman and indirect ancestor of Cosimo I was one of tremendous popularity, a notion no doubt designated by Cosimo in order to enhance the legitimization of his own rule – which was not without its tyrannical overtones – over mid-sixteenth century Florence. In so doing Vasari proposed, wittingly or not, an interesting historical parallel, and one which may not have been unknown to or unappreciated by either the protagonist of the painting or its patron.

In Vasari's painted portrait, as well as in the preliminary study for its composition [Fig. 2], prominent exposure is given to a giraffe which, among the other gifts being presented to Lorenzo, stands out not only for its scale and dimension but as well for its physical coloration. The presence of the giraffe is, in addition, critical to the composition of both painting and drawing, for in the curvature of its disposition it alone provides balance in the form of a harmonizing echo to the position of Lorenzo himself. There can be little doubt that this presence had

not only a historical motive, as specified in the instructions of Cosimo Bartoli, the designer of the program for the soffit of this chamber,[4] but, for this reason, a peculiar iconographical significance.

While this tallest of mammals, whose tongue is remarkable for its length and which is capable of galloping up to forty kilometers an hour, was little known in medieval bestiary and scientific tradition either as a living animal or as a fabulous beast,[5] it was, in fact, known to antique geographers, travellers, and natural historians from the 3rd century B. C., when giraffes were first exhibited in Alexandria.[6]

While, writing two centuries earlier, Aristotle does not refer to the giraffe in the scheme of his biological works,[7] the description of Strabo, writing his *Geography* in Hellenistic times:

"they are in no respect like leopards; for the dappled marking of their skin is more like that of a fawnskin, which latter is flecked with spots, and their hinder parts are so much lower than their front parts that they appear to be seated on their tail parts, which have the height of an ox, although their forelegs are no shorter than those of camels; and their necks rise high and straight up, their heads reaching much higher up than those of camels"[8]

clearly refers to giraffes. According to Strabo the occurrence of this animal, which "is not a wild beast, but rather a domesticated animal, for it shows no signs of wildness",[9] was restricted to southern and western Ethiopia. A different opinion regarding

1) Giorgio Vasari, «Lorenzo de' Medici Accepting Gifts from his Ambassadors», Florence, Palazzo Vecchio (Courtesy Alinari).

2) Giorgio Vasari, «Study for the Soffit of Sala di Lorenzo il Magnifico», New York, Pierpont Morgan Library, no. 1967. 25 (Courtesy of Pierpont Morgan Library).

the nomenclature of this animal is provided in the *World History* of Strabo's older contemporary, Diodorus of Siculus, written in the late 1st century B. C.:

"The camelopards, as they are called, represent the mixing of the two animals which are included in the name given to it [*sic*]. For in size they are smaller than the camel and have shorter necks, but in the head and the arrangement of the eyes they are formed very much like a leopard; and although they have a hump on back like the camel, yet with respect to colour and hair they are like leopards; likewise in the possession of a long tail they imitate the nature of this wild beast".[10]

In his *Natural History*, written in the early 1st century A. D., Pliny the Elder offers yet another variation on the physical characteristics of the giraffe: "The Ethiopians give the name of *nabun* to one that has a neck like a horse, feet and legs like an ox, and a head like a camel, and is of a ruddy colour picked out with white spots, owing to which it is called a camelopard".[11] The baffling nature of this animal in antiquity, whose existence was restricted to Eastern Africa south of the Sahara, most surely accounts for the fact that it was not a common subject in painted, mosaic, or sculptured representations of animals – as were for example, the lion, the eagle, and the horse – in antiquity. Consequently, it does not appear among the zoomorphic motifs popular in Renaissance art prior to 1488.[12] In this context the gift of a giraffe seems not only peculiar but extraordinary in 15th century Florence where this animal was virtually unknown. Indeed, while Vasari was able to rely on a model for his portrait, he was not so fortunate, as he himself admits, in the case of the giraffe:

"La gente indiana, che dice Vostra Eccelenza, vengono a far segno, con tanti ricchi varj doni, della benevolenza che alla virtu e grandezza di Lorenzo portava Caibeo, Soldano del Cairo, il quale fu allora grandissimo nelle imprese di guerra, che gli mando (come vedete) a presentare fino in Fiorenza que' vasi, gioie, pappagalli, scimmie, cammelli, e, fra gli altri doni, una giraffa, animale indiano non più visto di persona, e di grandezza, e di varieta di pelle, che in Italia simil cosa no venne mai; e tanto più era da tenere conto, quanto nè i Porthoghesi, nè gli Spagnuoli nell' India, e nel nuovo mondo, non hanno mai trovato tale animale […]".[13]

Though not the only one Vasari painted,[14] the giraffe of Lorenzo de' Medici is less unique for the inventiveness of its physical characteristics and for the role it plays in the design and composition of the painting than for the fact that it constituted a most unusual gift.

Entries in two Florentine diaries authored by contemporaries of Lorenzo essentially corroborate each other in describing this unparalleled gift and its effect on contemporary Florence. Luca Landucci describes the animals which arrived in Florence the 11th of November 1487 as supposed gifts from the Sultan of Egypt, obtained through the intervention of Lorenzo's friends and presented to Lorenzo by the ambassador of the Sultan on the 18th of the same month. Despite his mention of other animals (a lion, a goat, exotic sheep and other unspecified animals), Landucci's attention is focused on the giraffe, which he describes as, "molto grande e molto bella e piacevole; com' ella fussi fatta se ne puo vedere i' molti luoghi in Firenze dipinte".[15] The giraffe, he continues, remained alive in the city for several years.[16] Commenting on the death of Lorenzo, which occurred on the 8th of April, 1492, Bartolomeo Masi, a Florentine coppersmith, says that Lorenzo received gifts of "animali vivi, de' piu begli e de' piu maravigliosi che mai si vedessino in queste parte",[17] among which, he continues, "V' era uno animale che si chiamava giraffe, che aveva la testa sua come una vitella, sensa corna, e aveva el pelo rossigno, e aveva le gambe dinanzi alte circa di tre braccia […] e aveva la coda sua come una vitella, el colle lungo circa di quattro braccia […]".[18] The giraffe, which had, according to Masi, a variegated diet, died while trying to extricate its head from the projecting stone supports of the architrave of a portal.[19]

While these two entries, little noted by Lorenzo's biographers,[20] help us to establish the historical fact of the presentation of the giraffe to Lorenzo and its effect on the Florentine populace, they do not explain why such an unusual gift might have been chosen for this particular statesman. Nor do they offer any explanation for the labors of the Sultan of Cairo, if indeed he was the instigator of the idea, to procure such a specimen, indeed one even exotic for Egypt. While perhaps directed by its taste for Gothic culture and associated expressions of luxury and exotica,[21] the historical interest of the Medici family in animals – which can be traced back to the mysterious "storie di animali" which Vasari asserts were painted by Uccello for the Palazzo Medici in the 15th century[22] – eventually led to the formation of one of the most important menageries of 17th century Europe, indeed a predecessor of the zoological garden.[23] The absence, however, of reference to animal collecting in these accounts, as in the information provided by Vasari,[24] suggests rather that the gift of the giraffe was in the form of a special acknowledgment to Lorenzo and one that was meant to impress the Florentine populace.

Only once before had a giraffe been displayed in an Italian city, in 46 B. C. by Julius Caesar who, returning from an arduous and not entirely successful campaign in Africa, paraded a giraffe through the streets of Rome in expression of his 'triumph'. Descriptions of this event survive in the *Natural History* of Pliny the Elder and the *Roman History* of Dio. According to the account of Pliny, the camelopard was first displayed at Rome in the games accompanying the triumph of Caesar.[25] Dio is more specific. His description of the triumph, when, in his efforts to hold his power, Julius Caesar "entertained the populace splendidly, giving them grain beyond the regular amount and olive oil",[26] sets the stage for the appearance of the giraffe:

"The first days of the triumph he passed as was customary, but on the last day, after they had finished dinner, he entered his own forum wearing slippers and garlanded with all kinds of flowers; thence he proceeded homeward with practically the entire populace escorting him, while many elephants carried torches. For he had himself constructed the forum called after him, and it is distinctly more beautiful than the Roman Forum; yet it had increased the reputation of the other so that was called the Great Forum. So after completing this new forum and the temple to Venus, as the founder of his family, he dedicated them at this very time, and in their honour instituted many contests of all kinds. He built a kind of hunting-theater of wood, which was called an amphitheatre from the fact that it had seats all around without any stage. In honour of this and of his daughter he exhibited combats of wild beasts and gladiators; but anyone who cared to record their number would find his task a burden.[...] I shall accordingly pass over this and other like events that took place later, except, of course, where it may seem to me quite essential to mention some particular point, but I will give an account of the so-called camelopard, because it was introduced into Rome by Caesar for the first time and exhibited to all. This animal is like a camel.[...] Finally he produced a naval battle, not on the sea nor on a lake, but on land; for he hollowed out a certain tract on the Campus Martius and after flooding it introduced ships into it [...]".[27]

Evidently, the giraffe was considered by Dio to be one of the highlights of Caesar's triumph which, he asserts, was designed to indicate to the populace the magnitude of his accomplishments and, in that all Roman citizens were not rewarded, the extent of his power.

Clearly both descriptions suggest that for Julius Caesar, because it was exotic and rare rather than because it was bestial and wild, the giraffe provided a visible symbol of his extraordinary power to those, such as the jeering soldiers described by Dio,[28] who might have doubted his authority. Similarly difficult were the times for Lorenzo de' Medici. Following his outrage with the rebellion of Volterra and the cruel repression which followed in the mid-1470's, after his narrow escape from death in the Pazzi conspiracy in 1478 (in which the Pope himself was implicated) during which his Brother Giuliano was killed, and after his acquisition of Sarzana following a brutal siege against

the Genoese in August of 1487, Lorenzo had tightened his grip on the city of Florence.[29] Not only was he on bad terms with Pope Sixtus but as well with King Ferdinand, the Pisans, the Genoese, and the Venetians, among many others. Addressing the Florentine people in a language which, despite the atrocities committed by him in the city following the events of 1478, begs for the support of the populace, the words of Lorenzo, as supplied by Machiavelli, reveal his desire to involve the Florentine citizenry in the design to re-assert, in a manner more forceful than ever before, Medicean power:

"Whoever inquires into the truth of these matters, will find that our family has always been exalted by you, and from this sole cause, that we have endeavored by kindness, liberality, and beneficence, to do good to all [...]. If our enemies' conduct has been adopted, to gratify their sense of power [...] if they were actuated by envy and hatred of our authority, they offend you rather than us; for from you we have derived all the influence we possess".[30]

Reason does not exist to suggest that Lorenzo personally devised the strategy of the presentation of the giraffe; yet, to a learned entourage such as Lorenzo's the episode of Caesar's giraffe must have been well known, as to Lorenzo himself. Not only was Lorenzo an avid collector of Roman antiquities, including mementoes and images of Roman emperors, he was moreover interested in expressing his nostalgia towards the past through staging antique triumphs as well as through his literary interests.[31] The significance of these interests was conspicuously recognized in the fact that King Matthias Corvinus of Hungary, upon his death, left Lorenzo a major group of luxurious codices.[32] Indeed, the Medici collection of antique texts included an edition of Pliny's Natural History obtained by Lorenzo's father, Piero, in which, as we have seen, Caesar's triumph and the role of the giraffe are reported, and as well an edition of Caesar's Commentaries.[33] That Caesar's triumph was a subject dear to the Medici family is evident in the fact that Duke Alessandro de' Medici had, before his murder in 1537, already commissioned Vasari to paint, for the ground floor of the Medici palace, a series of four scenes from the life of Caesar, including his Triumph.[34]

Whether or not Caiebus, the Sultan of Cairo, had Caesar's triumph in mind in the considerable efforts he must have made to obtain for and transport to Lorenzo il Magnifico this exotic animal from the south of Ethiopia, the symbol he chose as an expression of extraordinary homage to this formidable princely tyrant – for Lorenzo had indeed become a tyrant – at least parallels Julius Caesar's exhibition of a giraffe in the city of Rome. Although we do not know the conditions under which Caesar's giraffe was obtained, Lorenzo himself must have been aware of this unique historical parallel. For the reign of Lorenzo de' Medici as that of Julius Caesar before him, both of whom had many internal as well as external enemies, both of whom were accused in their own times of abandoning republican principles in exercising a rule that was increasingly despotic, and both of whom were the object of assassination conspiracies,[35] was plagued by a strong political conservatism which felt that he deserved assassination.

Indeed, in his *De Libertate*, Alamanno Rinuccini, himself a long-time member of the the Medici entourage, praised the instigators of the Pazzi conspiracy, whom he described as of "truly magnanimous mind and noble character", in their action to champion the cause of liberty by opposing a tyrant.[36] "Their resolution [...] and action against which they embarked, deserve praise forever. Men of sound judgment will always rank them with [...] Brutus and Cassius of Rome".[37] Rinuccini's dialogue goes, indeed, further. Written in 1479, the year following the Pazzi conspiracy, Rinuccini specifically accuses Lorenzo of being a tyrant:

"This war [the opposition of the pope and others to Lorenzo]..was undertaken not against the Florentines but against Lorenzo de' Medici, the tyrant of Florence, for the liberty of the people [...] for their liberation from Lorenzo's fierce tyranny".[38]

In putting Lorenzo's tyrannical acts into the context of Florentine history and, while upholding the heroism of Pompey, relying heavily on Ciceronian example and Ciceronian argument in defense of republican values,[39] Rinuccini strongly suggests – although he avoids the direct comparison – that Lorenzo's role vis à vis Florentine republican institutions is philosophically equivalent to that of Julius Caesar in ancient Roman times. Indeed, his catalogue of indictments of the politics of Lorenzo,

"And I see people [...] bullied today by the whims of one young man. Many noble minds and men of eminent seniority and wisdom wear today the yoke of servitude and hardly recognize their own condition. Nor, when they do see it, do they dare avenge themselves. They become, and this is worst of all, the unwilling adversaries of those who try to liberate them [...]. Thanks to the arrogance of a few overbearing individuals [...] these few today usurp the power of all. Their impulses and ambitions decide everything, while almost no authority is left to the councils or the people [...]. He [Lorenzo] did not get reasonable advice from the citizens, nor did he listen to his own reason. He did everything according to the impulses of his willful spirit, and he dragged down the poor country. Spoiled in part of her wealth and altogether of her dignity, she has become the mockery of all

Italy for enduring such a destructive and cruel tyranny"[40]

is not unlike Suetonius' description of the reign of Julius Caesar.[41] Indeed, Rinuccini's complaint that the report he wrote for Lorenzo, apprising him of incidents of his responsibility that were not in line with the aims of the republic, recalls, in the arrogance with which it was scorned that was repeatedly described by Suetonius, the case of Caesar's reprimanding two tribunes of the people who had advised him of the dangers of allowing his statue to be crowned with a white fillet as a symbol of "kingship", an episode corroborated by Plutarch.[42] Rinuccini's appeal to the Florentines to protect their ancient liberties is not unlike the disapproval of tyranny reported by Suetonius to have been voiced by a number of Caesar's republican-minded contemporaries.[43]

The portrait of Lorenzo de' Medici painted by Vasari shows Lorenzo in the act of receiving homage and submission (not only gifts) from Italian princes and rulers as well as from foreign kings and dignitaries. As clearly stipulated by the painter, this composition does not refer to a single event in the life of Lorenzo; rather, as suggested by Vasari, always anxious to serve Medicean interests,[44] it refers to a conglomeration of episodes manipulated in their arrangement so as to suggest an eternal "condition" in which Lorenzo emerges pictorially as supreme statesman, military commander, arbiter of justice, prince of the faith, and paragon of virtue. Centrally located in the ceiling and surrounded by auxiliary images illustrating Lorenzo's supremacy in these categories, the portrait becomes the centralizing image of the entire *sala*. Focussed on Lorenzo in this painting are the interconnected complexities of his rule; more importantly, it can be considered a "fantasia" of Lorenzo's power.

Thus is the question Vasari addressed to himself relevant: "Belle fantasie; ma non volete voi che io sappia chi son coloro che stanno attorno a Lorenzo".[45] The power of Lorenzo, seated before his ambassadors, just as that of Caesar who, to the dismay of many of his contemporaries, remained seated before the Roman Senate,[46] is suggested in his movement which constitutes the main element of design in the painting, a design echoed in the presence of the giraffe. Whatever the inspiration behind so exotic a gift, certainly its awesome result as a symbol of the power of the tyrant was not different from the one time before in history when a giraffe had been presented to the Italian people.

Vasari's giraffe is a distinguished and balancing compositional accent in the painting; because of its uniqueness as subject matter and composition, the spectator's eye can assess its meaning immediately. In this sense, the human protagonists of the painting who surround Lorenzo, as well as those of the accompanying decorations are, without Vasari's guide in hand, resolved into a blur of subservient humanity among whom the presence of Alamanno Rinuccini, who maintained, "If I am unwilling to adore, to flatter and to bow before this man, can you blame me?" is, for good reason, lacking.[47]

The author would like to express sincere thanks to Serena Padovani for assistance with photographs.

[1] Lorenzo died (of illness) in 1492. The frescoes contained in the Quartiere di Leone X of the Palazzo Vecchio, extolling the memories of Lorenzo and his grandfather Cosimo de' Medici, were painted by Vasari, by his own account, shortly after 1555. See G. Vasari, *Le Vite de' più eccelenti pittori scultori ed architettori* (ed. G. Milanesi), Florence, 1906, VII, p. 699. Most probably those of the Sala di Lorenzo il Magnifico, based on "invenzioni" of Cosimo Bartoli, were begun in 1556. Regarding the Sala di Lorenzo il Magnifico and its contents, see A. Lensi, *Palazzo Vecchio*, Milan-Rome, 1929, pp. 161 ff., and E. Allegri, A. Cecchi, *Palazzo Vecchio e i Medici: Guida Storica*, Florence, 1980, pp. 136-142.

[2] Vasari specifically states that he based his portrait on one (or ones?) by Botticelli, "Questa gli ho ritratti da Sandro del Botticello, pittore, [...]". See Vasari, "Ragionamento secondo", in *op. cit.*, VIII, p. 112. Vasari also states that the protagonists in the painted representations of this *sala* were all based on previous portrait models (*ibidem*, VIII, p. 110). Despite Verrocchio's favored status in the employ of Lorenzo (discussed in M. Wackernagel, *The Word of the Florentine Renaissance Artist* (1938), trans. A. Luchs, Princeton, 1981, pp. 252-253), the possibility that he was insufficiently rewarded or not paid at all is raised in the fact that following the exile of the Medici in 1494, the younger brother of Verrocchio, Tommaso, protested to the deputies of the rebels in charge of the Medici possessions after the expulsion of the family the lack of payment that had been made to the artist. Listing the works in question, Tommaso requested reparation (see copy of document first published by Fabriczy and reprinted in M. Cruttwell, *Verrocchio*, London, 1904, pp. 242-244; see also comment of E. H. Gombrich, in "The Early Medici as Patrons of Art", first in *Italian Renaissance Studies. A Tribute to the Late Cecilia M. Ady* (ed. E. F. Jacob), London 1960, reprinted in *Norm and Form, Studies in the Art of the Renaissance*, London-New York, 1971, p. 53).

[3] The "invenzioni" are contained in a part of a letter written to Vasari by Cosimo Bartoli in the Spring of 1556: "[...] io vi farei Lorenzo che havessi atorno varij imbasciatori de potentati di Italia, che si governavono a suo senno, della quale egli indubitabilmente fu arbitro. Farevi uno con una toga rossa che gli presentassi il cappello del cardinale, suo figliolo, uno altro che gli presentassi cavagli per il regno di Napoli, uno altro, a guisa di soldato, che gli presentassi armi per il ducato di Milano; et per che s'intendessi, vi farei una celata con i serpi e putti di casa Sforzesca. Farevi poi per i Baglioni et per i Vitelli et per i Bentivogli, Petrucci Sanesi, per i Manfredi, che la maggior parte gli fussino atorno con bandiere o insegne loro, mentre che Lorenzo a sedere ricevessi i doni del soldano [...]. Et se havessi luogo da farvi dentro una Magnanimita et una Prudentia, ve la Farei". Other foreign ambassadors to be included, according to the letter, were those of King Matthias Corvinus of Hungary and Ferdinando of Aragon. The extract of the letter, first published by Frey in 1923-30, is printed with explanatory diagram in Allegri and Cecchi, *op. cit.*, p. 137. It should be noted, however, that in his description of this painting Vasari gives the impression that he had considerable latitude in working out the details of Bartoli's suggestions (*op. cit.*, VIII, pp. 103-122). Regarding the

program of the *sala* in general, see Vasari's own description in *loc. cit.*, Allegri, Cecchi, *op. cit.*, and Paola Barocchi, "Il Vasari Pittore", *Rinascimento*, 1956, pp. 208 ff.

[4] See notes 1 and 3 above.

[5] Its omission is to be noted, for example, in the 12th-century copy of a Latin prose bestiary preserved at the Cambridge University Library (no. II. 4. 26), as in the "Cloisters" Bestiary. An English translation of the former is provided in T. H. White, *The Bestiary, A Book of Beasts*, New York, 1960. While possibly due to constrictions of selection, the omission is nonetheless notable for the fact that its author or authors had knowledge of Pliny (cf. note 11 below), at least for the discussion of fish (*op. cit.*, p. 217). Regarding the latter see R. H. Randall, Jr., *A Cloisters Bestiary*, New York, 1960. On the subject of medieval bestiaries, a form of natural history normally containing an illustrated text which were in large part derived from the *Physiologus*, an anonymous early Christian source which summarized information about animals, birds, and reptiles derived from antique literary sources, see N. Henkel, *Studien zum Physiologus im Mittelalter*, Tübingen, 1976 (with an excellent bibliography on the subject in general); F. Mc Culloch, *Medieval Latin and French Bestiaries*, Chapel Hill, 1960 and 1962; G. C. Druce, "The Medieval Bestiaries, and their Influence on Ecclesiastical Decorative Art", *Journal of the British Archaeological Association*, December, 1919; and J. V. Carus, *Geschichte der Zoologie (Geschichte der Wissenschaften, XII)*, Munich, 1872. Limited information on history of this animal is contained in C. A. Spinage, *The Book of the Giraffe*, Boston, 1968 (including a useful bibliography), and A. I. Dagg and J. B. Foster, *The Giraffe; its Biology, Behavior, and Ecology*, New York, n. d. (c. 1976). Regarding the representation of wild animals in medieval sculptural programs and cosmographic traditions, see the discussion of R. van Marle, *Iconographie de l'Art Profane au Moyen-Age et à la Renaissance*, rep., New York, 1971, pp. 127-131.

[6] This information is cited in *Diodorus of Sicily* (ed. and trans. C. H. Oldfeather), Cambridge-London, 1967, II: 51, ed. note 2. Cf. note 12 below.

[7] The zoological treatises of Aristotle include the following works: *De incessu animalium*, *De partibus animalium*, *De motu animalium*, *De generatione animalium*, and the *Historia animalium*.

[8] *The Geography of Strabo* (ed. and trans. H. L. Jones), Cambridge-London, 1966, 16. 4. 16.

[9] *Loc. cit.*

[10] Diodorus of Sicily, *op. cit.*, II, 51. 1 (translation Oldfeather).

[11] Gaius Plinius Secundus (Pliny the Elder), *Natural History* (ed. and trans. H. Rackham), Cambridge-London, 1967, VIII. xxvii. 69-70.

[12] While the giraffe as a subject was not popular in the art of the Renaissance, neither was it unknown after 1487. Two Quattrocento examples dating after this time are to be found in the *Vulcan Scene* of the National Gallery at Ottawa painted by Piero di Cosimo and dated sometime after November 11, 1487 (E. Panofsky, "The Early History of Man in Two Cycles of Paintings by Piero di Cosimo", *Studies in Iconology* (1939), New York-Evanston, 1962, pp. 46-47), and in an engraving by Maso Finiguerra in which a giraffe is represented led by a turbaned figure (the Sultan of Egypt?) through a desert landscape (A. M. Hind, *Early Italian Engraving*, London 1938-48, Vol. V, p. 307 and VII, pl. 911). Another example by a painter primarily active in that century is in the painting of *St. Mark Preaching in Alexandria* by Gentile Bellini (completed by Giovanni Bellini), begun in 1504 for the Scuola Grande di San Marco in Venice and now in the Brera Gallery, Milan. The presence of a giraffe in an imaginary view of Alexandria may well suggest that the fact that giraffes were first exhibited in Alexandria (cf.

note 6 above) was known to Gentile. Another image of a giraffe is to be found in Bacchiacca's *Gathering of Manna* in the National Gallery in Washington. Grateful recognition is extended to Mark Zucker who most generously shared his expertise and interest in giraffes in early Italian art with me.

[13] *Op. cit.*, VIII, p. 114.

[14] In his autobiography Vasari mentions a triptych representing the *Adoration of the Magi* executed by him for the high altar of Sta. Maria di Scolca near Rimini which contained, according to his account, a vast processional suite including horses, elephants, and giraffes (*op. cit.*, VII, p. 684).

[15] L. Landucci, *Diario fiorentino dal 1450 al 1516* (ed. Iodoco del Badia), Florence, 1883, p. 52. Examples would be those by Piero di Cosimo and Maso Finiguerra cited in note 12 above.

[16] *Loc. cit.* With regard to the giraffe, the account reads as follows: "E a di 11 novenbre [1487], ci venne certi animali che si disse gle el soldano; poi s'intese ch'era stati pure certi amici di Firenze per avere qualche buona mancia. Gli animali furono questi: una giraffa molto grande e molto bella e piacevole; com'ella fussi fatta se ne puo vedere i' molti luoghi in Firenze dipinte. E visse qui piu anni. E uno lione grande, e capre e castroni, molto strani.[...] E a di 18 di novenbre 1487, el sopradetto anbasciadore del Soldano presento alla nostra Signoria la sopradetta giraffa, e lione, e l'altre bestie".

[17] B. Masi, *Ricordanze di Bartolomeo Masi, calderaio fiorentino, dal 1487 al 1526. Per la prima volta Pubblicate da Gius. Odoardo Corazzini*, Florence, 1906, ricordanza 68, p. 18.

[18] *Loc. cit.*

[19] *Loc. cit.* The entry reads as follows: "[...] animale vivi, de' piu begli e de' piu maravigliosi che mai si vedessimo in queste parte; fra' quali v'era uno animale che si chiamava giraffa, che aveva la testa sua come una vitella, sanza corna, e aveva el pelo rossigno, e aveva le ganbe dinanzi alte circa di tre braccia, e quelle di dietro circa a dua, e aveva la coda sua come una vitella, el collo lungo circa di quattro braccia; e mangiava d'ogni cosa, ed era agievole quanto uno aguiello. Mori el sopradetto animale in ispazio di poco tenpo, perche alzando el capo percosse in uno cardinale [quadrangular blocks supporting corners of architrave] d'uno uscio, e di quello si mori".

[20] The Landucci diary is listed in the bibliography of N. Rubinstein, *Il Governo di Firenzo sotto i Medici* (1434-1494), Florence, 1971, though Rubinstein does not discuss the incident of the presentation of the giraffe. Wackernagel lists the diary of Masi in his bibliography. In quoting a letter written to the wife of Lorenzo who was at the time in Rome (probably in connection with the marriage of their daughter, Maddalena, to the son of Innocent VIII which occurred earlier in the same month) by Pietro da Bibbiena, Lorenzo's secretary, Fabroni provides an inventory of the gifts from the Sultan; at the top of the list is "un bel cavallo bajo", which, since no horse is mentioned in other descriptions (nor is it included in the list of the Sultan's gifts from which Vasari worked, *op. cit.*, VIII, pp. 114-115), may possibly suggest that the giraffe was at first viewed as an exotic type of horse. (See A. Fabroni, "Pietro da Bibbiena a Clarice de' Medici", in his *Laurentii Medicis Magnifici Vita*, Pisa, 1784, II, doc. no. 199, pp . 337). Among the many biographers who refer to this event without citing sources are H. R. Williamson, *Lorenzo the Magnificent*, New York, 1974, p. 216, and M. Rowdon, *Lorenzo the Magnificent*, Chicago, 1974, p. 211. The preoccupation of such contemporary observers as Vespasiano da Bisticci, Guicciardini, Machiavelli, and Condivi with certain aspects of Lorenzo's life and rule perhaps provides sufficient explanation for the absence of the description of this event in their accounts. See Vespasiano da Bisticci (who does not provide a *vita* of Lorenzo but

whose *vita* of Donato Acciaiuoli includes an account of the Pazzi conspiracy which took place on Sunday, the 26th of April 1478), *Vespasiano, Renaissance Princes, Popes and Prelates, the Vespasiano Memoirs* (ed. M. P. Gilmore), New York-London, p. 286. Guicciardini's history opens in the period following the death of the giraffe and just prior to the death of its owner (F. Guicciardini, *The History of Italy* (ed. and trans. S. Alexander), New York-London, pp. 3 ff.). Machiavelli's text includes a perceptive and persuasive description of Lorenzo's politics (N. Machiavelli, *Le istorie fiorentine* (ed. E. Bianchi), Florence 1938, pp. 506 ff.). The information about Lorenzo in Condivi's biography of Michelangelo is restricted to relevant statements about his patronage (A. Condivi, *The Life of Michelangelo* (trans. A. S. Wohl, ed. H. Wohl, Baton Rouge, La., 1976, pp. 5-19).

[21] For discussion of Lorenzo's cultural tastes as a patron of literature and art see Wackernagel, *op. cit.*, esp. pp. 251-264, and Gombrich, *op. cit.*, esp. pp. 54-57.

[22] Of these paintings no trace remains. Their "mysterious" character is exacerbated by Vasari's report that they were painted on canvas: "In casa de' Medici dipinse in tela a tempera alcune storie di animale [...]". See Vasari, *op. cit.*, II, p. 208 and accompanying note of Milanesi.

[23] While Alexander of Macedon is considered to have been the first notable collector of animals gathered in his military campaigns, Roman emperors, following his example, gather imported animals in the *bestiaria*, a practice which fell into disuse after the fall of the Empire. Menageries, or collections of animals, popular during Renaissance times, were spurred by the interest in foreign geography which resulted from the number and diversity of explorations undertaken during this period. Early examples of such collections include ones at Parma and Venice; a developed example, dating from the late 1600's , was that of the Medici near the Piazza San Marco. On this subject see G. Loisel, *Historie des Menageries de l'Antiquité a nos Jours*, 3 vols., Paris, 1912, esp. Vol I, pp. 197-220, on animal collections in Renaissance Italy; H. Thetard, *Les Dompteurs: la Menagerie des Origines a nos Jours*, Paris, 1930; and G. Lepri, "Giardini Zoologici", *Enciclopedia Italiana*, Rome, 1949, XVII, pp. 76 ff. It appears that until the 17th century the interests of the Medici in animals were primarily expressed in painted representations such as, e. g., the life-sized series of double-headed sheep, calves, rare birds, and quadrupeds that decorated the rooms of Cosimo I's Villa Ambrogiana (Detroit Institute of Arts, City of Florence, *Twilight of the Medici*, cat., Detroit, 1974, p. 15).

[24] See note 13 above.

[25] Pliny the Elder, *loc. cit.*

[26] Dio Cassius, *Dio's Roman History* (ed. and trans.Earnest Cary), London-Cambridge, 1961, XLIII. 21.

[27] *Ibidem*, XLIII. 22-23.

[28] *Ibidem*, XLIII. 20.

[29] The rebellion of Volterra and its violent repression are described by Machiavelli in *op. cit.*, Bk. 7, Ch. 5; the acquisition of Sarzana, which Lorenzo claimed had been "bought" by his father (Lorenzo de' Medici, "Ricordi", in *Humanism and Liberty: Writings of Freedom from Fifteenth-Century Florence* (ed. and trans. Renee Neu Watkins), Columbia, S. C., 1978, p. 159), which followed the subjugation of Pietrasanta, by Vasari himself in *op. cit.*, VIII, p. 111.

[30] Machiavelli, *op. cit.*, (*History of Florence* (ed. and trans. F. Gilbert), New York 1960, pp. 368-79).

[31] Lorenzo himself, in his memoirs, tells of two antique marble portrait heads of Emperors Augustus and Agrippa that he brought back from Rome in September of 1471 (*Ricordi, op. cit.*, p. 161). He was not the first in his family to collect images of Roman emperors, for Filarete describes a favorite pastime of Lorenzo's father, Piero, who delighted in

the contemplation of his collection of "effigies and portraits of all the emperors and noble men who ever lived" (A. A. Filarete, *Treatise on Architecture* (ed. and trans. J. R. Spencer), New Haven, 1965, p. 320).

Regarding Lorenzo's strong interest in antiquarian artistic pursuits, including the collection and display of small-scale antique sculptures among more important specimens of statuary obtained from excavations, and his vast collection of antique medals, gems, and cameos, see E. Muntz, *Les Collections des Medicis au XVe Siècle*, Paris, 1888, *passim*; W. Roscoe, *The Life of Lorenzo de' Medici*, London 1889, *passim* (regarding collections of cameos, gems, and ancient inscriptions, see esp. pp. 311-312); W. Holzhausen, "Zum Schatz des Lorenzo Magnificos", *Mitteilungen des Kunsthistorisches Institut in Florenz*, III, pp. 104 f.; N. Dacos, A. Guiliano, U. Pannuti, eds., *Il tesoro di Lorenzo il Magnifico: Le gemme*, cat. Mostra Pal. Medici-Riccardi, Florence, 1972; D. Heikamp with A. Grote, ed., *Il tesoro di Lorenzo il Magnifico: I vasi*, cat. Mostra Pal. Medici-Riccardi, Florence, 1972. See also Wackernagel, *op. cit.*, p. 98 n. 87, pp. 102, 107, 252-255, and Gombrich, *op. cit.*, pp. 55-56. Lorenzo's collection of coins is discussed by A. von Reumont, *Lorenzo de' Medici il Magnifico*, II, Leipzig, 1883, pp. 155 ff. The staging of antique triumphs as a visible gesture of the "peace and plenty" of Lorenzo's reign is described by Machiavelli in *op. cit.*, p. 507.

Lorenzo's interests as a collector and appreciator of antique literature are well known. Condivi refers to his library as a "very noble" one, which he and his forebears had collected "from all over the world" (Condivi, *op. cit.*, pp. 11-2 trans. Wohl). In explaining the program of the decoration of the *sala* of Lorenzo, Vasari himself provides an elaborate description of the "uomini dottissimi" in Greek and Latin letters and "uomini litterati" who surrounded Lorenzo and were the recipients of his patronage in *op. cit.*, VIII, pp. 115-119. Lorenzo's library and his activities as a buyer of antique codices are discussed by Fabroni, *op. cit.*, I, esp. pp. 145-153. See also on this subject Wackernagel, *op. cit.*, p. 258, and Gombrich's hypothesis (*op. cit.*, p. 56) that because Lorenzo was so interested in reviving the past he had little use for works by contemporary authors.

[32] Regarding Lorenzo's acquisition of a significant collection of codices from Matthias Corvinus after the latter's death, see Wackernagel, *op. cit.*, p. 258 no. 14 and *passim*. See also the discussion of Gombrich, *op. cit.*, pp. 52 ff.

[33] See Gombrich, *op. cit.*, p. 51, and Fig. 83, and G. Pottinger, *The Court of the Medici*, London-Totowa (N. J.), 1978, p. 37. Regarding the friendship of King Matthias Corvinus and Lorenzo and its expression in terms of their common literary interests, see Vasari, *op. cit.*, VIII, p. 112, and Wackernagel, *loc. cit.*

[34] The scenes, now believed to have perished, included Caesar swimming with his *Commentaries* in his hand and a sword in his mouth; Caesar burning the papers of Pompey his enemy; Caesar revealing himself to a boatman when in danger; and the triumph of Caesar. Vasari, *op. cit.*, VII, p. 656.

[35] The republican opposition to the Medici, a condition which pre-existed the Pazzi revolt, is discussed by Rubinstein, *op. cit.*, p. 196. Cf. Rinuccini's reaction to the Pazzi conspiracy (notes 36-40 below) with Suetonius' statements regarding the many who felt Caesar deserved assassination (Gaius Suetonius Tranquillus, *Suetonius* (ed. J. C. Rolfe), London- Cambridge, 1970, I, pp. 3-119). Machiavelli, who despite the fact he suffered torture and was exiled by the Medici for his antidictatorial views is, in his subsequent attempts to flatter Lorenzo as supreme ruler (N. Machiavelli, *Il Principe*, in *Il Principe e Discorsi*, ed. S. Bertelli, 2nd ed., Milan, 1979) an example of those who viewed survival and service as co-equivalent. Savonarola, though not a statesman, was one who did not.

[36] A. Rinuccini, *Dialogus de libertate*, Fr. Adorno, ed., in *Atti e memorie dell'accademia toscana di scienza e lettere, La Columbaria*, XXII, N. S. VIII, 1957, pp. 265-303. Trans. Watkins, in *Humanism and Liberty, Writings on Freedom from Fifteenth-Century Florence, op. cit.*, p. 196.

[37] *Loc. cit.*

[38] *Ibidem*, p. 221.

[39] *Ibidem*, p. 204. Cicero, in the 1st *Philippic*, speaks of Brutus and Cassius as liberators of the Roman people from the loss of freedom they had suffered under Caesar; in the 5th *Philippic* he speaks of Brutus as having made Rome a "free city" in rendering a great service to the Roman people; in the 11th *Philippic* Brutus is described as the "light and glory of Rome". (Cicero, *Le Philippiques de Ciceron* (ed. P. du Ryer), Paris 1640).

[40] *Ibidem*, pp. 204-205 and 221.

[41] Suetonius, *op. cit.*, I, pp. 3-119.

[42] *Ibidem*, Secs. 77, 79. Cf. Plutarch, *The Lives of the Noble Grecians and Romans* (ed. J. Dryden, rev. A. Clough), New York, n. d., p. 890.

[43] Suetonius, *op. cit.*, Sec. 80.

[44] In his autobiography Vasari repeatedly refers to his close attachment to various members of the Medici family, notably Duke Alessandro de' Medici and Cardinal Ippolito de' Medici whom, he served in his early career, Ottaviano de' Medici whose care and protection he considered to be that of a father, Pope Clement VII, and Duke Cosimo I. Vasari, *op. cit.*, VII, pp. 649-724, *passim*.

[45] Vasari, *op. cit.*, VIII, p. 113.

[46] Suetonius, *op. cit.*, Sec. 78.

[47] Rinuccini, *op. cit.*, p. 221 (trans. Watkins).

JUDITH ZILCZER

"Color Music": Synaesthesia and Nineteenth-Century Sources for Abstract Art

During the late nineteenth century, the term "color music" was coined to describe a visionary new art form, created with colored lights and independent of easel painting.[1] The American color theorist Maud Miles spoke for many of her fellow inventors and artists when she claimed:

The truest parallel that I can conceive between direct light rays of color and music would be to lay aside all attempts to represent objects either in a natural or conventional way, in using the color. To simply use the color as music, might prove a genuinely new art. Perhaps some genius will invent a pipe organ behind a screen of colored lights. If these same lights could be operated by the same keys that play the organ, and if they could be reduced in brilliancy as the music grows softer, then a nearly perfect music and color parallel would be produced [...].[2]

By the late nineteenth century, a disparate group of artists, writers, and inventors had become convinced that "color music" represented the art of the future.

The idea of color music was symptomatic of a fundamental shift in aesthetic theory. As an outgrowth of the Romantic and Symbolist movements, music was elevated to a status of supremacy over all other forms of creative expression.[3] The other arts, notably poetry and painting, were said to aspire to the "condition of music." Artists came to believe that painting should be analogous to music. The American expatriate painter James McNeill Whistler proclaimed this new aesthetic doctrine of musical analogy in 1878:

As music is the poetry of sound, so is painting the poetry of sight, and subject matter has nothing to do with harmony of sound or of color [...]. Art [...] should stand alone, and [...] that is why I insist on calling my works "arrangements" and "harmonies."[4]

In one sense color music was the most extreme manifestation of this concept of musical analogy in the visual arts.

Proponents of musical analogy based their aesthetic theories on an abstraction of the idea of music, rather than on a clear understanding of musicology. For them music represented a non-narrative, non-discursive mode of expression. They reasoned that music, in its direct appeal to emotions and senses, transcended language. Just as music was a universal form of expression, so should the visual arts attain universality by evoking sensual pleasure or an emotional response in the viewer.

Advocates of musical analogy and color music also depended upon the related notion of synaesthesia; that is, they believed in the subjective interaction of all sensory perceptions. This common acceptance of synaesthesia resulted from two divergent philosophical positions. According to the more romantically inclined artists and writers, the interchangeability of the senses was evidence of mystical correspondence to a higher reality. On the other hand, some artists joined forces with scientific researchers to study synaesthesia as a phenomenon of human perception. These two schools of thought represent the quasi-mystical and the pseudo-scientific arguments for synaesthesia. Both interpretations deeply influenced the development of musical analogy in the visual arts.

Since the late nineteenth century, musical analogy in the fine arts has taken a variety of forms which range from simple parallels to more complex systems of correspondence between the visual and musical arts. First and perhaps foremost is the use of musical terminology in titling paintings. Secondly, music has provided direct inspiration for painting. Not only have artists incorporated allusions to specific musical compositions in their works, but they have also sought to create visual representations of musical scores. Finally, the most ambitious artists have attempted to emulate methods of musical composition in the visual arts. This essay will analyze the major modes from this wide spectrum of musical analogy and trace their influence on the development of the art of ''color music'' in the late nineteenth and early twentieth centuries.

The use of musical terminology in titling works of art originated with James McNeill Whistler. His early painting *The Girl in White* (*Symphony in White*), 1862 [Fig. 1], marked the beginning of his adaptation of musical analogy.[5] In later works such as *Nocturne in Black and Gold: Falling Rocket* [Fig. 2], Whistler sought to make color, line, and form predominate over subject matter. Musical terminology was meant to convey this subordination of representational to formal values.

Whistler's paintings and his aesthetic theories exerted an enormous influence in the U.S. American painters such as J. Alden Weir produced atmospheric and muted tonal paintings in response to Whistler's example.[6] At the same time, Whistler's theory of musical analogy found sympathetic adherents among American writers and critics. The Chicago collector and author Arthur Jerome Eddy published a biography of Whistler in which he stressed the concept of musical analogy in painting:

[...] there is a music of color even as there is a music of sound, and there should be a delight in color composition even as there is a delight in sound composition; and this delight should be [...] fundamentally distinct from any interest in the subject of the composition.[7]

The highly influential educator Arthur Wesley Dow disseminated the concept of musical analogy in his widely read book *Composition* [Fig. 3], originally published in 1899. Dow believed ''Music to be, in a sense, the key to the other fine arts, since its essence is pure beauty.''[8]

Dow's ideas, as well as those of Whistler, played a formative role in the aesthetics of the artists and photographers associated with the American photographer Alfred Stieglitz. The critic Sadakichi Hartmann relied on musical analogy in his critical essays published in Stieglitz's journal, *Camera Work*. Moreover the painter-photographer Eduard Steichen, Stieglitz's collaborator and associate at his gallery 291, produced Whistlerian

1) James McNeill Whistler, «The White Girl» («Symphony in White No. 1»). Oil on canvas 84 x 42 inches. Collection, National Gallery of Art, Washington, D. C. Harris Whittemore Collection.

Nocturnes incorporating the characteristic musical terminology.[9]

These American artists and critics all subscribed to the quasi-mystical argument for synaesthesia. Utopian idealism united the critics and artists of the Stieglitz circle. Charles Caffin spoke for the Stieglitz group when he observed that:

> The terms of music are borrowed by the pictorial and plastic arts [...]. A word is no longer a plane mirror, but [...] infinitely suggestive. Thought [...] is shaping itself into a new realization of the spiritual.[10]

Concurrently, European artists adopted musical analogy in response to Symbolist criticism and poetry. Under the influence of Guillaume Apollinaire, for example, the French painter Francis Picabia developed the concept of pure painting.[11] Picabia relied on musical analogy to develop this theory. Both his paintings and his ideas had a direct impact on the American avant-garde when he visited New York during the Armory Show. Picabia believed that:

> We understand without any difficulty the meaning and logic of a piece of music because this work is based on laws of harmony and composition [...].[12]

He predicted that abstract painting based on analogous laws of visual composition would result in a pure or absolute art form. His watercolor *Negro Song* [Fig. 4] exemplifies his dependence on musical analogy.

Picabia's idea of pure painting based on musical analogy was common to many European pioneers of abstract painting, notably Wassily Kandinsky [Fig. 5] and Frantisek Kupka [Fig. 6]. Both artists used musical terminology to denote their abstract compositions, and both subscribed to mystical theories of synaesthesia.[13]

Their works, in turn, influenced American modernist painters such as Marsden Hartley. Hartley was familiar with Kandinsky's paintings, and he was well aware of the importance of synaesthesia in Kandinsky's work. He once wrote his friend Rockwell Kent that, "Kandinsky is attempting to paint the color of sound [...]."[14] In his own abstractions such as *Musical Theme (Oriental Symphony)* [Fig. 7], Hartley combined a mystical search for universal expression with musical allusions:

> I am trying to express my emotions of the cosmic scheme in general [...] to present a sensation of cosmic bodies in harmony with each other by means of color and form [...]. With a sense also of the color of sound as I get these feelings out of music - I have even done something after a prelude of César Franck's [...].[15]

2) James McNeill Whistler, «Nocturne: Blue and Gold - Old Battersea Bridge», 1872-3. Oil on canvas, 26 x 19-3/4 inches. Collection The Tate Gallery, London.

Hartley's reference to the music of César Franck went beyond the simple use of musical terminology to suggest ane analogy between painting and music. Apparently, Hartley derived synaesthetic inspiration from listening to music. In this practice he was not alone. Other American painters incorporated direct allusions to pieces of music in their work or composed paintings while listening to music.

Modern technology enhanced the efforts of the early American modernists to translate musical sound into visual art. While the impulse to create synaesthetic paintings originated in the nineteenth century, the invention and commercial distribution of the gramophone and the radio facilitated early twentieth-century experiments in the transcription of music in painting. By the early 1890s, the American public had access to recordings of

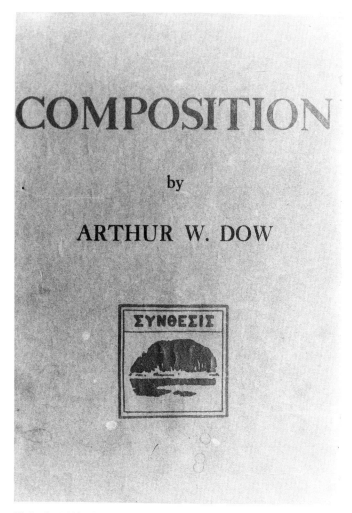

3) Arthur Wesley Dow, cover of «Composition», 1899.

4) Francis Picabia, «Negro Song» («Chanson Négre»), 1913. Watercolor on paper, 26 x 22 inches. Collection, The Metropolitan Museum of Art, New York. The Alfred Stieglitz Collection, 1949.

popular and classical music produced for a commercial market. With the introduction of the disc recording, distribution of recorded music to a mass market became a commercial reality at the turn of the century.[16] The phonograph literally brought music into the artist's studio. During the 1920s, the advent of commercial radio broadcasting [Fig. 8] provided modern painters with another readily accessible source of musical inspiration.[17]

Many of the American modernists who studied with Arthur Wesley Dow listened to music while painting. Georgia O'Keeffe has recalled that Dow's students at Columbia University were required to draw while listening to recorded music:

[...] one day [...] I heard the music from his classroom. Being curious I opened the door and went in. A low-tuned record was being played and students were asked to make a drawing from what they heard. So I sat down and made a drawing, too. [...] This gave me an idea that I was very interested to follow later - the idea that music could be translated into something for the eye.[18]

Bold but elegant color abstractions such as *Music - Pink and Blue*, 1919 (collection of the artist), and *Blue and Green Music* (1919) [Fig. 9] resulted from O'Keeffe's experiments with synaesthesia and musical analogy in painting.

Between 1912 and 1917, Max Weber, another graduate of Dow's classes, produced a group of abstract pastels [Fig. 10] and oil paintings [Fig. 11] devoted to musical themes. Weber's correspondence with the photographer Alvin Langdon Coburn

5) Wassily Kandinsky, «Improvisation No. 30» («Warlike Theme»), 1913. Oil on canvas, 43 x 43-3/4 inches. Collection, The Art Institute of Chicago. Arthur Jerome Eddy Memorial Collection.

6) Frank (Frantisek) Kupka, «Study for "Fugue in Two Colors"», 1912. Oil on Canvas, 39 x 29 inches. Collection, Philadelphia Museum of Art. The Louise and Walter Arensberg Collection.

7) Marsden Hartley, «Musical Theme» («Oriental Symphony»), 1912-13. Oil on canvas, 39-3/8 x 31-3/4 inches. Collection Rose Art Museum, Brandeis University, Waltham, Massachusetts. Gift of Mr. Samuel Lustgarten, Sherman Oaks, California.

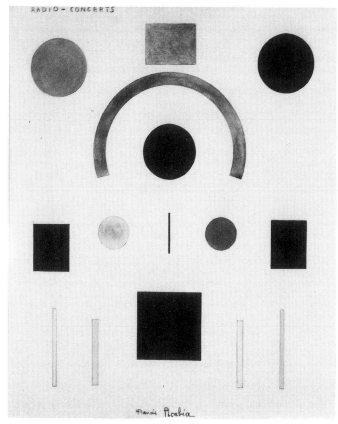

8) Francis Picabia, «Radio Concerts», ca. 1922. Ink and watercolor on composition board, 28 x 23 inches. Private collection (photography courtesy Richard Gray Gallery, Chicago).

reveals that his "music pictures" were intended to be visual translations of music.[19] In 1915, a newspaper reporter interviewed Weber and asked him:

> You spoke a while ago about painting impressions. Do you refer only to what you see, or do you mean you can paint what you hear? A piece of music for instance?

Weber replied:

> Why I've already done it. My picture called *Memory of a Symphony* [now lost] has been understood by many, for the change of public opinion in regard to the new movement in art is very remarkable.[20]

Weber's efforts to make synaesthetic equivalents of music in painting were closely tied to his larger aesthetic theory of the

fourth dimension. Briefly stated, Weber believed that the fourth dimension represented a higher spiritual reality.[21] The Symbolist concept of musical analogy enabled Weber to accept abstraction and envision the fourth dimension. In his first essay on the subject, Weber claimed that the fourth dimension "is somewhat similar to color and depth in musical sounds. It arouses imagination and stirs emotions."[22] Synaesthetic experiences made the fourth dimension tangible for Weber:

> The silent inner breathing of the atmosphere of the four dimension is audible, luminous music to the soul. It is the spirit symphony heard by the senses in attendance.[23]

Such assumptions typify the quasi-mystical arguments in support of synaesthesia.

In fact, Weber's artistic theory, published in his *Essays on Art*, relied on synaesthesia or the interchangeability of the senses. Weber believed that, "The highest development of

9) Georgia O'Keeffe, «Blue and Green Music», 1919. Oil on canvas, 23 x 19 inches. Collection, The Art Institute of Chicago. Gift of the artist.

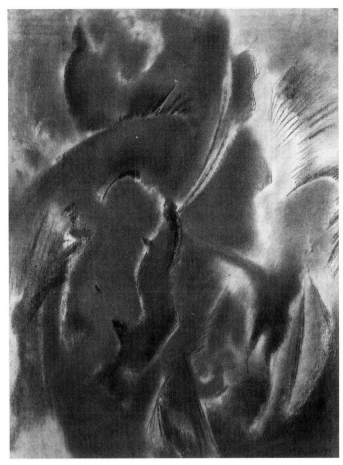

10) Max Weber, «Music», 1912. Pastel on paper, 25 x 19 inches. Collection, Forum Gallery, New York.

Through "spiritual tactility" Weber believed he could attain the fourth dimension.

Weber's abstract paintings embodied the twin principles of musical analogy and synaesthesia. In the five-year period between 1912 and 1917, he produced no fewer than a dozen paintings and pastels in which music served as the major thematic element. In one of the first of Weber's musical compositions, the pastel *Music*, 1912 [Fig. 10], the blue and red hues of the informal composition are barely inflected with lines. Weber subordinated the structural framework characteristic of his later Cubist abstractions to color.

11) Max Weber, «Interior with Music», 1915. Oil on canvas, 60 x 40 inches. Collection, Mr. and Mrs. Ahmet Ertegun (photograph courtesy Forum Gallery, New York).

perception and of sensitiveness will spring from the most tender interlacing, blending or correspondence of the several senses."[24] He claimed that this sensory interchange produced a state of higher consciousness which he called "spiritual tactility." Weber explained this heightened mode of perception:

This power of assimilation, of appreciation, of approach, of perception, depends largely upon the intensity of the spiritual tactility, or tactile intimacy, of creator or appreciator. To touch matter through sight, to color the invisible with memory of the visible, to hear through touch, to see through imagination, to prophesy or to evoke through memory; thus to interchange the functions of the senses in the process of perception while enlarging the spiritual range of the senses is the most real function of the spirit.[25]

12) John Covert, «Brass Band», 1919. Oil and string on composition board, 26 x 24 inches. Collection, Yale University Art Gallery, New Haven, Connecticut. Société Anonyme Collection.

In Cubist oil paintings such as *Interior with Music*, 1915 [Fig. 11], Weber focused on the spatial design of interpenetrating, transparent planes. He restricted color to a limited range of earth tones in the manner of Analytic Cubism. Unlike the Cubists, however, Weber sought to capture and make manifest the intangible. His paintings are not analytic reductions of still-life or landscape motifs, but painted analogues for musical sound.

To express moods that stir the emotion from within as does music, the plastic artist when he conceives of energetic rhythmic interlaced forms or units should be much more moved than even by music.[26]

Not all attempts at synaesthetic translations of music were mystical in source and purpose. Some artists sought a more concrete effect in painting. For example, in assemblages such as *Brass Band* (1919) [Fig. 12], John Covert attempted to evoke a specific musical sound with visual imagery. The repetitive textured banding and drum-like shapes in this monochromatic relief suggest the bombastic music of a brass band. In this case,

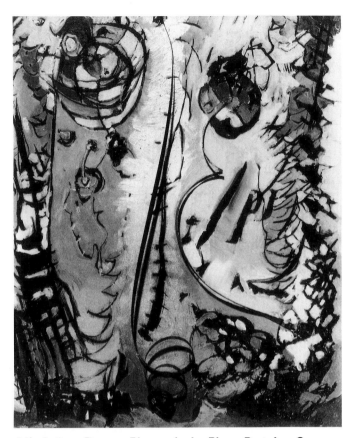

14) **Arthur Dove, «Rhapsody in Blue, Part I – George Gershwin», 1927. Collage of oil and metallic paint on aluminum with clock spring, 11-3/4 x 9-3/4 inches. Private collection.**

the substitution and confusion of the senses derived from a love of irrational juxtaposition. Covert appealed to an iconoclastic spirit of the absurd, rather than to spiritual mysticism.

Among the most successful of these early twentieth-century paintings inspired by music was a series of jazz compositions produced by Arthur Dove in 1927.[27] A member of the Stieglitz Circle, Dove continually sought inspiration from music. He was convinced that abstract painting could attain an emotive power comparable to that of music: "Art is nearer to music, not the music of the ears, just the music of the eyes."[28] Dove listened to music while painting and drawing. His wife recorded in her diary that he worked on his jazz paintings while listening to records of George Gershwin's music. His involvement with synaesthesia led him to devise a linear notation system for transcribing musical sound. The linearity of such paintings as *Improvision* [Fig. 13] resulted from this working method.[29]

In the collage *George Gershwin -Rhapsody in Blue; Part I* [Fig. 14], the central work in his jazz series, Dove used color and line

13) **Arthur Dove, «Improvision», 1927. Oil on building board, 15 x 14 inches. Collection, Mr. and Mrs. Donald Graham, Denver.**

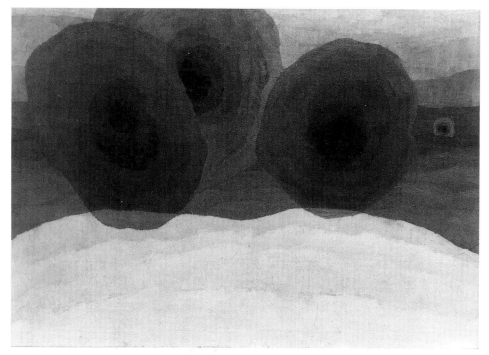

15) Arthur Dove, «Fog Horns», 1929. Oil on canvas, 17 x 25 inches. Collection, Colorado Springs Fine Arts Center. Anonymous Gift.

16) Arthur Dove, «Swing Music» («Louis Amstrong»), 1938. Encaustic on canvas, 17-5/8 X 25-7/8 inches. Collection, The Art Institute of Chicago, Alfred Stieglitz Collection.

to evoke the melody and tempo of jazz. The resulting vibrant composition represents Dove's symbolic tribute to George Gershwin's musical genius.[30]

Throughout his later career, Dove relied on musical analogy and synaesthesia in his paintings. In 1929, just two years after completing the jazz paintings, Dove produced one of his most successful abstractions based on synaesthesia. His painting *Fog Horns* [Fig. 15] evokes the sound and atmosphere suggested by the title. Although inspired by sound rather than music, the painting fuses the visual and auditory senses. In this composition both the muted hues of pink, blue, and gray and the repetition of three circular motifs with their concentric, wave-like emanations serve as effective visual analogues for sound. Dove explained his deliberate effort to evoke auditory experience through painting: "Anybody should be able to feel a certain state and express it in terms of paint or music."[31] By blending visual and auditory experience in *Fog Horns*, Dove achieved his ideal of painting as "music of the eyes."[32] This synaesthetic analogy of visual music served as a theoretical foundation for Dove's entire *oeuvre*. Moreover, specific musical themes recur in two important paintings produced during the last eight years of Dove's life. In 1938, Dove returned to jazz and popular music in a tribute to Louis Amstrong, another jazz musician-composer. The painting *Swing Music - Louis Swing* [Fig. 16] differs from the earlier jazz series. As in *Fog Horns*, Dove minimized his reliance on linear tracery in favor of a greater emphasis on bright color and fluid forms. Dove's wife, the painter Helen Torr, pronounced the finished painting "a perfect thing in mathematical beauty of color-paint."[33] *Swing Music - Louis Amstrong* is an eloquent summation of Dove's explorations of jazz motifs in painting.

Primitive Music [Fig. 17], Dove's last work based on direct musical reference, fuses synaesthesia with another powerful element of modern art – primitivism. Dove's masterful combination of earth tones and muted colors with jagged lines and angular forms evokes the elemental simplicity that was central to modernist fascination with tribal culture. The painting also embodies Dove's belief in the primal power of music. He regarded music as an elemental mode of expression. Dove once described his paintings in terms which reveal his dual fascination with synaesthesia and primitivism: "Two of the large paintings I feel have the sensation of sound in them – As though some primitive had hit a tree with a club."[34] *Primitive Music* represents the mature distillation of Arthur Dove's life-long preoccupation with musical analogy:

Then there was the search for a means of expression which did not depend upon representation. It should have order, size, intensity, spirit, nearer to the music of the eye.[35]

17) Arthur Dove, «Primitive Music», 1944. Wax emulsion on canvas, 18 x 24 inches. Collection, The Phillips Collection, Washington, D. C.

From Whistler to Dove, most artists who experimented with synaesthesia invoked musical analogy in order to emphasize the formal values of painting. Often their attempts at musical transcription resulted in abstract painting. In Alfred Stieglitz's case, musical analogy served as a compelling metaphor of the formal value of abstract photography. That many of the artists closest to Stieglitz chose to explore synaesthetic analogy inevitably affected Stieglitz's own creative efforts. Stieglitz not only supported their artistic experiments, but he also shared their ideal of aesthetic purity. During the period of renewed concentration after he closed his gallery in 1917, Stieglitz produced several series of abstract photographs devoted to clouds [Figs. 18 and 19]. Each series depended upon musical analogy. Stieglitz's cloud photographs served as photographic counterparts to the musical abstractions of the early American modernists.

Stieglitz explained the origin of his clouds series through direct musical analogy. He stresses that these photographs were meant to demonstrate that photography transcended subject matter. In 1923 he elaborated on this premise in an essay for *Amateur Photographer and Photography*:

I wanted to photograph clouds to find out what I had learned in 40 years about photography. Through clouds to put down my philosophy of life – to show that my photographs were not due to subject matter – not to special trees, or faces, or

18) Alfred Stieglitz, «Music: Clouds in Ten Movements, No. 1», 1922. Silver photographic print, 194 x 240 mm. Collection, National Gallery of Art, Washington, D. C. Alfred Stieglitz Collection. Gift of Georgia O'Keeffe and the Alfred Stieglitz Estate.

interiors, to special privileges, clouds were there for every-one – no tax as yet on them – free.

So I began to work with the clouds – and it was great excitement – daily for weeks. Every time I developed I was so wrought up, always believing I had nearly gotten what I was after – but had failed. [...] I had told Miss O'Keeffe I wanted a series of photographs which when seen by Ernest Bloch (the great composer) he would exclaim: Music! Music! Man, why that is music! How did you ever do that? And he would point to violins, and flutes, and oboes, and brass, full of enthusia-sm, and would say he'd have to write a symphony called *Clouds*. Not like Debussy's but *much, much more*.[36]

In the first series of cloud photographs, Stieglitz made explicit use of musical analogy in the title for the group of ten prints - *Music: A Sequence of Ten Cloud Photographs*, 1922 [Fig. 18].

19) Alfred Stieglitz, «Songs of the Sky», 1924(?). Silver print, 3-5/8 x 4-5/8 inches. Collection, National Gallery of Art, Washington, D. C. Alfred Stieglitz Collection. Gift of Georgia O'Keeffe and the Alfred Stieglitz Estate.

Two years later Stieglitz again used musical analogy in the title for a related cloud photograph, *Song on the Sky*, 1924, [Fig. 19]. In Stieglitz's mind, his search for a visual expression of the ideal corresponded to the aesthetic impact of music. He explained in a letter to Hart Crane:

> I know exactly *what* I have photographed. I know I have done something that has never been done. Maybe an approach occasionally found in music.[37]

Just as musical analogy inspired Stieglitz's exploration of abstract photography, so synaesthesia also served to transform the most realistic imagery of contemporary painting into abstract visual design. The pristine industrial landscapes of Charles Sheeler exemplify this idealization of reality through the synaesthetic medium of music. Since the 1930s, Sheeler repeatedly used musical titles to evoke the abstract visual structure in his deceptively straightforward factoryscapes.

20) Charles Sheeler, «Fugue», 1940. Tempera on canvas board, 11 x 13 inches. Collection, Museum of Fine Arts, Boston. Arthur Mason Knapp Fund.

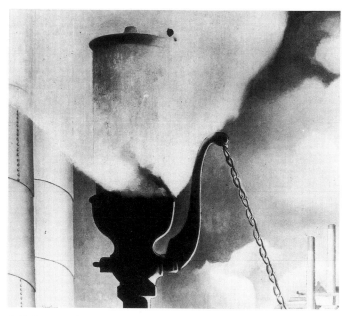

21) Charles Sheeler, «Music in the Air», 1941. Oil on gesso panel, 11 x 9 inches. Present location unknown. (Photograph: Downtown Gallery Papers, Archives of American Art, Smithsonian Institution, Washington, D. C.)

In *Fugue*, 1940 [Fig. 20], Sheeler merged musical analogy with machine aesthetics. He likened the vertical repetitive pattern of the smokestacks, which form the central motif of the composition, to successive thematic variations of a musical fugue. The parallel was not lost on a contemporary critic, who commented in 1940:

Webster's Dictionary defines "fugue" as a "polyphonic composition developed from a given theme according to strict contrapuntal rules." Sheeler has given this title to his painting, which is a recent addition to the collections of the Boston Museum of Fine Arts. Out of the component elements of the contemporary industrial theme with which we are all familiar, Sheeler has constructed a fugue with paint and canvas. By means of his selective vision, the artist has made us see the beauty of a New Bedford factory in the afternoon.[38]

Sheeler's "selective vision" was equally apparent in another synaesthetic oil painting, *Music in the Air*, 1941 [Fig. 21]. Incorporating much of Sheeler's imagery associated with music, the lost composition featured steam and clouds in the upper portion of the canvas. A girder-like chain linked this intangible realm to the industrial imagery in the lower portion of

the composition. Two smokestacks in the lower right area recalled the motif of *Fugue*. Each of the elements in *Music in the Air* would be isolated and recombined in numerous paintings and drawings. Not only did Sheeler favor musical titles such as *Counterpoint* and *Architectural Cadences*, but also his manipulation of Machine Age imagery resembled the composer's variations on musical melodies:

The idea is based on having realized that when we look at any object in nature [...] there is the memory of the object we have previously seen that carries over overtones on the present. I combine the immediate image with things previously seen.[39]

In his use of musical metaphor Sheeler imbued Machine Age materialism with spiritual idealism.

All of the foregoing examples of musical analogy represented essentially intuitive creative processes. Even an artist such as Arthur Dove, who engaged in synaesthetic transcriptions of music, did not believe that a mathematically exact correlation between painting and music was possible.

More systematically inclined artists sought to develop a mode of painting based on a supposed mathematical equivalence between color and sound. Two American painters working in Paris, Morgan Russell [Fig. 22] and Stanton Macdonald-Wright [Fig. 23], invented the style Synchromism, based on this pseudo-scientific premise of synaesthesia. The very name which they selected for their movement signified the musical analogy they espoused: Synchromism literally means with color, just as symphony signifies "with sound." Morgan Russell explained the implications of their new color theory:

In order to resolve the problem of a new pictorial structure, we have considered light as intimately related chromatic waves, and have submitted the harmonic connections between colors to a closer study. These "color rhythms" somehow infuse a painting with the notion of time: they create the illusion that the picture develops, like a piece of music, within a span of time, while the old painting existed strictly in space, its every expression grasped by the spectator simultaneously and at a glance. [40]

Macdonald-Wright believed that an exact correspondence between the color spectrum and the musical scale would provide a key to a new art. He later wrote:

For many years there has been growing a conviction that there is some deeply rooted, recondite analogy between color and sound. Both are demonstrably vibratory; both have a varied and defined emotional stimulus for us, and each is used as a medium for an art. [41]

Both men relied on this quasi-scientific analogy to produce pure color abstractions in painting.

Neither artist, however, was satisfied with the conventional easel painting as a medium for color expression. They envisioned instead a new art of color freed from the constraints of conventional painting. Over the years both Morgan Russell [Figs. 24 and 25] and Stanton Macdonald-Wright experimented

22) Morgan Russell, «Synchromy in Orange: To Form», 1913-14. Oil on canvas, 135 x 121 inches. Collection, Albright-Knox Art Gallery, Buffalo. Gift of Seymour A. Knox.

23) Stanton Macdonald-Wright, «Conception Synchromy», 1914. Oil on canvas, 36 x 30-1/8 inches. Collection, Hirshhorn Museum and Sculpture Garden, Smithsonian Institution, Washington, D. C. Gift of Joseph H. Hirshhorn, 1966.

24) Morgan Russell, «Study in Transparency», c. 1922. Oil on tissue paper, 18-3/4 x 13-7/8 inches [irregular]. Collection, The Museum of Modern Art, New York. Gift of Miss Rose Fried.

25) Morgan Russell, «Study for Kinetic Light Machine», c. 1916-23. Ink of paper, 8-8/9 x 6-3/4 inches. Collection, Montclair Art Museum, Montclair, New Jersey. Gift of Henry Reed.

with light projection equipment. They hoped to produce an art of colored light incorporating the element of time. In short, they conceived of an art of ''color music.''

The Synchromists were by no means the only artists or inventors in this period to attempt to create color music. Just as the quasi-mystical arguments for synaesthesia arose in the last century, so the pseudo-scientific research into color music evolved from nineteenth-century studies of optics and the psychology of perception.[42]

Virtually all experiments in color music rested upon one of two pseudo-scientific arguments for synaesthesia. Some artists and inventors postulated an exact physical correspondence between light and sound. Although the German scientist Hermann von Helmholtz had disproved this hypothetical analogy by the 1860's, the notion of an equivalence between the color spectrum and the musical scale persisted well into the twentieth century.[43] Secondly, psychological investigations of human perception were used to support associations of color with sound. Originally linked to the study of insanity, reports of cases of synaesthesia appeared in popular scientific literature throughout the later nineteenth century.[44] Systems of psychological correspondence between the color spectrum and the musical scale were based on the premise that synaesthesia was a common experience of human perception.

Alexander Wallace Rimington (1854 – 1918), a British inventor and professor of fine arts in London, designed and built one of the first successful instruments for color music [Fig. 26][45] His color organ, patented in 1893, was first used in a public performance in June 1895 in St. James Hall in London. Rimington believed in the physical equivalence of light and sound. He attempted to apply the three musical functions – time, rhythm, and combination – to color. Rimington equated

26) «Invents Color Organ.» Article in *The Enquirer* (Cincinnati), March 28, 1914 (photograph courtesy Library of Congress, Washington, D. C.).

27) Thomas Wilfred, «Vertical Sequence, Op. 137», 1941. Lumia composition (projected light on translucent screen). Form cycle 7 minutes; Color cycle 7 minutes 17 second. The two cycles coincide every 50 hours and 59 minutes. Screen, 15 x 15-3/8 inches. Collection, The Museum of Modern Art, New York.

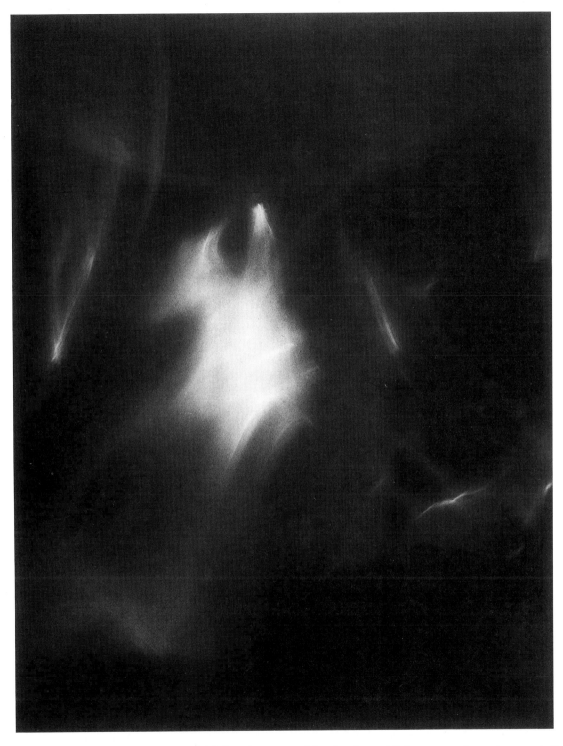

28) Thomas Wilfred, «Aspiration, Op. 145», 1955. Lumia composition (projected light on translucent screen). Duration 42 hours, 14 minutes, 11 seconds. Screen, 19 x 15 inches. Collection, The Museum of Modern Art, New York. Gift of Mr. and Mrs. Julius Stulman.

the seven spectrum bands of natural light with diatonic intervals which composed the musical octave. When color compositions were performed on the keyboard of Rimington's organ, moving colors were projected on a white drapery in his studio. Musical accompaniment lent a synaesthetic dimension to these visual performances. Rimington's invention captured the imagination of many artists in the U. S. and in Europe.[46] The Russian composer Alexander Scriabin even composed an orchestral work, *Prometheus* (*Poem of Fire*, opus 60), with an optional part for a keyboard of light. In 1915, the New York premiere of Scriabin's composition featured the first successful light performance in concert.[47]

Scriabin's *Prometheus* was not the only performance of color music in the United States during this period. The American architect Claude Bragdon, a staunch advocate of color music, was responsible for two performances of *Song and Light*, which he believed demonstrated the possibility of *Harnessing the Rainbow*. In collaboration with Harry Barnhard of the Rochester Community Chorus, Bragdon designed "a new kind of civic celebration," an evening festival of song and decorative electric illumination. Several outdoor performances were presented at Highland Park, Rochester, New York on September 30, 1915, and in Central Park in Manhattan on September 14, 1916. Bragdon based his notion of color music on the psychological, rather than the purely physical analogy between light and sound:

> If we are to have color symphonies, the best are not likely to be those based on a literal translation of some musical masterpiece into color according to this or any theory, but those created by persons who are emotionally reactive to this medium, able to imagine in color, and to treat it imaginatively.[48]

Bragdon emphasized the need for innate sensitivity to the new medium of kinetic color and light. He enlarged the concept of color music beyond a simple correspondence between color and music.

While Bragdon raised new social and aesthetic issues associated with color music, the Philadelphia pianist Mary Hallock Greenewalt also promoted the idea of color music through lectures and solo performances incorporating colored lighting. Mrs. Greenewalt shared Bragdon's belief in the psychological basis for musical analogy: "There is a whole literature on color audition and kindred association."[49] However, Mrs. Greenewalt cautioned that, in developing the new art of kinetic light, strict correspondence between color and music would be impossible:

> Light, in its very nature, is an atmosphere, a suffusion, an enveloping medium. To give it the sharpness of short succession, as with the notes of an instrument, is inconceivable. To give it a formful image on the flat, turns it into a kaleidoscope – certainly not a new thing. To play with intensities of light and tint without forcing them out of the groove to which they cling, that will be a new joy for the artist as it once was the Creator's.[50]

Mrs. Greenewalt's argument is particularly striking in view of the fact that she herself performed piano concerts with light accompaniment. Nevertheless, her insight into the distinct nature of "mobile color" accorded with Bragdon's views. Together they introduced the issue of "truth to materials" into the debate about color music.

In technological terms, the most successful instrument for color music invented during this period was the clavilux. Its originator was Thomas Wilfred (1889-1968), a Danish-American singer, artist, and inventor. A student of both music and the fine arts, Wilfred was convinced that the physical correspondence of the color spectrum and the musical scale was a false analogy. Wilfred concluded that an art of colored light should be based on the intrinsic properties of the medium: form, color, and motion. He envisioned building a new light projection instrument. After immigrating to the United States in 1916, he found patronage and support for his research through Claude Bragdon, who designed his first studio. In 1919, the two men launched the Prometheans, a cooperative group dedicated to the new art of light. That same year, Wilfred built the first of a series of successful light projection instruments, to which he gave the generic name "clavilux." Wilfred called his newly invented light performances *Lumia* [Figs. 27 and 28]. The title, which derives from the Latin word for light, symbolized his separation of the art of light from the older idea of color music.[51] In 1930 Wilfred wrote:

> Through twenty-two years of research work I have helped to lay the foundation for an independent Art-form of Light – first by establishing its three basic factors as Form, Motion, and Color – second by inventing and building a number of instruments with which I have succeeded in proving beyond refute my much contested statement that an artist can create and give a completely satisfying message of beauty solely through the medium of Light projected on a white screen from an instrument that gives him control over Form, Motion, and Color.[52]

Despite his insistence that *Lumia* was an independent art form, Wilfred designed collaborative lighting performances for the theater, particularly the dance. Performances on the clavilux sometimes incorporated music. The titles for many of Wilfred's light compositions for clavilux retain a residual analogy with music. *Counterpoint in Space* (1938, opus 96), *Crescendo*

29) Mark Tobey, «Brodway Melody», 1945. Tempera on hard-board, 24 x 17 inches. Collection, University of Michigan Museum of Art, Ann Arbor. Gift of Mr. and Mrs. Roger L. Stevens.

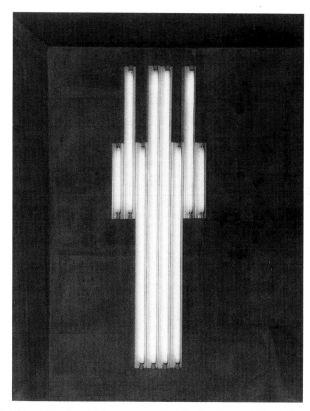

30) Dan Flavin, «Monument for V. Tatlin», 1969. Fluorescent light, 8 light fixtures joined together and 8 light tubes, 96-1/8 x 28-3/8 x 4 inches. Collection, University Art Museum, University of California, Berkeley. Gift of Mr. and Mrs. Frederick Weisman.

(1939) or *The Firebird* (1934, opus 91) are typical examples.

Wilfred's clavilux was the product of technological developments in electronic engineering. His invention was matched by those of Adrian Bernard Klein and the Strand Electronic and Engineering Company in London.[53] All such efforts to create an art of projected light depended upon electronic engineering.

Although the concepts of musical analogy, synaesthesia and color music arose in the nineteenth century, these closely related ideas have had a continuing influence on twentieth century art. In abstract painting musical analogy has persisted. Artists such as Hans Hofmann, an influential teacher, relied on musical analogy and often used musical titles for their abstract canvases.[54] Analogy with music is an underlying assumption of much critical writing about abstract art. Musical terminology has been appropriated in the critical vocabulary of modern art. While musical analogy usually signifies the predominance of formal over narrative values, in the later twentieth century several abstract painters have used musical allusions to endow abstract compositions with tangible meaning. Mondrian's *Broadway Boogie Woogie* (1942-43, The Museum of Modern Art) and Mark Tobey's *Brodway Melody* [Fig. 29] are but two examples of this variation of musical analogy.[55]

Finally, experiments in color music and light projection foretold the late twentieth-century light and laser art created by artists such as Dan Flavin [Fig. 30] and Rockne Krebs. In the 1920s the critic Sheldon Cheney, speaking of color music, had predicted a "purely abstract art of light."[56] By abandoning the synaesthetic analogy with music, artists of the 1960s and 1970s, have continued the work of Thomas Wilfred and have realized Cheney's dream of an art of pure light.

[1] This article is an expanded version of a paper presented at the Nineteenth-century Seminar of the Joseph Henry Papers, Smithsonian Institution, Washington, D. C., on April 26, 1985. I am grateful to Nathan Reingold, Senior Historian of the National Museum of American History and former editor of the Joseph Henry Papers, for the lecture invitation which provided the initial forum for the presentation of this research. Portions of this study were also presented at the University of Delaware's biennial symposium, "American Art of the Twentieth Century: Vision and Revision," May 1, 1987. Specials thanks are due to Professor William I. Homer for his encouragement and support.

[2] M. Miles, *Short talks to Art Students on Color from an Artist's Standpoint, Also Dealing with the Relations of Color to the Musical Scale*, Kansas City, Missouri, 1914, p. 97.

[3] The pervasive influence of synaesthesia in European modern art and literature has been investigated in greater depth than has the American phenomenon. For synaesthesia and Symbolist aesthetics in literature, see A. G. Lehmann, *The Symbolist Aesthetic in France, 1885 – 1895*, Oxford, 1950. Major contributions to the study of synaesthesia in European painting include S. Ringbom, "Art in 'The Epoch of the Great Spiritual': Occult Elements in the Early Theory of Abstract Painting," *Journal of the Warburg and Courtauld Institutes*, XXIX, 1960, pp. 386-418; P. Vergo, "Music and Abstract Painting: Kandinsky, Goethe and Schoenberg," *Towards a New Art: Essays on the Background to Abstract Art 1910-20*, ed. M. Compton, London, 1980, pp. 41-63; J. Bowlt, "The Spirit of Music," *The Isms of Art in Russia*, 1907-30, Cologne, 1977, pp. 5-17; N. J. Troy, "Theo van

Doesburg: From Music into Space,'' *Arts Magazine*, 56, February 1982, pp. 92-101; and A. Kagan, *Paul Klee: Art & Music*, Ithaca-London, 1983. For an introduction to musical analogy in early American modernist painting, see J. Zilczer, ''The Aesthetic Struggle in America, 1913-1918: Abstract Art and Theory in the Stieglitz Circle,'' unpublished Ph. D. dissertation, University of Delaware, 1975, pp. 43-110. In August 1985 the Neue Staatsgalerie in Stuttgart presented a major exhibition exploring the interrelationship between music and painting in the twentieth century. See K. von Maur, ed. *Vom Klang der Bilder*, Stuttgart, 1985.

[4] J. A. McNeill Whistler, letter to *The World*, May 22, 1878, reprinted in the *Gentle Art of Making Enemies*, New York: Dover, 1967, pp. 127-8. See also R. Johnson, ''Whistler's Musical Modes: Symbolist Symphonies and Numinous Nocturnes,'' *Arts Magazine*, 55, April 1981, pp. 167-76.

[5] Cf. B. Borelius, *Oscar Wilde, Whistler and Colours*, Lund, 1968; C. P. Barbier, *Correspondence Mallarmé-Whistler*, Paris, 1964.

[6] W. Corn, *The Color of Mood: American Tonalism, 1880-1910*, San Francisco, 1972.

[7] A. J. Eddy, *Recollections and Impressions of James A. McNeill Whistler*, Philadelphia-London, 1903, pp. 183-4.

[8] A. W. Dow, ''Introductory Note,'' in *Composition*, 3rd ed., New York, 1900, p. 5. For the sources of Dow's theories, see L. Chisholm, *Fenollosa: The Far East and American Culture*, New Haven-London, 1963; C. Lancaster, ''Synthesis in the Artistic Theory of Fenollosa and Dow,'' *Art Journal*, XXVIII, 1969, pp. 286-7; F. C. Moffatt, *Arthur Wesley Dow (1857-1922)*, Washington, D. C., 1977.

[9] For the influence of Symbolism on the Stieglitz circle, see R. P. Hull, ''*Camera Work*, an American Quarterly,'' unpublished Ph. D. dissertation, Northwestern University, 1970; S. Hartmann, ''A Tuesday Evening at Stéphane Mallarmé's,'' *The Art Critic*, I, no. 1, 1893, pp. 9-11, reprinted in the *Sadakichi Hartmann Newsletter*, II, no. 2, Fall, 1972, pp. 4-5.

[10] Ch. Caffin, ''Symbolism and Allegory,'' *Camera Work*, no. 18, April, 1907, pp. 17-20. For a study of Caffin's criticism, see S. Underwood, ''Charles H. Caffin: A Voice for Modernism, 1897-1918,'' unpublished Ph. D. dissertation, Indiana University, 1981. While Underwood acknowledged Caffin's dependence on musical analogy, she disputed Roger Hull's contention that Caffin's aesthetic theories reflected the influence of Dow and Fenollosa. Cf. Hull, *op. cit.*, pp. 110-3.

[11] W. A. Camfield, *Francis Picabia: His Art, His Life, His Times*, Princeton, New Jersey, 1979, pp. 26-39.

[12] Francis Picabia, undated manuscript, on Hotel Brevourt Stationery, Alfred Stieglitz Archives, Yale Collection of American Literature, Beinecke Rare Book and Manuscript Library, Yale University, New Haven, Connecticut. (Translation from the original French by the author.)

[13] See P. Weiss, *Kandinsky in Munich: The Formative Jugendstil Years*, Princeton, New Jersey, 1979, pp. 81-103. According to Jonathan Fineberg, the pervasive influence of Symbolist aesthetics and utopian idealism was a crucial factor in the development of European vanguard painting. See his incisive review article, ''Kandinsky: Through the Scholar's Glass,'' *Art in America*, 70, December, 1982, pp. 11-3; 153-5.

[14] Marsden Hartley (Paris), letter to Rockwell Kent, [undated, c. 1912], Rockwell Kent Papers, Archives of American Art, Smithsonian Institution, Washington, D. C., Box 41.

[15] Marsden Hartley (Paris), letter to Rockwell Kent, Christmas Eve, December 24, 1912, Rockwell Kent Papers, Box 41.

[16] See R. Gelatt, *The Fabulous Phonograph*, 1877-1977, 2nd revised ed., New York-London, 1977. J. R. Smart, J. W. Newson, ''Wonderful Invention'': A Brief History of the Phonograph from Tinfoil to the LP, Washington, D. C., 1977.

[17] J. F. MacDonald, *Don't Touch That Dial! Radio Programming in America Life*, 1920-1960, Chicago, 1979.

[18] G. O'Keeffe, *Georgia O'Keeffe*, New York, 1976, unpaginated.

[19] Alvin Langdon Coburn, letters to Max Weber, February 12, March 17, and July 8, 1914, Max Weber Papers, Archives of American Art, Smithsonian Institution, Washington, D. C., microfilm roll no. N69-85, frames 292-293, 364, 383.

[20] ''Maker of Curious Pictures in Town. Weber Unburdens Soul and Discusses His Rivals,'' *Baltimore Evening News* [March 1915], Bound clippings, Max Weber Papers, microfilm roll no. Ny59-6, frame 359.

[21] L. D. Henderson, *The Fourth Dimension and Non-Euclidean Geometry in Modern Art*, Princeton, New Jersey, 1983, pp. 167-82. See also *eadem*, ''Mabel Dodge, Gertrude Stein, and Max Weber: A Four-Dimensional Trio,'' *Arts Magazine*, 57, September 1982, pp. 106-11; W. Bohn, ''In Pursuit of the Fourth Dimension: Guillaume Apollinaire and Max Weber,'' *Arts Magazine*, 54, June 1980, pp. 166-9.

[22] M. Weber, ''The Fourth Dimension From a Plastic Point of View,'' *Camera Work*, no. 31, July 1910, p. 25.

[23] M. Weber, ''Preparing to See,'' *Essays on Art*, New York, 1916, pp. 39-40.

[24] Weber, ''Spiritual Tactility,'' *Essays on Art, op. cit.*, p. 13.

[25] *Ibidem*, p. 15.

[26] Weber, ''The Equilibrium of the Inanimate,'' *Essays on Art, op. cit.*, p. 69.

[27] See J. Zilczer, ''Synaesthesia and Popular Culture: Arthur Dove, George Gershwin, and the 'Rhapsody in Blue','' *Art Journal*, 44, no.4, Winter 1984, pp. 361-6.

[28] A. G. Dove, ''Notes by Arthur G. Dove,'' December 19 [1928] and March 5 [1929], in *Dove Exhibition*, New York, The Intimate Gallery, April 9-28, 1929.

[29] See S. M. Smith, G. Smith, ''Music of the Eye: The Development of an Idea,'' unpublished lecture, American University, Washington, D.C., 1950, reedited 1976, Suzanne Mullett Smith Papers, microfilm roll no. 1043, frame 1274.

[30] Zilczer, ''Synaesthesia and Popular Culture,'' *op. cit.* p. 365.

[31] A. G. Dove, ''Notes by Arthur G. Dove,'' December 19 [1928], in *Dove Exhibition*, New York, The Intimate Gallery, April 9-28, 1929.

[32] *Ibidem*.

[33] Helen Dove, diary entry, Sunday, March 13, 1938, Helen Dove Papers, Archives of American Art, Smithsonian Institution, Washington, D. C., microfilm roll no. 39, frame 684.

[34] Arthur Dove, letter to Alfred Stieglitz and Georgia O'Keeffe, undated [c. 1927-28?], page 3, numbered leaf 1035, Arthur Dove Correspondence, Alfred Stieglitz Archives, Yale Collection of American Literature, Beinecke Rare Book and Manuscript Library, Yale University, New Haven, Connecticut.

[35] A. Dove, letter to S. M. Kootz, undated [1929-30], published in S. M. Kootz, *Modern American Painters*, n. p.: Brewer & Warren. Inc., 1930, p. 36.

[36] A. Stieglitz, ''How I Came to Photograph Clouds,'' *Amateur Photographer and Photography*, 56, September 19, 1923, p. 255. See also S. Greenough, J. Hamilton, *Alfred Stieglitz: Photographs & Writings*, Washington, D. C., 1983, pp. 24, 206-8.

[37] Alfred Stieglitz, letter to Hart Crane, December 10, 1923, published in Greenough, Hamilton, *op. cit.*, p. 208.

[38] H. H. A., "The Home Forum," *The Christian Science Monitor*, undated clipping [1941], Charles Sheeler Papers, Archives of American Art, Smithsonian Institution, Washington, D. C., microfilm roll no. 1811, frame 363.

[39] Charles Sheeler, undated letter to Mr. Rae, Sheeler Papers, microfilm roll no. 1811, frame 363.

[40] M. Russell, "Introduction," *Les Synchromistes: S. Macdonald-Wright et Morgan Russell*, Paris: Bernheim-Jeune & Cie, October 27-November 8, 1913, translated from the French by M. Laing, and republished in G. Levin, *Synchromism and American Color Abstraction, 1910-1925*, New York, 1978, p. 130.

[41] S. Macdonald-Wright, *A Treatise on Color*, Los Angeles, 1924, p. 14.

[42] The interaction of scientific theories of synaesthesia with analogy of sound and color in the arts actually can be traced to the eighteenth century. See E. von Erhardt-Siebold, "Harmony of the Senses in English, German, and French Romanticism," *Publication of the Modern Language Association of America*, XLVII, no. 2, June 1932, pp. 577-92. I am grateful to Thomas Hankins of the University of Washington for bringing Erhardt-Siebold's research to my attention.

[43] For Helmholtz's refutation of the analogy of color and sound, see L. Koenigsberger, *Hermann von Helmholtz*, tr. by F. A. Welby, New York, 1965, pp. 174-5. Arthur Herber Church, a professor of chemistry at the Royal Academy of Arts in London, disseminated the results of Helmholtz's optical research to English-speaking artists through his book *Colour: An Elementary Manual for Students*, originally published in 1872. An enlarged edition appeared in 1897, and republication in 1911 brought still wider distribution of Church's work in New York and Toronto.

[44] A comprehensive bibliography of the psychology of synaesthetic perception is included in Annelies Argelander, *Das Farbenhören und de synästhetische Faktor der Wahrnehmung*, Jena, 1927, pp. 153-72. Typical articles include Henri de Parville, "Association of Colors with Sounds," *The Popular Science Monthly*, 23, August 1883, pp. 490-2; B. F. Underwood, "Association of Color with Sounds," *Science*, 21, no. 541, June 16, 1893, pp. 329-30; L. Dauriac, "Des images sugérées par 'Audition Musicale,'" *Revue philosophique*, 54, October 1902, pp. 488-503. Alfred Binet, one of the investigators to develop intelligence tests, also applied statistical methods to research in synaesthesia. See A. Binet, "L'application de la psychometrie a l'étude de l'audition colorée," *Revue philosophique*, 36, 1893, p. 334. For later studies, see especially R. H. Wheeler, T. D. Cutsforth, "Synaesthesia and Meaning," *The American Journal of Psychology*, 33, no. 3, July 1922, pp. 361-84; T. Karkowski, H. S. Odbert, "Color-Music," *Psychological Monographs*, 50, no. 2, 1938, pp. 1-60 published for the American Psychological Association, Ohio State University, Columbus, Ohio, J. F. Dashiell, ed.

[45] A. W. Rimington, *A New Art: Colour Music* (A Paper Read at St. James Hall, [London], June 6, 1895). Rimington's was not the first such invention. Color organs were originally invented in the eighteenth century. See E. von Erhardt-Siebold, "Some Inventions of the Pre-Romantic Period and Their Influence Upon Literature," *Englische Studien* 66, no. 3, 1932, pp. 347-63.

[46] Arthur Jerome Eddy devoted a chapter to color music in his book *Cubists and Post-Impresionism*, Chicago, 1914, pp. 140-6. A comprehensive bibliography of critical notices about Rimington's invention was compiled by A. B. Klein [Cornwall-Clyne], *Coloured Light: An Art Medium*. Third enlarged edition of *The Art of Light: Colour Music*, London, 1937, Appendix I, 235-9.

[47] Klein, *op. cit.*, p. 9. See also "'Color Music' in 'The Poem of Fire'," *New York Times*, March 21, 1915; R. Doyle, "Will Colour Music Become an Art?," *Bookman*, 41, June 1915, pp. 399-401.

[48] C. Bragdon, *Architecture and Democracy*, New York, 1918, p. 139. See also C. Bragdon, "Song and Light," *The Architectural Record*, 4, no. 9, September 1916, pp. 169-72. For Bragdon's role in the dissemination of the idea of the fourth dimension in the United States, see Henderson, *The Fourth Dimension...*, *op. cit.*, pp. 186-201.

[49] M. Hallock-Greenewalt, *Light: Fine Art the Sixth. A Running Nomenclature to Underlay the use of Light as a Fine Art*, Philadelphia, 1918, p. 10. This monograph was originally presented as an address before the Illuminating Engineers' Society, Engineers' Club, Philadelphia, April 19, 1918. (See also *Transactions of Illuminating Engineers' Society*, 13, no. 7 [October 10, 1918].) In 1903 Thomas Eakins painted a portrait of Mrs. Greenewalt, now in the Wichita Art Museum. Since they shared an interest in science and music, Mrs. Greenewalt tried unsuccessfully to interest Eakins in the "fourth dimension." See L. Goodrich, *Thomas Eakins*, 2 vols., Washington, D. C.: National Gallery of Art and Cambridge, Mass., 1982; vol. II, pp. 13, 211-3, fig. 248.

[50] Greenewalt, *Light...*, *op. cit.*, p. 17. Mrs. Greenewalt also wrote a longer monograph on her researches. See M. E. Hallock-Greenewalt, *Nourathar: The Fine Art of Light Color Playing*, Philadelphia, 1946. Klein, in the preface to the second edition of *Coloured Light*, cited Mrs. Greenewalt's patents for color projection and mentioned that her Gold Medal Award at the 1926 Sesqui-Centennial International Exposition in Philadelphia was the first public award for the new art of light projection. See Klein, *op. cit.*, pp. via-vib., 21-2.

[51] See D. M. Stein, *Thomas Wilfred: Lumia, A Retrospective Exhibition*, Washington, D. C., The Corcoran Gallery of Art, 1971.

[52] T. Wilfred, "A Personal Statement," December, 1930, published in Stein, *op. cit.*, p. 60. For contemporary accounts of Wilfred's invention, see "The Color Organ," *Science and Invention*, 10, May 1922, No. 22-3; S. Young, "The Color Organ," *Theater Arts Magazine*, 6, January 1922, pp. 20-32; S. Cheney, *A Primer of Modern Art*, revised edition, New York, 1958, pp. 177-88. Klein believed that "No living experimenter has done more to advance the art of colour-music than Thomas Wilfred [...]." (Klein, *op. cit.*, p. 16.)

[53] See Klein, *op. cit.*

[54] Hofmann's color theory depended on musical analogy. See, for example, his essay "Search for the Real", 1948, reprinted in S. T. Weeks, B. H. Hayes, Jr., eds., *Search for the Real and Other Essays*, Cambridge, Mass., 1967. See also E. G. Landau, "The French Sources for Hans Hofmann's Ideas on the Dynamics of Color-Created Space," *Arts Magazine*, 51, no. 2, October 1976, pp. 76-81.

[55] See E. Rathbone, "The Role of Music in the Development of Mark Tobey's Abstract Style," *Arts Magazine*, 58, no. 4 (December 1983), pp. 94-100.

[56] Cheney, *A Primer of Modern Art*, p. 177.

PAUL F. WATSON

On a Window in Parnassus

At the center of a famous engraving depicting Mount Parnassus, created in Rome toward 1520 by Marcantonio Raimondi, rises the upper part of a window [Fig. 1]. This man-made addition to the landscape frames a cartellino that presents the engraver's monogram, MAF, set beneath an inscription, "RAPHAEL PINXIT IN VATICANO." What Raphael did paint in the Vatican, where these engraved words direct us, is an equally famous fresco in celebration of Mount Parnassus and the art of poetry, part of the decorations of the Stanza della Segnatura undertaken between 1509 and 1511 [Fig. 2]. But the engraving hardly duplicates the fresco. Sparsely populated and severely composed, Marcantonio's print reproduces instead Raphael's first version of the subject. At the same time Marcantonio fashions with care what is also present in the Vatican, the window around which Raphael was obliged to compose Parnassus. It is this window in Parnassus, as Raimondi presents it, that becomes a means to consider his print as a record of Raphael's thinking as he sets about the task of presenting Parnassus. The window also helps to reveal the richly poetic content of that first thought, related to but distinct from that of the fresco. Marcantonio's window serves as well to define his print as a distinguished work of art in its own right, and one well calculated to appeal to its immediate audience, the papal court of the High Renaissance.

The engraving presents Mount Parnassus as the throne of Apollo and the haunt of distinguished poets. Their world is harsh; only a few laurel trees rise in these steep, rocky hills. At the center sits Apollo who strikes a lyre. Around him gather the Muses, a canonical nine although only a few can be identified by name, such as the Muse of epic poetry, Calliope, who displays her trumpet at Apollo's proper right. To Calliope's left as we

scan the print stands a compact group of poets, Dante, Virgil and Homer who dictates verses to a seated youth. Other poets occupy escarpments of Parnassus, some to converse, other to expostulate and one to contemplate. None of these is immediately identifiable. All, however, wear crowns of laurel, as does Apollo. More laurel wreaths are offered by several cupids, wheeling in the sky above, even though no poet here stands in need of one. All this happens on a small scale, for the print measures only 358 by 472 mm. These dimensions also mean that the viewer may hold Parnassus comfortably in his or her hand and that the engraved sheet has sufficient room for details that are precise and evocative.

Apollo also occupies the center of Parnassus frescoed in the Vatican [Fig. 2]. There, however, he plays a Renaissance viol, just as the attending Muses gain other instruments and attributes. Many poets now crowd the slopes of Parnassus to make a continuum of movement across the painted surface. Many of these can also be recognized at a glance, such as Sappho who sits at the lower left or the poets who look outwards at the right, presumably Raphael's distinguished contemporaries. Parnassus takes on specificity, as these passages show, but it also becomes complex and charmingly collegial because the poets converge upon the center to brush against Raphael's enchanting Muses, the gentle sponsors of their art. At the same time no putti fly through the sky of frescoed Parnassus.[1]

The richness of the fresco and the simplicity of the print suggest that the latter preserves a preliminary version of the former. Such was the contention of Giovanni Pietro Bellori in 1695. More recently John Shearman has investigated evidence not at Bellori's command, such as surviving drawings for the

127

1) Marcantonio Raimondi after Raphael, «Parnassus», The Art Institute of Chicago, Chicago, Illinois. Photo: Museum.

fresco and Raphael's full-dress but small-scale drawings for other projects, to argue that the engraving is an exact record of a lost *modello* for Parnassus. Shearman is also among the few to consider that *Parnassus I*, as he calls the print, preserves Raphael's first conception of what Parnassus implies, the nature of poetry, but in this case thoughts that generalize rather than specify.[2] Shearman's reconstruction of Raphael's working procedure has now found general acceptance and a particular endorsement by two students of Marcantonio and his art, Innis H. Shoemaker and Elizabeth Brown. They date his print around 1517 to 1520. They also draw renewed attention to a rare trial proof, preserved in Cleveland, where large stretches of Parnassus remain unfinished [Fig. 3]. The proof also reveals that Marcantonio worked with an assistant, whose efforts appear on the right-hand side.[3] It is also a collaboration extended through time. At the very least the engravers did their work six years after Raphael finished his fresco and at the most a full decade afterwards. One question these facts raise is why Raphael gave what amounts to his imprimatur to a project that he himself had set aside. Obviously the master deemed it worthy of publica-

2) Raphael, «Parnassus», Stanza della Segnatura, Vatican, Rome. Photo: Musei Vaticani.

tion. Even so: why, and why in this particular form?

The latter question, that of formal presentation, follows from that object so conspicuously set on Parnassus, the Vatican's window. Presumably Marcantonio might have suppressed it, just as he ignores another part of the pictorial field at the Vatican, the semicircular top of the Segnatura's window wall [Fig. 2]. Provision, however, is made for the window even in the proof where it figures as a great rectangular void scored here and there by guide lines [Fig. 3]. In the completed print that void is filled by architecture, a window framed in marble and closed by wooden shutters. Marcantonio takes care to show the textures of stone and wood, suggest the complex profiles of frame and shutters, and even acknowledge the art of metalwork in the form of the shutters' hinges. In consequence his window becomes an artifact set against nature, Apollo's landscape of rock and trees.

The engraved window is also set within nature. Rocky plateaux overlap its marble frame at the lower left and right. A similar situation prevails in the fresco, where a painted frame is partially masked by segments of landscape and by its inhabi-

3) Marcantonio after Raphael, «Parnassus», trial proof, The Cleveland Museum of Art, Cleveland, Ohio, Gift of the Print Club of Cleveland.

tants, such as Sappho. The print can be regarded, then, as a commemoration of pictorial difficulties readily overcome, Raphael's first response to a given and potentially distracting obstacle, the Vatican's window. Dramatizing Raphael's feat, Marcantonio also aligns the window with a rocky shelf, rising at the left, and permits Parnassus' central height to rise behind it to the crest where Homer stands. Consequently, as Shearman observes, the window serves to indicate distances within the landscape with which it is integrated.[4]

Marcantonio preserves Raphael's obstacle, but he takes liberties with it that give the window other functions to perform. His architecture, for example, differs in detail from that to be seen in the Segnatura; the engraved window frame is thick and curving, sculptural by contrast with the thinly moulded border that Raphael paints. The engraver also changes the existing architecture of the room. In the Segnatura the window where Parnassus appears illuminates a relatively deep embrasure, as

Fig. 2 indicates, which is provided with seats. In the engraving that embrasure becomes quite shallow as the shutters' hinges clearly show. With depth denied, the visual role of the window as a closed plane becomes all the more evident. It contrasts with the faceted rockfaces of the landscape before and behind it to stress the authority of the general picture plane, that of the engraved sheet. The window also emphasizes another flat plane, the inscribed cartellino that it encloses. The cartellino, the shutters behind it and the marble frame are all rectangular shapes, as is the engraving itself where Marcantonio gives the scene two borders outlined with the burin, a rectangle nestled within a rectangle. As engraved, the Vatican's window dramatizes an orchestration of geometric forms.

The window suggests that a simple geometry underlies the structure of the print as a whole. Its shuttering even directs us to seek it out. Marcantonio swings the shutters closed upon a mullion whose raised surface is also stippled, and hence

4) Marcantonio after Raphael, «Parnassus», Diagram A.

emphasized. The mullion also receives a thin vertical line dividing it in half. A slip of the burin carries that line downwards a millimeter or so into the plane of the cartellino where it stops just above the second "I" of "PINXIT." The inscription, in other words, is centered upon the line of the mullion. That line also divides the entire window plane into equal halves. Perhaps it may so divide the entire print as well.

What the unassisted eye senses, geometric order, can be easily demonstrated with compasses and a ruler. That exercise begins by designating the corners of the inner border as ABCD, clockwise from the upper left [Fig. 4]. Extend the central line that Marcantonio marks on the window's mullion to the full height of the print to become EF. It yields two important observations. It does divide the print in two, but not into two equal halves because DF is greater than FC. The window is, in fact, then, slightly off-center, as are the various apertures of the Segnatura itself. Although EF shows that geometric analysis has

its limits, it also indicates that it can be illuminating. EF rises to pass through the body of Apollo and the trunk of the tree growing just behind his head. Conforming to what the eye readily senses, EF encourages the construction of other parallels, as indicated by the architecture of the window. Extend its outer marble frame upwards to mark GH and IJ. Although the latter line indicates only an unknown poet laboring through the landscape and thus seems a disappointment, the former passes directly through Homer. GH almost defines his center of gravity. Consequently a geometric scaffolding begins to take on meaning because at two key points it coincides with the most significant figures on Parnassus, antiquity's god of poetry and antiquity's foremost poet.[5]

Further analysis of Marcantonio's print begins with the upper window frame. This is a massive horizontal shape whose unbroken contour also figures in the trial proof [Fig. 3]. Let the upper contour of the lintel be extended to the inner border at

131

5) Marcantonio after Raphael, «Parnassus», Diagram B.

points K and L [Fig. 5]. KL immediately creates a gridwork, like the surface of a Renaissance drawing squared for transfer, to indicate four areas of nearly equal size, each of the shutters and the segments of landscape at either side. KL also yields two vertical units of equal length, KD and LC. At the top corners of the print, A and B, mark lines equal to KD and LC to make AM and BN, respectively. If M is connected to N, the resulting line establishes an upper rectangle matching that generated below by the window: ABNM = KLCD. But line MN also passes just above the head of Homer and just beneath the feet of the putti flying above. Expressed geometrically, MN marks the upper border of a grand rectangle, MNCD, which includes all the earthbound figures of Parnassus, the essential details of their surroundings, and the window. Geometry thus reveals much about Marcantonio's methods as he prepares to engrave. It also evokes Raphael at work.

What geometry defines, MNCD, is a pictorial field matched by other drawings for the Stanza della Segnatura by Raphael or his followers. One analogy is presented by Raphael's own cartoon for the *School of Athens*, a rectangular drawing preserved in the Ambrosiana which confines itself to the

painting's philosophers, their groupings, and the steps where they stand. It corresponds to the lower half of the fresco's pictorial field.[6] An even closer comparison is offered by a drawing in Oxford, an early copy after Raphael for the lower part of Parnassus, but one that records a later stage in the creation of the fresco than the print preserves. Oxford's drawing centers on the void that is the window, the poets standing just to its right and left, and the figures on the hill above. It stops just above the heads of Homer and the standing Muses.[7] This drawing also resembles the area defined by MNCD in Fig. 5, as does the cartoon in Milan. Both drawings document Raphael working in the Segnatura, as he gives his chief attention to complexities of figural composition at the expense of the upper parts of the painting in question, which are the subject, presumably, of other drawings. The evidence for the way Raphael actually proceeds gives weight to what geometry maps out. What the engraved window generates, MNCD, corresponds to a lost *modello* by Raphael for Parnassus.

This conclusion is clouded by a problem because it suggests a crude division of labor. Applied geometry threatens to split the print in two, giving the lower part to Raphael and relegating the

E

K

Q

L

F

6) Marcantonio after Raphael, «Parnassus», Diagram C.

upper section to Raimondi to complete as he pleases. Such a situation has, in fact, been suggested by some who see the putti, confined here by ABNM, as mere filling devices. Others, however, have sensed that they serve an iconographic purpose consistent with the scene as a whole.[8] At this stage the question can be resolved by other means, stylistic analysis and a final geometric exercise.

The cupids Marcantonio engraves are characteristic of Raphael's art at the time of the Segnatura, and they perform functions consistent with the decoration of that room. In engraved Parnassus they twist and spiral through the air, like the earthbound Christ Child of the Bridgewater Madonna, painted just before Raphael came to Rome late in 1508, or the seaborne Eros who guides the chariot of Galatea in the Farnesina, frescoed toward 1512.[9] The cupids just above Homer also resemble the putti who bear the Gospels in the *Disputà*, the first of Raphael's frescoes in the Stanza della Segnatura. The laurel-bearing putti thus echo that fresco, just as Dante is carried over from it and set on Parnassus in reverse. The cupids also correspond to five earth-bound putti who assist three Virtues in the fresco that faces Parnassus.[10] One cupid

makes a more particular liason. He flies at the upper right, looking over his left shoulder; if painted in the Segnatura, he would acknowledge the scene set at the right of Parnassus, the *School of Athens*. He and his companions, like Dante below them, reflect Raphael's response to the situation confronting him in his room, how to connect frescoes of varied subject with one another.

The engraved putti fit in with the Segnatura and Raphael's style of that time, but these circumstances do not by themselves prove that they would fit into the area reserved for Parnassus. That field is a lunette whose form Raphael emphasizes by a proscenium arch painted in perspective [Fig. 2]. Since that arch also reduces wall space, there seems to be little or no room for putti here. The gridwork of Fig. 5, however, suggests other possibilities. In that diagram two of the lines generated by the window, EF and KL, intersect like some inverted cross just below Apollo's feet. Let that point of intersection be O [Fig. 6]. The result resembles the radii of a circle whose circumference has yet to be traced. That is not actually the case because the off-centering of the window ensures that KO is greater than OE. Nevertheless, an experiment conducted with compasses pro-

133

duces an illuminating result. Let O be the center of a circle whose radius is KO. Swing the compasses to produce an arc passing through EF at P to end at Q in the right outer border. KPQ is a semicircle that matches the proscenium arch Raphael paints in the Segnatura; they spring from the same place, exactly opposite the upper contour of the window frame. KPQ also does violence to the topmost cupids, slicing through wings, garlands, and even heads. With some adjustments, however, all these figures could find room to fly in the projected lunette.

The question of the cupids so resolved, we may return to the engraving proper to assess its archaeological value as a trace of Raphael at work. His hand is present in the earthbound parts of Parnassus, the area around the window, which has counterparts in the study preserved at Oxford and in other compositional drawings. What geometry creates, rectangle MNCD in Fig. 5, corresponds to Raphael's major *modello*. What lies above, the putti, reflects the master's hand equally well. In this instance, however, it seems prudent to suppose several smaller drawings because the cupids echo one another, as in the case of the putto second from the right, the putto at top left and his companion, who is also his mirror image. These all derive from a single model, a small drawing like those surviving for the putti of the *Disputà* and the ceiling above.[11] The engraver combines several such drawings to adapt what was designed for a lunette to this field, an engraved rectangle. Along the way there are compromises and adjustments, as in the relative positions of the cupids. The engraving, after all, represents a collaboration but in this case one between an artist who invents by drawing and an artist who understands the logic of those inventions very well.

The sense of collaboration is heightened by the trial proof at Cleveland [Fig. 3]. It reads almost as a sketch, thanks in large part to the blank void of the window. The sketchiness in part reflects Marcantonio at work, as the finished plate further indicates. There is a pentimento, for example, in the upper left corner where a laurel tree bursts into foliage. First Marcantonio brings it to a careful enough finish in the proof, stopping its growth just beneath the upper border, and then changes his mind to rework the tree and let it continue under the frame. This reworking is Marcantonio's particular concern because, as Fig. 6 indicates, the left corner would have disappeared under the proscenium arch. Shoemaker and Brown have observed another pentimento at the lower right where a poet makes his way up Parnassus. In the proof he is wedged between two trees, but in the finished version he gains weight and movement thanks to a wind-tossed drape.[12] The change corrects an engraver's flaw. It may also indicate an amendment to Raphael's original design which perhaps at this point remained unfinished. Unmarked, too, is the window which must reflect Raphael at work, leaving it

blank because it is an architectural given. With due caution, then, the proof can be seen as a closer approximation to Raphael's original design than the final engraving is.

The proof must now undergo surgery to reveal Raphael's first thoughts for Parnassus. Apply the area bounded by MNCD in the engraving to the proof, which does indicate the contours of the window with precision and hence is susceptible to geometric analysis. Crop the proof at these points, MNCD, to make Fig. 7. The result brings Raphael's original design for Parnassus into a sharp focus. The void of the window is matched by the blankness of the backdrop to give the sense of drawing, carefully detailed to be sure but preliminary nevertheless, where the figures predominate.

To see Parnassus abbreviated in this way is also to sense the artist's mandate, depict Apollo with many poets, and the literary sources underlying the commission. At the left, for example, Dante follows in the footsteps of Virgil, just as he does in the *Divine Comedy* and its innumerable Renaissance illustrations, and, as in that poem, these two cross Homer's path.[13] Virgil indicates the Muses with Apollo, centered above the window. They evoke the florid words of Statius:

> [...] cantu musarum nobile mulcens
> concilium citharaeque manus insertus Apollo
> Parnassi summo spectabat ab aethere terras.

Which is to say: with song Apollo was charming the noble council of the Muses and, with one hand placed upon his lyre, was gazing down upon the lands from the heavenly peak of Mount Parnassus.[14] At this stage Raphael visualizes with directness what he reads, or is directed to read, to create the pictorial counterpart of an anthology of verses.

To impose visual order upon his textual sources and give them a common theme, Raphael fashions a configuration that is stately and symmetrical. Groups are deployed around the window's void and above it in a way that recalls the most familiar and majestic of Renaissance picture types, the altarpiece called then and now a *sacra conversazione*. Just as the Virgin Mary sits at the center of such an altarpiece to reign over her eternal court of Heaven, so does Apollo command the heights of his. Just as angels may surround the Virgin who is their queen, so do the Muses envelop Apollo. Just as saints from many times and places may expand Mary's court to make matching groups at left and right, so do the poets marshal themselves into balancing clusters on the peripheries of Parnassus.[15] The general type to which Raphael turns, the *sacra conversazione*, is also combined with a more particular variant, the *Disputà* of the Stanza della Segnatura. Apart from quotations, such as Dante, the composition of Fig. 7 recalls that fresco's earthbound parts, a semicircular grouping and then sub-groupings of prelates, and its celestial focus, Christ seated

7) Marcantonio after Raphael, «Parnassus», trial proof, detail.

between the Virgin and the Baptist. It is as if that latter motif, the Deesis, were brought down to earth to join with the exponents of the Godhead, the theologians, on either side. There are structural borrowings as well in the form of flanking figures gesturing inwards toward the center, although their placement here is determined by the Vatican's window, which confines them to the foreground.[16]

The blank of the window also emphasizes the visual autonomy that each group enjoys, despite the authority of the underlying compositional type. A generous fissure of blank paper, for example, separates Dante's pilgrimage from the Statian council of the Muses. This is a confederation of forms but not yet a union. One group is even capable of independence, that of Apollo with the Muses, as its afterlife in the Cinquecento indicates. In 1562, for example, Giulio Sanuto published a remarkable print in which he lifted the Muses from Raphael's engraved Parnassus, deleted Apollo, and set them down in a landscape to preside over the flaying of Marsyas, which their lord undertakes.[17] Sanuto's task was made easy by Raphael. As he assembles the Muses, he devises strong visual boundaries

for them as a group, a drapery fluttering at the left, a veil inflated into a curve at the right. These forms, the visual clichés of ancient art and testimony as well to the breezes stirred by the putti above, echo one another to define the Muses as a self-contained unit. Raphael's art gives them an authority virtually architectural; his forms in movement are like the curving volutes of a Renaissance church facade.

Raphael's formation of the Muses reflects the singular task he faced in the Segnatura, that of combining old forms in new ways. The Muses are an instructive example. They had made their way into art long before Raphael's time, of course, but never in the way they are depicted here. In classical art the Muses often form a frieze to adorn a sarcophagus where each stands to display her particular attribute; on occasion one goddess may turn to converse with a companion. During the early Renaissance they figure in pictures painted in series, such as panels devised in Urbino by Giovanni Santi, Raphael's father, who follows Quattrocento precedent by depicting each Muse and her attribute in isolation. Much more rarely do the Muses appear as a group on Parnassus with Apollo. A charming instance is a cassone panel painted in Siena around 1470 [Fig. 8]. Although it has been cut down at the right, it presents the surviving Muses with everything else associated with Parnassus, such as the god of poetry, a poet who reclines on the steps of a fountain, and twinned peaks. Each Muse here, however, occupies herself with her particular art so that each exists in some invisible capsule of space. As this panel, Santi's series and other works indicate, the chief precedent for depicting the Muses was a mode essentially additive.[18] An alternative involves choreography, in which the Muses discard their instruments and with them separate identities to link hands in a dance, as in Mantegna's *Parnassus* and its late medieval sources.[19] Both the choreographic and additive modes demonstrate antecedents for Raphael's group, but no true precedent. Thinking about Parnassus, Raphael devises a new way to present the Muses, consistent with his general conception of Parnassus as a disguised *sacra conversazione* and inspired perhaps by Statius' verses, *nobile [...] concilium*. Raphael groups his Muses in repose.

Raphael creates his new entity, the Muses in council, by establishing a strong external boundary and fashioning equally strong internal links. Some of Apollo's audience he subjects to the most loving and gentle of bonds. At the left, for example, three Muses stand in mutual embrace, touching one another on arms and shoulders. Three more link themselves at the right and intimately so, for one Muse touches her sister on her breast. These sub-groups imitate the actions of the Graces. Those goddesses, the three handmaidens of Venus, are also the subject of an early panel by Raphael who may recall, too, astrological charts from the late Quattrocento in which the Graces are associated with the planets and the Muses under the rule of Apollo. But there the relationship between Muses and Graces is only intellectual, not visual.[20] What Raphael does here, to make some Muses behave as the Graces do, has the effect of uniting all in a loving unity whose focus is Apollo and the music he makes.

Raphael's reference to the Graces partakes of a broader pattern that unites his central group: composing by threes. There are three Muses, for example, who devote their entire attention to Apollo: two press against trees to regard him, just behind a third who sits at his left, face turned in his direction. She is also one of three – and only three – Muses to bear an instrument. The rest have none, an utter departure from precedent. Here only Calliope displays her trumpet, a Muse at the left whose dance-like step may indicate that she mimes the part of Terpsichore has an unstrung lyre, and a third sits to display a panpipe. That instrument is not a traditional attribute for any Muse, although Euterpe sometimes plays a single pipe, sometimes two. But there may be other candidates.[21] What can be said is that only three goddesses on Parnassus have

instruments. But there is a fourth musician, Apollo striking his lyre to charm the others, as Statius says. Enthroned at the center, he also completes a triad of seated figures.

Another and more powerful pattern underlies Apollo's court, an order imposed by hierarchy. Unlike his Renaissance predecessors, such as the author of the Sienese cassone [Fig. 8], Raphael creates a distinction between those who may sit and those who must stand. Among the most privileged of the former group is Calliope, who occupies the position of honor on Apollo's right. She sits, in fact, upon a natural throne: a block of stone whose front face is smooth and polished and whose cubic form is further stressed by the straight fall of her robe. Calliope's counterpart, placed on Apollo's left and therefore less honored, must make do with a sloping ridge upon which she props herself. These distinctions of rank and precedence, inherent in Raphael's general model, the *sacra conversazione*, are echoed by differences in instruments. The panpipe, for example, is the most primitive of instruments because, as Ovid's myth of Pan and Syrinx shows, it is merely hollow reeds plucked from some riverbank and joined together with melted beeswax. Nobler is Calliope's attribute, metal shaped by fire and art to make stirring music and serve as the sign of eternal fame. But nobler still is Apollo's stringed lyre. As the comic judgment of Midas or the tragic fate of Marsyas demonstrate, plucked strings make a music more divine than that of wind-blown pipes.[22] A Muse also possesses a lyre, but she cannot play it, for it is unstrung. Only Apollo has the honor here of making music. He stands highest in the hierarchy of this council, just as he occupies its center to become focus of meditation.

The instruments on Parnassus contribute to another ordering pattern that allies the Muses with the poets on either side. Panpipes, lyres and the trumpet are classical in form, not absolutely so by any archeological standard but demonstrably so by comparison with precedents from the recent past, such as the Sienese cassone whose musicians play modern lutes, organs and viols [Fig. 8]. Classicism manifests itself more generally in matters of dress. The Muses all wear himations and chitons, while Apollo clothes himself *all'antica* in a short tunic and a long mantle, thrown over a muscular shoulder. What Apollo wears becomes the dress of the poets nearby. Some wear only a tunic kilted round the waist, like the author gesturing second from the right, others such as Homer have very long tunics, as befits that poet's age, and nearly all wrap mantles round themselves in varied ways. All, that is, except Dante. But his Trecento costume stresses the general rule, a unifying classicism of dress and feature.

From Raphael in Rome around 1510 we may expect nothing less than a classical Parnassus. In Rome the monuments of classical art inspire him to a classicism that goes beyond form to the inner life of antique art. The Muses resemble those carved

8) Benvenuto di Giovanni, «Apollo and the Muses», Detroit Institute of Arts, Founders Society Purchase, Membership Fund. Photo: Daris.

on Roman sarcophagi, but as the sculptor first created them, noble but animated. Raphael's seated Muses are adapted from a particular sarcophagus installed in the Vatican in these years, marked by seated captives whose rhythmic pose the Muse with the pipes quite clearly and Calliope more subtly echo. Calliope's majesty owes even more to a famous classical sculpture, the *Ariadne* of the Vatican, installed there in 1512 but recorded in Rome by 1508. Similarly, the youth seated opposite Calliope paraphrases the Spinario, displayed then and now upon the Capitoline Hill. Even when more modern models are studied, such as Michelangelo's unfinished St. Matthew, a book-bearing athlete in heroic contrapposto who is the source both for Virgil and a poet standing at the extreme left, they are assimilated to the norms of classical art.[23] One consequence is to restore the subject to its classical origins, especially by contrast with Quattrocento precedents, such as the cassone from Siena [Fig. 8]. Another is to impose what is peculiar to classical art, its sense of the general and the ideal, upon this company so that the poets who so greatly resemble one another in feature, dress and pose, register as just that, classical poets but seemingly no poet in particular. Dante becomes the exception that proves a generalizing rule.

Visual classicism may generalize but it can also specify with illuminating results. Homer's scribe provides a notable instance. This muscular youth crosses his legs in the manner of the Spinario to reveal that he wears trousers, loosely fitted. No one else on Parnassus does. His pantaloons, however, are authentic ancient dress, for they are also worn by the captive barbarians of the Vatican's sarcophagus cited just above. The same costume appears in an equally classical context on the wall where Parnassus is painted [Fig. 2]. To the lower left is a grisaille panel painted toward 1520 which shows Alexander the Great depositing his copy of Homer's *Iliad* in the tomb of Achilles [Fig. 9]. The actual work is performed by a bearded man in trousers.[24] He is there because Achilles, so it is believed, lies buried in Sigeum on the southern shore of the Hellespont, near Troy and Phyrgia, whose natives in antiquity were trousered.[25] Costume, then, denotes ethnicity and place. It performs an equally precise function in engraved Parnassus, where a trousered figure serves a Greek poet. Homer, it was believed, came from Smyrna, set on the eastern shores of the Aegean not far from Phrygia and Troy. That location is specified in a pictorial cycle that Raphael knew well, a series of famous men painted by Justus van Ghent in the Ducal Palace of Urbino, where Homer who gropes in his blindness is designated as "OMERO SMYRNAEO."[26] The Phyrgianic trousers that Raphael gives Homer's servant become the pictorial counterpart to Justus' epithet, showing that he is a Greek from Asia Minor, like his Ionian master, and hence "Smyrnaeo."

Homer's scribe and his costume make other equally specific contributions to this generalized scene. His attentive pose, his Asiatic trousers and his lack of a laurel crown all demonstrate that he is a servant, expert in Homer's native dialect, and nothing more. Raphael stresses that he is no poet, even though commentators from Vasari onward have persisted in identifying him as one and in the case of the fresco, even by name.[27] Attending Homer, this youth also sharpens the viewer's sense of Homer's particular time, place and language, which is heightened by the poet's neighbours, Dante and Virgil. These three poets do nothing less than epitomize the history and geography of poetry: first Homer, far away in ancient Smyrna; then Virgil, the foremost Latin poet of Augustian Rome; and last,

9) Raphael, with assistance, «Alexander at the Tomb of Achilles», Stanza della Segnatura, Vatican, Rome. Photo: Musei Vaticani.

Dante, for modern Italy and its Tuscan vernacular. Homer's trousered scribe documents, almost in the manner of a footnote, Raphael's poetic history.

Homer's group also stands for the history of a poetic genre. These three are all epic poets, who occupy the highest part of Parnassus, as Fig. 7 demonstrates, and who stand close to the Muse of Epic poetry, Calliope, with her trumpet. They also raise a possibility for Parnassus as a whole that figural grouping and spatial placement connote poetic categories arranged in a certain order.

Another oddity of costume indicates that Raphael does compose by genres. Just beneath Homer's scribe stands an author who leans against a tree to observe a conversation. At first glance this figure is no different from the others, all barefoot, mantled, tuniced and crowned. This particular laureate, however, wears a loosely sleeved tunic which breaks over a pair of breasts. These rounded forms, to be sure, are delicate in scale and veiled by shadow. They exist, nevertheless, and their existence Raphael draws attention to. This writer is associated closely with two others who are masculine; tightly fitted tunics model chests that are broad and flat. By comparison their companion has surprisingly narrow shoulders, even when foreshortening is taken into account. Moreover, this writer echoes the pose and proportions of the Muse standing at the extreme left of Apollo's court who turns her head to observe the epic poets. The formal rhyme that Raphael makes is deliberate, suggesting that the deity on the summit and the laureate in the foreground belong to the same sex. On Parnassus Raphael sets a poetess. She is his first version of that poetess who occupies such a prominent place in the fresco, Sappho of Lesbos [Fig. 2].

Engraved Sappho, it must be observed, is by no means as recognizable as her frescoed successor. She dresses like her male companions, wears her hair as they do, and allows herself no feminine frills. Though she echoes a distant Muse, she is hardly as voluptuous as the goddesses of poetry. Sappho's muted femininity is, however, perfectly consistent with her portrayal in classical poetry. Horace by way of famous example calls her ''mascula Sappho,'' an epithet interpreted in antiquity and the Renaissance to mean that a virile spirit animated her verses or that her talent was as good as any man's.[28] Raphael's manlike poetess becomes the visual counterpart to these commentaries and their Horatian source: Sappho is defined as *mascula*. Perhaps Sappho's proximity to the poets at the left, the direction of her gaze and the languor of her pose may also characterize her as classical poets and Renaissance scholars did, as a poetess who not only writes about love but is possessed by love, a love that directs itself towards men: Sappho *amatrix*.[29]

Sappho's identity suggests a collective identity for her associates. It is prompted by the author whom Raphael consults, Horace, who on this occasion links himself with Sappho and others, including Alcaeus and Archilochus, to encapsulate the history of a genre, lyric verse. Sappho, in other words, is famed as a lyricist.[30] Here on Parnassus Sappho is intimately allied with authors who form an autonomous sub-unit, centered around a tree and framed by a great shelf of rock. Theirs is a group as tightly-knit as Homer's above, where visual autonomy implies a common poetic endeavor. In this instance the presence of Sappho specifies what that endeavor is: lyric verse.

No other poet here or on the other side of the window reveals his name. Poetic identity, nevertheless, can be established in a general way and with it a sense of poetic ordering in the landscape. The means are suggested by the way that Raphael himself identifies Sappho. He lights upon a verbal paradox that lends itself to depiction, and he relies upon a convention of poetic biography that confuses artistic with human personality. Raphael's imagination is guided by the writings of poets and the ways in which those poets were read. The figure of Dante offers an even more obvious case in point. He acts, as observed above, as he does in his poem, a pilgrim guided by Virgil: ''Allor si mosse, e io li tenni retro,'' and then he moved and I came on behind him.[31] On Raphael's Parnassus, however, Virgil the guide points Dante the pilgrim not to scenes in the afterlife that bring spiritual salvation but rather to Apollo's court and the trumpet that Calliope displays. Here Raphael adapts what there is to read in the *Divine Comedy*, a poetic mime described by a poetic voice.

The notion of the poetic voice was also a commonplace of Renaissance literary criticism. An instance is given by the

Florentine Bartolommeo della Fonte, whose *De poetice*, of ca. 1490, typifies the poetic theories of humanism. Concerning himself with poetic genres in Book III, della Fonte categorizes poetry by voice to establish, among others, what he calls the common mode where both the poet and his characters speak – as Dante converses with Virgil in the *Divine Comedy*.[32] Raphael was neither a critic nor a theorist, but as a painter he understood the power of the poet's voice at first hand. There are verses by Raphael in which he writes in the first person to assume a role like Petrarch in his *Canzoniere*, the lover who sighs and aspires. They are preserved on the working drawings for the *Disputà*, undertaken before Parnassus. Raphael's verses are in a sense working drawings as well because he writes poetry, as John Onians argues, to learn the art of poetry for himself, to grasp through experience its laws and patterns, and in a more pragmatic way to prepare for the task of depicting poets on Parnassus.[33] That experience equips Raphael for a particularly daunting commission, for never before in the history of Renaissance art, as the Sienese cassone shows [Fig. 8], had so many poets gathered on Parnassus.

What Raphael understands by versifying, the role a poet assumes as he speaks, finds particular expression at the right side of Parnassus where a poet receives a hillock of his own. Utterly still, feet pressed together with no attempt at counterpoise or motion, he occupies himself in looking. This laureate contemplates the summit of Parnassus to fix his gaze on one object there, the pipes of Pan held by a seated Muse. He also has an object of his own, not a bound codex like those which other poets at the left bring to Parnassus, but a slender tube-like implement, held casually in his left hand. It is difficult to identify because two poets conversing before him mask it. It can be read as a wand or switch, perhaps, or a musical instrument like the modern piccolo, or even as a rolled-up scrap of paper. These alternatives are supplied by Virgil in his capacity as a bucolic poet, the author of the *Eclogues*. In these ten short works the narrator and his companions are solitary dwellers in nature, shepherds and rustics equipped with staff and crook who also make music, usually with a slender reed in imitation of Pan their god, as well as penning verse on stray pieces of paper. What Virgil here creates is a composite portrait of the pastoral poet.[34] It is that verbal portrait which Raphael recreates here in the person of his solitary poet who contemplates the instrument peculiar to rustic poets, the pipes of Pan, just as Virgil himself on the other side directs Dante to the attribute of epic art, Calliope's trumpet.[35]

In establishing the *persona* of a pastoral poet, Raphael creates an identity for the Muse he singles out. Rustic poets, so Virgil says, do have a Muse of their own, not someone grand like Calliope but rather a goddess like them, rural and sylvan. In his sixth *Eclogue*, a masterly evocation of bucolic poetry in history,

Virgil names her: Thalia.[36] That is a name usually associated with comedy, but in antiquity, as Virgil suggests, and during the Renaissance Thalia had other arts to nurture. She is the patroness of rustic poets because she is the most earthbound of all the Muses, sometimes personifying nature in her most verdant aspect. She is also a Muse who keeps silent. Raphael's pastoral Muse rests her body upon the earth and even presses her hand against its soil to become earthbound. Even though she has an instrument, it can make no music because the reeds of her pipe, as Eugene Winternitz observes, are not cut diagonally to produce tones. Keeping silent, Raphael's Muse is also Virgil's Thalia.[37]

Poetic mime and poetic voice suggest a role for the men who stand before the pastoral poet. They have a territory of their own, a grassy knoll unsurely rendered by Marcantonio's assistant. They are further isolated by two trees rising directly behind the bearded man at the right, which emphasize where these poets are and what they do. They converse, but in an expansive fashion characteristic of this side of Parnassus, generally more active than the opposite static side, a contrast that Raphael was to develop as a governing principle in the Stanza d'Eliodoro.[38] Here the energy of these poets also takes on a histrionic air; they resemble dramatic actors as depicted in late antique and early medieval manuscripts of Terence.[39] There is also something theatrical about their juxtaposition, a concentrated contrasting of youth and maturity, repose and energy, contemplation and exhortation. By association, this pair seems to enact the particular conditions of dramatic poetry, divided into two forms, comedy and tragedy, which alternate upon a single stage. The pointed contrast of ages, more strongly marked here than anywhere else, evokes an observation Horace makes in the *Ars Poetica* that tragedy preceded comedy in time and is thus the senior dramatic art.[40] A senior poet here in similar fashion assumes a commanding and dramatic role.

The sense of poetic category that mime indicates depends as well upon the landscape and the stages it makes. Parnassus rises to be riven into four discrete parts, whose divisions the engravers deepen as they complete their task. In the trial proof, for example [Figs. 3, 7], the bucolic poet stands behind a slight declivity in the landscape which in the final print becomes a miniature chasm. Similarly, and as noted previously, the shelf before which Sappho stands becomes aligned with the window. As Raphael first designed it, or as the engraver first fashioned it, this is a formidable enough obstacle. It is difficult to imagine that poets even as muscular as she could easily scale it. In the final print Marcantonio adjusts its right contour, nocking it so that it can accommodate the window frame in the manner of mortise-and-tenon construction. As a result, all of Parnassus takes on the sense of barriers established and compartments formed where poets take their places in an ordering as hierarchical as that of the Muses around Apollo. Lyric outpost, epic summit, pastoral knoll, dramatic ledge these areas might be named. As Horace says, ''Let each form of Poetry occupy the proper place allotted to it.''[41]

The fourfold partitioning of Parnassus finds an echo at its summit, where Apollo sits. He is one of four to possess an instrument, two of which can also be linked to specific poets and poetic genres. Above him grow four laurel trees, present even in the truncated proof [Fig. 7]. In the print as completed, however, the trees rise to form one dense canopy of laurel, a foliate crown for a single and magisterial god, Apollo himself. In similar fashion, as poets observe, there may be many forms of poetry, but ultimately it is an art that speaks with a single voice. Even Apollo comes to encourage those who play the pipes of Pan, as Virgil affirms in his *Eclogues*.[42]

Equally evocative of the condition of poetry as a whole is a mime enacted on the right side of Parnassus. Three poets draw near Apollo and the Muses. The decorum of place that Horace lays down suggests that they be considered epic poets. If so, they are obliged to labor their way up to the summit. An author turns in mid-journey to gesture toward that goal and encourage his colleague, set behind two trees, who lags behind. Theirs is the situation of Dante and Virgil, wayfarer and guide, repeated in reverse but made more difficult. The poet framed by trees puts his right hand behind his guide, as if to grasp his mantle or clutch his arm. Exhorted to scale this mountain, he needs help to find his way. Even more arduous is the situation confronting the third member of this group. Moving to the left of his gesturing colleague, this poet wraps his mantle round his body as he climbs the far slopes of Parnassus. He also looks downward and to his right. It is as if he sees some deep chasm opening beside him as he negotiates a narrow mountain track. What he does is also emphasized by the grid that underlies this print [Fig. 4] and is further stressed by the engravers who clarify his action and magnify his role in yet another revision of the proof [Fig. 7]. This poet in difficulty becomes important, then, even if he has no name. That is because he acts out a poetic commonplace, as do his companions, that poetry is extraordinarily difficult to write, whether it be a multivolumed epic or a two-line epigram. The pangs of composition are expressed by metaphors of travel. Narrow is the poet's path, Horace asserts. Echoing him, Propertius notes that the road that leads to the Muses is not broad. For Virgil the slopes of Parnassus are steep and lonely: ''Sed me Parnasi deserta per ardua dulcis / raptat amor.''[43] Mountaineering becomes a prime metaphor for poetic difficulty and aspiration, which Raphael and Marcantonio depict by these precipitous slopes which poets strive to climb.

The mountaineering poets participate in a more general play of form that suggests the larger significance of the scene as a whole. Leftwards they move to contribute to visual accents that counter the general rightward descent of the mountain itself. These begin with the pastoral poet who closes the composition in his corner, continue with sweeping gestures before and behind him, and then crest with the Muses, some of whom turn to their right. Thalia and Calliope do this, as does Apollo. He looks toward Homer as he declaims his verses. As the poet speaks the god strikes his lyre, not merely to charm the Muses as Statius says, but to accompany the poet and perhaps to inspire him. Apollo surrenders some of his majesty to honor Homer, singled out by other means as well, such as the left-moving accents to which mountaineering poets contribute and the underlying grid [Fig. 4], to become the true narrative focus of Parnassus.

What does Homer say? One answer is given by his trousered Smyrnean scribe. Folding his mantle over crossed legs to make an impromptu desk, he raises a pen and cocks his head to catch his master's words and dash them down. He prepares to take dictation. If Homer has just begun to speak, then he must make an invocation: ''Sing, Muse,'' opens the *Iliad*: ''Sing, Muse'' begins the *Odyssey*. But the Muse who inspires him will not sing of the wrath of Achilles or the voyage of Ulysses, as Homer himself indicates. His right hand moves in concert with his speech, but as it does its index finger points downwards. That gesture within a gesture is enough to show that Homer's epic voice celebrates the very soil upon which he stands.

Elsewhere on Parnassus others echo Homer's theme. The poets standing at the extremities of left and right point downwards to their particular haunts of turf and rock. The bearded poet at the right dramatizes the tale to include all Parnassus in his gesturing. At its summit Homer's particular Muse, Calliope, allows her left hand to relax and by so doing draw attention to the crest she occupies. The pastoral Muse, Virgil's Thalia, presses an index finger to this same earth. So Raphael suggests a common discourse whose subject unites all poets, epic, lyric, dramatic or pastoral: Parnassus itself.

The meaning of that general discourse is revealed by a particular conversation conducted by the lyric poets on their ledge. Around a single tree they gather. One poet points downwards to its roots and the soil sustaining them, albeit with some difficulty, as he must hold his book of verses at the same time. A companion counters his gesture to point upwards and touch this same tree's bark. His act focuses poetic discourse on this laurel, where it grows and what it may signify. Perhaps these poets tell the poetic fable of Daphne, living nymph once but laurel now, whose would-be lover Apollo first fell in love with her on this very spot and then took her foliage as his own crown, as he still does on the summit, an evergreen emblem of victory, fame and art.[44] That conversation's tone is suggested by the poet touching the tree: grave but gentle is his countenance. Against that laurel Sappho rests. Her stance, in fact, requires its support. There is an echo here of the Sienese cassone of a generation before, where another poet reposes on Parnassus, but in his case on the steps of a fountain [Fig. 8]. In engraved Parnassus, however, a tree sustains a poetess. To her right another laureate who indicates its roots also supports a book in his pointing hand, as if to make a connection between folios of verse, a tree bearing foliage and the leaves he wears. The lyric poets suggest that the laurel is a mystery.

A formal maneuver completes the mystery of the laurel. Upward grows this single laurel to rise above the lyric poets and shade the epic writers behind. As it grows, a branch divides to make two arching curves, one dipping down toward Homer, the other ascending rightwards to Apollo's central grove. There a putto flies leftwards burdened by laurel wreaths. As engraved, he comes from behind that cluster of foliage but his twisting flight also suggests that he emerges from it. From Apollo's grove come the poets' crowns, all this says, wreaths that are the true poet's due reward as tokens of eternal glory. Many poets from antiquity to Raphael's time say that in their verses, among them Propertius who cites Homer as a chief instance of poetry's evergreen fame. But Apollo's gift, the laurel, is also a talisman. It can give inspiration to those who seek its shade or wear its leaves, as Statius says, who calls his own poetic frenzy laurel-wreathed, *laurigero*.[45] The repose of Sappho, who leans against a laurel to make it her staff and prop, evokes this same belief but in the restrained way that marks this Parnassus.

Sappho's particular tree inaugurates a grander and even more mystic pattern. As noted earlier, Marcantonio revises it to let it grow under the print's border. It becomes the tallest tree on Parnassus. Consequently it begins a gentle visual progress through clusters of laurel across the page and downward to the right. There arboreal movement concludes with the overlapping branches of paired laurels. What begins with one tree ends in two. In between rise the four laurels crowning Apollo. The flora of Parnassus, in other words, grow in patterns. Their ordering can be expressed as simple numbers, as in the laurels framing the scene at left and right: $1 \times 2 = 2$. The central copse, when factored in, creates an order $- 2 \times 2 = -$ that is harmonic. The eye perceives an arithmetical accumulation as well: $1 + 2 + 4 = 7$. Those organic forms whose texture the engraver so skillfully renders culminate in the most evocative of all numbers.

Seven is also a sum that can be computed beneath the trees. The pipes of Pan, Thalia's instrument, have exactly seven reeds. And Apollo's own lyre, completed after Marcantonio engraved the trial proof, sounds with seven strings [cf. Fig. 3]. These instruments connect the figure seven with music and with Apollo whose shrine seven-laurelled Parnassus is. In Apollo, then, precise meanings for the print's numerical pattern should be sought and can be found.[46]

It is Virgil who guides the artist's hand in matters of numerical detail. In his capacity as a pastoral poet, he gives a fellow poet panpipes composed of seven uneven hemlock-stalks, transposed here to the pastoral Muse but left uncut.[47] Composing as an epic poet, Virgil depicts the Elysian Fields, laurel-groved, the haunt of a Thracian priest who strikes his lyre to make seven clear notes. Virgil's image is explained by Servius, his most influential commentator, who identifies the Thracian as Orpheus, the fabled inventor of music and poetry and the first to discover the harmony made by the spheres, not all nine of them because our earth and the *primum mobile* make no sound, but rather seven; so the music struck by Orpheus, seven clear notes, is the music of the universe.[48] But Apollo's lyre has seven strings, too, as Macrobius asserts.[49] Divine musicians like Apollo need no more and no less to sound what Pliny the Elder on the authority of Pythagoras calls the *diapason*, that harmony reflecting the musical intervals separating the planets as they move.[50] Such a harmony even Thalia might sound on her pipes, if they were to be cut. And such a harmony is evoked on a grander scale by the laurel trees that grow on Apollo's mountain. They rise to image what Sir Philip Sidney would call ''the planet-like Musicke of *Poetrie*.''[51]

Sidney's phrase and Virgil's verse conjure up an even grander idea: poetry as an art truly divine because poets speak through inspiration. That is an old belief, for which Plato in *Ion* gives a classical formulation, and in Raphael's time it remained the prevailing view among those concerned with poetics, such as Bartolommeo della Fonte, cited earlier, or that more fervid Platonist, Cristoforo Landino, who speaks of poetry as a *furore divino*. In a general way, as Landino proposes, the image of Apollo upon Parnassus is a figure for that doctrine.[52] Engraved Parnassus and the *modello* it reflects, however, downplay any expression of Platonic exaltation; even inspired Homer remains dignified in his uttering. If there is little of *furore* in Landino's sense, there is much that is *divino*: the mysteries suggested by the laurel, the insistence on numbers, and above all the governing figural pattern, the *sacra conversazione*, the Renaissance image of the court of Heaven. Perhaps there are intimations of divinity as well in the odd number of poets laureate on Parnassus, exactly thirteen as were Christ and his apostles, an association encouraged by the view that the poetic vocation is a priesthood. Where these poets take their stand is also enchanted, perhaps even holy, ground. Here trees grow in Pythagorean harmonies, here the earth sustaining them shapes itself into natural niches and stages and here at the summit rise ''seats in the living stone,'' as Virgil says.[53]

Raphael's mountainous landscape, which the poets encourage us to examine, reflects an oddly playful approach to poetic descriptions of Parnassus. His seats in the living stone, such as

Calliope's, are occasioned by the decision to amass the Muses into a stately council on the one side and to include a scribe for Smyrnean Homer on the other. As a consequence the crest of Parnassus has two peaklets, in conformity with that which poetic fiction and geographic fact both maintain, that Parnassus has two summits. They also appear as miniature mountains in the Sienese version of Parnassus [Fig. 8]. Apollo makes one summit his shrine; the Muses by their fabled spring occupy the other. Virgil's ascent to Parnassus, *Sed me Parnasi deserta*, maps out a traditional terrain: first steep slopes, then lonely heights rapturously traversed, and at the last "a narrow track … which turns down by a gentle slope to the Castalian spring."[54] Where Virgil ends his journey, the Muses' spring, is yet another metaphor of poetic inspiration, or at least refreshment, and as such it figures prominently in the Sienese cassone. On Raphael's first Parnassus, however, there is no spring whatsoever, even though there is ample room here for it to flow. The poets point out a landscape that, in the light of poetic orthodoxy, seems capricious, twin summits reduced to convenient seats, rising in an arid place where no poet can refresh himself.

All that singular landscape is the theme debated by the poets who conclude Parnassus, the dramatic figures at the lower right, who also indicate a new topic of conversation. Pausing in mid-stride, a youthful laureate points down to their particular place, just as a lyric poet opposite indicates his particular corner. His bearded companion, whose pose Raphael studied with great care as several drawings show,[55] pivots, spreading his arms and opening his hands to indicate both his stage and what rises behind it. Where we move, he says, and where Apollo sits are as one. At the same time, this same poet points out a place of equal importance. As the trial proof and its abbreviation clearly indicate [Fig. 7], he is gesturing toward the void that is the Vatican's window. This too, he seems to say, is Parnassus.

If painted in the Stanza della Segnatura on the wall reserved for Parnassus [Fig.2], Raphael's dramatic poet would have indicated an equally dramatic view. In Raphael's time, the window provided a view of Bramante's Cortile del Belvedere and with it a prospect across terraces and staircases to the villa that gave the courtyard its name. Constructed by Innocent VIII, the Belvedere crowns a hill within the confines of the Vatican. What Raphael's poet on Parnassus points out is a distant eminence that is, by courtesy, a mountain.[56]

In the early sixteenth century the Belvedere became a place of papal recreation whose style and decor, as Elisabeth Schöter frequently observes, were Parnassian. Among sculptures installed there during the reign of Raphael's patron, Julius II, were such famous antiquities as the sleeping Ariadne, shortly to become the centerpiece of a fountain which includes the

sarcophagus whose seated captives inspired Raphael's Virgilian Thalia, the heroic Torso Belvedere and, most important, the Apollo Belvedere from the private collection of Julius II, installed there on 12 July 1511. That particular installation also constituted a restoration, of sorts, because in antiquity Apollo's cult flourished on the Vatican's hills. On the Belvedere his cult was remembered and renewed in Renaissance pageants. 11 November 1512, for example, witnessed a play at the Belvedere in which Apollo and the Muses acted their accustomed roles, then a coronation in which Julius himself gave laurel crowns to two Italian poets, and finally a recitation, verses chanted by an old blind man to the sounds of a lyre.[57] He sounds like Raphael's Homer brought to life, just as the first act of the Belvedere's pageant recalls the central section of his Parnassus. The festivities at the Belvedere and the design intended for the wall in the Segnatura facing it are connected by something grander and more moving, the belief that papal Rome had created a renewal of the ancient world, a renewal in which the Cortile del Belvedere, the enterprise of St. Peter's and the frescoes of the Segnatura all played their parts.[58] On a smaller scale the same part is played by Raphael's dramatic poet who concludes Parnassus with a gesture that is epideictic: what lies beyond and behind us, he says to his thoughtful companion, is Apollo's home as much as our mountain is.

The bearded poet also concludes a larger pattern within Raphael's Parnassus which, like his gesture, implies renewal in Rome. He and his colleague pause in movement, as if they were about to leave Parnassus. Their interrupted journey is Virgilian because, like Virgil, they move down a gentle slope, perhaps to seek that Castalian spring for which the fountains of the Belvedere, which inspired Raphael's own art, are the living counterpart. Other poets behind them enact the first stage of Virgil's journey, laboring over arduous slopes. Virgil's depicted journey, as Raphael shows it, takes him to the highest place of Parnassus where he acts as Dante's guide, a duty that also places him closest of all these poets to the Muses and makes him the only laureate privileged to bring his works to Apollo's side. But in those works Virgil speaks of removal from Parnassus. He essays a path, he says in that same poem, *Georgics III*, where he attains Parnassus, whereby he might rise from the earth but afterwards, "First, if life but remain, I will return to my own country, bringing the Muses with me in triumph from the Aonian peak."[59] By this Virgil means that he renews the art of poetry, invented first by the Greeks, but in the Latin tongue and by so doing brings glory to his Roman home. That sense of renewal runs through the texts that illuminate Raphael's first Parnassus, such as Virgil's reflection on pastoral poetry, removed now to Italian woods, or Horace's assessment of his lyric art in relation to Sappho's. These Latin poets, of whom Virgil is the chief and for this Parnassus the most influential, raise the hope of triumphant renewal in Rome. The bearded poet embarked on his particular journey suggests its corollary, the renewal of a renewal.

The sense of poetic renewal animates frescoed Parnassus as well, but there it takes other forms and a different direction [Fig. 2]. Parnassus now enjoys its Castalian spring, just at Apollo's feet, so that the landscape may be regarded as complete in itself. Its waters may refresh a greater number of poets, many of whom are moderns who write either in Latin or Italian, or both. All poets now crowd against Apollo and his court. Poets and Muses throng together because Raphael makes all the rough places of his earlier landscape smooth, as the utter suppression of Sappho's cliff shows; Parnassus becomes one mountain for all. With the erasure of spatial compartments, the need to order by genres also diminishes. Instead Raphael suggests a deeper sense of the loving unity of poetic art through a sustained compositional movement. Sappho sits now by herself against a window frame, less to signal the distant prospect of the Belvedere than to initiate a general progression, moving leftwards at first and then reversing to ascend a gentle hill, advance with Virgil, descend to Apollo, disperse at the right and then in a flourish of energy resume with poets who now point out the very room where the viewer stands, the Stanza della Segnatura. This new concluding conversation implies that if Parnassus lives anew, it is here.[60]

The particular orientation of the fresco is confirmed in other ways. One of these is the multiplication of seated figures, first Apollo and the flanking Muses, then Sappho and her vigorous counterpart in the right foreground. Creating links between laureates and deities, these seated poets also flank the window embrasure. They draw attention to it but also to its internal function, a place where the visitor may sit and, looking at this and other frescoes, find his or her physical situation duplicated on a heroic scale. Seated in this or the opposite window embrasure the viewer must also look up at the frescoes where, on the right side of Parnassus, several poets turn to meet his glance. But these attentive figures look straight ahead, downwards. The direction of their eyes serves to elevate the spectator they acknowledge, and place him in imagination on their level, atop some lofty eminence: an ideal Parnassus, in this room, of this room.

Several years after Raphael finished his work in the Segnatura, Marcantonio Raimondi undertook his, reworking the master's old drawings to create engraved Parnassus [Fig. 1]. With this remarkable print he also restores Raphael's original orientation of Parnassus, via the gesticulating poet, toward the Belvedere. Marcantonio's sense of timing was shrewd. In these same years, around 1517 to 1520, the reigning pontiff was Leo X, himself a poet and the patron of poets, Leo Musagetes as some called him, a new Apollo whose hillside retreat, the

10) Maffeo Olivieri, «Augusto da Udine», medal, National Gallery of Art, Washington, Samuel H. Kress Collection. Photo: Museum.

Belvedere, was celebrated outright as the new Parnassus. As the poet Marco Girolamo Vida writes around 1517, all the chaste sisterhood of the Muses and father Apollo have migrated from their ancient home to Leonine Rome, where poetic song sounds anew.[61] Reason enough, it seems, to publish Raphael's *modello*.

In reworking Raphael's first Parnassus, Marcantonio exploits what the master did not need to depict, the Vatican's window, by inscribing it. Its rich textures, in fact, become a gigantic frame for the acknowledgment "RAPHAEL PINXIT IN VATICANO." To a knowledgeable observer of the time these words are enough to indicate where Raphael did paint and why one of Marcantonio's poets seems almost to embrace a window. More immediately, the engraved words evoke a pun. It involves the poetic Latin word for poet, *vates*, meaning an inspired seer, as is the English term "bard" in its original sense. Virgil's Thracian musician, for example, strikes his seven-stringed lyre near pious bards whose words are worthy of Apollo, "pii vates et Phoebo digna locuti" (*Aeneid* VI, 662). What bards do, *vaticinare*, suggests a play on *Mons Vaticanus* so that the viewer holding the print sees *in Vaticano vates*. The pun has particular force in Marcantonio's time, when modern poets claimed the old honor of bardship. One instance is Augusto da Udine, the subject of a medal contemporary with Marcantonio's print [Fig. 10], honored by the Muse Urania, the laurel crown and the title *vates*. His medal suggests that the print be read as the place, Parnassus, where bards assemble according to Raphael's invention, where bards once gathered under Apollo in ancient times, and where modern bards like Augusto or those laureated by Julius in 1512 still assemble, nearby on the Belvedere, *in Vaticano*.[62]

The window enshrines words that reflect a shrewd marketing strategy on Marcantonio's part and no doubt Raphael's as well, but it also, by its form, serves the artist's original intentions. Marcantonio's architecture of wood and stone alerts the viewer, as we have seen, to the structures that underlie this Virgilian vision of Parnassus. The very fact of panelling the shutters into four severe rectangles, set just beneath Apollo's court, further alerts the observer to what Raphael depicted above it, four instruments, four trees, four divisions of landscape and, by extension, four genres of poetry. In its abstract order Marcantonio's window completes the equally severe order that underlies Raphael's first Parnassus.

And yet the window strikes a discordant note, or perhaps a merely playful one. Its forms are revealed by light projected from the left, as is everything else on Parnassus. Everything else, however, casts shadows as it accepts light, as Sappho and her cliff-face indicate. Marcantonio's window, however, receives no shadow from those forms set before it at the left, nor does it project any shadow into the landscape behind it on the right. The window is exempt from the prevailing pictorial norm. We may see it as an apparition, a plane that hovers in the landscape, but if that is true there are those in the landscape who acknowledge its presence. Since the window is so substantial, however, its reality can also be understood as differing from that of the landscape enveloping it to indicate that the window only abuts upon a picture. The viewer is confronted with a picture of a picture, in this case a picture that never was, just as the inscription asserts that Raphael painted the picture in the Vatican. The visual paradox that Marcantonio creates may play upon a Latin verb, PINXIT. Since it is a paradox, however, the alternative interpretation, apparition, holds equally true. There are other possibilities as well. What Marcantonio's art does accomplish can be more surely stated: it draws attention to that very window and provokes curiosity on what it may conceal and reveal.[63]

The window is matched by another pictorial game in the landscape itself. Parnassus, as noted, has no spring and the dramatic poets must debate its whereabouts. The fresco remedies that seeming defect [Fig. 2]. In the corresponding passage in the proof as abbreviated [Fig. 7], there are only geological accidents, folds of rock merely outlined but in the final print Marcantonio fashions a dark crevice, much like that in the fresco, but lets his rocks remain dry. With this pentimento,

the engraver plays with the fresco and by so doing, raises expectations that are not met. The engraver teases the spectator burdened with iconographic orthodoxy and encourages him to look elsewhere for Pierian springs. Here Marcantonio merely elaborates a game that Raphael, years before, began.

Play erupts in the skies above where cupids dive and soar. First designed by Raphael and reconsidered by Raimondi, they add a blithe note to this stately tableau, as well as movement unhindered. The putti also make their contribution to Raphael's sense of poetry on Parnassus because by bearing garlands from above they suggest the old notion that the gifts of poetry descend from the heavens. They become what Plato suggests an inspired poet is, "a light and winged and holy thing."[64] The cupids also bring comic relief. They are there, after all, to enact what amounts to an airborne coronation, the poetic counterpart to the laureations performed by the popes at the Belvedere. But these putti have no one here to crown. Just above Homer and Virgil wheel two cupids, holding poets' garlands and hovering to find suitable candidates. To no avail. The only uncrowned person here is the trousered Smyrnean who sits there only to take down words, not compose them. A putto at the right, emerging from Apollo's own copse, redirects this squadron's mission. He turns rightward to observe two more putti, flying just above the muses. The lower cupid looks up to his partner who looks over his left shoulder. His deed was intended for the Segnatura, to perform functions of visual liason, but as engraved here on this scale it seems instead that he has glimpsed somewhere someone worthy of Apollo's laurel crown. To parts unknown he and his fellows soon will speed.

They do not have far too go. As the viewer holds this Parnassus in his hand, he senses that the observant cupid looks in his direction, just over his right shoulder. Laurel-bearing cupids straight from Parnassus are about to invade his world, a notion encouraged by what the window suggests, that this is a fiction in which all may participate. If these putti can do so, so Raphael and Marcantonio seem to say, then Parnassus is at once a mountain in Greece or a picture in Rome or an idea that lives everywhere. Presented to the eye, Parnassus lives in the viewer's mind.[65]

[1] For a serviceable account of the fresco and the circumstances leading up to it, see R. Jones, N. Penny, *Raphael*, New Haven-London, 1983, pp. 68-74; also L. Dussler, *Raphael: A Critical Catalogue of his Pictures, Wall-Paintings and Tapestries*, London-New York, 1971, pp. 74-76, with full bibliography.

[2] J. Shearman, "Raphael's Unexecuted Projects for the Stanze," *Walter Friedlaender zum 90. Geburtstag*, ed. G. Kauffmann, W. Sauerländer, Berlin, 1965, pp. 158-80. See also G. P. Bellori, *Descrizzione delle imagini dipinte da Raffaelle d'Urbino delle Camere del Palazzo Apostolico Vaticano*, Rome, 1695, reprinted Farnborough, 1968, p. 25.

[3] I. H. Shoemaker, E. Brown, *The Engravings of Marcantonio Raimondi*, Lawrence, Kansas, 1981, pp. 155-7, with bibliography and a helpful review of problems. See also R. M. Mason, *Raphael et la seconde main*, Geneva, 1984, pp. 53-4.

[4] Shearman, *op. cit.*, 1983, pp. 161-3.

[5] For a similar geometric exercise and a similar subject, see J. Brink, "Simone Martini, Francesco Petrarca, and the Humanist Program of the Virgil Frontispiece," *Mediaevalia*, 3, 1977, pp. 106-9 and Diagram 1.

[6] K. Oberhuber, *Polaritt und Synthese in Raphaels "Schule von Athen"*, Stuttgart, 1983, pp. 33-9.

[7] See J. Pope-Hennessy, *Raphael*, New York, 1970, Fig. 84 on p. 96 and also pp. 97-100.

[8] Among those who see the cupids as fillers are Jones, Penny, *op. cit.*, pp. 68-74, and Mason, *op. cit.*, p. 54. Opposing views are given by Bellori, *op. cit.*, p. 25, and at greater length, Shearman, *op. cit.*, p. 159.

[9] See Dussler, *op. cit.*, pl. 60 and 157, respectively. In both cases the twisting pose is derived from Leonardo's Burlington House cartoon.

[10] See Jones, Penny, *op. cit.*, pp. 49-80, for these works and the room as a whole, with further references.

[11] Consult E. Knab, E. Mitsch, K. Oberhuber, *Raphael: Die Zeichnungen*, Stuttgart, 1983, p. 583 and Abb. 298, a drawing for the putti in the *Disputà*, and p. 586, Abb. 329, a drawing for one of the putti attending Theology above.

[12] Shoemaker, Brown, *op. cit.*, p. 155. These and other authorities argue that the apprentice reworks Marcantonio's suggestions, but the reworking, too extensive for a beginner, suggests instead the master's intervention to clarify a received and faulty design.

[13] As in *Inferno*, IV, 70-103.

[14] Statius, *Thebaid*, VI, 355-7. My translation is indebted to that of J. H. Mozley in the Loeb Classical Library edition of Statius, 2, Cambridge (Mass.)-London, 1969, p. 87.

[15] See R. Goffen, "*Nostra Conversatio in Caelis Est*: Observations on the *Sacra Conversazione* in the Trecento," *Art Bulletin*, 61, 1979, pp. 198-222, for the general type and its nomenclature. A specific and instructive instance is the high altar of S. Marco in Florence, as in J. Pope-Hennessy, *Fra Angelico*, 2nd ed., Ithaca, 1974, pls, 48-55: the court of, Heaven is set before a landscape where trees are selected to mark a precise order and where the foreground is marked by an aperture as well, in this case a tabernacle whose shutters depict the Crucifixion. Other religious prototypes are suggested by E. Schröter, "Raffaels Parnass: Eine ikonographische Untersuchung," *Actas del XXIII Congreso internacional de historia del arte*, Granada, 1973, 3, pp. 593-605.

[16] There are other transfers, including the figure of Dante and the motif of flying putti, to be discussed more fully below, as well as the scholarly note of a seated scribe taking dictation.

[17] Mason in *op. cit.*, pp. 54-56, no. 64: the background group of the Muses is inscribed EX PARNASI /RAPHAELIS /PICTURA, VT VACVVM /HOC IMPLERETVR. Another variant is an anonymous copy after Marcantonio's print which, in the manner of my Fig. 7, truncates the original but in this case omitting the zone of the door and the upper section to concentrate upon the central group. That group is also translated as statuettes to adorn an Italian table desk, appropriately enough, of 1584 now in the Metropolitan Museum of Art, New York: see W. M. Watson, *Italian Renaissance Maiolica from the William J. Clark Collection*, London, 1986, p. 160. For the engraved copy see K. Oberhuber, *The Illustrated Bartsch, 26: The Engravings of Marcantonio Raimondi and his School*, New York, 1978, p. 245.

[18] For the cassone, consult G. Coor, "Quattrocento-Gemälde aus der Sammlung Ramboux," *Wallraf-Richartz Jahrbuch*, 31, 1959, p. 91 and for the general traditions it reflects, the invaluable dissertation by E. Schröter, "Die Ikonographie des Themas Parnass vor Raffael," Friedrich-Wilhelms-Universität, Bonn-Hildesheim-New York, 1977. For the Muses in ancient art, see L. D. Ettlinger, "Muses and Liberal Arts: Two Miniatures from Herrad of Landsberg's *Hortus Deliciarum*," *Essays in the History of Art Presented to Rudolf Wittkower*, ed. D. Fraser, H. Hibbard, M. J. Lewine, London, 1967, pp. 29-31 and Figs. 3, 10, as well as O. Bie, *De musarum imaginibus quaestiones selectae*, Berlin, 1887, still the most valuable compilation of classical texts. For the muses at Urbino, see R. Dubos, *Giovanni Santi*, Bordeaux, 1971, pls. XXXVI-XLV. As Dubos points out, Santi and his collaborator Timoteo Viti derive their imagery from the so-called Tarocchi prints, a series engraved at Ferrara around 1465, for which see the discussion by J. A. Levenson, K. Oberhuber, J. L. Sheehan, *Early Italian Engravings from the National Gallery of Art*, Washington, 1973, pp. 100-13.

[19] See the exhaustive discussion by P. Williams Lehmann in *Samothracian Reflections: Aspects of the Renewal of the Antique*, Princeton, 1973, pp. 90-115.

[20] See the frontispiece to *Pratica musica* by Gafurius, printed in 1496, and discussed by E. Wind, *Pagan Mysteries in the Renaissance*, rev. ed., Harmondsworth, 1967, pl. 20 and pp. 265-9. There the Muses are co-ordinated with their respective planetary spheres and the Graces are a separate unit, standing at the upper left beside Apollo: one of these is named THALIA, as is one of the Muses. Perhaps these circumstances stimulated Raphael's thoughts. For his own version of the Graces, now at Chantilly, see Dussler, *op. cit.*, pl. 15 and pp. 6-7.

[21] Euterpe plays two pipes in the Ferrarese engraving of ca. 1465, illustrated in Levenson *et al.*, *op. cit.*, (as in n. 18), p. 110, no. 32; but see also n. 37 below. For the Muse with the stringless lyre, I can offer no exact identification. Although her pose evokes the art of Terpsichore, Muse of the dance, a similar dancing pose distinguishes Erato, as in Giovanni Santi's panels at Urbino (as in n. 18); a filial debt to this dancing Muse has been observed by P. de Vecchi, "*The Coronation of the Virgin* in the Vatican Pinacoteca and Raphael's Activity Between 1502 and 1504," *Raphael Before Rome* (Studies in the History of Art, 17), ed. J. Beck, Washington, 1986, p. 77 and Figs. 5-6. But in Santi's picture and the Ferrarese series (Levenson, *op. cit.*, pp. 104-5), Erato's own instrument is a tambourine. This note demonstrates that Renaissance Museography awaits further scholarly work and that Raphael's role in it is singularly inventive. Iconographic tradition is respected, however, in the figure of Calliope, so identified by her trumpet, a consistent attribute in the series just named and a feature in the Sienese cassone as well, where Calliope stands on Apollo's right side (Fig. 8).

[22] See further E. Winternitz, "The Curse of Pallas Athena," *Musical Instruments and their Symbolism in Western Art*, New York, 1967, pp. 160-5; also pp. 190-1 for the engraved Parnassus. See further K. Mayer-Baer, *Music of the Spheres and the Dance of Death; Studies in Musical Iconology*, Princeton, 1970, pp. 137-8.

[23] On Raphael's antique sources, see especially Pope-Hennessy, *op.*

cit., 1970, pp. 139-44. The sarcophagus with seated captives, who mirror one another, is in H. H. Brummer, *The Statue Court in the Vatican Belvedere*, Stockholm, 1970, pp. 160-1 and Figs. 138-40.

[24] For this component of frescoed Parnassus and its date, see Dussler, *op. cit.*, pp. 76-7.

[25] Cicero locates Achilles' tomb in the Troad in *Pro Archia Poeta*, X, 24. A more famous Phrygian with trousers is Paris as a shepherd, so depicted in a Roman sarcophagus discussed by E. Panofsky, *Problems in Titian, Mostly Iconographic*, New York, 1969, Fig. 184 and pp. 169-70, and shown with Phrygian cap and trousers in part set aside in the famous *Judgment of Paris*, discussed by Shoemaker and Brown, *op. cit.*, pp. 146-7.

[26] For Homer by Justus van Ghent, see J. Lavalleye, *Les primitifs flamands, VII: le palais ducal d'Urbin*, Brussels, 1964, p. 59, pl. CXXV. See now L. Cheles, *The Studiolo of Urbino: An Iconographic Investigation*, University Park, Pa., 1986, especially p. 93 and n. 5. The inscription here follows a Renaissance consensus treated by G. Finsler, *Homer in der Neuzeit: Von Dante bis Goethe*, Leipzig-Berlin, 1912, p. 37, beliefs that in turn follow ancient precedent as in Cicero, *op. cit.*, VIII, 19, or Strabo, *Geography*, XIII, 3, 27, a text that also locates Smyrna for those unfamiliar with the Aegean and whose discovery in the Renaissance, an exciting chapter in the history of humanism, is treated by A. Diller, *The Textual Tradition of Strabo's Geography*, Amsterdam, 1975, pp. 101-34.

[27] The usual designation nowadays is Ennius: see Dussler, *op. cit.*, p. 74 with further references.

[28] Horace, *Epistles*, I, xix, 28: "temperat Archilochi Musam pede mascula Sappho," an epithet borrowed by Ausonius, VIII, 24-5. For what Horace may mean, see the Renaissance commentaries by Antonio Mancinelli and Iodocus Badius Ascensius, both contemporaries of Raphael, in Horace, *Poetae amoenissimi*, Paris, 1519, fols. cclx-cclxv.

[29] See Horace, *Odes*, IV, ix, 10-12, and above all Ovid, *Heroides*, XV and for their consequences, a view of Sappho's sexuality not corrected until fragments of her verse came to light in the mid-Cinquecento, H. Rüdiger, *Sappho: Ihr Ruf und Ruhm bei der Nachwelt*, Leipzig, 1933, pp. 17-23. I have signalled a Quattrocento portrayal of Sappho as poetess and as a lover in *The Garden of Love in Tuscan Art of the Early Renaissance*, Philadelphia-London, 1979, p. 114.

[30] See, for example, Ausonius, *Epigrams*, LI: "I, Lesbian Sappho, adopted sister of the Muses, /am ninth of the lyrists, tenth of the Aonides," in *Ausonius*, ed. and tr. H. G. E. White, Cambridge-London, 1967, 2, pp. 186-7; also Mancinelli, who types as *lyrici vates* Sappho, Alcaius and Pittacus, as reported by Rudiger, *op. cit.*, p. 23.

[31] *Inferno*, I, 136.

[32] C. Trinkaus, *The Scope of Renaissance Humanism*, Ann Arbor, 1983, pp. 118-9 with abundant documentation, and more generally pp. 88-139.

[33] J. Onians, "On How to Listen to High Renaissance Art," *Art History*, 7, 1984, p. 429. Raphael's poems are in V. Golzio, *Raffaello nei documenti*, Vatican City, 1936, reprinted Westmead, 1971, pp. 181-7; see also the discussion by G. Morolli in *Raffaello: Elementi di un mito*, Florence, 1984, pp. 76-9.

[34] The *Eclogues* establish these traits: (1) the poet who speaks is a rustic, usually a shepherd or cowherd: I, 9-10, and hence has the tools of these trades: II, 30; (2) other tools are flutes and reeds: I, 2 and I, 9-10; V, 88-90 and VIII, 21; (3) rustic solitude is a *sine qua non*, as in I, 1-2. All these ideas are restated in VI, in which Virgil defines the history and dignity of bucolic poetry, poetry that is brief or as he puts it, keep the songs thin, *deductum dicere carmen*: VI, 5. I owe that rendering to

E. W. Leach, *Vergil's "Eclogues": Landscapes of Experience*, Ithaca-London, 1974, p. 232. See also her discussion of authorial voice and poetic role-playing on pp. 232-45, 247. She is preceded by Servius, who as early as the 4th century identifies the shepherd Tityrus with Virgil himself: see *Servii Grammatici Commentarii*, eds. G. Thilo, H. Hagen, Hildesheim, 1961, 3, pt. i, p. 64.

[35] For the pan-pipes, see *Eclogues* II, 31-3, 36-7 and VIII, 24.

[36] *Eclogues*, VI, 1-2: "Prima Syracosio dignata est ludere versu / nostra nec erubit silvas habitare Thalia," a reference particularly important because, as noted above, this poem defines Virgil's pastoral art.

[37] See Winternitz, *op. cit.*, p. 191. For the association of Thalia with the earth, see Wind, *op. cit.*, pp. 266-99, who cites Ficino on identifying this Muse with *viriditas*, that is, Nature in her most verdant aspect. That is also the view of Virgil's Renaissance commentators, such as Mancinelli and Ascensius, who call Thalia the *florida Musa*: see Virgil, *Opera*, Venice, 1533, fols 30r-31v. A Ferrarese print also associates her with the earth: see Levenson, *op. cit.*, p. 107, where Thalia who plays a viol sits upon the earth like a Madonna of Humility. None of the authorities cited here associates Thalia with comedy, but she is identified as a comic Muse in the Urbino series: see Dubos, *op. cit.*, pl. XXXVII, by Timoteo Viti who gives her, however, a cornucopia, so that the Virgilian identification with the earth predominates over the association given in the titulus below.

[38] See further S. K. Freedberg, *Painting of the High Renaissance in Rome and Florence*, Cambridge, Mass., 1961, pp. 151-7.

[39] See L. W. Jones, C. R. Morey, *The Miniatures of the Manuscripts of Terence prior to the Thirteenth Century*, Princeton, 1931, vol. 2 in general but in particular Fig. 64, where two actors compose themselves as Raphael's poets do. This is Rome Bibl. Apol. Vaticana, Cod. Lat. 3868, fol. 9v, a text discussed by Jones and Morey in *op. cit.*, 1, pp. 27-45. It becomes important because the MS, although produced in Lorraine early in the 9th century, is a Carolingian recension of late antique models; moreover, it was in the Vatican Library by 1475 and hence available; see K. Weitzmann, *Late Antique and Early Christian Book Illumination*, New York, 1977, pp. 13 and 30 with further references.

[40] Horace, *Ars poetica*, 275-84. See also the Renaissance commentaries in the 1519 Horace cited in n. 28, where Ascensius, for one, notes that tragedy first and then comedy derive from Homer's epics as a form (fol. CLX). Perhaps the fact that one of Raphael's paired poets is bearded implies a similar connection in that he resembles Homer in that regard, but no one else. But he is younger than Homer, his beardless friend younger still.

[41] Horace, *Ars poetica*, 92: "singula quaeque locum teneant sortita decentem." I owe the translation to N. De Witt as given in *Classical Literary Criticism*, eds. A. Preminger *et al.*, New York, 1974, p. 160. Renaissance literary criticism and the attempt to classify genres by voices and other standards are discussed by Trinkaus, *op. cit.*, also B. Weinberg, *A History of Literary Criticism in the Italian Renaissance*, Chicago, 1960, i, pp. 71-91, and O. B. Hardison, Jr., *The Enduring Monument: A Study of the Idea of Praise in Renaissance Literary Theory and Practice*, Chapel Hill, 1962, pp. 68-106. The latter points out on p. 69 that until the rediscovery and assimilation of Aristotle's *Poetics*, an event of the mid and late 16th century, epic poetry usually ranked as the highest genre, a situation that Aristotle's influence was to reverse, but also a situation matched by Raphael's Parnassus.

[42] See *Eclogues* VI, 2-5 and X, 21. In both instances Apollo's advent is comic as he comes to warn poets to stick to their last. But see also VI, 64-66, a moving passage in which the choir of the Muses rises to honor

the pastoral poet Gallus.

[43] Virgil, *Georgics*, III, 291-2, lines that Petrarch made the text for his coronation as poet laureate in 1343: see the translation in E. H. Wilkins, *Studies in the Life and Works of Petrarch*, Cambridge, Mass., 1955, pp. 300-13. See also Horace, *Epistles*, II, ii, 79-80: "Tu me inter strepitus nocturnos atque diurnos / via canere et contracta segui vestigia vatum?", and Propertius, III, 1, 15: "Non datur ad Musas lata via," together with the beautiful edition of 1487 (Venice) in which Filippo Beroaldo the Elder glosses this passage in the light of Hesiod to liken the poet's narrow path to the path that leads to virtue. The motif of ascent is burlesqued by Catullus, 105, 1-2, on the poet Mentula who strives to climb Parnassus only to be driven away by Muses wielding pitchforks. Given the reference to the metaphor of poetic difficulty in this section of the design, it might be possible to interpret a related passage, the poet who follows his colleague, in the light of Statius, *Thebaid*, XII, 810-19, in which he speaks of his poem as following in the footsteps of Virgil's epic.

[44] Ovid, *Metamorphoses*, I, 452-567, and for the general significance of the laurel as suggested by Ovid's fable, Petrarch's Coronation Oration (as in the preceding note).

[45] Statius, *Thebaid*, I, 32-3, "Cum laurigero tua fortior oestro / facta canam," as cited by Petrarch, *op. cit.*, and glossed upon, pp. 309-11. Petrarch here accepts a corrupt medieval reading, given, however, by all but one of the surviving MSS., and preserved in Renaissance editions as well. Modern editors prefer "Pierio" to *laurigero*, as in *P. Papiri Stati Thebaidos Libri XII*, ed. D. E. Hill, Leyden, 1983, p. 4 and n. 32; for this and other philological problems, see A. Klotz, ed., *Thebais*, rev. T. C. Klinnert, Leipzig, 1973, pp. i-lxxii. See also Propertius, III, 1-35 on Homer and the laurel's shade.

[46] The sum total of trees, if not their subdivisions, has been observed, especially with regard to the fresco. See H. B. Gutman, "Zur Ikonologie der Fresken Raffaels in der Stanza della Segnatura," *Zeitschrift für Kunstgeschichte*, 21, 1958, pp. 32-4 and, following him, Pope-Hennessy, *op. cit.*, 1970, p. 139. Gutman relates the fresco to Dante's vision in the Earthly Paradise of seven golden candlesticks, the gifts of the Holy Spirit, as in *Purgatorio*, XXIX, 44-51; a closer reading of Dante does not support Gutman because Dante first thinks he sees trees and then perceives that they are not.

[47] Virgil, *Eclogues*, II, 36-7: "Est mihi disparibus septem compacta cicutis / fistula."

[48] Virgil, *Aeneid*, VI, 645-8: "Nec non Threicius longa cum veste sacerdos / obloquitur numeris septem discrimina vocum, / iamque eadem digitis, iam pectine pulsat eburno." See also Servius, *op. cit.*, pp. 89-90, especially: "septem sunt, quorum sunum deprehendit Orpheus, unde uti septem fingitur chordis."

[49] Macrobius, *Saturnalis*, I, xix, 14.

[50] Pliny, *Natural History*, II, 20. See further W. Burkert, *Lore and Science in Ancient Pythagoreanism*, tr. E. L. Minar, Sr., Cambridge, Mass., 1972, pp. 350-5 and 474, as well as S. K. Heniger, Jr., *Touches of Sweet Harmony, Pythagorean Cosmology and Renaissance Poetics*, San Marino, California, 1974, pp. 91ff and 178-9; also Winternitz, *op. cit.*, p. 200. Visual equivalents to the engraving and its septenary patterns in Raphael's other works are ably discussed by B. F. Davidson, *Raphael's Bible: A Study of the Vatican Logge*, University Park-London, 1985, pp. 73-4.

[51] Sir Philip Sidney, *An Apology for Poetry*, ed. F. G. Robinson, Indianapolis-New York, 1970, p. 89. Frescoed Parnassus has undergone its share of numerical analysis, as n. 46 indicates; see also Schröter, *op. cit.*, p. 603. Numbers seem more evident in the engraving. The cupids, for example, are half the sum of Apollo and the Muses, but the wreaths they bear multiply their own total by two to equal that of the central group. Similarly, the total number of humans around them doubles the sum of the trees – but one of these is only Homer's scribe. There are limits, therefore, to this form of interpretation which in its turn opens up possibilities that go on forever, as Philo says: "I doubt whether anyone could adequately celebrate the properties of the number seven for they are beyond all words": cited by Davidson, *op. cit.*, p. 74.

[52] See Landino's commentary on Dante, *Paradiso*, I, 13-33, in *Comedia*, Florence, 1529, reprinting Landino's first edition of 1481. See also C. Landino, *Scritti critici e teorici*, ed. R. Cardini, 2 vols.

[53] Virgil, *Aeneid*, I, 167: "vivoque sedilia saxo," denoting an enchanted place, the home of rymphs, and for an earlier depiction of Virgil's landscape, see E. Callmann, *Apollonio di Giovanni*, Oxford, 1974, pl. 43. Virgil's imagery elsewhere in the *Aeneid* evokes the sacerdotal vocation of poets and even suggests why Raphael's Homer wears such a long tunic: see VI, 645-8, cited in n. 48.

[54] Virgil, *Georgics*, III, 292-3: "qual nulla priorum / Castaliam molli devertitur orbita clivo." Raphael's seeming failure to show two mountain tops in the fresco has been repeatedly stressed by Schröter, *op. cit.*, p. 605, and *idem*, "Raffaels Parnass," *Kunstchronik*, 30, 1977, pp. 76-7. On the traditional topography of Parnassus, consult Strabo, *Geography*, IX, 2, 25 and 3, 1; also Virgil, *Eclogues*, X, 11, and Dante, *Paradiso*, I, 16-8. For the fabled spring, see the excellent commentary on Persius, *Prologus* 1 by R. A. Harvey, *A Commentary on Persius*, Leiden, 1981, pp. 8-10.

[55] In addition to the drawing after Raphael in Oxford (see n. 7), there is a drawing by the master himself in the British Museum which studies the pose of the bearded poet, with alterations in dress and features, to make his gestures all the more telling; see Knab, *et al.*, *op. cit.*, pp. 589-90 and Abb. 363.

[56] The fresco's orientation was first observed by Giorgio Vasari: see *Le vite de' più eccellenti pittori scultori ed architettori*, ed R. Bettarini, P. Barocchi, Florence, 1972, 1, pt. 4, p. 170: "Nella facciata dunque di verso Belvedere, dove è il monte Parnaso ed il fonte d'Elicona" (1550 ed.). Its orientation is also stressed by Schröter, as in the studies cited in n. 54 and most recently, *idem*, "Die Vatican als Hügel Apollons und der Musen. Kunst und Panegyrik von Nikolaus V. bis Julius II," *Römische Quartalschrift für christliche Altertumskunde und Kirchengeschichte*, 75, 3-4, 1980, pp. 208-40. In this and her other papers Schröter considers chiefly the fresco but, as this essay indicates, her findings apply more directly to the engraving and the project it preserves.

[57] Cited by Schröter, *op. cit.*, 1980, pp. 237-8; also A. Luzio, "Federigo Gonzaga, ostaggio alle corte di Giulio II," *Archivio della società romana di storia patria*, 9, 1886, p. 544. For the Belvedere's decor, see in general Brummer, *op. cit.*, and for Ariadne as a fountain, Brummer, pp. 154-69, and E. B. MacDougall, "The Sleeping Nymph: Origins of a Humanist Fountain Type," *Art Bulletin*, 67, 1975, pp. 357-65.

[58] There is a vast literature to be cited on the High Renaissance in Rome as a renaissance. See in particular J. W. O'Malley, "The Vatican Library and the School of Athens: A Text of Battista Casali, 1508," *Journal of Medieval and Renaissance Studies*, 7, 1977, pp. 271-87; and P. Fehl, "Poetry and the Art of Raphael," *Raphael and the Ruins of Rome: the Poetic Dimension*, Urbana-Champaign, Illinois, 1983, pp. 5-13.

[59] *Georgics*, III, 10-1: "Primus ego in patriam mecum, modo vita supersit, / Aonio rediens deducam vertice Musas."

[60] By rethinking the lower right corner, Raphael reduces the role of

the Belvedere to something almost sensed subliminally. The fresco also becomes richer by itself and in relation to the adjoining frescoes of the Segnatura, topics that I treat in a forthcoming essay, "To Paint Poetry: Raphael on Parnassus."

[61] "Una omnes hac tunc castae ex Helicone sorores, / Migrassent Phoebusque pater, tunc laeta sonarent / Carmina, tum vates veterum decore alta virorum / Aequassent cantuque animos super astra tulissent," in *The De Arte Poetica of Marco Girolamo Vida*, New York, 1976, p. 248, and for the Leonine references in the 1517 version (the revised poem was not published until 1529), pp. xxxviii-xl, 209-10. Other panegyrics connecting the Belvedere, Parnassus and Pope Leo are cited by Schröter, *op. cit.*, 1980, p. 240, and MacDougall, *op. cit.*, p. 363 and n. 71. For an elegant evocation of Leo, see now Davidson, *op. cit.*, in general and in connection with Apollo, p. 74.

[62] For Augusto da Udine, see G. F. Hill, *A Corpus of Italian Medals of the Renaissance Before Cellini*, London, 1930, 1, p. 128, no. 485; also *idem* and G. Pollard, *Renaissance Medals from the Samuel H. Kress Collection at the National Gallery of Art*, London, 1967, p. 33. The term "vates" is treated by Landino in *Scritti critici* (as in 52), 1, pp. 142-3, 142; see also the full documentation in vol. 2. The play on "vates" and Vatican has been treated repeatedly by Schröter, as in *op. cit.*, 1980, p. 235.

[63] See further M. Wundrum, "Raum-Fläche-Bild: Beobachtungen zur Entwicklung der autonomen Form in der Fresken Raffaels," *Art the Ape of Nature*, ed. M. Barasch, L. F. Sandler, New York, 1981, pp. 213-4.

[64] *Ion*, 534, as cited in *Classical Literary Criticism* (see n. 41).

[65] This elaborates on Shearman, *op. cit.*, p. 159: "Five putti who carry five laurel crowns reinforce the idea of inspiration in action, of poesia in the making, rather than accomplished in an assembly of identifiable notables." I am also indebted to an instructive essay on the art of the print by D. Rosand, "Raphael, Marcantonio, and the Icon of Pathos," *Source*, 3, 2, 1984, pp. 33-52. To colleagues and friends I owe even greater debts; my thanks to Georgianna Ziegler, John W. McCoubrey, Robert Turner, Victoria Kirkham, and Elizabeth A. Anderson.

JOSEPH F. CHORPENNING

Another Look at Caravaggio and Religion

**I. Caravaggio's art and devotion
in the Counter-Reformation: the state of the question**

The starting-point for any serious consideration of Caravaggio's relationship to his religious milieu is Walter Friedlaender's discussion of this topic. Developing suggestions made earlier by P. Francastel and R. Hinks,[1] Friedlaender hypothesized that the direct communication Caravaggio establishes between the spectator and the sacred scene in altarpieces such as the *Madonna di Loreto* [Fig. 1] and *Conversion of St. Paul* [Fig. 2] has an affinity, on the one hand, with the informal mysticism and humility of St. Philip Neri and the Oratorians and, on the other, with the ideas and meditative practices of St. Ignatius Loyola's *Spiritual Exercises*. Moreover, according to Friedlaender, Caravaggio was probably introduced to the *Exercises* by the Oratorians.[2]

Friedlaender's hypothesis has had a very mixed reception by Caravaggio scholars. R. Wittkower, M. Fagiolo dell'Arco, and R. Spear agree that Caravaggio's religious paintings are close in spirit to both Neri and Loyola.[3] However, while R. Jullian, A. Zuccari, and A. Moir admit Caravaggio's affinity only with Neri and the Oratory and either explicit or implicity exclude any parallels between Caravaggio and Loyola,[4] G. Cozzi, H. Röttgen, and H. Hibbard reject the suggestion that Caravaggio was somehow influenced by Oratorian ideals.[5] F. Bologna denies that there was any connection between Caravaggio and either Neri and the Oratory or Loyola and the Jesuits.[6] Objections to the contrary notwithstanding, M. Cinotti, J. Gash, and T. Thomas are unwilling to dismiss the relevance of Neri's religious reform for understanding Caravaggio's religious art.[7]

Some observations should be made about Friedlaender's hypothesis and its reception.

1. There is no evidence to support Friedlaender's assumption that Caravaggio was introduced to the *Exercises* by the Oratorians. It is more likely that Caravaggio became familiar with the *Exercises* through the Augustinians, who were strong advocates of Ignatian spirituality.[8] Hibbard noted that "There may have been some connection between Caravaggio and the Augustinians, whose headquarters were in Lombardy";[9] he also detected "Augustinian" elements in Caravaggio's religious imagery, e. g., his use of light suggests an Augustinian emphasis on man's total dependence on divine grace and mercy.[10] Caravaggio did three paintings for Augustinian churches – the *Conversion of St. Paul*, the *Crucifixion of St. Peter* [Fig. 3], and *Madonna di Loreto* – and two of these, the *Conversion* and *Madonna*, were singled out by Friedlaender for being in accord with the ideas and practices of the *Exercises*.[11] Although Neri confessed "that all he knew about mental prayer he had learned from St. Ignatius,"[12] the Oratorians were not corporately committed to any particular method of meditation.[13] By contrast, the Augustinians were renowned as propagators of the *Exercises*, and hence Ignatian elements in two of the paintings Caravaggio produced for their churches would have been very appropriate.

2. Something more needs to be said about the *Exercises'*, meditative practices, which Friedlaender and others have considered relevant to Caravaggio's religious art. The "composition of place" and "application of the senses" aim to make Christian mysteries actual and tangible by having the meditator employ his imagination and senses to become and active participant in a gospel scene.[14] Although the *Exercises* are the *locus classicus* of the description of the composition of place and application of the senses,[15] these practices antedate Loyola; they are found in the works of medieval spiritual writers

like St. Anselm, St. Bernard, St. Bonaventure, and many others, as well as in the Carthusian Ludolph of Saxony's fourteenth-century *Vita Christi*, from which Loyola learned them.[16] These practices are also contained in the works of countless other spiritual authors of the sixteenth and seventeenth centuries. For example, in Italy during Caravaggio's lifetime they were available in the Italian translation of the Spanish Dominican Luis de Granada's *Book of Prayer and Meditation* (1554), and instructional manual on prayer;[17] the number-one best-seller of the entire Spanish Golden Age (it ran through well over one hundred editions between 1554 and 1679),[18] this work was translated into Italian in 1556 and went through two dozen editions between that date and 1610, the year of Caravaggio's death.[19] Instructions concerning the composition of place and use of the senses in meditation were also accessible in native Italian sources, such as the Theatine Lorenzo Scupoli's *Spiritual Combat*;[20] noteworthy too is that Scupoli's humanized image of the Virgin Mary is identical to Loyola's and Caravaggio's.[21] Between 1589, when it first appeared in Venice, and 1610, also the year of Scupoli's death, over thirty editions of the *Combat* were published in Italian; translated into all the major European languages, it was also enormously popular throughout Europe, appearing in more than 250 editions between 1589 and 1750.[22] Across the Alps, St. Francis de Sales included the composition of place and application of the senses in the method of meditation he offers in his *Introduction to the Devout Life* (1609);[23] as P. Askew has pointed out, although De Sales' writings could not have served as a source for Caravaggio, they, nevertheless, are relevant to his art because De Sales and Caravaggio were nurtured in the same religion climate, and hence De Sales' works provide information about the milieu in which the artist lived and worked.[24] However, these meditative techniques were not only recommended in books on prayer but also in preaching manuals of the period as ways of communicating the gospel and Christian doctrine more effectively to the faithful,[25] and we know that they were actually used for this purpose.[26] In short, the composition of place and application of the senses were part and parcel of a widely disseminated, and specifically Catholic, method of meditation during the Counter-Reformation.[27] One church historian has gone so far as to attribute the success of the Catholic reform to methodical meditation, which was an integral component of priestly formation in the Tridentine seminary and of the rules of both the new and old religious orders.[28] All of the orders for whose churches Caravaggio produced paintings – the Augustinians, Oratorians, Capuchins, Dominicans, and Discalced Carmelites – not only practiced methodical meditation but popularized it through preaching and the pastoral ministry.[29]

3. One of the principal objections raised by Cozzi, Bologna, and Röttgen against Caravaggio's ties with the Oratory was that the artist's breaches of decorum would have been offensive to the Oratorians, whose taste in art was conservative.[30] Thomas has perceptively observed that the flaw in this argument is that while it explains how the Oratory may have reacted to Caravaggio's paintings, it tells us nothing of how Caravaggio may have responded to and internalized the oratorian concept of humility.[31] Jullian's and Bologna's arguments against Caravaggio's affinity with Loyola suffer from a similar weakness: they explain how the Jesuits may have reacted to Caravaggio but say nothing about how the artist may have responded to the *Exercises*, or, to be more precise, Counter-Reformation meditative practices.[32] Equally off the mark is the distinction Bologna makes between the life and experience of Loyola and Caravaggio (i. e., that Loyola and Caravaggio could not be more different – Loyola's conception of Christians mysteries in terms of the actual and tangible originated in his mystical experience and sought to move the exercitant to contrition, asceticism, and ecstasy, three things very foreign to Caravaggio[33]) because, again, it ignores Caravaggio's response to the *Exercises* and leads to facile conclusions about Caravaggio's complex and unconventional personality. Given the wide diffusion and popularity of Counter-Reformation meditative practices, Caravaggio was certainly aware of their importance, particularly for the orders for whose churches he did paintings. Furthermore, I contend that the hallmarks of Caravaggio's religious art identified by Friedlaender and others – the direct contact the artist establishes between the sacred scene and the spectator and his consistent humanization of Christ, the Virgin, and the saints, as well as the population of his religious paintings with apparently poor, common, and very human types[34] – are primarily Caravaggio's artistic response to, and interpretation of, these practices. This contention is supported by a combination of various factors: the positive correlation between the character of Caravaggio's religious work and the purpose and content of Counter-Reformation meditative techniques; the interest in these practices by the orders for whose churches Caravaggio painted; the liturgical context of the artist's altarpieces and the liturgical piety of his age; and the close relationship between art and devotion in the Counter-Reformation.

II. Caravaggio's art and the religious climate of his time

Counter-Reformation meditative techniques prescribed that the meditator imagine a religious scene as if it were taking place before him "now," or as if he were present at the historical moment, and then participate in it by means of the senses, or, more exactly, their analogues in the imagination. Caravaggio's religious paintings are the pictorial equivalent of these methods.

1) Caravaggio, «The Madonna di Loreto», Rome, Cavaletti Chapel, Sant'Agostino.

2) Caravaggio, «The Conversion of St. Paul», Rome, Cerasi Chapel, Santa Maria del Popolo.

3) Caravaggio, «The Crucifixion of St. Peter», Rome, Cerasi Chapel, Santa Maria del Popolo.

In both his early and mature works, the artist consistently portrays Christ, the Virgin, and the saints as human beings; he also often includes poor spectators alongside sacred persons, as, e. g., in the *Madonna di Loreto* and *Madonna of the Rosary*. The result is that sacred scenes are represented as human dramas.[35] Thus Caravaggio makes the supernatural actual and establishes a direct rapport between the scene and the spectator, enabling the spectator to identify with the mystery being portrayed. Consequently, just as meditative practices engaged the meditator immediately in Christian mysteries, Caravaggio's religious art achieves the same effect by bringing the supernatural "near to the spectator, almost to the degree of physical tangibility."[36]

The prevalence of the humanization of sacred persons and scenes in Caravaggio's early and mature paintings suggests that the artist's response to the meditative practices of his period underwent a prolonged process of gestation and development. Caravaggio likely first came into contact with these practices in Lombardy, probably through the Augustinians and/ or preaching.[37] However, the full potential of the meditative quality of Caravaggio's religious art was not realized until the artist began to execute altarpieces for the churches of the orders that popularized these practices. To appreciate Caravaggio's achievement in this regard, it is necessary to understand the close relationship that existed between religious art and piety in the Counter-Reformation.

The lives and writings of various Counter-Reformation saints reveal that during this period art was considered to be an aid to prayer and devotion. Loyola not only used pictures to help himself meditate on the mysteries of Christ's life, but asked the Jesuit Jerome Nadal to compose an illustrated book of gospel meditations to assist young Jesuits with the practice of the composition of place.[38] Similarly, St. Teresa of Avila recognized the important role of religious art in the life of devotion. For example, Teresa relied heavily on images as aids to prayer, especially in the early stages of her spiritual life; she not only had a preference for particular religious paintings but commissioned paintings of Christ, the Virgin, and her favorite saints of her monasteries because they helped worship and awakened the love of God; she lamented the devotional impoverishment caused by the Lutherans and others who condemned the use of images; and, as the depositions given at the processes of Teresa's beatification and canonization testify, she often had raptures while looking at religious paintings.[39] Neri wished the altarpieces of the Chiesa Nuova to be used for meditation,[40] and he himself would "all unconsciously be rapt into a sweet ecstasy" as he sat contemplating Federico Barroci's altar painting in the Chapel of the Visitation in the Chiesa Nuova.[41] During his student days in Paris, De Sales had a great esteem for a black statue of the Virgin in the church of Saint Etienne des Grès; when he struggled with his great temptation to despair of his salvation, he was delivered from this trial as he prayed the Memorare before this statue.[42] Moreover, De Sales recommended images as a possible remedy for the dryness sometimes experienced in meditation because they are able to arouse the heart.[43]

The impact of Caravaggio's altarpieces as devotional images can be grasped only when they are considered in the liturgical context for which they were intended. Caravaggio's conception and interpretation of religious subjects is in complete harmony with Counter-Reformation liturgical piety, of which meditative prayer was an integral part. By the end of the Middle Ages, the so-called "private mass" was firmly established as the model for its public celebration; the Council of Trent canonized and universalized this model. Consequently, until the restoration of the Second Vatican Council, the laity acted as spectators rather than as participants at the liturgy.[44] To keep the laity engaged in activity during mass, devotional writers encouraged them to meditate or to pray the rosary. For example, De Sales tells Philothea in the *Introduction to the Devout Life* that if she wishes to hear Mass properly, she should keep herself recollected by meditating on the mysteries of Christ's life or some other mystery of her choice.[45] The saint himself, when about to receive episcopal consecration, made a pious resolution always to pray the rosary when his duties required him to attend a public mass.[46] When prayed correctly, the rosary was to be a meditative prayer, a point insisted upon in rosary books of the sixteenth and seventeenth centuries.[47] These books typically included an illustration, composition of place, and points for meditation for each of the fifteen mysteries of the rosary.[48] Again, turning to De Sales' *Introduction*, the saint gives Philothea this advice about the rosary: "The rosary is a very useful form of prayer, provided you know how to say it properly. To do this, get one of the little books that teach us the way to recite it."[49] M. A. Graeve related the rosary program of the Chiesa Nuova and Caravaggio's *Entombment of Christ* to an early sixteenth-century rosary book by the Dominican Alberto Castellano that was in Neri's personal library.[50]

Friedlaender attributed the "spiritual relationship" Caravaggio establishes between the sacred scene and the spectator to the fact that "Almost all of Caravaggio's religious works, beginning with the San Luigi series, were altarpieces designed for the worship of the Christian community and its members [...]."[51] The liturgical piety of the age and the interrelationship between Counter-Reformation art prayer suggest that Caravaggio's altarpieces were intended to help worshippers to meditate while they attended mass. A passage from Granada's *Brief Memorial and Guide of the Duties of a Christian* (1561), which specifies the correspondence between the composition of place and painting, gives an idea of how Caravaggio's altar-

4) Caravaggio, «The Stigmatization of St. Francis», Hartford, The Ella Gallup Sumner and Mary Catlin Sumner Collection, Wadsworth Atheneum.

pieces may have served as meditative aids: "Each day the Christian should select one or two or three episodes of the life of Christ for his meditation. He should represent each mystery as present to him here and now. The representation of these mysteries is a function of the imagination, which knows how a painter would portray them."[52] By depicting Christian mysteries in human terms so that the spectator could identify with them,

Caravaggio's altarpieces would have assisted worshippers with meditative techniques such as the composition of place.

There is yet another dimension of Counter-Reformation liturgical piety that coincides with Caravaggio's emphasis on the tangibility of the supernatural in his altarpieces. As already indicated, while attending mass, the laity meditated or prayed the rosary. The part of the mass that was the main focus of the people's attention and devotion was the consecration, particularly the elevation of the host by the priest. This focus came about as a result of the medieval controversies over how and when Christ became present in the Eucharist. Consequently, a "moment of consecration" was defined, and the importance of the canon was reduced to the words of institution.[53] A bell called the congregation's attention to this moment when the supernatural became present.[54] Caravaggio's altarpieces, which made the supernatural actual and tangible, were completely in keeping with the Eucharistic piety of his age. The example *par excellence* of this harmony is Caravaggio's *Entombment*: when the priest elevates the newly consecrated host for the adoration of the congregation, the host is perfectly juxtaposed with Christ's body in Caravaggio's altarpiece.[55]

Finally, there remains the untidy problem of the rejection of some of Caravaggio's altarpieces. If they were in such harmony with Counter-Reformation meditative practices and liturgical piety and the interests of the orders for whose churches he produced paintings, why were some of them rejected? (Presumably the immediate commissioners of Caravaggio's altarpieces would have had a particular sympathy for the interests of the orders with which they were associated.[56]) Caravaggio responded to the meditative techniques and liturgical piety of his day by consciously and consistently representing the human reality and significance of sacred scenes and persons. To achieve this humanization of the supernatural, the artist ignored conventional rules of decorum, and this led to the refusal of some of his work.[57] Caravaggio's concern with portraying the literal sense of sacred events is sometimes linked to the spirit of the Protestant return to Scripture.[58] However, this concern was shared by several contemporary orthodox Catholic biblical scholars who also ran foul of ecclesiastical authorities for insisting on the biblical or historical truth of sacred events and persons precisely because this truth contradicted the way in which such events and persons were conventionally portrayed by religious paintings.[59]

In summary, Caravaggio's religious painting were nourished by, as well as nourished, Counter-Reformation meditative techniques and liturgical piety. While Caravaggio initially responds to these techniques in his early religious works, the full potential of the meditative quality of his interpretation of Christian mysteries is not realized until the artist begins to produce altarpieces for the churches of the orders that disseminated these practices among the laity. Caravaggio's altarpieces are perfectly integrated into the liturgical context for which they were intended: they serve to help the spectator/worshipper meditate and be conscious of the presence of the supernatural.

Finally, it should be pointed out that the preceding discussion, of course, does not exhaust the topic of Caravaggio and religion. Rather, it has focused on issues raised by the most studied and controversial aspect of this topic, namely, Friedlaender's hypothesis and its reception. Another important aspect, which has received much less attention, is Caravaggio's creation in the *Stigmatization of St. Francis* [Fig. 4] and *Magdalen in Ecstasy* of vivid pictorial equivalents for the description of ecstasy found in the writings of the great Counter-Reformation mystics.[60]

I should like to thank Prof. Donald Posner for the guidance and encouragement he offered in the preparation of this article.

[1] P. Francastel, "Le réalisme de Caravage", *Gazette des Beaux-Arts*, LXXX, 1938, pp. 45-62; and R. Hinks, *Michelangelo Merisi da Caravaggio: His Life, His Legend, His Work*, London, 1953, p. 75.

[2] W. Friedlaender, *Caravaggio Studies*, Princeton, 1955, pp. 117-35.

[3] R. Wittkower, *Art and Architecture in Italy, 1600 to 1700*, New York, 1958 (rpt. 1982), p. 56; M. Fagiolo dell'Arco, "Le 'Opere di Misericordia': contributo alla poetica del Caravaggio", *L'Arte*, N. S., I, no. 1, 1968, pp. 37-61, esp. 41-3 and 47; and R. Spear, *Caravaggio and His Followers*, New York, 1975, pp. 6, 10-11, and 13.

[4] R. Jullian, *Caravage*, Lyon-Paris, 1961, pp. 111 and 136, nn. 35 and 36; A. Zuccari, "La politica culturale dell'Oratorio romano nella seconda metà del Cinquecento", *Storia dell'arte*, XLI, 1981, pp. 77-112; and A. Moir, *Caravaggio*, New York, 1982, pp. 13, 22, 56 and 128.

[5] G. Cozzi, "Intorno a cardinale Ottavio Paravicino, a monsignor Paolo Gualdo e a Michelangelo Caravaggio", *Rivista storica italiana*, LXXIII, no. 1, 1961, pp. 36-68, esp. pp. 62-5; H. Röttgen, *Il Caravaggio: richerche e interpretazioni*, Rome, 1974, pp. 236-40; and H. Hibbard, *Caravaggio*, New York, 1983, p. 313.

[6] F. Bologna, "Il Caravaggio nella cultura e nella società del suo tempo", in *Colloquio sul tema Caravaggio e i Caravaggeschi, organizzato d'intesa con le Accademie di Spagna e di Olanda*, Rome, 1974, pp. 149-87, esp. pp. 163-6 and 175-6.

[7] M. Cinotti, with a critical essay by G. A. Dell'Acqua, *Michelangelo Merisi detto il Caravaggio*, Bergamo, 1983 (excerpted from *I pittori bergamaschi: Il Seicento*, I), p. 223; J. Gash, *Caravaggio*, London, 1980, p. 15; and T. Thomas, "Expressive Aspects of Caravaggio's First *Inspiration of St. Matthew*", *Art Bulletin*, LXVII, 1985, pp. 637-52.

[8] See D. Gutiérrez, "Ermites de Saint-Augustin", *Dictionnaire de spiritualité*, Paris, 1960, IV, no. 1, cols. 983-1018, esp. 1002.

[9] Hibbard, *op. cit.*, p. 184.

[10] *Ibidem*, pp. 101-2 and 125-31.

[11] Friedlaender, *op. cit.*, p. 122.

[12] V. J. Matthews, *St. Philip Neri: Apostle of Rome and Founder of the Congregation of the Oratory*, London, 1934 (rpt. Rockford, Ill., 1984), p. 72.

[13] *Ibidem*, p. 71; and L. Ponnelle, L. Bordet, *St. Philip Neri and the Roman Society of His Times (1515-1595)*, trans. R. F. Kerr, London, 1932, pp. 386.

[14] The "composition of place" entailed using the imagination to visualize a particular scene in the life of Christ in all its details. The "application of the senses" goes further: the exercitant is to apply each of the five senses (or rather, their analogues in the imagination) to the scene in question.

[15] See, e. g., *The Spiritual Exercises of St. Ignatius*, trans. L. J. Puhl, Westminster, Md., 1951, pars. 47, 65-70, 91, 103, 106-7, 112, 114, 116, 121-5. Friedlaender, *op. cit.*, discusses several of these passages on p. 121.

[16] See J. Maréchal, "Application des sens", *Dictionnaire de spiritualité*, Paris, 1932, I, cols. 810-28, esp. 822-6; L. Spear, "Prayer with Images", *The Way*, XIII, 1973, pp. 236-44; J. Walsh, "Application of the Senses", *The Way Supplement*, XXVII, 1976, pp. 59-68; and D. M. Stanley, "Contemporary Gospel-Criticism and 'The Mysteries of the Life of Our Lord' in the *Spiritual Exercises*", and E. H. Cousins, "Franciscan Roots of Ignatian Meditation", in *Ignatian Spirituality in a Secular Age*, ed. G. P. Schner, Waterloo, 1984, pp. 26-50, esp. 28-30, and pp. 51-64, resp.

[17] See *Summa of the Christian Life: Selected Text from the writings of Venerable Louis of Granada, O. P.*, 3 vols., trans. J. Aumann, St. Louis, 1954-8, vol. II, p. 317.

[18] K. Whinnom, "The Problem of the 'Best-Seller' in Spanish Golden-Age Literature", *Bulletin of Hispanic Studies*, LVII, 1980, pp. 189-98, esp. p. 194.

[19] M. Llaneza, *Bibliografía del V. P. M. Fray Luis de Granada*, 4 vols., Salamanca, 1926-8, vol. I, nos. 15-145, *passim*; and G. M. Bertini, M. A. Pelazza, *Ensayos de literatura espiritual comparada hispano-italiana*, Turin, 1980, pp. 204-8. In fact, of all the Spanish spiritual works published and disseminated in Italy during the sixteenth and seventeenth centuries, the editions of Granada's works were the most numerous (St. Teresa of Avila's works occupy a distant second place): see Bertini, Pelazza, *op. cit.*, p. 214. The popularity of Granada's writings in sixteenth-century Italy is well attested; for example, St. Charles Borromeo (1538-84), whose spirit dominated not only the Milan of Caravaggio's youth but the entire Counter-Reformation Church, often preached from Granada's works: see A. Huerga's introduction to the *Summa of the Christian Life, op. cit.*, vol. I, pp. xvii-lxxxvii, esp. lxxix.

[20] L. Scupoli, *The Spiritual Combat and a Treatise on Peace of the Soul*, trans. W. Lester and R. Mohan, New York, 1978, pp. 46-7, 69-70, 72-3, 138, and 147-8.

[21] Cf. *ibidem*, pp. 141-4; and Friedlaender, *op. cit.*, p. 122.

[22] H. A. Hodges, "A History of *Unseen Warfare*", in *Unseen Warfare, Being the Spiritual Combat and Path to Paradise of Lorenzo Scupoli*, trans. E. Kadlubovsky and G. E. H. Palmer, London, 1963, pp. 227-81. The popularity the *Combat* attained outside Italy is often attributed to the recommendation given it by St. Francis de Sales in the *Introduction to the Devout Life*, trans. J. K. Ryan, Garden City, 1972, p. 108, and letters of spiritual direction: cf. St. Francis de Sales, *Selected Letters*, trans. E. Stopp, New York, 1960, pp. 61, 138, and 142-3. Moreover, De Sales himself testifies that he carried a copy of the *Combat* in his pocket for more than eighteen years and read from it daily: see *ibidem*, p. 138; and J.-P. Camus, *The Spirit of St. Francis de Sales*, trans. C. F. Kelley, New York, 1952, p. 43.

[23] De Sales, *Introduction to the Devout Life, op. cit.*, p. 87.

[24] P. Askew, "The Angelic Consolation of St. Francis of Assisi in Post-Tridentine Italian Painting", *Journal of the Warburg and Courtauld Institutes*, XXXII, 1969, pp. 280-306, esp. 288-9.

[25] See H. D. Smith, *Preaching in the Spanish Golden Age: A Study of Some Preachers of the Reign of Philip III*, Oxford, 1978, p. 67.

[26] *Ibidem*, pp. 67-8; and E. Orozco, *Manierismo y Barocco*, 3rd ed., Madrid, 1981, pp. 89-91.

[27] Catholic meditative techniques aimed at having the meditator "apply himself to the subject, so that he participates in it; he imagines a scene vividly, as if it were taking place in his presence, analyzes the subject, and stirs up emotions appropriate to the scene or event or personal spiritual condition. The typical Protestant procedure is very nearly the reverse: instead of the application of the self to the subject, it calls for the application of the subject to the self - indeed for the subject's location in the self [...]"; from B. K. Lewalski, *Protestant Poetics and the Seventeenth-Century Religious Lyric*, Princeton, 1979, p. 151. M. Deutsch Carroll has related Rembrandt to Counter-Reformation meditative techniques: cf. "Rembrandt as Meditational Printmaker", *Art Bulletin*, LXIII, 1981, pp. 585-610. Recently, however, D. R. Smith has challenged that connection and argued for Rembrandt's relationship to Protestant meditative methods: cf. "Towards a Protestant Aesthetics: Rembrandt's 1655 *Sacrifice of Isaac*", *Art History*, VIII, 1985, pp. 290-302.

[28] L. Cristiani, *L'Église a l'époque du Councile de Trente*, Paris, 1948, pp. 253-4.

[29] See Gutiérrez, *op. cit.*, cols, 1007-8; A. Cistellini, "Oratoire philippin", *Dictionnaire de spiritualité*, Paris, 1982, XI, cols. 853-76, esp. 860; J. Smet, *The Carmelites: A History of the Brothers of Our Lady of Mt. Carmel*, 4 vols., Darien, Ill., 1975-82, vol. II, pp. 229-30; and O. de Veghel, "Spiritualité franciscaine aux 16e et 17e siècles", *Dictionnaire de spiritualité*, Paris, 1964, V, cols. 1347-91, esp. 1349-53. The Dominicans promoted the rosary as a meditative prayer: cf. below; and D. Abbrescia, "Frères prêcheurs en Italie du 16e siècle à nos jours", *Dictionnaire de spiritualité*, Paris, 1964, V, cols. 1445-64, esp. 1450 and 1457.

[30] Cozzi, *op. cit.*, pp. 62-5; Bologna, *op. cit.*, pp. 175-6; Röttgen, *op. cit.*, pp. 236-40.

[31] Thomas, *op. cit.*, pp. 642-3. At the same time Thomas notes that the virtue of humility was emphasized not only by Neri but also by other Counter-Reformation spiritual masters such as Loyola and De Sales (p. 647). To this list should also be added the names of Grenada and Teresa of Avila. For Granada, "humility is the foundation of all the virtues and the disposition for the reception of all graces" (*Summa of the Christian Life, op. cit.*, vol. II, p. 398). Moreover, Granada enumerates six degrees of humility: cf. *ibidem*, vol. II, pp. 400-5. Similarly, Teresa considered humility to be the foundation of the whole spiritual life: cf. *The Collected Works of St. Teresa of Avila*, 3 vols., trans. K. Kavanaugh and O. Rodriguez, Washington, D. C., 1976-85, vol. I, p. 86, and vol. II, p. 447. Recently, it has even been argued that Teresa's autobiography is essentially a practical treatise on humility: see R. Senabre, "Sobre el género literario del Libro de la vida", in *Actas del Congreso Internacional Teresiano*, eds. T. Egido *et al.*, 2 vols., Salamanca, 1983, vols. II, pp. 765-76.

[32] Jullian, *op. cit.*, p. 136, no. 35; and Bologna, *op. cit.*, pp. 163-6.

[33] Bologna, *op. cit.*, p. 166.

[34] See, e. g., Friedlaender, *op. cit.*, p. 120 and 129; Wittkower, *op. cit.*, p. 56; Spear, *op. cit.*, p. 6; Moir, *op. cit.*, pp. 56-7; and Gash, *op.*

cit., p. 10.

[35] See, e. g., Friedlaender, *op. cit.*, pp. 122, 126-7, and 129; and Spear, *op. cit.*, pp. 5-6 and 10-11.

[36] Friedlaender, *op. cit.*, p. 120.

[37] Editions of the Latin translation of Granada's preaching manual, *Ecclesiastical Rhetoric* (1576), in which he encourages preachers to use the composition of place to make their subject more vivid and immediate for their audience, were published in Venice in 1578 and Milan 1585 and 1588: see Llaneza, *op. cit.*, vol. III, no. 2845 and nos. 2847-7; and Smith, *op. cit.*, p. 67.

[38] T. Buser, "Jerome Nadal and Early Jesuit Art in Rome", *Art Bulletin*, LVIII, 1976, pp. 424-33, esp. 425.

[39] M. Florisonne, *Esthétique et mystique d'après Sainte Thérèse d'Avila et Saint Jean de la Croix*, Paris, 1956, pp. 49-86; and J. Rhodes, "St. Teresa and Devotion to Christ's Passion", *Mount Carmel*, XXVII, 1979, pp. 108-37, esp. 119-20.

[40] M. A. Graeve, "The Stone of Unction in Caravaggio's Painting for the Chiesa Nuova", *Art Bulletin*, XL, 1958, pp. 223-38, esp. 234.

[41] F. Haskell, *Patrons and Painters: Art and Society in Baroque Italy*, New Haven, 1980, p. 69.

[42] M. Henry-Coüannier, *St. Francis de Sales and His Friends*, trans. V. Morrow, Staten Island, 1973, pp. 33-6.

[43] De Sales, *Introduction to the Devout Life*, *op. cit.*, p. 93.

[44] T. Klauser, *A Short History of the Western Liturgy: An Account and Some Reflections*, 2nd ed., trans. J. Halliburton, New York, 1979, pp. 94-152; and W. H. Willimon, *Word, Water, Wine, and Bread: How Worship Has Changed Over the Years*, Valley Forge, 1980, pp. 51-74.

[45] De Sales, *Introduction to the Devout Life*, *op. cit.*, pp. 104-5.

[46] L. Bouyer, *Liturgical Piety*, Notre Dame, 1955, p. 2.

[47] Abbrescia, *op. cit.*, cols. 1440 and 1457; and J. Rhodes, "The Rosary in Sixteenth-Century England II", *Mount Carmel*, XXXII, 1984, pp. 4-17, esp. 7-10.

[48] Abbrescia, *op. cit.*, col. 1450; and Rhodes, *op. cit.*, 1984, pp. 7-10.

[49] De Sales, *Introduction to the Devout Life*, *op. cit.*, pp. 82-3.

[50] Graeve, *op. cit.*, pp. 235-6.

[51] Friedlaender, *op. cit.*, p. 129.

[52] My translation. *Obras del V. P. M. Fray Luis de Granada, III* (Biblioteca de autores espanoles, vol. 11, Madrid), 1945, p. 197.

[53] Willimon, *op. cit.*, pp. 54-8.

[54] J. A. Jungmann, *The Mass of the Roman Rite: Its Origins and Development*, trans. F. A. Brunner, 2 vols., New York, 1951-5, vol. II, pp. 209-10.

[55] See G. Wright, "Caravaggio's *Entombment* Considered in *Situ*", *Art Bulletin*, LX, 1978, pp. 35-42; and Hibbard, *op. cit.*, p. 174. Caravaggio's humanization of the supernatural would have also been in keeping with the Roman Catholic doctrine of the communion of saints. According to this doctrine, because of Christ's conquest of death by his resurrection, not only the Church militant on earth but also the Church triumphant in heaven is present at the sacrifice of the mass: see, e. g., De Sales, *Introduction to the Devout Life*, *op. cit.*, pp. 103-4.

[56] Gash, *op. cit.*, pp. 15-6.

[57] Thomas, *op. cit.*, p. 643.

[58] See, e. g., Hibbard, *op. cit.*, p. 126.

[59] See C. P. Thompson, "*En la Ascensión*: Artistic Tradition and Poetic Imagination in Luis de León", in *Mediaeval and Renaissance Studies on Spain and Portugal in Honour of P. E. Russell*, eds. F. W. Hodcroft *et al.*, Oxford, 1981, pp. 109-20, esp. 111-2.

[60] This aspect of Caravaggio's religious art has been briefly commented on by Askew, *op. cit.*, pp. 287-8; Gash, *op. cit.*, p. 14; and Hibbard, *op. cit.*, pp. 58-61 and 211.

FERDINANDO BOLOGNA

Alla ricerca del vero *San Francesco in estasi* di Michel Agnolo da Caravaggio per il cardinale Francesco Maria Del Monte[1]

Fra gli scrittori seicenteschi che consideriamo "fonti" per la ricostruzione dell'attività del Caravaggio, nessuno ha tramandato notizie di dipinti del maestro raffiguranti san Francesco d'Assisi o storie della sua vita. Ciò nonostante, la critica moderna ha individuato tre quadri di tal soggetto attribuibili al Caravaggio stesso o derivati con sicurezza da sue idee originali; in secondo luogo, ha recuperato una serie di documenti scritti, di varia natura ma tutti databili entro la prima metà del XVII secolo, che menzionano quadri di soggetto sanfrancescano attribuiti al pittore; in terzo luogo, si è studiata di mettere in rapporto i dipinti con le testimonianze. Eppure, a parte un breve saggio di F. G. Pariset risalente all'ormai lontano 1952,[2] e un passaggio ben documentato, ma neanch'esso esauriente, che s'incontra in uno studio di Luigi Spezzaferro di data più fresca,[3] non si può dire che il problema sia mai stato affrontato espressamente e nella sua interezza.

Poiché il presente scritto nasce dall'intento di provare che il *San Francesco in estasi* entrato da poco nella Barbara P. Johnson Collection a Princeton [Figs. 1 - 3], è opera autografa di Michelangelo Merisi da Caravaggio,[4] ed è anzi una sua opera storica, suscettibile di un'identificazione precisa; l'occasione sollecita a procedere in via preliminare alla verifica e alla più accurata valutazione di tutto quanto si sa finora in proposito. Ritengo, infatti, che un'indicazione d'importanza basilare per il miglior raggiungimento dello scopo prefisso, emerga proprio da un attento riesame del materiale disponibile.[5]

A)

I dipinti finora individuati dagli studi, che abbiano titoli effettivi per esser presi in considerazione nella questione, sono i seguenti (li enumero in base a una descrizione quanto più

precisa possibile, ricapitolando anche i dati della loro storia esterna più utili all'identificazione)[6]:

1) *San Francesco svenuto dopo aver ricevuto le stimmate, sorretto da un angelo* (di solito descritto più genericamente come "San Francesco che riceve le stimmate", o "Estasi di san Francesco", o "San Francesco in estasi"); olio su tela di 92,5 x 127,8 cm., ora al Wadsworth Atheneum di Hartford (Conn.). Agli inizi di questo secolo l'opera passò da una collezione privata di Malta, dove non è accertato da quanto tempo si trovasse, al signor Guido Grioni di Trieste. Dopo una sosta presso l'antiquario Seligman di New York, pervenne alla sede attuale nel 1943. E' ritenuta autografa quasi all'unanimità ed è databile fra le opere giovanili del maestro nel corso degli anni 1590. Se ne conoscono varie copie (cinque, fino a ora), la più importante e documentata delle quali – a lungo creduta l'originale – è quella del Museo Civico di Udine (olio su tela di 93 x 129 cm.), lì giunta nel 1894 dalla chiesa di San Giacomo a Fagagna. A tale chiesa essa era stata donata nel 1852 dal conte Francesco Fistulario, ultimo erede della famiglia udinese dei Tritonio, presso la quale questo specifico esemplare era (o si crede fosse: manca una documentazione incontrovertibile) dagli inizi del XVII secolo.[7]

2) *San Francesco in meditazione sul teschio che tiene tra le mani, con una croce a terra* (descritto anche come "San Francesco in meditazione"); olio su tela di 125 x 93 cm., appartenente alla chiesa di San Pietro a Carpineto Romano e ora in deposito presso la Galleria d'Arte antica di Palazzo Barberini a Roma, dopo esserlo stato presso il Museo di Palazzo Venezia, sempre a Roma. E' opera priva di qualsiasi documentazione antica non puramente presuntiva, ed è quasi certo che anche la

sua ubicazione nella chiesa di San Pietro a Carpineto, la cui fondazione è del 1609, non sia quella originaria. Recuperata fisicamente e criticamente nel 1968, è ritenuta da molti – ma non senza autorevoli e insistenti contrasti – la redazione autografa del tema noto dall' esemplare appartenente alla chiesa di Santa Maria della Consolazione dei Cappuccini di Roma (olio su tela di 128 x 94 cm.). Anche di quest'ultimo, da taluni declassato a copia nonostante abbia qualità degne di un originale (ma non saranno, i due dipinti in questione, buone copie entrambi di un prototipo ancora da ritrovare ?), manca la documentazione antica. In ogni caso, anche il quadro dei Cappuccini dovette trovarsi in origine in una sede diversa dall'attuale, perché questa fu fondata nel 1626; ed è attestato che, secondo quanto recava un cartellino seicentesco applicato sul rovescio della tela e letto nel 1908, ma non più esistente da tempo, l'opera fu donata ai Cappuccini di Roma, con la clausola ''che non si possi dare a nisuno'', da un ''Signore Francesco de Rustici'', forse identificabile con il pittore senese Francesco Rustici, detto il Rustichino, la cui presenza e attività a Roma sono accertate per il biennio 1617-19.[8]

3) *San Francesco raccolto a meditare in ginocchio, con il mento appoggiato alle mani intrecciate, dinanzi a un crocifisso posto fra le pagine di un libro aperto, accanto a un teschio* (descritto comunemente come ''San Francesco penitente''); olio su tela di 130 x 90 cm., appartenente ora alla Pinacoteca del Museo Civico di Cremona. E' pervenuto in tale sede con il lascito del marchese Filippo Ala di Ponzone, discendente del marchese Sigismondo, la destinazione pubblica della cui raccolta risale a un testamento del 1836, aggiornato nel 1842. Privo pur esso di qualsiasi altra documentazione, è stato solo nel 1943 che Roberto Longhi ha proposto di riconoscervi una buona copia da un originale perduto del Caravaggio. In seguito, sebbene con la riserva del cattivo stato di conservazione, Denis Mahon ha proposto per primo di rivalutarlo come originale, ottenendo adesioni significative.[9]

B)

I documenti scritti – incluse, ovviamente, le testimonianze inventariali, purché non più tarde della prima metà del XVII secolo –, in cui si ritiene siano menzionate esplicitamente o implicitamente opere del Caravaggio raffiguranti in qualche modo ''San Francesco'', sono quelli dai quali, in estratto e secondo la successione cronologica, ricavo le seguenti attestazioni:

6 agosto 1606. Il genovese Ottavio Costa, residente a Roma, lascia per testamento a Ruggiero Tritonio di Udine, abate commandatario di Pinerolo e segretario del cardinale Montalto,

un quadro a sua scelta fra questi due: ''San Francesco'' e le ''Sante Marta e Maddalena''; il quadro che rimarrà, andrà a Giovanni Enriquez de Herrera (socio del Costa in affari, e futuro committente degli affreschi che Annibale Carracci e discepoli eseguiranno nella cappella appartenente allo stesso Herrera nella chiesa romana di San Giacomo degli Spagnuoli):

''legavit multo ill.mi D. Rogerio Abbati Tritonio a secretis ill.mi et r.mi Car[dina]lis Montisalti unum ex duobus quadris ipsius D. testatoris i[d est] quadrum *S.ti Francisci* seu *S.tarum Marthae et Magdalenae* ad electione[m] ipsiius D. abbatis, alterum vero legavit m.to ill. D. Jo(‹poc›hann]i Enriquez de Herrera''.[10]

25 ottobre 1607. Con testamento di tale data (non del 1597, come era stato creduto in precedenza), e che sarà pubblicato solo alla morte del testatore, il 13 luglio 1612,[11] Ruggiero Tritonio lascia al nipote Francesco, ordinandogli di non cederlo o venderlo a chicchessia, il dipinto con ''*San Francesco*'', *opera di Caravaggio*, che gli aveva donato Ottavio Costa:

''*divi Francisci signum a Caravagio* celeberrimo pictori summa cum diligentia affabre *pictum*, quod mihi dominus Octavius Costa [...] donavit, perpetue asservari nec ulli unquam concedi aut alienari iubeo''.[12]

21 febbraio – 18 maggio 1627. L'inventario, redatto nei giorni indicati, dei dipinti facenti parte dell'eredità del cardinale Francesco Maria Del Monte in Roma, elenca ben sette opere del Caravaggio, distribuite nelle varie sale del palazzo Del Monte a Ripetta. Fra queste, nella ''Galleria piccola, che va nella loggia'', sono registrate insieme le seguenti: ''Una S. Caterina della Ruota opera di Michel Agnolo da Caravaggio con cornici d'oro rabescate di palmi sette. Un' [sic] *S. Francesco in Estasi di Michel Agnolo da Caravaggio* con cornici negre di palmi quattro''.[13]

25 maggio 1628. Nel ''Giardino di Ripetta'' in Roma, per settanta scudi e in un lotto che comprende solo questo dipinto, è messo in vendita dall'eredità del cardinal Del Monte ''un *S. Fran.co del Caravaggio*'', sicuramente lo stesso descritto nell'inventario Del Monte del 1627 come ''S. Francesco in Estasi''.[14] L'acquirente non è nominato, né è stato ancora possibile identificarlo. E' comunque da escludere l'ipotesi che questi fosse il cardinale Antonio Barberini, perché, a differenza della ''Santa Caterina della ruota'', inventariata in casa Del Monte nel 1627 insieme al ''San Francesco'' (si veda più sopra) e acquistata effettivamente dal cardinal Barberini alla stessa vendita, un'opera identificabile con il ''San Francesco'' descritto nei documenti del 1627 e 1628 non ricompare in nessuno dei due inventari seicenteschi di quadri barberiniani (rispettivamente del 1644 e del 1671) editi dalla Aronberg Lavin.[15]

1) Caravaggio, «San Francesco in estasi», Barbara P. Johnson Collection, Princeton, N. J.

1631. Antoniotto Costa, figlio di Ottavio, invia da Roma a Malta alcuni quadri dei quali non è indicato il nome dell'autore (o degli autori), ma i cui temi iconografici hanno indotto qualche studioso a supporre che potesse trattarsi di dipinti del Caravaggio. Fra questi è un ''San Francesco''.[16]

18-24 gennaio 1639. Nell'inventario dei quadri di Ottavio Costa, redatto in tali giorni in Roma alla morte di Ottavio stesso (il quale era dunque sopravvissuto sia al testamento fatto in punto di morte nel 1606, sia allo stesso Tritonio, morto – come s'è già detto – nel 1612), è menzionato, insieme a ''un quadro grande con l'imagine di Judit'' e a ''un altro quadro con l'imagine di S. Gio.Batta nel diserto'', entrambi del Caravaggio, ''un altro *quadro di S. Francesco fatto dall'istesso Caravaggio*''. E' degno di nota, in proposito, che in un ulteriore testamento, dettato sette anni prima del definitivo, nel 1632, Ottavio Costa includesse per il futuro erede l'ordine di non alienare in nessun caso ''tutti li quadri del Caravaggio particolarmente la Giuditta''.[17]

Prima del 1641. Secondo le indicazioni che egli stesso afferma essergli state fornite, di ritorno da Napoli, da Teofilo Gallacini (noto scrittore senese anche di cose architettoniche, morto nel 1641), l'anonimo autore delle postille alla copia fiorentina del manoscritto delle ''Considerazioni sulla Pittura'' di Giulio Mancini con vite di artisti, aggiunge, per quanto ''appartiene alla vita di Michelagnolo da Caravaggio'', una lista di opere del maestro che ''si ved[ono] in Napoli''; fra queste, nella chiesa di Sant'Anna dei Lombardi, e nella stessa cappella di detta chiesa dove, del Caravaggio, si trovava anche ''una tavola d'un Christo resurgente bellissima'' (la ''Resurrezione'', della cappella Fenaroli), è indicato testualmente (corsivo mio): un ''*S. Francesco in atto di ricever le stimate*''.[18]

C)

Collazionando i dati documentari riferiti nella precedente sezione B), con i dipinti elencati nella sezione A), la critica moderna ha finora ritenuto di poter trarre le seguenti conclusioni, e prospettare le seguenti ipotesi di collegamento.[19]

Il dipinto ora a Hartford, riconosciuto universalmente come unico autografo fra quanti ripresentano la medesima iconografia,[20] è lo stesso che Ottavio Costa, testando il 6 agosto 1606, donava, in alternativa al quadro delle ''Sante Marta e Maddalena'', a Ruggiero Tritonio. E' pertanto anche lo stesso che il 25 ottobre dell'anno dopo, testando a sua volta, Tritonio lasciava in eredità al nipote, indicandolo giusto come l'opera del Caravaggio che gli era stata donata da Ottavio Costa.[21] Si tenga tuttavia presente fin d'ora, che a questo punto di vista, e ai due seguenti

che ne derivano, ne è stato opposto un altro, che ricorderò più sotto e discuterò, insieme al resto, a suo luogo.

Poiché dall'eredità ottocentesca della famiglia Tritonio è pervenuto al Museo di Udine un dipinto raffigurante la stessa iconografia del dipinto di Hartford, e tale esemplare per un verso risulta inoppugnabilmente copia di quello, per un altro ha caratteristiche di fattura che lo fanno giudicare non posteriore agli inizi del XVII secolo; i più ritengono che, nonostante Ruggiero Tritonio ordinasse al nipote suo erede di non vendere il quadro,[22] questi non solo lo vendesse (e, molto probabilmente, già alla morte dello zio, avvenuta nel 1612), ma lo facesse anche sostituire con la copia che ci è pervenuta dalla sua eredità.

Tenendo presente che l'inventario delle collezioni Del Monte redatto nel 1627 include fra i quadri posseduti dal cardinale anche un ''San Francesco in estasi'' del Caravaggio,[23] una parte della critica ha argomentato che il nipote di Tritonio, fatta eseguire la copia di cui s'è detto, vendesse l'originale proprio a Francesco Maria Del Monte, già protettore del Caravaggio, come si sa, e collezionista di sue opere.[24] Morto Del Monte nel 1626, e andata in vendita due anni dopo una parte importante delle sue raccolte,[25] il ''San Francesco'' sarebbe stato riacquistato dal suo committente e primo proprietario, Ottavio Costa; e ciò perché nel 1631 un ''San Francesco'' era in possesso del figlio di Ottavio, Antoniotto Costa.[26] Avendo per altro Antoniotto inviato quell'anno da Roma a Malta, insieme ad altri quadri, anche un ''San Francesco'',[27] questo sarebbe lo stesso quadro che, circa due secoli e mezzo dopo, pervenne da Malta a Trieste e poi emigrò a Hartford.[28]

Una diversa parte della critica, evidentemente sconcertata da un'ipotesi così romanzesca, ha invece sostenuto che il dipinto ora a Hartford andrebbe identificato certamente con il dipinto dell'inventario Del Monte, ma senza bisogno di ricorrere al giro vizioso di una vendita semiclandestina fatta dall'erede del Tritonio al cardinale: basta credere che l'autografo ora a Hartford fosse dipinto dal Caravaggio per lo stesso Del Monte (Frommel ha supposto addirittura che il san Francesco raffigurato in quel quadro sarebbe un ritratto del cardinale),[29] e che il quadro donato da Ottavio Costa a Ruggiero Tritonio sarebbe stato, dall'origine, una copia: la stessa, appunto, pervenuta dai discendenti del Tritonio al Museo di Udine.[30]

In quanto l'inventario dei quadri Costa redatto nel gennaio 1639 cita ancora un ''quadro di San Francesco fatto dall'istesso Caravaggio'',[31] è stato supposto che tale ulteriore ''San Francesco'' sia identificabile o con il dipinto di Carpineto (in eventuale alternativa con il suo gemello dei Cappuccini a Roma),[32] o con quello di Cremona[33]: entrambi, del resto, simili per dimensioni e, secondo l'opinione di chi ha avanzato questa proposta, anche per epoca.[34]

2) Caravaggio, «San Francesco in estasi», particolare, Barbara P. Johnson Collection, Princeton, N. J.

Al riguardo, infine, del ''San Francesco in atto di ricevere le stimmate'', citato sulla fede del Gallaccini nella cappella Fenaroli a Sant'Anna dei Lombardi in Napoli dal postillatore del Mancini,[35] non solo non sono stati addotti riscontri convincenti, ma s'è addirittura dato dentro a gravi confusioni. Caduta e ormai abbandonata da tutti la tesi, del resto presentata come estremamente incerta dallo stesso Friedländer che la prospettò per primo,[36] secondo cui in quest'opera si sarebbe potuto ravvisare l'originale del *San Francesco* di Cremona, allora giudicato copia[37] – ma l'infondatezza dell'ipotesi era evidente già dalla discrepanza che corre fra il soggetto del dipinto descritto e quello del dipinto chiamato a riscontro –; non poggia che su una catena di errori anche la tesi più recente, cresciuta per tappe successive e per differenti vie da Raffaello Causa a Vittorio

Casale, secondo cui una derivazione diretta dall'opera in questione (Causa), o, comunque, da un prototipo perduto del Caravaggio (Casale), sarebbe da riconoscere in un *San Francesco* noto da due versioni dipinte e da una terza a stampa[38]: la prima, al Monteoliveto di Napoli, attribuita dallo Strazzullo, con il consenso del Causa, a Filippo Vitale[39]; la seconda, al monastero di San Quirico ad Assisi, già attribuita al Cigoli[40]; e l'ultima, in un'incisione in controparte, che, con la firma dell'incisore seicentesco Pieter Claesz. Soutman, reca l'annotazione: ''Michael Agnolo Caravaggio pinxit''.[41] Premesso che la giusta descrizione iconografica del dipinto riflesso in tutte e tre queste versioni non può essere altro che ''San Francesco in meditazione davanti al Crocifisso'' (quanto meno, ''San Francesco orante''), e non ''San Francesco in atto di ricever le stimate'', come invece recita la descrizione del quadro visto dal Gallaccini a Napoli – donde una divergenza insanabile, che già di per sé mette fuori giuoco l'identificazione con quest'ultimo –; fu Alfred Moir a rilevare per primo che nella stampa di Pieter Soutman l'atteggiamento del santo deriva da un dipinto attribuito a Francesco Bassano nel Kunsthistorisches Museum di Vienna.[42] In realtà, il rapporto iconografico-compositivo con il dipinto di Vienna non si limita alla stampa di Soutman, né riguarda soltanto l'atteggiamento del santo. Estendendosi a tutti i particolari della rappresentazione, esso coinvolge anche e specialmente le due versioni pittoriche, le quali ripropongono la medesima composizione ancor più fedelmente: nel verso giusto e in ogni dettaglio, con la sola eccezione – per esser precisi fino in fondo – del filaterio, che è aggiunta peculiare del dipinto di Assisi. Poiché il ''San Francesco orante'' di Vienna reca l'attribuzione a Francesco Bassano il giovane dal 1783, dopo aver portato quella a Jacopo almeno dal 1659; e per giunta è compagno di una ''Santa Giuliana Falconieri'' la cui caratterizzazione stilistica tra Jacopo e Francesco junior è ancor più manifesta[43]; non è a pensare (come non è ancora venuto in mente ad alcuno, ma potrebbe) che anch'esso sia eventualmente copia da un perduto originale del Caravaggio. Essendo Francesco Bassano morto il 3 luglio 1592, appena cinque mesi dopo il padre Jacopo, i tempi lo escludono in modo perentorio. Così come occorre escludere senza perplessità – e in questo caso per manifeste ragioni di principio –, che fosse il Caravaggio a trarre copie da un Francesco Bassano ! Non risulterà allora di poco interesse, che nel 1692, dopo aver descritto sull'altar maggiore giusto della chiesa napoletana di Sant'Anna dei Lombardi una tavola di Fabrizio Santafede, il canonico Carlo Celano aggiungesse questa testuale indicazione: ''i quadri laterali a detta tavola, in uno dei quali sta espresso S. Francesco, nell'altro una Santa Vergine, sono stimati del Bassan vecchio, e veramente sono cose degne d'esser vedute''.[44] Dal momento che questi due dipinti, pur presentando soggetti identici a quelli di Vienna (la dizione: *una* Santa Vergine'', e non *la* Santa

Vergine'', nel contesto del Celano indica sicuramente che lo scrittore definiva ''Santa Vergine'' la santa Giuliana Falconieri che non aveva identificato), non possono essere gli stessi di Vienna, perché questi si trovavano nella collezione dell'arciduca Leopoldo Guglielmo d'Absburgo da prima del 1659[45]; si è costretti ad ammettere che ne fossero versioni o copie fedeli. E poiché è risaputo che dopo il 1798, in seguito al crollo della chiesa dove tali versioni si trovavano, almeno alcuni dei quadri superstiti passarono a Monteoliveto,[46] si è altres indotti a ritenere verosimile, se non addirittura certo, che la versione/copia della ''Santa Giuliana'' anadasse distrutta o dispersa, come tante e importanti altre opere presenti nella stessa sede, ma che quella del ''San Francesco'', rimasta indenne, fosse fra le poche passate a Monteoliveto, e dunque sia identica con l'esemplare in questione, che in quella chiesa si trova tuttora. Ne consegue di necessità che sia gli studiosi moderni via via ricordati, sia lo stesso Soutman, che pure era stato collaboratore di Rubens dal 1620, e mor nel 1657 – dunque a non grande distanza di tempi dagli avvenimenti –, in definitiva han solo confuso Caravaggio con Francesco Bassano. Senza dire dell' infortunio, indubbiamente più lieve, di chi ora risulta aver preteso di collegare un documento buono, il pagamento del 1613 a Filippo Vitale, con un dipinto sbagliato: voglio dire con un dipinto che con Filippo Vitale non ebbe, né ha a che fare, più che con Caravaggio.[47]

Tornando a cose pertinenti, è opportuno non trascurare un' ultima nota: che il ''San Francesco in atto di ricever le stimate'' del Caravaggio segnalato a Sant'Anna dei Lombardi, non può aspirare a esser connesso o identificato nemmeno con ''l'historia di S. Francesco col compagno, del pittore Caravaggio'', che gli inventari dell'eredità del cardinale Ascanio Filomarino citano a Napoli nel 1685 e nel 1700.[48] Se, infatti, l'enunciato di ''historia di S. Francesco col compagno'' questa volta potrebbe rispondere bene a una scena con san Francesco che riceve le stimmate, dove la presenza del ''compagno'', alias frate Leone, è d'obbligo; si oppone all'identificazione il fatto che il dipinto caravaggesco di Sant'Anna dei Lombardi si trovava sicuramente ''in situ'' ancora sullo scorcio del XVIII secolo.

Orbene, uno scrutinio ragionatamente critico di tutta questa materia (e anche dopo averne espunto la poco istruttiva questione intrecciata intorno al *San Francesco stimmatizzato* di Napoli), autorizza a ricavare una sola evidenza affidabile: che, tra le diverse proposte di collegamento fra quadri e dati documentari, l'unica meritevole di essere giudicata conclusiva è quella che identifica nel dipinto ora a Hartford il ''quadrum Sancti Francisci'' che nel 1606 apparteneva a Ottavio Costa, e l'anno dopo, per dono del Costa, a Ruggiero Tritonio. Non può, infatti, non esser giudicata inattendibile proprio la tesi che, all'apparenza (ma solo all'apparenza) sembrerebbe la più lineare: vale a dire che Costa donasse a Tritonio una copia del quadro ora a

3) Caravaggio, «San Francesco in estasi», particolare, Barbara P. Johnson Collection, Princeton, N. J.

Hartford, quella di Udine, e che l'originale ora a Hartford fosse dipinto dal Caravaggio per il cardinal Del Monte. L'inattendibilità di una supposizione del genere nasce dal fatto che Tritonio, menzionando in testamento il quadro donatogli dal Costa, volle accreditarlo con una impegnativa dichiarazione di paternità, e con un elogio di merito, il cui valore di testimonianza è incontrovertibile. Alla data del 1607; a Roma; Caravaggio appena fuggito di città, ma sempre vivo e stimato; affermare che quel "divi Francisci signum" era stato "a Caravagio celeberrimo pictori summa cum diligentia affabre pictum",[49] comportava infatti un grado di convinzione, nonché un'assunzione di responsabilità, che si giustificano solo in presenza di un autografo comprovato. Una smentita del Caravaggio in persona era troppo a portata di mano per sfidare il rischio di esser colti, come si dice, con le mani nel sacco. Né pare lecito insinuare la solita celia sulla circostanza che Ottavio Costa era ... genovese, o addirittura, come ha fatto Carlo Volpe, muovere l'accusa d'un inganno deliberato. Nel 1606, Costa testava in punto di morte, anche se poi tornò in salute; e non curò minimamente di affermare che i quadri che donava a scelta, a Tritonio e a Herrera, fossero o non del Caravaggio: tanto più sostenere che un appassionato ammiratore e protettore del maestro quale Costa fu senza possibilità di smentita, donasse in punto di morte copie e non originali di lui, a due dei suoi più intimi soci in fatto di preferenze pittoriche, pare una supposizione che sorpassa di troppo i limiti, pur ristretti, che dobbiamo porre alla sfiducia negli uomini. E aggiungiamo ancora che, gettare dubbi su un sistema di testimonianze di prima mano quale emerge a date ancora alte dai testamenti privati di un Costa e di un Tritonio, è poco corretto innanzitutto dal punto di vista del metodo nell'uso storiografico delle fonti. Il quadro Costa-Tritonio è quello ora a Hartford, proprio perché il quadro di Udine ne è copia letterale. Copia, fatta certo per aggirare il vincolo di non-alienabilità imposto agli eredi dal geloso testatore, per altro in un momento in cui (si doveva essere nel 1612, a due anni dalla morte del Caravaggio) proprio la morte del Caravaggio aveva notoriamente rinfocolato la ricerca di sue opere da parte di molti.

Quanto al rimanente (come, del resto, nel caso che s'è appena finito d'illustrare), la critica ha dimostrato nient'altro che la tendenza a comprimere la varietà del materiale documentario sui soli tre dipinti identificati in precedenza. E' già difficile credere che quadri di destinazione chiesastica quali sono senza dubbio i *San Francesco* di Carpineto, dei Cappuccini a Roma e di Cremona, siano riducibili ragionevolmente sotto l'etichetta di un quadro "da collezione" quale dovette essere quello presente nella raccolta Costa nel 1639. Né si trascuri che, se il *San Francesco* dei Cappuccini di Roma fu effettivamente donato a tale chiesa da Francesco Rustici fra il 1617 e il 1619, ciò esclude perentoriamente qualsiasi altra identificazione, almeno per quell'esemplare. Figurarsi quanto possa esser credibile la catena di supposizioni secondo cui il quadro uscito dall'eredità Tritonio dopo il 1612, quello presente nella collezione Del Monte fino al 1627 e andato in vendita nel 1628, e ancora il "San Francesco" spedito a Malta da Antoniotto Costa nel 1631, sarebbero sempre lo stesso quadro.

Dopo la fuga del Caravaggio da Roma, non è provato affatto che il cardinal Del Monte acquistasse quadri del maestro da altri. Al contrario, pare certo che quel prelato possedesse dipinti del Caravaggio acquisiti esclusivamente negli anni in cui il maestro era stato presso di lui; e se si dà l'eccezione del "quadro di San Giovanni Battista", che entrò nella collezione del cardinale verso il 1624 provenendo da quella di Ciriaco Mattei, ciò non fu per un acquisto ma per un lascito, e con la seguente, esplicita motivazione da parte del figlio di Ciriaco, Giovanni Battista Mattei: "item lascio all'illustrissimo Signor Cardinale

Del Monte come unico mio signore e padrone il quadro di San Giovanni Battista del Caravaggio".[50]

Quanto a Ottavio Costa, è provato ancor meno, anzi non esiste sintomo alcuno, che dopo il 1628 acquistasse quadri del Caravaggio provenienti dalla collezione Del Monte; così come sono mere e infondate congetture sia che il "San Francesco" inviato nel 1631 a Malta dal figlio Antoniotto fosse opera del Caravaggio (il documento, come s'è avuto cura di ricordare a suo luogo, non ne fa il nome),[51] sia che fosse addirittura l'opera del Caravaggio donata da Ottavio a Tritonio nel 1606. Per altro, se nel 1628 Costa avesse recuperato effettivamente il quadro donato a Tritonio nel 1606 – dimostrando così un interesse per esso veramente eccezionale –, non si capisce come, e perché mai, l'avrebbe poi sottovalutato al punto di consentire che, solo tre anni dopo, il figlio lo esportasse a Malta; tanto più che nel 1632, come si ricorderà, si preoccupava di ingiungere per testamento al futuro erede di non disfarsi in alcun modo di "tutti li quadri del Caravaggio".[52]

Ma al fine di ribadire questo già consistente cumulo di sintomi contrari, il punto decisivo è ancora un altro. E' che il quadro Costa-Tritonio-Hartford rappresenta San Francesco nel momento successivo a quello della stigmatizzazione, quando, ricevute le stigmate, il santo tramortito è consolato dall'angelo (la dimostrazione datane anni a dietro da Pamela Askew è, sotto questo aspetto, ineccepibile)[53]; il dipinto elencato nel 1627 nell'inventario Del Monte è descritto invece come un "San Francesco in estasi", vale a dire come un dipinto nel quale, a rigor di termini, siamo autorizzati a supporre un'unica e sola figura, in atto estatico.

Prende così a farsi finalmente strada un interrogativo finora non posto o evitato dalla critica: se il Caravaggio, oltre a quelli noti, non abbia eseguito altri dipinti di soggetto sanfrancescano; e, in particolare, se il "San Francesco in estasi" posseduto dal cardinal Del Monte, sicuramente distinto dal quadro ora a Hartford, non sia opera tuttora da ritrovare.

S'è anche trascurato di osservare, in oltre, che nell'inventario Del Monte i dipinti del Caravaggio s'incontrano in sale distinte, radunati per gruppi che sembrano cronologicamente omogenei[54]; e il "San Francesco in estasi" è menzionato nella stessa sala (la "Galleria piccola che va sulla loggia") della "Santa Caterina della ruota", anzi di seguito a essa. Poiché, come si sa, quest'ultima è con certezza il dipinto già dei Barberini conservato attualmente nella collezione Thyssen-Bornemisza alla Castagnola presso Lugano, che la critica considera opera – chiave nello svolgimento del Caravaggio verso il "ringagliardire gli oscuri" di cui parlò Bellori,[55] pare legittimo domandarsi se il nuovo "San Francesco in estasi" che viene profilandosi, non solo fosse diverso dal quadro finito a Hartford, ma anche più svolto nelle ricerche stilistiche e perciò più simile, eventualmente, alla *Santa Caterina* Thyssen.

In fine, non vorremo rinunciare a trarre profitto dall'argomento esposto da Frommel quando, tentando di collegare il quadro di Hartford al quadro dell'inventario Del Monte, ha sostenuto che il cardinale facesse dipingere un "San Francesco" perché egli stesso portava il nome del santo, e che, nell'intento di far risaltare meglio l'identità onomastica, volesse che nel dipinto il santo avesse le sue stesse fattezze fisiche.[56] Ebbene, un'ipotesi del genere, esistenzialmente assai verosimile, può risultare vera a due precise condizioni: la prima, che nel quadro del quale andiamo in cerca, la figura del santo appaia in un'evidenza dominante, pressoché assoluta: comunque, maggiore che nel quadro di Hartford, dove il santo divide il ruolo di protagonista con l'angelo, con la scena schizzata nel fondo e con lo squarcio di paese; la seconda è che tale quadro appartenga a un momento dell'arte caravaggesca nel quale – giusto come nella *Santa Caterina*, il cui modello fisico è così bene individuato, che s'è potuto riconoscerlo anche in altri quadri coevi del maestro[57] –, l'istanza ritrattistica in senso stretto sia condotta più avanti di quanto non fosse in tutte le opere risalenti ai primi anni romani del Caravaggio, e anche nel dipinto di Hartford, che al novero di quelle appartiene ancora di diritto.

Se poniamo la questione in questi termini, s'impone subito l'evidenza che il dipinto entrato nella collezione Johnson raffigura alla lettera un *San Francesco in estasi* e ha le caratteristiche stilistiche e tipologiche richieste dalle condizioni illustrate. Malauguratamente, non conosciamo ancora quali fossero le fattezze fisiche del cardinal Del Monte; perciò almeno l'ipotesi di un suo ritratto nelle vesti dell'omonimo santo di Assisi non può che rimanere congetturale; nondimeno non è una congettura che nel nuovo dipinto la forza di caratterizzazione e d'individuazione fisiognomica sia sospinta tanto avanti, da soddisfare a pieno anche all'ultima condizione sopra descritta. Il *San Francesco* Johnson, in altri termini, ha tutti i requisiti necessari per essere identificato esso, a preferenza di ogni altro, con il "*San Francesco in Estasi di Michel Agnolo da Caravaggio*" elencato nell'inventario Del Monte del 1627, e andato in vendita nel maggio dell'anno dopo, per settanta scudi, con la reiterata menzione di "*San Fran[ces]co del Caravaggio*".

Mentre ci disponiamo ad attendere che tornino alla luce dati idonei a colmare, almeno in parte, la prolungata mancanza di notizie che dal 1628 arriva fino a noi, veniamo ora a costatazioni più analitiche, per un verso, più addentrate in profondità, per un altro, al fine di consolidare su un terreno più specifico l'identificazione appena proposta.

Un primo passo può esser fatto lavorando a un controllo ragionato delle dimensioni del dipinto, in rapporto ai modi con cui furono rilevate in passato. La critica ha già costatato che, in materia di rilevamento delle misure, l'inventario Del Monte impiegò di volta in volta criteri differenti: impiegò addirittura, com'è stato scritto, "un sistema molto misto, ora specificando che si tratta di altezza o di lunghezza, ora senza precisazioni", e sempre senza dichiarare se la misura rilevata includesse o non la cornice, a onta che in qualche caso, pur raro, la includesse sicuramente.[58] Nondimeno, la stessa critica ha accertato che per taluni quadri ricorre un particolare tipo di approssimazione fra le misure riscontrabili oggi, quelle date per la sola altezza (e presumibilmente senza cornice) nell'inventario Del Monte, e quelle date nell'inventario Barberini del 1671. Mia Cinotti, che di recente ha prestato un'attenzione speciale al problema nel suo complesso, ha stabilito che nei casi in discorso, e dato il "palmo" romano pari a 22,34 cm., "le misure Del Monte, se assunte in altezza, sono alquanto inferiori a quelle attuali senza cornice, quelle Barberini sono un poco superiori".[59] A prova, ha fatto costatare che un'opera ben conosciuta del Caravaggio, quale la già ricordata *Santa Caterina della ruota* oggi nella collezione Thyssen-Bornemisza, e che è menzionata con le misure e nelle condizioni descritte in entrambi gli inventari presi in esame, dà comparativamente il seguente stato di cose:

altezza attuale effettiva: 173 cm.;
altezza Del Monte: "palmi sette", pari a 156,38 cm.;
altezza Barberini: "circa palmi otto", pari a c. 178,72 cm..

Il "San Francesco in estasi" non ricompare negli inventari Barberini; evidentemente, perché non entrò mai in quella collezione, come già sappiamo; e ciò ci priva di uno dei termini di paragone. Ma nell'inventario Del Monte è elencato nella stessa stanza della *Santa Caterina*, subito di séguito a essa; e ciò autorizza a credere, senza dubbi possibili, che le misure dei due quadri furono rilevate nello stesso momento, con gli stessi strumenti e in base allo stesso criterio di misurazione. Ebbene, nell'inventario del 1627 il "San Francesco" Del Monte è dato di "palmi quattro", ossia, in base al solito computo, di 89,36 cm.; mentre quello Johnson è alto 103 cm. Costatiamo così che, rispetto alle misure Del Monte, il *San Francesco* Johnson accusa una differenza di 13,64 cm. in più, che, in termini di proporzione, corrisponde bene ai 16,62 cm. in più che le misure reali della *Santa Caterina* Thyssen-Bornemisza (173 cm.) hanno rispetto a quelle attribuite allo stesso dipinto nello stesso inventario ("palmi sette" 156,38 cm.). Il rapporto proporzionale 103 : 89,36 173 : 156,38 dà infatti, nel primo caso 1,152, nel secondo 1,106, con uno scarto irrilevante. Nel medesimo contesto, per contro, vale la pena di notare che il quadro di Hartford è alto 92,5 cm.; presenta, cioè, uno scarto di soli 3,14 cm. in più rispetto ai "quattro palmi", pari a 89,36 cm., indicati nell'inventario Del Monte. Per quanto possa apparire paradossale in base a valori assoluti, ciò risulta molto distante da quel che le costatazioni fatte fin qui reclamerebbero per confermare l'identità con il "San Francesco" Del Monte che alcuni hanno voluto sostenere.

Ma v'è ancora un altra e forse più stringente ipotesi da prospettare in proposito, ed è che quando l'inventario Del Monte dà una sola misura, in realtà intenda indicare il massimo ingombro del quadro, vale a dire rilevi la misura del suo lato più lungo: per alto, se il quadro è verticale; per largo, se orizzontale. Poiché abbiamo la prova che fu sicuramente così almeno nel caso della *Santa Caterina* Thyssen, ne discende in via definitiva che il "San Francesco in estasi" non può nemmeno in tal caso aver fatto tutt'uno con il dipinto di Hartford. Quadro notoriamente orizzontale, questo, sul lato lungo, raggiunge attualmente addirittura 127,8 cm., pari a poco meno di sei palmi (5,721): ciò vuol dire che rispetto all'unica misura nota del quadro Del Monte ("quattro palmi", pari a 89, 36 cm.), e anche senza tener conto dei sopra illustrati scarti di valore relativo, esso eccede in larghezza molto, anzi troppo di più, di quanto non faccia in altezza il ritrovato *San Francesco* Johnson (127,8 –89,36 38,44; 103 – 89,36 13,64).

Stabilito questo primo punto, resta però che gli argomenti capaci di dare una concretezza storiografica effettiva alle indicazioni provenienti dall'analisi dei documenti e dei dati di fatto in essi registrati, sono pur sempre e innanzitutto quelli storico-artistici, sia stilistici (nel senso dell'ordinamento compositivo e della realizzazione pittorica), sia tecnici (nel senso dei procedimenti operativi). E' tempo, perciò, di venire a essi.

Che il tema iconografico del dipinto in esame sia "San Francesco in estasi", è fuori discussione. Ma, posto il fatto fra le cose assodate, occorre passare subito a mettere in risalto in qual modo, e con quale sottile originalità, quel tema – che, com'è risaputo, non era inedito – qui figura assunto ed elaborato. Negli ultimi decenni del XVI secolo, il motivo figurale del santo di Assisi con le braccia incrociate al petto, una mano sorreggente una piccola croce, l'altra più o meno in vista con lo stigma, e il volto levato al cielo, aveva conosciuto una sua particolare fortuna. Anche a fondarsi sul solo materiale illustrato nel catalogo della mostra romana dedicata alcuni anni fa all' iconografia di San Francesco nella Controriforma, si possono indicare non meno di quattro esempi specifici, tre dei quali presenti o relativi a Roma e tutti radunati fra il 1574 circa e la fine del secolo; nonché pochi altri di epoca non dissimile, che o variano o arricchiscono lievemente l'assetto reciproco degli stessi motivi su descritti.[60] Fra i primi, per altro, due versioni appaiono iconicamente tanto vicine a quella adottata nel nostro dipinto, da lasciar supporre un rapporto men che generico: il mosaico di Paolo Rossetti del 1594, a Santa Maria di Loreto; e il

disegno del Pomarancio agli Uffizi, da taluni messo in relazione con gli affreschi della cappella Mattei all'Aracoeli, di qualche anno prima[61]: ciò, per giunta, anche a prescindere dal divario – però non del tutto irrilevante ai fini del significato religioso – per cui in entrambe queste versioni il santo non sorregge la croce con la mano nascosta, bensì con la stessa della quale (destra o sinistra che sia) è messo meglio in vista lo stigma – ora in primo, ora in secondo piano, e pur con diverse angolazioni della croce. Nondimeno, indipendentemente dalle singole varianti tematiche eventualmente preferite, e a prescindere, per ora, anche dal fatto che tutti gli esempi fin qui addotti appartengono di diritto al terzo dei "temi" principali su cui "l'immagine di S. Francesco nella Controriforma" si sarebbe fondata: "il ritiro, la meditazione e l'estasi"[62]; s'impone l'evidenza che la totalità delle medesime versioni iconografiche chiamate al riscontro risulta improntata a un tipo d'impaginazione compositiva del tutto tradizionale: tale, comunque, da non lasciar supporre un qualsiasi intento di ricerca, con significato iconografico o di valore espressivo, affidata alla collocazione della figura del santo nello spazio entro cui la si vuol far apparire o muovere. Nel *San Francesco* Johnson, invece, è proprio una ricerca del genere, per altro acutissima, che occorre avvertire per prima.

Una volta stabilito che il campo dipinto dell'opera, del resto pervenutoci in uno stato di conservazione perfetto anche sotto gli altri aspetti, risulta intatto lungo tutti e quattro i margini originali, non si tarda ad avvedersi che in esso la figura del santo è collocata leggermente più a sinistra della linea mediana della composizione, ed è angolata di poco, con una rotazione di non più che quarantacinque gradi verso sinistra, rispetto al piano di fondo e a quello parallelo di superficie. Questa sottile scentratura, con disposizione angolata, sarebbe già di per sé un'invenzione figurativa di non comune intelligenza. Ma occorre passar subito a percepire che essa è anche il prodotto di un calcolo compositivo portatore di un potenziale d'innovazione non minore sotto almeno due aspetti: al confronto delle simmetrie canoniche in fatto di ordinamento della scena, a cui la tradizione cinquecentesca – inclusa quella, come s'è accennato, rispecchiata negli esempi iconografici ricordati più a dietro – non aveva ancora cessato di tributare omaggi; ma soprattutto in rapporto e in funzione del tema iconografico, l'estasi, a cui la medesima invenzione è manifestamente addetta. Tale accorgimento compositivo, infatti, fa sì che il santo paia come se avanzasse verso sinistra, incamminato alla volta della fonte di luce rimasta fuori del quadro, in alto da quel lato. In termini più precisi, l'accorgimento genera la sensazione che il santo sia stato colto dal pittore (il quale, in questo come in altri casi, s'identifica con il riguardante) nel momento in cui, scorta la lama di luce trapelata or ora, si è volto verso di essa e ha preso ad avvicinarlesi, levando gli occhi e la faccia.

168

Ebbene, è evidente che tutto ciò implica in prima istanza un'interpretazione dell'estasi dissenziente dalle (comunque, non allineata con le) posizioni ortodosse intese a concepirla come *rapimento* – cioè, come assunzione catartica, e passiva, del *chiamato*, in una sfera mistico/ascetica dove non si dà che *visione*, o contemplazione trasumanante, magari a occhi chiusi –; e invece fautrice di una concezione innovante che nell'estasi vuol cogliere il momento di una *scoperta* vera e propria –, l'operazione attiva di un soggetto il quale, al richiamo, risponde con un gesto corrispondente a un'esigenza di costatazione (se non addirittura di verifica), e insomma con la decisione di muoversi per andare a vedere, *a occhi aperti*, quel che ha attirato la sua attenzione –. Tutto questo non potrebbe essere più caravaggesco. E caravaggesco nel senso che, lungo una linea interpretativa non priva di precedenti autorevoli, chi scrive ha procurato di chiarire ripetutamente, e di nuovo nella prima parte del libro a cui il presente capitolo appartiene, in materia di raffigurazioni caravaggesche del sacro, come, del resto, del profano e del mitologico. Nel senso, voglio dire, che in tutte le rappresentazioni di tal genere, il proposito del maestro fu costantemente quello di ricondurle al grado zero della dimensione esistenziale, anzi alla condizione di testimonianza, assumendo la storia e l'immagine giusto nel momento bruciante in cui l'evento storico era stato solo un accadimento umano costatabile, e l'immagine era stata, com'è tuttora, innanzitutto un oggetto dell'esperienza: entrambe le volte al di là della metafora idealisticamente amplificante, nonché di schemi mentali troppo rigidamente pre-costituiti o sclerotizzati nella "routine" della ripetizione rituale, e sia che appartenessero alla normativa religiosa (specie in accezione post-tridentina), sia che derivassero dai repertori colti della simbologia mitologica di tradizione umanistica.[63]

Venendo alla realizzazione pittorica, il *San Francesco* Johnson si dimostra improntato a un carattere che è caravaggesco in senso ancor più stringente, anzi finalmente specifico. Esso prende infatti figura da un processo rappresentativo per il quale gli aspetti più integri dell'esistente, svincolati e riscattati dalla mera selezione disegnativo-coloristica che tutta la pittura tardo-cinquecentesca continuava a considerare essenziale, sono recuperati senza residui alla pura e semplice evidenza ottica. E ciò grazie al potere non meno rivelatore che plasmante attribuito alla luce, ora intesa non più come fattore di accordo cromatico classicamente "tonale" al modo veneziano, ma come fattore visivo di stacco e di distinzione percettiva, causa prima della ricezione ottica dei valori timbrici, secondo la sperimentazione pittorica lombarda da Foppa a Savoldo, a Lotto, ai bresciani, e a certi loro ascendenti fiamminghi.[64] Di qui, nel nostro quadro, quel "timbro" universale di argento non ossidato, pungente e pulito come l'aria del mattino, che per un

verso esalta l'impatto della lama di luce dove percuote più direttamente, per un altro valorizza al massimo la percettibilità delle mezze luci e delle luci riverberate nelle ombre. Di qui l'istaurarsi di quel chiarore ad alta trasparenza, che, mentre consente di prendere il più completo possesso ottico delle parti esposte alla luce piena, permette di distinguere nitidamente anche dentro le penombre: lì dove balùginano taluni particolari minori (sebbene non irrilevanti, né per l'iconografia, né per il risultato pittorico), quali i sommari punti di cucitura con cui sono applicate al saio le toppe di colore leggermente diverso, le tacche della corda attorta che funge da cingolo, il taglio netto e fresco dei legni che formano la croce. Aggiungo ancora che il momento in cui questa straordinaria vicenda di luci e di ombre, e anche di riverberi e di chiarori, riesce a esprimere la sua più alta virtù rappresentativa, è nel vero e proprio dramma d'ombre che si svolge attorno all'occhio sinistro del santo: nel luogo pittorico, cioè, in cui un colpo di luce passante prende all'interno, e quasi di sotto in su, la parte superiore della cavità oculare, e sùbito incomincia a suscitare riflessi dove l'ombra era all'origine più fonda, nella pozza dell'occhio; percorrendo questa con un tale andirivieni di mezze luci, sempre più tenui, ma nitidissime, da permettere di scrutarvi dentro distintamente.

Quest'ordine di acute considerazioni pittorico-luministiche, e l'elevato livello d'arte con cui i risultati descritti risultano raggiunti, sono per altro attribuibili al Caravaggio non solo in senso generale, bensì in rapporto con il particolare momento della sua attività in cui, pur continuando ad approfondire le esperienze giovanili delle opere "in chiaro", egli prese per la prima volta a rinforzare le ombre e a orientare più risolutamente le luci, innescando in "crescendo" la serrata dialettica, appunto di ombre e di luci, che negli anni finali lo indurrà a concentrarle, come scrisse Roberto Longhi, nel puro "fotogramma". Per accordo unanime, l'opera esemplare di tale momento, e a proposito della quale, come s'è ricordato più a dietro, Giovan Pietro Bellori scrisse l'ormai famosa osservazione circa il "ringagliardire gli oscuri" a cui il pittore prese a volgersi d'allora in avanti, è la *Santa Caterina della ruota* già Del Monte, poi Barberini, ora Thyssen-Bornemisza alla Castagnola.[65] E a essa la critica suole accomunare anche il *Ritratto femminile* di Berlino, andato distrutto alla fine dell'ultima guerra mondiale; l'originale della *Marta e Maddalena* già costa e Herrera, da taluni identificato nell'esemplare – però guastissimo, anzi sfigurato, e perciò assai mal giudicabile – ora Detroit; il *San Giovanni Battista con il capro* già Mattei e poi Del Monte, ora ai Musei Capitolini; e la *Giuditta che decapita Oloferne* posseduta in origine da Ottavio costa, ora identificata dai più, ma non senza la perplessità di alcuni, nell'esemplare pervenuto alla Galleria nazionale d'arte antica di Roma[66]: opere tutte nelle quali, giusto come nella *Santa Caterina*, la pienezza di una forma umana giovane, al colmo del vigore, è esaltata appunto dalla funzione rivelatrice delle luci e dei chiarori riverberati, a contrasto con il buio di base degli scuri "ringagliarditi" di cui s'è detto; per giunta sullo sfondo di un nero unito che, rispetto allo svolgimento complessivo dell'opera del maestro, fa la sua comparsa più antica (è utile precisarlo a questo punto) proprio in tali dipinti.

Ora, non è dubbio che il *San Francesco* Johnson solleciti e sostenga bene un riscontro stilistico-tipologico molto addentrato innanzitutto con l'opera capo-lista della serie francescana da cui abbiamo preso le mosse, il *San Francesco stigmatizzato* di Hartford; al quale è infatti vicinissimo specialmente nel taglio della veste del santo e nella distribuzioni dei lumi sulle pieghe di essa. Ma per ciò che riguarda tutto quanto è stato finora l'oggetto della nostra analisi, esso trova corrispettivi convincenti, anzi punti di esauriente identità, solo nelle opere connesse con la *Santa Caterina* Thyssen, e con la *Santa Caterina* medesima. A lasciar da parte per un momento le pur evidenti coincidenze interne relative ai fatti di forma e di luce, per concentrare invece l'attenzione su di un solo particolare, ma capace di funzionare con valore d'esponente, non può non colpire la totale identità morfologica e di scrittura pittorica che accomuna il taglio degli occhi, il voltar delle pupille e il modo d'illuminarle, del *San Francesco* in discorso, con quelli di Marta nel quadro di Detroit, della donna dai fiori d'arancio nel quadro un tempo a Berlino, dello stesso Oloferne nella *Giuditta* di Roma, e, specialmente, della *Santa Caterina*; la quale, per giunta, offre al nostro *San Francesco* il riscontro di altri due tratti molto particolari: il sottile cerchio di luce, che, librandosi nel buio in uno scorcio acutissimo sul capo di entrambi i raffigurati, prende il luogo dell'aureola (e che in tale assetto e funzione, in anticipo su quello identico del Cristo nella *Chiamata di san Matteo* a San Luigi dei Francesi e sui numerosi altri analoghi venuti in seguito, probabilmente fa qui la più antica apparizione reperibile finora nel "corpus" del maestro); e ancora un tocco di eccezionale percezione ottica, voltata subito in testimonianza pittorica pura, grazie al quale il bianco lattescente e luminoso delle sclerotiche, nella *Santa Caterina* come nel *San Francesco*, si vena lievemente d'azzurro.

Se da questo punto torniamo a quanto s'è osservato più a dietro a proposito del fatto che nella raccolta del cardinal Del Monte la *Santa Caterina* si trovava nella stessa stanza (e, magari, sulla stessa parete) del *San Francesco in estasi*, dal che s'era già delineata la probabilità che le due opere fossero stilisticamente omogenee, e fossero percepite come tali già dal loro proprietario-committente; quel che è venuto emergendo si rivela idoneo a confermare sia che il *San Francesco* Johnson è identificabile davvero con il quadro presente nella raccolta Del Monte fino al 1627, sia che esso fu dipinto dal Caravaggio in tempi sostanzialmente coevi alla *Santa Caterina*, e comunque che è prossimo ad essa nei dati di fatto decisivi della

"authorship" e dei connotati stilistici.

Traducendo questi collegamenti in termini di cronologia assoluta, tale duplice conferma rimarrebbe valida sia se ci acconciassimo a datare la *Santa Caterina* anteriormente al 1596-97 (e tuttavia, a mio parere, a non prima del 1595); sia se, accogliendo la cronologia più ritardata proposta a suo tempo da Denis Mahon per tutta la produzione caravaggesca precedente ai quadri Contarelli, la *Santa Caterina* la datassimo al 1596-97 (meno probabilmente al 1598-99),[67] e nel *San Francesco* in discorso – come il Mahon stesso mi consigliava verbalmente, se ho bene inteso il suo pensiero – dovessimo scorgere riscontri stilistici lievemente più avanzati, indirizzati piuttosto verso la successiva fase Contarelli, quanto meno al tempo della *Chiamata*. Posso aggiungere, infatti, due altre osservazioni, entrambe in grado d'inquadrare la questione cronologica entro maglie solo un un poco più larghe, e proprio perciò compatibili con tutti e due i riferimenti temporali or ora addotti.

La prima osservazione, di tipo induttivo, deriva dal fatto che l'origine accertatamente "Del Monte" (per committenza, evidentemente, oltre che per provenienza) di un *San Francesco in estasi* diverso dal quadro di Hartford; nonché la verosimiglianza che un tale *San Francesco*, in rapporto pressoché certo con il nome di battesimo del cardinale-committente, ne ritraesse in qualche modo anche le fattezze fisiche[68]; comportano due "post quem non" molto precisi: vale a dire, la data di conclusione del soggiorno del Caravaggio presso il cardinal Del Monte, che il nuovo documento pubblicato nel 1985 da N. Randolph Parks fissa a prima del giugno 1601, quando il pittore, che nel novembre dell'anno precedente era ancora "in casa dell'Ill.o e R.o Cardinale De Monte", ormai risulta "commorans in Palatio Ill. et R.mi D. Cardinalis Matthei"[69]; e l'età di Francesco Maria Del Monte stesso, il quale, nato il 5 luglio 1549,[70] non poteva che apparire poco meno o poco più che cinquantenne in un dipinto dove fosse stato ritratto anteriormente al luglio 1601. Due circostanze che il *San Francesco* Johnson non solo non contraddice, ma conferma proprio nel dato che si sarebbe giudicato più sfuggente: l'età mostrata dall'uomo ritratto nelle vesti del santo, il quale non supera di certo la cinquantina, e forse ne è lontano ancora qualche anno.

La seconda osservazione è invece di tipo deduttivo, e si fonda sul fatto che il prototipo caravaggesco in vario modo postulato dalla critica alla base sia della cosiddetta *Estasi di san Francesco* (o *San Francesco consolato dagli angeli*) di Giovanni Baglione, ora in collezione privata a Chicago,[71] sia, e ben più, del *San Francesco in estasi in braccio ad un angelo* di Orazio Gentileschi nelle versioni della Galleria nazionale d'arte antica a Roma [Fig. 4],[72] e del Prado a Madrid [Fig. 5],[72] a questo punto, pur al di là dell'ipotesi intenibile di una copia letterale, non può non essere identificato giusto nel *San Francesco in estasi* Johnson. Poiché il *San Francesco* di Baglione reca iscritta la

4) Orazio Gentileschi, «San Francesco in estasi in braccio ad un angelo», Galleria Nazionale d'Arte Antica, Roma.

5) Orazio Gentileschi, «San Francesco in estasi in braccio ad un angelo», Museo del Prado, Madrid.

data 1601, e i due di Orazio Gentileschi sono stati datati – come devono per ragioni di stile, oltre che per sintomi documentari – rispettivamente al 1600-1603 e al 1603-1605,[73] ne deriva al nostro dipinto un altro "post quem non" perfettamente compatibile con tutto quanto s'è detto in precedenza.

Se poi, accantonando per un momento le questioni strettamente cronologiche, ci risolviamo a badare anche a quelle riguardanti le eventuali aree di risonanza e di efficacia culturale del dipinto in esame, non tarda ad imporcisi un altro fatto di grande importanza: che il rapporto di dipendenza accusato nei confronti del *San Francesco* Johnson dai due *San Francesco* del Gentileschi, in realtà comporta un rapporto di dipendenza addentrato soprattutto nell'ordine delle ascendenze culturali; anzi, interferente in termini decisivi sulla stessa capacità di orientamento del Gentileschi, al momento critico delle scelte di

campo. La critica ha chiarito da tempo che, all'inizio del nuovo secolo, Orazio non solo stava abbandonando le radici manieristiche per voltarsi al Caravaggio; bens che lo fece, secondo quanto scrisse Longhi già nel lontano 1916, in base alla "ripresa ch'egli assunse dello stile di Caravaggio primitivo".[74] "He was also attracted to – ha soggiunto di recente R. Ward Bissel – and given deeper spiritual guidance by the earlier works of the master [...]. In other words, Orazio found in Caravaggio's pictures of the 1590s the initial means of adapting Caravaggio's mature style to his own artistic temperament".[75] Ebbene, il solo punto che resta ancora da specificare in proposito, è che, mentre la concezione compositiva dei due *San Francesco* del Gentileschi risulta, a guardar bene, un libero adattamento in controparte del primo *San Matteo* del Caravaggio (nell'esemplare di Spagna non meno che in quello di Roma, dove la cosa è più evidente; ma, in entrambi i casi, incluso il "par d'ale" dell'angelo che sovrasta il gruppo); tutte e due le redazioni della figura del santo svenuto, con un'accentuazione più evidente nel quadro di Spagna, s'improntano a un punto delle ricerche caravaggesche degli avanzati anni 1590, rivolte – come s'è ripetuto più volte con il Bellori – "ad ingagliardire gli oscuri", che coincide in tutto giusto con quello attestato – più che da qualsiasi altra opera del maestro – dal *San Francesco* Johnson. Del quale, certo, nei due dipinti di Orazio non è compreso affatto, né è tenuto in considerazione, il tratto più acuto: la scentratura dell'immagine del protagonista, in funzione del suo muoversi dal fondo per risalire verso la luce. Ma la versione di Spagna attesta che, dei motivi qualificanti di quel dipinto, Orazio tenne ben presente la rappresentazione, stupendamente impressionante nella sua oggettività, dello "stigma" sul dorso della mano: e a preferenza della truculenta ferita con il chiodo ancora infisso, raffigurata nella versione di Roma, nella quale il motivo dovette essere suggerito da un intento, poi abbandonato, di più scoperta e pietosa devozione. Né ci lasceremo sfuggire che l'altro gran tema pittorico del quadro Johnson, la faccia del santo presa dalla luce nel momento in cui si leva verso di essa, fu non meno evidentemente la fonte di quello che Gentileschi, adattandolo a volti femminili, rielaborerà in varie altre opere degli anni 1610, e principalmente nella *Giovine violinista* (forse "Santa Cecilia"?) del Detroit Institute of Arts.[76] Non sembrerà esagerato, perciò, se, per tutte queste ragioni, ora traiamo la conclusione che il *San Francesco* Johnson costituì uno dei principali punti di riferimento, se non il principale, per la trasformazione caravaggesca di Orazio Gentileschi agli inizi del nuovo secolo: e ciascuno vede da sé come una conclusione del genere torni a convalida del diritto a riassumere la propria identità storico-artistica che il *San Francesco* Johnson può ormai accampare senza contrasti: d'essere non solo opera autografa del Caravaggio, ma, comunque se ne voglia calcolare il tempo, anteriore al 1600.

Un ultimo "test", che i più recenti studi caravaggeschi hanno reso ineludibile in materia di opere autografe del maestro, riguarda la presenza, o meno, nel tessuto pittorico del dipinto in esame, di tracce graffite nella preparazione, ovvero, come altri ha preferito definirle, "incisioni contornanti, tracciate con una punta nella mestica ancora fresca".[77] Come si sa, tracce del genere furono rilevate per la prima volta nel 1922 da Matteo Marangoni, il quale, vero riscopritore moderno della particolarità, la segnalò innanzitutto nella *Santa Caterina* Thyssen-Bornemisza (uno dei dipinti più antichi, rispetto alla cronologia caravaggesca, a mostrarla con evidenza), e ancora in opere più tarde del maestro, quali il secondo *San Matteo*, la *Conversione di san Paolo* a Santa Maria del Popolo e la *Madonna dei Palafrenieri*.[78] Con l'estendersi delle conoscenze, le costatazio-

ni di tali tracce si sono estese anch'esse, e attraverso le tappe riassunte particolarmente bene da Mia Cinotti nel 1983,[79] si è pervenuti al "census" sistematico fornito nel settembre 1986 da Keith Christiansen.[80] Quanto alla funzione tecnico-operativa e, più in generale, al significato storico-artistico delle incisioni descritte, l'opinione di Marangoni, che dovessero interpretarsi come sintomo di uso da parte del Caravaggio di disegni preparatori su cartoni, simili a quelli impiegati negli affreschi, non ha avuto seguito; è risultata di gran lunga più pertinente, invece, la valutazione data da Roberto Longhi, quando, a proposito della *Conversione di san Paolo* Odescalchi, scrisse testualmente: "la tavola reca, incisi sulla preparazione, quei tratti che il Caravaggio usò spesso, non già come vero e proprio 'disegno' dell'opera, ma piuttosto come traccia della 'posa'".[81] Infatti, giusto nel solco di questa interpretazione di "tratti" usati come "traccia della *posa*" si è rimesso il più recente studioso del problema; il quale, pur intendendo tali incisioni "as an aid in composing", ha scritto che "the most interesting and original use of these incised lines is a direct response to Caravaggio's habitual practice [...] of painting from models".[82] In altri termini, è "the consequence of a technique that emphasized 'dipingere con l'avere gli oggetti naturali davanti'", è lo strumento del dipingere con "l'esempio davanti del naturale": posto che il Caravaggio, pittore non già di "disegno", bensì di percezione pittorica diretta, dovette nondimeno esser costretto dalle contingenze operative a fissare preventivamente almeno i confini delle cose che avrebbe reso per "similitudine".

D'altra parte, fino a qual punto la presenza in un dato dipinto di procedimenti tecnici propri del Caravaggio può garantire la paternità caravaggesca di quel medesimo dipinto? fino a qual punto essa è di per sé un indizio di autografia? La critica si è posto da tempo anche tale quesito, e mentre in un passato abbastanza recente ha dimostrato la tendenza a rispondere in termini sempre positivi, almeno Christiansen, il quale ha dovuto costatare la presenza di tali incisioni anche in dipinti di attribuzione fortemente dubbia, ha profilato una soluzione non certo opposta alla precedente, ma più sfaccettata e probabilista. "If the issue is the simple presence or the absence of incisions, the answer is that such occurence is of very limited consequence. If, on the other hand, we are talking not about a technical feature *per se*, but about its character and function in the production of a picture, then the matter must, I believe, be taken seriously, the more so in that Caravaggio apparently had no pupils (his technique certainly did not admit workshop assistance in the traditional sense), and his followers imitated the surface appeareance of his pictures – the results of a highly personal method".[83] Né credo sia impossibile trovare un accordo di ordine più generale e al tempo stesso più pragmatico, assumendo che vi possano essere opere di istituzione caravaggesca, ma non per questo necessariamente autografe del maestro e magari frutto di contraffazione!, che presentino tracce di incisioni simili a quelle in discorso (il caso più esplicito, in tal senso, è dato dal *Cavadenti* di Firenze, che, a parere mio e di molti altri, non tollera la riesumazione della vecchia attribuzione al Caravaggio voluta da Mina Gregori); ma si dànno raramente (anche se è indubbio che si diano) opere prive di tali incisioni che possano aspirare a essere riconosciute autografe del Carvaggio, almeno a far data dal 1595 circa. Non per nulla, ad esempio, come mi fa notare Patrick Matthiesen su indicazione di Ward Bissel da lui appositamente consultato, nessun'opera di Orazio Gentileschi reca segni di ''scratchings'' o ''scoring, so closely associated with Caravaggio''.

Ebbene, mentre ai fini dell'attribuzione al Caravaggio stesso viene da osservare che la presenza di segni graffiti e di incisioni è, quanto meno, un buon segno, e dunque un segno fortemente ambito se non addirittura condizionante, l'esame a luce radente condotto a suo tempo sulla superficie pittorica del *San Francesco in estasi* ora della Signora Johnson, fece rilevare che, oltre a un ''pentimento'' in corrispondenza del pollice della mano destra, il dipinto mostra sotto pelle, per tutto il suo sviluppo, delle tracce graffite nella preparazione. In oltre, a un esame reiterato, e in buona analogia con pressoché tutti i rilevamenti

pubblicati da Keith Christiansen relativi a opere sicure del Caravaggio, il dipinto lascia vedere anche a occhio nudo un'intera serie di altri graffiti, che ora riguardano la parte superiore della fronte del santo, ora i margini del suo orecchio destro, ora il taglio del braccio della croce rivolto verso l'alto, ora numerose parti del saio; graffiti, per altro, che nel loro complesso risultano addetti a definire piuttosto alcuni punti di riferimento per l'ingombro generale delle forme, da ritrarre poi su natura, che non, secondo la selezione disegnativa tradizionale, profili definiti di cose e di aspetti umani.

Che tutto questo sia il segno di un ''highly personal method'', non pare dubbio; e che tale metodo altamente personale sia quello del Caravaggio, il quale ''apparently had no pupils'', pare dubbio ancor meno. In oltre, non posso astenermi dal richiamare l'attenzione sul fatto che la complessità, e anche la tendenziale irregolarità, delle incisioni osservate nel *San Francesco*, hanno molto a che fare con quanto è stato rilevato soprattutto nella *Santa Caterina* Thyssen[84]: la quale, come sappiamo, in casa Del Monte pendeva giusto accanto, un posto avanti sulla stessa parete, al ''San Francesco in Estasi di Michel Agnolo da Caravaggio, con Cornici negre, di Palmi quattro''.

[1] Il saggio che qui si pubblica costituisce un capitolo del volume *Nuovi studi sul Caravaggio*, che l'autore ha in corso di pubblicazione presso la casa editrice ''Giulio Einaudi'' di Torino, e che vedrà la luce nei primi mesi del prossimo anno 1988. *Artibus et Historiae* e l'autore ringraziano vivamente l'editrice Einaudi per aver consentito a questa ''ante prima''. A titolo personale, l'autore ringrazia ancora il dottor Józef Grabski, direttore di *Artibus et Historiae*, per l'obbligante e amichevole insistenza con cui gli ha offerto di pubblicare sulla sua rivista il saggio presente.

[2] F. G. Pariset, ''Le Caravage et saint François'', *Annales. Economie-Societé- Civilisation*, 1952, pp. 39-48.

[3] L. Spezzaferro, ''Ottavio Costa e Caravaggio: certezze e problemi'', in AA. VV., *Novità sul Caravaggio*, Milano 1975, pp. 103-118.

[4] Il dipinto, raffigurante a due terzi di figura ''San Francesco in estasi'' – le braccia incrociate al petto, la mano destra con lo ''stigma'' bene in vista, e una croce nella mano sinistra –, è eseguito a olio su tela di 103 x 65,5 cm., ed è entrato nella raccolta di Mrs. Barbara P. Johnson a Princeton, U. S. A., per le cure della Matthiesen Art Gallery di Londra. Prima di pervenire alla sede attuale, l'opera aveva soggiornato a lungo a Ginevra, in Svizzera; e fu a Ginevra, fra la fine del 1981 e gli inizi dell'82, che io potei esaminarla nell'originale, raggiungendo fin da allora le conclusioni che espongo nel testo.

Con l'occasione, esprimo la mia gratitudine alla Signora Johnson per aver voluto confermare a me il privilegio di pubblicare l'opera. Ringrazio Mr Patrick Matthiesen, il titolare della casa londinese che s'è occupata del dipinto, per le innumerevoli forme di aiuto, di facilitazione e di collaborazione che ha voluto prestarmi durante la preparazione del presente scritto. Soprattutto, e in modo affatto particolare, desidero ringraziare il decano, oltre al più autorevole tra gli studiosi del Caravaggio oggi viventi, Sir Denis Mahon: il quale non solo ha accettato di discutere con me molti dei punti relativi al dipinto in questione, specialmente in materia di cronologia, ma è stato il primo a confortarmi del Suo ambito assenso nel riconoscimento che l'opera è autografa del Caravaggio.

[5] Poiché, a tutt'oggi, il più informato e più affidabile ''corpus'' di dati sul Caravaggio – ancorché neanch'esso completo – resta la monumentale monografia di M. Cinotti e G. A. Dell'Acqua, *Caravaggio* (''I pittori bergamaschi. Il Seicento'', vol. I, Banca Popolare di Bergamo, 1983), d'ora in avanti, a meno d'indicazione diversa, utilizzerò quest'opera come punto di riferimento preferito, anche in materia di bibliografia.

[6] Com'è ovvio, escludo dall'elenco la ben nota tela del 1601 con una composizione definita di solito, ma affrettatamente, ''San Francesco in estasi'' o ''San Francesco consolato dagli angeli'' – passata via via dalla Galleria Borghese a quella del cardinal Fesch, quindi in proprietà Breval a Parigi, dell' Earl of Drogheda a Dublino, del dott. M. De Benedetti a Roma, e ora in collezione privata a Chicago negli U. S. A. –, che tutti, unanimemente, sulla base del parere espresso da Roberto Longhi fin dal 1930, ormai considerano opera di Giovanni Baglione: e non del Caravaggio, al quale era stata attribuita con una certa insistenza durante il XVIII e il XIX secolo. Per le notizie relative alla storia esterna

del dipinto, il referto più completo è ancora quello incluso nel catalogo della *Mostra del Caravaggio e dei Caravaggeschi*, Milano 1951, pp. 37-38, n. 51, tav. 50.

E' quasi superfluo aggiungere che escludo dall'analisi anche quei pochissimi dipinti del Caravaggio, come la ben nota tela dell'oratorio di San Lorenzo a Palermo (rubata) e quella commissionatagli a Napoli nell'ottobre del 1606 da Niccolò Radolovic (finora non ritrovata), nei quali la figura di san Francesco compare (o compariva) insieme ad altri santi. Rimando infine a più avanti la menzione (e la parziale utilizzazione) di tesi, del resto già contraddette dalla critica, che, pur senza alcun supporto documentario, hanno presunto la dipendenza da originali perduti del maestro di dipinti d'argomento sanfrancescano dovuti ad altri pittori (cfr., ad esempio, A. Moir, *Caravaggio and his Copyists*, New York 1976, p. 122 n. 180-III, contraddetto da R. Ward Bissel, *Orazio Gentileschi*, The Pennsylvania State University Press 1981, p. 141).

[7] Per i dati analitici e la bibliografia di tutto, cfr. Cinotti, in Cinotti e Dell'Acqua, *op. cit.*, scheda n. 19, p. 440.

[8] Dati e bibliografia ancora in Cinotti, *op. cit.*, scheda n. 6, pp. 417-18.

[9] Dati e bibliogafia sempre in Cinotti, *op. cit.*, scheda n. 9, p. 423; avvertendo però che Mahon espose fin dal 1951 l'opinione ricordata nel testo (cfr. "Egregius in Urbe Pictor: Caravaggio revised", in *The Burlington Magazine*, XCIII, 1951, p. 234 nota 125) e che tale opinione, secondo quanto lo stesso Denis Mahon mi comunica d'aver appreso dalla professoressa Mina Gregori, è stata confermata dai risultati del restauro eseguito recentemente. Per altre, ma assai meno fondate congetture relative all'origine dell'opera, si veda più avanti nel testo, nonché, e specialmente, quanto espone M. Gregori in *Caravaggio e il suo tempo*, catalogodell'edizione italiana della mostra newyorkese *The Age of Caravaggio*, Electa Napoli, 1985, pp. 310-12.

[10] Cfr. Spezzaferro, *op. cit.*, pp. 104-06, 113. I corsivi nel testo sono di chi scrive.

[11] Cfr., per tutto, di nuovo Spezzaferro, *op. cit.*, p. 114. I corsivi, sempre di chi scrive.

[12] Il testo completo del testamento è in *Miscellanea di storia veneta*, vol. XII, 1984, appendice, p. 41; in estratto, era già in W. Friedländer, *Caravaggio studies*, Princeton 1955, p. 294. Corsivi, sempre miei.

[13] Cfr. Archivio di Stato di Roma, 30 Notai Capitolini, Paulus Vespignanus, ufficio 28, vol. 138, f. 580r, edito da Chr. L. Frommel, "Caravaggios Frühwerk und der Kardinal Francesco Maria del Monte", *Storia dell'Arte*, n. 9/10, 1971, p. 34. Corsivi, c. s.

[14] Cfr. W. Chandler Kirwin, "Addendum to Cardinal Francesco Maria del Monte's Inventory: the Date of the Sale of Various Nobles Paintings", *Storia dell'Arte, op. cit.*, p. 53. Corsivo, sempre mio.

[15] Per i passaggi di proprietà della *Santa Caterina* oggi riconosciuta unanimemente nella tela della collezione Thyssen-Bornemisza, nonché per la bibliografia degli inventari barberiniani, cfr. Cinotti, *op. cit.*, scheda 19, p. 440.

[16] Cfr. A. Bertolotti, "Esportazione di oggetti di Belle Arti da Roma nei secoli XVI, XVII, XVIII", *Archivio storico artistico, archeologico e letterario della città di Roma*, I-II, 1877, p. 45; e Cinotti, *op. cit.*, p. 440. Corsivo mio.

[17] Cfr. Spezzaferro, *op. cit.*, rispettivamente pp. 118 e 109. Corsivo, sempre mio.

[18] Cfr. Cod. Palat. 597, della Biblioteca nazionale centrale di Firenze, terza pagina dalla fine del manoscritto. Com'è noto, la postilla in questione fu pubblicata per la prima volta da R. Longhi, "Ultimi studi sul Caravaggio e la sua cerchia", *Proporzioni*, I, 1943, pp. 36-37, bensì con il riferimento inspiegabilmente erroneo al "Ms. vat. barber. lat. 4315, f. 145r". Successivamente, fu D. Mahon, *Studies in Seicento Art and Theory*, Londra 1947, (cfr. ora reprint: Greenwood Press, Publishers, Westport, Connecticut, 1971), pp. 285-86 nota 16, che identificò l'effettiva ubicazione del passo, stabilì che esso era dovuto a un postillatore anonimo del Mancini e non al Mancini stesso, come sempre Longhi aveva supposto, e precisò l'identità storico-storiografica dell'informatore, Teofilo Gallaccini, citato espressamente dall'anonimo ("secondo la relazione datami dal signor Dr Gallaccini nel ritorno da Napoli"). Su tutto ciò, cfr. anche G. Mancini, *Considerazioni sulla pittura*, ediz. a cura di A. Marucchi, con note di L. Salerno, Roma 1956-57 (testo: vol. I, 1956, p. 340; note: vol. II, 1957, p. 217, nn. 1664-66); e ancora Cinotti, *op. cit.*, scheda n. 113, pp. 572-73.

[19] Quando non è indicato diversamente, la bibliografia delle singole opinioni è ovviamente la stessa richiamata nelle sezioni A e B, in rapporto ai dipinti e ai dati documentari in esse via via elencati.

[20] Cfr. sopra, A, 1.

[21] Cfr. sopra, B, 6 agosto 1606 e 25 ottobre 1607.

[22] Cfr. sopra, B, 25 ottobre 1607.

[23] Cfr. sopra, B, 21 febbraio – 18 maggio 1627.

[24] Con il necessario rinvio a una precedente opinione analoga di R. Spear, *Caravaggio and his Followers*, catalogo della mostra, Cleveland 1971, p. 68, cfr. specialmente Spezzaferro, *op. cit.*, p. 114.

[25] Cfr. sopra, B, 25 maggio 1628.

[26] Cfr. sopra, B, 1631.

[27] Cfr. *ibidem*.

[28] Bibliografia della questione in Cinotti, *op. cit.*, p.440.

[29] Cfr. Frommel, *op. cit.*, p. 24. Un'analoga opinione (edita insieme e nella stessa sede di quella di Frommel, e perciò non si sa fino a qual punto indipendentemente da essa) fu adombrata anche da L. Spezzaferro, "La cultura del cardinal Del Monte e il primo tempo del Caravaggio", *Storia dell'Arte*, n. 9/10, 1971, p. 85, il quale scrisse: "si noti […] la coincidenza del nome del cardinale con quello del santo rappresentato".

[30] Cfr. C. Volpe, "Annotazioni sulla mostra caravaggesca di Cleveland", *Paragone*, n. 263, gennaio 1972, pp. 57-58; e ora di nuovo M. Gregori, *The age of Caravaggio*, catalogo della mostra di New York, ediz. inglese, Milano, Electa International, 1985, pp. 221-22 (cfr. altresì: *id.*, *Caravaggio e il suo tempo*, catalogo della mostra di Napoli, ediz. ital., Electa Napoli, 1985, p. 221).

[31] Cfr. sopra, B, 18-24 gennaio 1639.

[32] Cfr. sopra, A, 2.

[33] Cfr. sopra, A, 3.

[34] Cfr. Spezzaferro, *op. cit.*, pp. 114-15: "tornando ora al Costa, appare chiaro come il S. Francesco indicato nel suo inventario del 1639 debba essere, con tutta probabilità, un esemplare degli altri due tipi oggi noti".

[35] Cfr. sopra, B, "prima del 1641".

[36] Cfr. W. Friedländer, *op. cit.*, p.224.

[37] Cfr. Cinotti, *op. cit.*, scheda n. 9, p. 423, e scheda n. 113, pp. 572-73. Per il dipinto di Cremona, cfr. sopra, A, 3.

[38] Il cammino completo e la bibliografia della questione, che saranno richiamati via via anche qui appresso, si trovano ricapitolati e discussi (sebbene, com'è ovvio, in funzione della propria tesi) da V. Casale, nella scheda n. 123 inclusa in AA. VV., *Pittura del Seicento e del Settecento. Ricerche in Umbria, 2*, Treviso 1980, pp. 398-99; dove l'autore, "prescindendo da problemi attributivi inerenti [ai dipinti presi in considerazione], e dalla questione del *S. Francesco* di Caravaggio per Sant'Anna dei Lombardi", propone appunto "l'ipotesi di una derivazione diretta da un originale perduto del Merisi".

[39] Cfr. F. Strazzullo, *Documenti inediti per la storia dell'arte a Napoli*, Napoli 1955, p. 60, il quale collegò il dipinto in questione con la ricevuta di un pagamento di dieci ducati, fatto in data 18 maggio 1613 dall'Abate di Monteoliveto in Napoli a Filippo Vitale, per "un quadro della figura di San Francesco" (documento, per altro, pubblicato anonimamente fin dal 1939: cfr. "Documenti estratti dall'Archivio storico del Banco di Napoli: pittori", *Rassegna economica del Banco di Napoli*, IX, 1939, fasc. 2, p. 518). R. Causa, "La pittura del Seicento a Napoli dal Naturalismo al Barocco", *Storia di Napoli*, vol. V, Napoli 1972, pp. 963 e 169, nota 27, non solo ritenne fondato il collegamento proposto dallo Strazzullo, accettando l'attribuzione del dipinto al Vitale che ne derivava; ma, supponendo che l'opera avesse "caratteri di strettissima derivazione caravaggesca, quasi di copia", avanzò la tesi che in essa si potesse ravvisare, come s'è detto nel testo, una copia del "San Francesco" del Caravaggio a Sant'Anna dei Lombardi. Circa l'attribuzione del dipinto a Filippo Vitale, assolutamente da escludere per ragioni di qualità e di stile oltre che di circostanze storico-documentarie, si veda più avanti.

[40] Cfr. Casale, in *Ricerche in Umbria*, *op. cit.*, *ibidem*, n. 123, tav. XVIII.

[41] Cfr. A. Moir, *op. cit.*, p. 122, fig. 13. Il testo completo della scritta che accompagna la stampa è il seguente: "Cum priv. Michael Agnolo Caravaggio Pinxit P. Soutman Effigiavit et excud."

[42] Cfr. la nota precedente.

[43] Per la storia critica dei due dipinti (nn. 287 e 288 della Gemäldegalerie del Kunsthistorisches Museum di Vienna), cfr. E. Arslan, *I Bassano*, seconda ediz., Milano 1960, vol. I, p. 225. A dire il vero, Arslan, dopo aver ricordato che le opere recavano l'attribuzione a Jacopo nel 1659 (quando si trovavano nella collezione dell'arciduca Leopoldo Guglielmo), furono spostate a Francesco dal Mechel nel 1783, e dopo d'allora (con l'eccezione di J. F. Willumsen nel 1927, il quale riprese l'attribuzione a Jacopo almeno per il *San Francesco*) rimasero assegnate a Francesco unanimemente; ricorda anche che una seconda versione della *Santa Giuliana Falconieri*, già nella collezione Remak a Berlino come opera di Francesco, poi passata alla galleria della University of Southern California a Pasadena, ha rivelato la firma: "Leander a Ponte Bass[anen]sis Eques F." (cfr. *ibidem*, e anche a p. 267). Ma che da ciò debba derivare la necessità di trasferire a Leandro anche i dipinti di Vienna, come finiva col prospettare lo stesso Arslan pur continuando a tenerli nelle liste di Francesco, non sembra confermato dal carattere della loro fisionomia stilistica. In proposito, a ogni modo, sarebbe importante controllare (il che a chi scrive non è ancora riuscito) se e quale "invenit" rechino le incisioni che dai due quadri viennesi trasse nel tardo XVII secolo Lucas Vorsterman junior (1624-1667), secondo quanto indica sempre Arslan, *ibidem*, p. 225.

[44] Cfr. C. Celano, *Notizie del bello dell'antico e del curioso della città di Napoli*, 1692, ediz. con aggiunzioni di G. B. Chiarini, introduzione di G. Doria e L. De Rosa, e uno scritto di B. Croce, a cura di A. Mozzillo, A. Profeta e F. P. Macchia, Napoli 1970, vol. II, p. 866.

[45] Cfr. E. Arslan, *op. cit.*, vol. I, p. 225, e quanto è stato già ricordato nella precedente nota 43.

[46] Per la data precisa della distruzione di Sant'Anna dei Lombardi e per la sua storia, oltre che per il passaggio dei quadri superstiti alla vicina chiesa di Monteoliveto, cfr. AA. VV., *Carlo Sellitto*, Napoli 1977, pp. 63-64, nota 2.

[47] Dell'impossibilità specificamente storico-artistica (a cui ho già accennato alla fine della precedente nota 39) di assegnare il dipinto ora a Monteoliveto a Filippo Vitale, tratterò diffusamente nella monografia sul maestro a cui lavoro da tempo, e che fu argomento di un mio corso universitario tenuto a Napoli alla fine degli anni 1970. Continuando a considerare qui solo i dati oggettivi esterni, aggiungo l'osservazione che le fonti e le guide antiche ricordano a Monteoliveto altri dipinti "colla figura di S. Francesco" (per esempio, ne indica uno, con un'attribuzione a Carlo Sellitto che potrebbe non essere la giusta, lo stesso Celano: cfr. *Notizie*, *op. cit.*, II, p. 867). Donde la conclusione ultima che nulla áncora di necessità il "San Francesco" dipinto da Vitale nel 1613 a quello di cui abbiamo discorso finora.

[48] Per tali inventari, cfr. R. Ruotolo, "Aspetti del collezionismo napoletano: il cardinale Filamarino", *Antologia di Belle Arti*, n. 1, marzo 1977, pp. 75 e 80; e Cinotti, *op. cit.*, p. 573.

[49] "Dipinto dal celeberrimo pittore Caravaggio ponendo la massima diligenza nell'esprimervi la propria maestria": *affabre* in Cicerone (Verr., I, 14), e *affaber*, *-bra*, *-brum* nell'epitome da Festo di Paolo Diacono, ricorrono appunto con il significato di "fatto con arte, con maestria" (cfr. Georges-Calonghi, *Dizionario latino-italiano*, terza edizione rifusa e aggiornata a cura di F. Calonghi, Torino 1965, col. 93.

[50] Cfr. i dati storici e bibliografici in Cinotti, *op. cit.*, scheda n. 59, p. 521.

[51] Cfr. sopra: B, 1631.

[52] Cfr. i dati forniti sopra, a conclusione di B, 18-24 gennaio 1639.

[53] Cfr. P. Askew, "The angelic consolation of St. Francis of Assisi in posttridentine italian paintings", *Journal of the Warburg and Courtauld Institutes*, XXXII, 1969, pp. 280-306.

[54] Prendendo a base l'inventario pubblicato da Frommel, *op. cit.*, *Appendix*, pp. 30 ss., e redatto secondo la successione degli ambienti "nel Giardino et Palazzo a Ripetta", si osserva che: 1) "Nella Galleria contigua" alla "Galleria Nova stretta", sono riuniti *Un quadretto nel quale vi è una caraffa*, *Un gioco*, una *Zingara* e *Un S. Giovanni Battista*, ossia la perduta "natura morta" degli esordi descritta anche dal Bellori, i *Bari* già Sciarra (e ora, pare, ritrovati, nell'esemplare entrato nel Kimbell Museum di Fort Worth), la *Buona ventura* nella redazione pervenuta al Museo Capitolino di Roma con il fondo Pio, e il *San Giovanni Battista*, pur esso oggi al Museo Capitolino con il medesimo fondo, ma che è senza dubbi quello già di Ciriaco Mattei, donato al Del Monte nel 1624 dal figlio dello stesso Ciriaco, Giovanni Battista: tutti quadri che si scalano nei primi anni della presenza del Caravaggio presso il Del Monte, ad eccezione dell'ultimo, il quale per altro, sebbene entrasse nella collezione solo nel 1624, appartiene anch'esso ad un momento ancora abbastanza precoce del Caravaggio, essendo, com'è stato detto, "opera-limite" subito prima della fase Contarelli; 2) "Nella Galleria Piccola, che va sula loggia", sono insieme "Una S. Caterina della Ruota" e "Un S. Francesco in Estasi", ossia i dipinti di cui parliamo qui appresso nel testo, e dei quali non è dubbio che la "Santa Caterina" appartenga a una fase successiva a quella dei quadri riuniti nella galleria precedente, in contiguità col "San Giovanni Battista" già Mattei; 3) nella "prima Stanza dell'appartamento novo", sta sola "Una musica", la quale, se ha a che fare – come i più dicono – con il *Concerto* ora al Metropolitan di New York (e che tuttavia lo scrivente ritiene copia, non originale del Caravaggio), apparterrebbe al tempo più antico del maestro e perciò interromperebbe la sequenza cronologica fin qui rilevata: se non si potesse invece ribattere che, così isolata nella "prima Stanza dell'appartamento novo", poteva costituire un'estrapolazione volontaria. Per quanto riguarda lo stato delle conoscenze e le fonti bibliografiche relative ai dipinti via via richiamati, si rinvia, come al solito, alle schede della Cinotti, *op. cit.*, disposte nell' ordine alfabetico dei luoghi di ubicazione.

[55] Cfr. specificamente Cinotti, *ibidem*, scheda n. 7, pp. 418-19.

[56] Cfr. la precedente nota 29.

[57] Cfr. quanto ricavano dalla bibliografia precedente la Cinotti, *op. cit.*, p. 419, e la Gregori, *op. cit.*, ediz. ital., p. 248.

[58] Cfr. Cinotti, *op. cit.*, scheda n. 24, pp. 447-48.

[59] Cfr. *ibidem*, p. 418.

[60] Con riferimento al catalogo della mostra ricordata, *L'immagine di San Francesco nella Controriforma*, Roma 1982, i quattro esempi specifici ivi reperibili sono: il San Francesco nella pala di Girolamo Siciolante già in San Pietro Vaticano e ora in San Tommaso in Formis a Roma, databile sul 1574 (cfr. *ibidem*, p. 49, fig. 13); il San Francesco a mosaico di Paolo Rossetti in Santa Maria di Loreto a Roma, del 1594 (*ibidem*, p. 51, fig. 17); il disegno dell'Empoli raffigurante *San Francesco con il crocifisso e studi vari*, del Gabinetto dei Disegni agli Uffizi in Firenze, relativo a un dipinto non identificato ma databile "nel periodo tardo" del maestro (*ibidem*, p. 84, n. 49, fig. 49); e il disegno di Cristoforo Roncalli detto il Pomarancio, con *San Francesco che porta la croce*, pur esso agli Uffizi, riferibile insieme ad altri due disegni analoghi conservati a Siena e a una figura di uguale iconografia – con la quale è soprattutto connesso-affrescata nella cappella Mattei all'Aracoeli a Roma, agli anni 1583-86 cfr. *ibidem*, p. 89, n. 71, fig. 71). Per la seconda classe di esempi, possono essere indicati almeno: il "San Francesco" di Gerolamo Muziano nella volta della cappella Ruiz a Santa Caterina dei Funari a Roma (c. 1570), che reca la croce ma non ha le braccia incrociate al petto (cfr. *ibidem*, p. 52, fig. 18); il *San Francesco* nel disegno del Gabinetto nazionale delle Stampe a Roma n. d'inv. FC 130.572, del marchigiano Giovan Battista Lombardelli, che, oltre alla croce, reca anche il libro, ma neanch'esso ha le braccia incrociate (*ibidem*, p.82, n. 43, fig. 43); e finalmente l'importante incisione con *San Francesco in meditazione* di Annibale Carracci, datata 1585, che elabora autonomamente i vari motivi del tema, nell'intento, perfettamente riuscito, di esaltare al massimo il momento ascetico della rappresentazione (*ibidem*, p. 173-74, n. 102, fig. 102). Nel medesimo contesto, può essere indicato ancora il san Francesco stigmatizzato con le braccia conserte incluso da Santi di Tito nella *Pietà* della chiesa di San Biagio a Scrofiano, a Sinalunga presso Siena, la cui data frammentaria "I5[...]" si suole completare in 1580 o poco più (cfr. sempre *ibidem*, p. 83, n. 46, fig. 46).

[61] Cfr. i riferimenti nella nota precedente.

[62] Cfr. Cfr. L. Bracaloni, *L'arte francescana nella vita e nella storia di settecento anni*, Todi 1924, p. 304, citato da C. Strinati, "Riforma della pittura e riforma religiosa", *L'immagine di San Francesco nella Controriforma*, *op. cit.*, p. 48.

[63] Per quanto riguarda l'analisi di ciascuno di tali problemi, i quali comportano ovviamente una precisa presa di posizione storica nei confronti delle ben note interpretazioni oggi correnti sia in materia di cultura caravaggesca presuntamente allegorico-simbologica, sia e ancor più in materia di posizione del Caravaggio – personale non meno che artistica – rispetto al problema religioso, e in particolare rispetto al cattolicesimo della Chiesa romana definito dal Concilio di Trento e sostenuto normativamente dai pur diversi indirizzi della Controriforma, rinvio all'intera prima parte del libro di cui il presente saggio costituisce un capitolo. In tale parte, dove ho inteso riprendere, aggiornare, documentare e ampliare di molto il saggio del 1973, *Il Caravaggio nella cultura e nella società del suo tempo*, che lessi a un convegno promosso a Roma dall'Accademia dei Lincei, si troverà anche un più motivato riferimento all'interessante saggio di J. F. Chorpenning, "Another Look at Caravaggio and Religion", che vede la luce in questo medesimo numero di *Artibus et Historiae* e che per ciò stesso ho potuto vedere solo all'ultimo momento: un saggio, a ogni modo, che, sebbene appartenga a un indirizzo culturale e interpretativo del tutto diverso da quello che a me sembra da preferire, va segnalato almeno

per la novità di aver posto al centro della discussione l'ipotesi non inedita, ma non ancora esaminata espressamente e con il rigore necessario in materia di "Caravaggio and Religion", che le opere del maestro d'argomento sacro, nella loro "emphasis on the tangibility of the supernatural", rifletterebbero le "meditative techniques" indicate dalla "liturgical piety" della pratica religiosa controriformata.

[64] Anche per l'analisi di questi aspetti della cultura caravaggesca, che non si esaurisce nella –, ma presuppone in modo determinante la – ben nota impostazione del problema prospettata a più riprese da Roberto Longhi, rinvio a un capitolo del libro a cui il presente saggio appartiene: quello che ne apre la seconda parte con il titolo: *La scelta e l'elaborazione delle sue* [id est: del Merisi] *scelte figurative: la cultura pittorica lombarda secondo la testimonianza di Paolo Pino e il "disegno" del Caravaggio*.

[65] Per i dati bibliografici e critici della questione, cfr. Cinotti, *op. cit.*, scheda n. 7, pp. 418-19.

[66] Per tutto, incluse le riproduzioni fotografiche relative, e anche a colori, cfr. Cinotti, *ibidem*, rispettivamente: scheda n. 2, p. 411; scheda n. 10, pp. 424- 27; scheda n. 59, pp. 521-23; scheda n. 55, pp. 515-17. Tuttavia, per un giudizio recente del tutto sfavorevole sull'esemplare di "Marta e Maria" ora a Detroit, cfr. G. Previtali, "Caravaggio e il suo tempo", recensione alla mostra di New York e di Napoli, *Prospettiva*, n.41, aprile 1985, p. 74; per uno recente del tutto favorevole (e, devo ammettere, molto ben appoggiato a convincenti osservazioni tecniche) sull'esemplare della *Giuditta e Oloferne* di Roma, cfr. K. Christiansen, "Caravaggio and «l'esempio davanti del naturale»", *The Art Bulletin*, vol. LXVIII, n. 3, September 1986, pp. 427-29.

[67] Cfr. lo stato della questione e i dati bibliografici riassunti da Cinotti, *op. cit.*, p. 419, e da Gregori, *op. cit.*, ediz. ital., p. 248.

[68] Cfr. quanto è stato supposto in proposito più a dietro, anche sulla base di suggestioni già avanzate ad altro proposito dal Frommel.

[69] Cfr. N. Randolph Park, "On Caravaggio's «Dormition of the Virgin» and its setting", *The Burlington Magazine*, CXXVII, n. 988, luglio 1985, p. 441: "Die 14 mensis Junii 1601. D. Michelangelus q. fermi Marisij de Caravaggio Pictor in Urbe commorans in Palatio Ill. et R.mi Cardinalis Matthei ecc.". Per la testimonianza, del resto ben nota, relativa al 1610, si veda la querela presentata il 19 novembre 1600, al Governatore di Roma contro il maestro, da Girolamo Stampa da Montepulciano, dove il Caravaggio risulta ancora "pittore in casa dell'Ill.o e R.o Cardinale De Monte" (cfr. Bertolotti, *Artisti Lombardi a Roma nei secoli XV, XVI e XVII*, vol. II, Milano 1881, p. 50, riferito anche in Friedländer, *op. cit.*, p. 269). Non si può non tener presente, per altro, che a onta del già avvenuto allontanamento da casa Del Monte, ma trasparendone ora anche i probabilissimi motivi, il 24 agosto 1605 Fabio Masetti scriveva da Roma alla corte estense di Modena quanto segue: "havendo inteso che il Caravaggio è comparso a Roma per la speranza della pace [da Genova, dove s'era rifugiato in contumacia per ferite inferte a un sostituto del notaio Spada], sono ricorso all'ill.mo Del Monte chefaccia comandargli l'ispedizione del Quadro di S. A., che me l'ha con molta prontezza promesso anchorché s'assicura poco di lui, dicendo che è uno cervello stravagantissimo, ecc." (cfr. L. Venturi, in *L'Arte*, 1910, pp. 281-84, riferito anche in Friedländer, *ibidem*, p. 310).

[70] Cfr. le fonti e la bibliografia indicate da Spezzaferro, "La cultura...", *op. cit.*, p. 58, nota 14.

[71] Per questo dipinto, si confrontino i dati forniti nella precedente nota 6.

[72] Cfr. le riproduzioni e la storia critica di entrambe (inclusa l'opinione di Moir già ricordata nella precedente nota 6) in Ward Bissell, *Orazio Gentileschi*, *op. cit.*, pp. 140-42, nn. 8 e 9, figg. 19 e 20. Per l'attribuzione al Gentileschi della versione ora a Madrid, non posso non

ricordare che essa mi parve evidente già nel 1952, quando la studiai nell'originale presso il Museo Provincial di Gerona (dov'era esposta sotto una generica attribuzione a scuola dei Carracci) e me ne procurai anche una riproduzione fotografica presso l'Archivio Mas.

[73] Cfr. di nuovo quanto riassume Ward Bissell, *ibidem*. Il sintomo documentario è quello che si ricava dall'affermazione del Gentileschi stesso al ben noto processo intentato nel 1603 dal Baglione, secondo cui Caravaggio "ha mandato a casa mia per una veste da cappuccino che gliela imprestai et un par d'ale che mi rimandò deve essere 10 giorni".

[74] Cfr. R. Longhi, "Gentileschi, padre e figlia", 1916; ora in *Opere complete di Roberto Longhi*, vol. I, *Scritti giovanili. 1912 – 1922*, Firenze 1961, tomo I, p. 223.

[75] Cfr. Ward Bissell, *op. cit.*, p. 16.

[76] Cfr. in Ward Bissell, *op. cit.*, le figg. 44, 45, 47, e specialmente 48 e 49.

[77] Cfr. Cinotti, *op. cit.*, p. 418.

[78] Cfr. M. Marangoni, "Note sul Caravaggio alla Mostra del Sei e Settecento", *Bollettino d'Arte del M. P. I.*, 1922-23, p. 226.

[79] Cfr. Cinotti, *op. cit.*, specialmente p. 418, con bibliografia.

[80] Cfr. Christiansen, *op. cit.*, pp. 421-45.

[81] Cfr. R. Longhi, *Caravaggio*, 1952: cito dalla riedizione postuma curata da G. Previtali, Roma 1982, p. 187.

[82] Cfr. Christiansen, *op. cit.*, p. 427.

[83] Cfr. *ibidem*, p. 435.

[84] Cfr. ancora *ibidem*, pp. 439-40.

Summary:

JÓZEF GRABSKI

The Corsini *Flagellation* Group by Alessandro Algardi

Based on the analysis of the recently rediscovered Corsini *Flagellation* group, till now known only from older literature, this paper reconsiders the authorship of the different versions of this, in the past highly regarded and often executed, three-figure group. Art historians which studied the different versions in the past (Planiscig, Schlosser, Nava Cellini, up to Jennifer Montagu) attributed various figures alternatively to two sculptors: A. Algardi or F. du Quesnoy.

Jennifer Montagu in both her studies on the problem (1967 and 1985) proposed a hypothesis that some figures are by A. Algardi (e.g. the so-called type "B"), and other version (e.g., type "B") by both authoes, Algardi and du Quesnoy. Reconsidering the old problem of two authors in the light of the newly rediscovered work, the author's opinion is that there is the same basic conception underlying all known examples. The different versions seem to reflect inner struggles in the creative process of the same artist, Alessandro Algardi, who attempts different approaches to the theme, in search of the best possible solution. He also offers to patrons and goldsmiths a possible choice of castings to fit the varying demands, both commercial and aesthetic, of the market.

LEO STEINBERG

"How Shall This Be?" Reflections on Filippo Lippi's *Annunciation* in London - Part I

Not only Christian philosophs but also artists concerned themselves with the *quomodo* of the Incarnation. Painters often represented the *spiritus sanctus* in the form of a dove from whose beak divine rays sometimes emanated. The critical questions of the dove's position in relation to the Virgin and at what point on the Virgin's body it should aim its divine rays were rethought with astonishing independence of mind by Lippi in his London *Annunciation*. The dove has relinquished its normal high-flying station and is level with the Virgin's womb. The rare golden motes emitted from its beak are directed at the Virgin's belly. The Virgin's dress parts over the abdomen, and the opening releases a burst of similar gold-dotted rays. This "How" of Mary's impregnation is in symbolic analogy to the process of vision as understood in 15th-century Florence: visual rays exiting from the eye mingle with oncoming rays to constitute sight. Lippi suggests light as the sole and sufficient symbol of fecundation. As light is the world's noblest substance and its cognate, vision, the noblest sense, so their mutual coupling is fittest to serve as a symbol of sacred union.

SAMUEL Y. EDGERTON, JR.

"How Shall This Be?" - Part II

Antonino Pierozzi, Archbishop of Florence in the mid-15th century, described extensively the miraculous *in utero* conception of Jesus. Lippi, in his London *Annunciation,* superseded theological interpretation and ventured into optics: namely Roger Bacon's theory of the "multiplication of *species*", which had been excerpted by Ghiberti in Book III of his *Commentarii* and was therefore well known to artists. The evidence is convincing that Lippi thought out the pictorial solution to this painting with Bacon in mind. When he painted the dove opposite Mary's womb, he was thinking that distinct vision occurs only when the visual object confronts the eye and the visual rays are able to enter at right angles. The second hint of Lippi's debt to Bacon's optics is the way he represented the *species* coming from the dove to the Virgin. Only one ray issuing from the dove connects with the center of the light emanating from the Virgin's womb. It is also the most nearly perpendicular. The little cut in Mary's garment represent: the pupil of an eye.

WALTER CAHN

Moses ben Abraham's *Chroniques de la Bible*

In The Royal Library in The Hague is a little-known manuscript with illustrations of the prophecies of Daniel, probably executed in northeastern France around 1300. The text is a French paraphrase of the Bible with special emphasis on the Books of Daniel and Maccabees, compiled by Moses ben Abraham, a Jew, for his patron William X of Auvergne. The express purpose of the work is to trace the lineage of noble clans and peoples to their Biblical origins, to speculate on struggles of ancient empires and marvels still to come. Despite the Christian reading the translator gives to Hebrew prophecy, there are discrepancies with the Latin Vulgate text which also come to light in the illustrations. It can be determined, on the basis of historical analysis, that the work in The Hague is a copy of an original made some fifty years earlier, and that it must have been the object of eschatological speculation and was therefore acutely topical for an audience entering a new century.

JOSEPH GUTMANN

The Sacrifice of Isaac in Medieval Jewish Art

The dramatic narrative of *Genesis 22* has always been one of the most important themes in Judaism. There are two known versions of the Sacrifice of Isaac in early Jewish art, but they have no relationship to the twenty-seven extant illustrations from the 13th to the 15th century. Most are found in prayer-books and reveal so many variations in detail that it is impossible to posit one source. It is not astonishing to discover that many of the miniatures were made by Christian artists or Jews copying medieval Christian models. Novel are the many distinct Jewish iconographic features.

CHRISTIANE L. JOOST-GAUGIER

Lorenzo the Magnificent and the Giraffe as a Symbol of Power

In Vasari's painted portrait of Lorenzo the Magnificent, painted for the apartments of Duke Cosimo I in the Palazzo Vecchio in Florence, prominent exposure is given to a giraffe, one of the gift presented to Lorenzo by his ambassadors. The article shows that the giraffe, which is critical to the composition of the painting, has not only a historical motive but also an iconographical significance. The admiration of Lorenzo for Julius Caesar is reflected in this demonstration, the second time in history when the giraffe was presented to the Italian people. It may therefore be interpreted as a symbol of the power of the tyrant.

JUDITH ZILCZER

''Color Music'': Synaesthesia and Nineteenth-Century Sources for Abstract Art

Coined in the late nineteenth century, the term ''Color Music'' described a visionary art form created with color lights and independent of easel painting. This idea of color music was symptomatic of a fundamental shift in aesthetic theory, where-

by music served as an ideal model for the visual arts. The twin doctrines of musical analogy and synaesthesia provided the foundation for theories of color music. Advocates of synaesthesia were divided into two distinct schools – the quasi-mystical and the pseudo-scientific. This paper analyzes the evolution of these two traditions and their influence among American artists and critics of the early modern period.

PAUL F. WATSON

On a Window in Parnassus

The window on Parnassus is the shuttered object that figures in Marcantonio Raimondi's engraved *Parnassus*, after Raphael (ca. 1517-20). This preserves Raphael's first thought or modello for the fresco in the Segnatura (1509-11), as scholarly consensus maintains and geometric analyses also demonstrate. Simpler in form than the final fresco, engraved *Parnassus* also differs in content: a tightly-worked out demonstration of poetry, its genres, hierarchies and activities, derived from a body of classical texts (Virgil, Horace) consistently Augustan. Raphael's classicized Parnassus also serves an epideictic function, directing attention to that new and Roman Parnassus, the Villa of the Belvedere, an orientation stressed by the engraver and the window on Parnassus that anchors his reworking of Raphael's first composition.

JOSEPH F. CHORPENNING

Another Look at Caravaggio and Religion

This article, the point of departure for which is W. Friedlaender's controversial hypothesis that there is an affinity between Caravaggio's altarpieces and the spirituality of St. Philip Neri and *Spiritual Exercises* of St. Ignatius Loyola, is divided into two parts. In part I, after a summary of the state of the question of this hypothesis and its reception, there is a critique of several ideas of Friedlaender, his supporters, and his critics: Caravaggio was probably introduced to the *Exercises* by the Augustinians, not the Oratorians; the *Exercises* are not the only place where the artist could have come into contact with the meditative practices of the composition of place and application of the senses; and although the Oratorians and Jesuits may have found Caravaggio's breaches of decorum offensive, that does not mean that the artist did not respond to and internalize elements of the spirituality of Neri and Loyola. Part II puts forth the view that the hallmarks of Caravaggio's altarpieces identified by Friedlaender and other – the direct contact the artist establishes between the sacred scene and the spectator and his consistent humanization of Christ, the Virgin, and the saints, as well as populating his religious paintings with apparently poor, common, and very human types – are primarily Caravaggio's artistic response to, and interpretation of, Counter-Reformation meditative practices. This view is substantiated by an examination of Caravaggio's religious art in relation to the liturgical context for which it was intended and the liturgical piety of his age, of which meditative prayer was an integral part.

FERDINANDO BOLOGNA

Searching for the true *St. Francis in Ecstasy* by Caravaggio for the Cardinal Francesco Del Monte

A thorough examination of all the available artistic and documentational material connected with Caravaggio's works on the subject of St. Francis of Assisi, leads to the conclusion that the "St. Francis in Ecstasy" mentioned in the 1627 inventory of Cardinal Del Monte's belongings, cannot be identified with any of the works known of so far. Not even the *The Stigmatization of St. Francis*, now in Hartford, since the subject of this work is not the same at all and the history of the painting is completely different. For some Caravaggio most likely must have done the work mentioned in the inventory for Del Monte himself and with the saint in the likeness of the Cardinal whose first name in baptism was in fact Francesco. If this supposition is true we should expect that the work we are looking for, besides fitting as closely as possible the subject in the title in the inventory, should highlight the figure of the saint as much as possible (and not as it is a fact in the Hartford painting), while being more clearly a portrait. The painting now in the Mrs. Barbara P. Johnson collection fulfills all these requirements quite good: it is of the dimensions given in the Del Monte inventory, the composition and unique use of iconography indicate that this interpretation of the ecstasy must be by Caravaggio himself. The preparatory graffiti are like what are quite often found in ones we are surest are Caravaggio's works. Furthermore the execution is of the highest quality, and typical of the personal and autographic style of Caravaggio. This style also coincides precisely with that of the painter in the years just before the *Calling of St. Matthew* for the Contarelli Chapel, and not at all after 1600-1601 when Caravaggio left Del Monte's house. Finally, confirming the value of the work and its importance in art history, it should be noted that at the turn of the next century the style of the Johnson *St. Francis* was to become an example for Orazio Gentileschi to follow when turning to Caravaggism in his own career. At which point he did

two paintings of, as a matter of fact *St. Francis*, one now in Rome and the other in Madrid. Both, though without preparatory graffiti (though Orazio never used these) quite obviously derive from the masterpiece here in question.

Zusammenfassungen:

JÓZEF GRABSKI
Die Corsini *Geißelungs*-Gruppe von Alessandro Algardi

Sich auf die Analysen der unlängst wieder entdeckten Corsini *Geißelungs*-Gruppe stützend, die bis jetzt nur aus der älteren Literatur bekannt war, stellt der Aufsatz nochmals die Frage nach dem Schöpfer der unterschiedlichen Versionen dieser in der Vergangenheit sehr geschätzten und oft ausgeführten Drei-Personen-Gruppe. Kunsthistoriker, die in der Vergangenheit diese Versionen studierten (Planiscig, Schlosser, Nava Cellini bis zu Jennifer Montagu), haben die verschiedenartigen Figuren abwechselnd zwei Bildhauern zugeschrieben: A. Algardi oder F. du Quesnoy.

Jennifer Montagu stellte in ihren beiden Studien zu diesem Problem (1967 und 1985) die Hypothese auf, daß manche Figuren von A. Algardi (z. B. der sog. Typ "B") und andere Versionen (z. B. Typ "A") von beiden Bildhauern, A. Algardi und F. du Quesnoy, stammen. Angesichts des kürzlich wieder entdeckten Werkes und unter der Berücksichtigung des alten Problems der beiden Schöpfer, vertritt der Autor die Meinung, daß es eine allen bekannten Beispielen gemeinsame Grundkonzeption geben muß. Die verschiedenen Versionen der Skulptur scheinen ein inneres Ringen im schöpferischen Prozeß ein und desselben Künstlers, nämlich A. Algardi, widerzuspiegeln, der sich – auf der Suche nach der bestmöglichen Lösung – diesem Thema von verschiedenen Seiten zu nähern versuchte. Er bietet auch den Mäzenen und Goldschmieden eine eventuelle Auswahl von Abgußformen an, um sich den Forderungen des Marktes – den kommerziellen und den ästhetischen – anzupassen.

LEO STEINBERG
"Wie soll das geschehen?" – Gedanken zu Filippo Lippis
Verkündigung in London - 1. Teil

Nicht nur christliche Philosophen, auch Künstler interessierten sich für das *quomodo* der Menschwerdung Christi. Maler stellten den *spiritus sanctus* oft in Gestalt einer Taube dar, aus deren Schnabel zuweilen göttliche Lichtstrahlen kommen. Die entscheidende Frage nach der Position der Taube in Bezug auf die Jungfrau und nach der Körperstelle, auf die sich die göttlichen Strahlen richten sollen, hat Lippi in seiner Londoner *Verkündigung* mit erstaunlicher Unabhängigkeit neu überdacht. Die Taube befindet sich jetzt auf gleicher Höhe mit dem Schoß der Jungfrau; dem Schnabel des Vogels entströmen vereinzelte goldene Stäubchen. Aus einer Öffnung im Gewand Mariens dringen ähnliche Strahlen, die sich mit den aus dem Schnabel der Taube kommenden vereinen. Dieses "Wie" der Empfängnis steht in symbolischer Analogie zum Ablauf des Sehprozesses, wie er in Florenz des 15. Jahrhunderts verstanden wurde: Sehstrahlen verlassen das Auge und verschmelzen mit ankommenden Strahlen, wodurch das Sehen entsteht. Lippi suggeriert Licht als einiges, angemessenes Symbol der Befruchtung. Da Licht die edelste Substanz der Welt und die ihm verwandte Sehkraft der erhabenste Sinn ist, eignet sich ihre Verbindung am besten, als Symbol der Heiligen Vereinigung zu dienen.

SAMUEL Y. EDGERTON, Jr.
"Wie soll das geschehen?" – 2. Teil

Antonino Pierozzi, in der Mitte des 15. Jh. Erzbischof von Florenz, beschrieb ausführlich die wunderbare *in utero*-Empfängnis Jesu. Lippi versucht in seiner Londoner *Verkündigung* an Stelle der theologischen Interpretation des Themas eine optische, und zwar mit Hilfe einer Theorie, die vom englischen Franziskanermönch Roger Bacon in seinem Traktat *De multiplicatione specierum* entwickelt worden war, wonach physikalische aber auch spirituelle Objekte ihnen eigene Kraft mittels eines sichtbaren Strahls (*species*) abgeben. Ghiberti hatte Bacons Lehre im dritten Buch seiner *Commentarii* exzerpiert, und es ist anzunehmen, daß sie daher Künstlern wohlbekannt war. Es gibt einige überzeugende Beweise dafür, daß sich Lippi bei der bildlichen Lösung zu diesem Gemälde der Baconschen Theorie bediente. Indem er die Taube auf gleicher Höhe mit Marias Schoß malte, übernahm er Bacons Satz, daß ein klares Bild nur dann entsteht, wenn sich das sichtbare Objekt dem Auge genau gegenüber befindet und die Sehstrahlen rechtwinklig einfallen können. Der zweite Hinweis auf Lippis Verpflichtung gegenüber Bacons Optik ist die Art und Weise in der er die von der Taube zur Jungfrau übergehende *species*

darstellt. Nur ein Strahl, der von der Taube ausgeht, verbindet sich mit dem aus dem Schoß der Jungfrau kommenden Leuchten. Dieser Strahl ist auch am ehesten als rechtwinklig anzusehen. Der kleine Ausschnitt im Marias Gewand ist mit einer Pupille zu vergleichen.

WALTER CAHN
Chroniques de la Bible von Moses ben Abraham

In der Königlichen Bibliothek in Den Haag befindet sich ein wenig bekanntes Manuskript mit Illustrationen der Prophezeiungen Daniels, das wahrscheinlich um 1300 im nordöstlichen Frankreich angefertig wurde. Der Text ist eine freie Übertragung der Bibel ins Französische, unter besonderer Hervorhebung der Bücher Daniels und der Makkabäer, zusammengestellt von dem Juden Moses ben Abraham für seinen Mäzen, Wilhelm X. Graf von Auvergne. Das Werk ist bestrebt, die Abstammung der Völker auf biblische Ursprünge zurückzuführen und über das Ringen früher Reiche und Wunder, die noch kommen sollten, nachzusinnen. Trotz der christlichen Deutung der hebräischen Prophezeiungen gibt es Unstimmigkeiten mit der lateinischen Vulgata, wie auch aus den Abbildungen ersichtlich wird. Historische Analysen ergeben, daß es sich bei dem Manuskript in Den Haag um die Kopie eines etwa fünfzig Jahre früher angefertigten Originals handelt, das ein Objekt eschatologischer Spekulationen und daher auch für den Leserkreis des damals anbrechenden neuen Jahrhunderts besonders aktuell gewesen sein muß.

JOSEPH GUTMANN
Die Opferung Isaaks in der mittelalterlichen jüdischen Kunst

Der dramatische Bericht der "Genesis 22" ist immer schon eines der wichtigsten Themen im Judentum gewesen. Obwohl es zwei bekannte Versionen der Opferung Isaaks in der frühen jüdischen Kunst gibt, besteht zwischen ihnen und den siebenundzwanzig noch vorhandenen Abbildungen aus dem 13. bis 15. Jh. keine Verwandtschaft. Die meisten sind in Gebetbüchern vorhanden und zeigen so viele Abweichungen im Detail, daß es unmöglich ist, eine gemeinsame Quelle vorauszusetzen. Es verwundert daher nicht, daß viele der Miniaturen von christlichen Künstlern oder Juden angefertigt worden sind, die mittelalterliche christliche Vorlagen kopiert haben. Ungewohnt aber sind viele ausgesprochen jüdische ikonographische Merkmale.

CHRISTIANE L. JOOST-GAUGIER
Lorenzo der Prächtige und die Giraffe als ein Symbol der Macht

In dem von Vasari gemalten Porträt Lorenzos des Prächtigen, einem Gemälde, das für die Gemächer Herzog Cosimos I. im Palazzo Vecchio bestimmt war, kommt einer Giraffe, die Lorenzo von seinen Gesandten geschenkt bekommt, besondere Bedeutung zu. Die vorliegende Arbeit zeigt, daß diese Giraffe, die kompositionell eine entscheidende Stellung einnimmt, nicht nur historisch sondern auch ikonographisch relevant ist. In ihrer Darstellung spiegelt sich Lorenzos Bewunderung für Julius Cäsar wider: zum zweiten Mal in der Geschichte wurde hier eine Giraffe dem italienischen Volk vorgeführt, sie kann daher als ein Symbol der Macht des Tyrannen verstanden werden.

JUDITH ZILCZER
"Farbmusik": Synästhesie und Quellen der abstrakten Kunst im 19. Jahrhundert

Der im 19. Jahrhundert geprägte Begriff "Farbmusik" bezeichnet eine visionäre Kunstform, die mit Farblichtern und unabhängig von der Staffeleimalerei geschaffen wurde. Diese Idee der Farbmusik war charakteristisch für den fundamentalen Wandel jener ästhetischen Theorie, wonach die Musik als ideales Modell für visuelle Künste galt. Die beiden miteinander verwandten Doktrinen der Musikanalogie und der Synästhesie legten den Grundstein für die Theorien der Farbmusik. Die Verfechter der Synästhesie waren in zwei verschiedene Schulen gespalten: eine quasi-mystische und eine pseudo-wissenschaftliche. Im vorliegenden Artikel wird die Entwicklung der beiden Schulen und ihr Einfluß auf die amerikanischen Künstler und Kritiker der frühen Moderne analysiert.

PAUL F. WATSON
Das Fenster in Raphaels *Parnaß*

Raimondis Kupferstich *Parnaß* (ca. 1517-1520) nach Vorbild des Raffaelschen Freskos in der Stanza della Segnatura, stützt sich wie die übereinstimmende Meinung der Forschung und geometrische Analysen in der vorliegenden Studie beweisen, auf Raffaels ersten Entwurf für sein vatikanisches Fresko. Während Raimondis Kupferstich einfacher ausgeführt ist und in erster Linie das Wesen der Dichtkunst und ihre Gattungsarten an Hand einer Darstellung klassischer Texte (Vergil, Horaz) abbildet, sollte die erste Version von Raffaels *Parnaß* das Interesse des Betrachters auf den neuen, römischen Parnaß, die Villa Belvedere lenken.

JOSEPH F. CHORPENNING
Neue Aspekte zu Caravaggios Verhältnis zur Religion

Der Ausgangspunkt dieses Artikels bildet die umstrittene Hypothese Friedlaenders, wonach zwischen Caravaggios Altarbildern, der Spiritualität des Hl. Philippo Neri und den *Geistigen Übungen* des Hl. Ignatius von Loyola eine Affinität besteht.

Im ersten Teil folgt einer kurzen Zusammenfassung des Untersuchungstandes dieser Hypothese und ihrer Aufnahme eine Kritik einzelner Ideen Friedlaenders, seiner Anhänger und seiner Gegner: Caravaggio wurde wahrscheinlich durch die Augustiner und nicht durch die Oratorianer in die *Geistigen Übungen* eingeführt. Die *Übungen* sind aber nicht der einzige Berührungspunkt des Künstlers mit den meditativen Praktiken der Raumkomposition und der Anwendung der Sinne; wenn auch Jesuiten und Oratorianer Caravaggios Verletzung der Schicklichkeit als anstößig empfunden haben, bedeutet das nicht, daß der Künstler nicht auf die Elemente der Spiritualität Philippo Neris und des Hl. Ignatius von Loyola nicht eingegangen wäre und sie nicht verinnerlicht hätte.

Der zweite Teil des Artikels vertritt die Ansicht, daß die von Friedlaender und anderen identifizierten charakteristischen Merkmale Caravaggios von Altarbildern – nämlich der direkte Kontakt, den der Künstler zwischen dem Betrachter und der heiligen Szene herstellte, seine Vermenschlichung Christi, der Jungfrau und der Heiligen, ebenso wie das Bevölkern seiner religiösen Gemälde mit sichtlich armen, einfachen und sehr menschlich wirkenden Gestalten – in erster Linie Caravaggios künstlerische Antwort auf die meditativen Praktiken der Gegenreformation und zugleich ihre Interpretation sind.

Bestätigt wird diese Ansicht durch eine Untersuchung der religiösen Kunst Caravaggios in ihrer Beziehung zum liturgischen Umfeld, für das sie gedacht war, ebenso wie zur liturgischen Frömmigkeit seiner Zeit, für die das meditative Gebet ein integrierender Bestandteil war.

FERDINANDO BOLOGNA
Auf der Suche nach dem von Caravaggio für Kardinal Francesco Del Monte geschaffenen *Hl. Franziskus in Ekstase*

Eine vollständige Untersuchung aller zugänglichen künstlerischen und dokumentarischen Materialien zum Thema des heiligen Franz von Assisi, die mit Caravaggios Werk verbunden sind, führt zu der Schlußfolgerung, daß der *Hl. Franziskus in Ekstase*, erwähnt 1627 im Bestandsverzeichnis des Kardinals Del Monte, mit keinem der bisher bekannten Werke identifiziert werden kann, nicht einmal mit der *Stigmatisierung des Hl. Franziskus*, derzeit in Hartford, weil dieses Gemälde thematisch und historisch gänzlich verschieden ist. Einige sind der Meinung, daß Caravaggio das im Bestandsverzeichnis Del Montes erwähnte Werk höchstwahrscheinlich selbst gemalt hat, und daß der Heilige eine Ähnlichkeit mit dem Kardinal aufweist, dessen erster Taufname ebenfalls Francesco war. Wenn diese Vermutung stimmte, sollten wir erwarten, daß nicht nur das Thema des gesuchten Werkes so deutlich wie möglich durch den Titel im Verzeichnis ausgedrückt, sondern auch die Gestalt des Heiligen möglichst stark herausgehoben sein müßte, so daß – im Unterschied zum Hartforder Bild – es eher einem Porträt glieche. Das Gemälde indes, das sich jetzt in der Sammlung von Mrs. Barbara P. Johnson befindet, erfüllt eigentlich alle diese Erfordernisse: Es hat Maße, wie sie im Bestandsverzeichnis Del Montes angegeben sind; sowohl die Komposition als auch der einzigartige Gebrauch der Ikonographie weisen darauf hin, daß diese Interpretation der Ekstase von Caravaggio selbst stammen muß. Die vorbereitenden Graffiti gleichen denjenigen, die ziemlich oft in den eindeutig von Caravaggios Hand stammenden Werken gefunden werden. Ferner ist die Ausführung von höchster Qualität und typisch für den persönlichen und autographischen Stil Caravaggios. Dieser Stil stimmt genau mit dem des Malers in den Jahren knapp vor der für die Kapelle Contarelli geschaffenen *Berufung des Hl. Matthäus* überein und paßt keinesfalls zu seinem Stil von 1600-1601, als Caravaggio das Haus Del Montes verlassen hat. Schließlich, muß man um den Wert des Werkes und seine Bedeutung in der Kunstgeschichte zu bestätigen, noch betonen, daß an der Wende zum nächsten Jahrhundert der Stil des *Hl. Franziskus* aus der Johnson-Sammlung zum Vorbild für Orazio Gentileschi werden sollte, als sich dieser in seiner eigenen Karriere Caravaggio zuwandte. Zu diesem Zeitpunkt malte er tatsächlich zwei Bilder des Hl. Franziskus: das eine hängt derzeit in Rom und das andere in Madrid. Beide, obwohl ohne vorbereitende Graffiti (weil Orazio sie nie verwendet hat), stammen ziemlich unverkennbar von dem hier angesprochenen Meisterstück ab.

Information about the authors - nota informativa sugli autori del presente numero - über die Autoren - les auteurs:

JÓZEF GRABSKI

Art Historian. Director of the IRSA (Vienna-Florence).
Editor of ARTIBUS ET HISTORIAE.

LEO STEINBERG

Benjamin Franklin Professor of the History of Art at the University of Pennsylvania. He has published widely in the fields of Renaissance and modern art. His most recent book is "The Sexuality of Christ in Renaissance Art and in Modern Oblivion".

SAMUEL Y. EDGERTON

Professor of Art History, Williams College, Williamstown, Mass., USA.

WALTER CAHN

Professor of Art History, Yale University, New Haven, Conn., USA.

JOSEPH GUTMANN

Professor of Art History, Wayne State University, Detroit, Michigan, USA.

CHRISTIANE L. JOOST-GAUGIER

Professor of Art History, University of New Mexico, Albuquerque, New Mexico, USA.

PAUL F. WATSON

Professor of Art History, University of Pennsylvania, Philadelphia, Penn.

JUDITH ZILCZER

Historian, Hirshhorn Museum and Sculpture Garden, Smithsonian Institution, Washington, D.C.

JOSEPH F. CHORPENNING

Allentown College of St. Francis de Sales, Center Valley, Penn., USA.

FERDINANDO BOLOGNA

Professor of Art History, University of Rome, Italy.

Photographic sources:

D. Posner, New York University; Gabinetto Fotografico Nazionale, Roma; Joseph Szaszfai, Branford, Conn.; Wadsworth Atheneum, Hartford, Conn.; National Gallery of Art, Washington D. C; Musei Vaticani, Archivio Fotografico; Founders Society Detroit Institute of Art, Detroit; The Cleveland Museum of Art, Cleveland, Ohio; The Art Institute of Chicago, Chicago, Ill.; Mrs. Barbara P. Johnson Collection, Princeton, N. J.; University Art Museum, University of California, Berkeley; J. Zilczer, Washington, D. C.; Museum of Modern Art, New York; Whitney Museum of American Art, New York; Hirshhorn Museum and Sculpture Garden, Smithsonian Institution, Washington, D.C.; Albright-Knox Art Gallery, Buffalo, N. Y.; Museum of Fine Arts, Boston; The Phillips Collection, Washington, D. C.; Colorado Springs Fine Arts Center; Andrew Crispo Gallery, New York; Helga Photo Studio, New York; Archives of American Art, Smithsonian Institution, Washington, D. C.; Yale University Art Gallery, New Haven, Conn.; Forum Gallery, New York; Richard Gray Gallery, Chicago, Ill.; Rose Art Museum, Brandeis University, Waltham, Mass.; Philadelphia Museum of Art, Philadelphia, Penn.; The Metropolitan Museum of Art, New York; The Tate Gallery, London; The Pierpont Morgan Library, New York; Alinari, Firenze; Samuel Y. Edgerton; Bibliothèque Nationale, Paris; Walter Cahn; Musée des Beaux-Arts de Dijon, Dijon; Arte Fotografica, Roma; Leo Steinberg, New York; A. C. Cooper, London; Villa I Tatti, Firenze; Photo Reali; Robert Dance, Fine Art, New York; The Frick Collection, New York; Germanisches Nationalmuseum, Nürnberg; National Gallery, London; Agnew & Sons, London; Courtauld Institute, London; Galleria Doria, Roma; Joseph Gutman; Rheinisches Bildarchiv, Köln; Kölnisches Stadtmuseum, Köln; Bodleian Library, Oxford; Frank J. Darmstaedter, New York; Jewish Theological Seminary of America, New York; Scansani Walter, Milano; Biblioteca Ambrosiana, Milano; E. Jekel, Wien; Kunsthistorisches Museum, Wien; Musées Royaux d'Art et d'Histoire, Bruxelles; Galleria Borghese, Roma; Statens Museum for Kunst, Copenhagen; Darmstadt, Hessisches Landesmuseum; Wedgwood Museum, Barlaston; Victoria and Albert Museum, London; Royal Library, The Hague; Koninklijke Bibliotheek, The Hague; Bayrische Staatsbibliothek, München; Israel Museum, Jerusalem; Universitätsbibliothek, Leipzig; British Library, London; Biblioteca Palatina, Parma.

artibus et historiae

PREVIOUS ISSUES

artibus et historiae nr 8 (IV), 1983

David Alan Brown - Raphael's *Small Cowper Madonna* and *Madonna of the Meadow:*
Their Technique and Leonardo Sources
Russell Panczenko - Cultura umanistica di Gentile da Fabriano
Augusto Gentili - Per Lorenzo Lotto e i suoi contesti storici: due episodi
ridocumentati, tra polemica e progetto
Patrick M. de Winter - Castle and Town Residences of Philip the Bold, Duke of
Burgundy (1364-1404)
Maurizio Marini - Equivoci del caravaggismo 2: A) Appunti sulla tecnica del
" naturalismo" secentesco, tra Caravaggio e " Manfrediana methodus ". B) Caravaggio
e i suoi " doppi ". Il problema delle possibili collaborazioni
Alicja Helman - The Present-Day Meaning of a Work of Art

artibus et historiae nr 9 (V), 1984

George Kubler - Les sources écrites de la cosmogonie andine
Adam S. Labuda - Wort und Bild im späten Mittelalter am Beispiel des Breslauer
Barbara-Altars (1447)
W. R. Rearick - Observation on the Venetian Cinquecento in the Light of the Royal
Academy Exhibition
Alessandra Ottieri - Laguna di Venezia, mare di Galilea: la *Vocazione dei figli di
Zebedèo* di Marco Basaiti
Saul Levine - Michelangelo's Marble *David* and the Last Bronze *David:* the Drawings
Christoph Stöcker - Dürer, Celtis und der falsche Bischof Achatius. Zur Ikonographie
von Dürer *Marter der Zehntausend*
Elizabeth Hutton Turner - Who is in the Brothel of Avignon? A Case for Context
Karsten Harries - Space, Place, und Ethos: Reflections on the Ethical Function of
Architecture

artibus et historiae nr 10 (V), 1984

Jan Białostocki - A New Look at Rembrandt Iconography
Julius S. Held - A Rembrandt "Theme"
Margaret Deutsch Carroll - Rembrandt's *Aristotle*: Exemplary Beholder
Cecil Gould - Raphael's *Double Portrait* in the Louvre: an Identification for the Second
Figure
Norman E. Land - On the Poetry of Giovanni Bellini's *Sacred Allegory*
Erasmus Weddigen - Jacopo Tintoretto und die Musik
Milly Heyd - Dali's *Metamorphosis of Narcissus* Reconsidered
Dieter Wuttke - Die Emigration der Kulturwissenschaftlichen Bibliothek Warburg und
die Anfänge des Universitätsfaches Kunstgeschichte in Großbritannien
Mieczysław Porębski - Les avant-gardes

artibus et historiae nr 11 (VI), 1985

Carlo Del Bravo - Quadri a lume di notte. Georges de La Tour e Sant'Agostino
Józef Grabski - On Seicento Painting in Naples: Some Observations on Bernardo
Cavallino, Artemisia Gentileschi and Others
Dieter Wuttke - Humanismus als integrative Kraft. Die Philosophia des deutschen
'Erzhumanisten' Conrad Celtis. Eine ikonologische Studie zu programmatischer
Graphik Dürers und Burgkmairs
Edward J. Olszewski - Distortions, Shadows, and Conventions in Sixteenth Century
Italian Art
Jindrich Chalupecký - Marcel Duchamp: a Re-evaluation
Teřesa Grzybkowska - The Pseudojapanese in «Young Poland» Art
Pietro Montani - Scritti sull'arte di S. M. Eisenstein. Nota introduttiva
S. M. Eisenstein - Scritti sull'arte. Il montaggio in pittura (su Serov, Repin e altri)